4TH EDITION
OAHU REVEALED
THE ULTIMATE GUIDE TO
HONOLULU, WAIKIKI & BEYOND

ANDREW DOUGHTY
PHOTOGRAPHS BY ANDREW DOUGHTY & LEONA BOYD

WIZARD
PUBLICATIONS
INC

Oahu Revealed
The Ultimate Guide to Honolulu, Waikiki & Beyond; 4th Edition

Published by Wizard Publications, Inc.
Post Office Box 991
Lihu'e, Hawai'i 96766–0991

ISBN: 978–0–9838887–0–3   1032
Library of Congress Control Number 2012932974
Printed in China

Cataloging-in-Publication Data

Doughty, Andrew
    Oahu revealed : the ultimate guide to Honolulu, Waikiki and beyond / Andrew Doughty – 4th ed. Lihue, HI : Wizard Publications, Inc., 2012
        304 p. : col. illus., col. photos, col. maps ; 21 cm.
        Includes index.
        Summary: A complete traveler's guide to the Hawaiian island of Oahu, with full-color illustrations, maps, directions and candid advice by an author who resides in Hawaii.
        ISBN 978-0-9838887-0-3
        LCCN 2012932974

    1. Oahu (Hawaii) – Guidebooks. 2. Oahu (Hawaii) – Description and travel. I. Title

DU628.03   919.69'3_dc22

All photographs (except the cover and page 209) taken by Andrew Doughty and Leona Boyd. Photo on page 209 courtesy of Tom Sanders.
Cover imagery courtesy of Earthstar Geographics (www.earth-imagery.com).
Cartography by Andrew Doughty.
All artwork and illustrations by Andrew Doughty and Lisa Pollak.

Pages 2–3: A kayaker loses herself in the beauty of Kane'ohe Bay.

We welcome any comments, questions, criticisms or contributions you may have, and we will incorporate some of your suggestions into future editions. Please send to the address above or e-mail us at **aloha@wizardpub.com**.

Check out our website at **www.hawaiirevealed.com** for up-to-the-minute changes. Find us on **Facebook**, **YouTube** and **Twitter** (@hawaiirevealed).

Although the author and publisher have made every effort to ensure that the information was correct at press time, the author and publisher do not assume and hereby disclaim any liability to any party for any loss or damage caused by errors or omissions, whether such errors or omissions result from negligence, accident or any other cause. Information has been obtained from sources believed to be reliable, but its accuracy and completeness, and the opinions based thereon, are not guaranteed.

Dedicated to the wizard that exists in all of us...

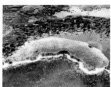

CONTENTS

7

WAI'ANAE & CENTRAL O'AHU SIGHTS
95

BEACHES
123

ACTIVITIES
159

ATTRACTIONS
109

8

CONTENTS

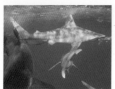

O'ahu: land of myths. We're not talking about ancient Hawaiian myths. We're talking about the myths that exist about this island, both for visitors and for those who live on the neighbor islands (including me before I moved here to do this book). The biggest myth is that O'ahu is Waikiki and Waikiki is O'ahu. *Nothing* could be further from the truth. O'ahu has all the wonder, adventure and discovery that a person could ever ask for—and far more.

Most travel publishers send a writer or writers to a given location for a few weeks to become "experts" and to compile information for guidebooks. To our knowledge, we at Wizard Publications are the only ones who actually *live* our books.

We hike the trails, ride the boats, eat in the restaurants, explore the reefs and do the things we write about. It takes us two *years*, full time, to do a first edition book, and we visit places *anonymously*. We marvel at writers who can do it all in a couple weeks staying in a hotel. Wow, they must be *really* fast. Our method, though it takes much longer, gives us the ability to tell it like it is in a way no one else can. We put in many long hours, and doing all these activities is a burdensome grind. But we do it all for you—only for you. (Feel free to gag at this point.)

Longtime locals have been surprised at some of the items described in our book. We have found many special places that people born and raised here didn't even know about because that's *all we do*—explore the island. Visitors will find the book as valuable as having a friend living on the island.

In this day of easy-to-access online reviews from countless sources, you can get "ratings" for nearly every company out there. What you get from our reviews is a single source, *beholden to none*, and with a comprehensive exposure to all of the companies. There are two critical shortcomings to online reviews. One is that you don't know the source or agenda of the reviewer. Nearly every company that offers a service to the public *thinks* they are doing a good job. (But as you know, not everyone does.) So who can blame a company for trying to rig the system by seeding good reviews of their company at every opportunity or having friends write good reviews? Many also encourage *satisfied* customers to write favorable online reviews (obviously *not* encouraging *unhappy* customers to do so). But maybe their enemies or competitors retaliate with bad reviews. The point is, you never *really know* where those reviews come from, and it's almost impossible to reconcile terrible reviews right next to glowing ones for the same company. Which do you believe?

The other problem is a lack of a frame of reference. A visitor to Hawai'i goes on a snorkel boat and has a great time. (Hey, he snorkeled in Hawai'i, swam with a turtle—*cool!*) When he goes back home, he posts good reviews all around. That's great. But the problem is, he only went on *one* snorkel boat. We do 'em all. If only he'd known that another company *he didn't even know about* did a much better job, had way better food, and a much nicer boat for the same price.

We are also blessed with hundreds of thousands of readers—from our books as well as our smartphone apps—who alert us to issues with companies and places. *Every single message* from our readers is received, placed in a special database that we constantly have available while we're out and about, and we personally follow up on every observation made by our readers. So when we walk into a business or restaurant, we check to see what our readers say and tips that they send us, and we use them to our advantage. (Thanks for the head's up to that incredible coconut cake at so-

and-so restaurant—I know what *I'll* be ordering for dessert today.) With such a resource, and after two decades reviewing companies in Hawai'i full-time, there ain't much that's gonna get past us.

A quick look at this book will reveal features never before used in other guidebooks. Let's start with the maps. They are more detailed than other maps you will find, and yet they omit extraneous information that can sometimes make a chore out of reading a map. We've also used a technique to highlight only the roads we think are relevant to you and left the countless ancillary roads faint, but still visible, so you'll know they're there but won't be overwhelmed when you read the maps. Where needed, we've drawn legal public beach access in yellow, so you'll *know* when you're legally entitled to cross someone's land. Additionally, we repeatedly drove and GPSed every inch of every road and trail on the maps. This is important because *many* of the roads and trails represented on existing maps have been shifted, moved or eliminated. You could become very frustrated trying to find certain beaches or other scenic spots using other maps. We physically check every place and often use aerial photography and a GPS to determine the best methods for getting to certain places.

Slick (and not so slick) free magazines and publications are strewn throughout the island. Most claim to point you to assorted wonders. There's nothing wrong with that. But the adage, "You get what you pay for," applies. Let's put it this way: If all the companies in this book were companies that we had to solicit for advertising, how much candor do you think we could provide? That's why *you* pay for the book, not the companies we describe. We're free to be as brutally honest as we want to be. Since we accept no advertisements, our allegiance is to our readers, not advertisers.

As you read this book, you will also notice that we are very candid in assessing businesses. Unlike some other guidebooks that send out questionnaires asking a business if they are any good (gee, they *all* say they're good), we've had personal contact with the businesses listed in this book. One of the dirty little secrets about guidebook writers is that they sometimes make cozy little deals for good reviews. Well, you won't find that here. All businesses mentioned in this book are here by *our* choosing. Not one has had any input into what we say, and we have not received *a single cent* from any of them for their inclusion. What we've seen and experienced is what you get. If we gush over a certain company, it comes from personal experience. If we rail against a business, it's for the same reason. We review businesses as anonymous visitors to ensure that we are treated the same as you. (Amazingly, most travel writers *announce* themselves.) What you get is our opinion on how they operate. Nothing more, nothing less.

Sometimes our candor gets us into trouble. More than once we've had our books pulled from shelves because our comments hit a little too close to home. That's OK, because we don't work for the people who *sell* the book; we work for the people who *read* the book.

O'ahu Revealed is intended to bring you independence in exploring O'ahu. We don't want to waste any of your valuable time by giving you bad advice or bad directions. We want you to experience the best that the island has to offer. Our objective in writing this book is to give you the tools and information necessary to have the greatest Hawaiian experience possible.

We hope we succeeded.

Andrew Doughty
Kailua, O'ahu

Four million years ago, before the dawn of man, the island of O'ahu emerged from a warm, frothing sea.

HOW IT BEGAN

Sometime around 70 million years ago an event of unimaginable violence occurred in the Earth's mantle, deep below the ocean floor. A hot spot of liquid rock blasted through the Pacific plate like a giant cutting torch, forcing liquid rock to the surface off the coast of Russia, forming the Emperor Seamounts. As the tectonic plate moved slowly over the hot spot, this torch cut a long scar along the plate, piling up mountains of rock, producing island after island. The oldest of these islands to have survived is Kure. Once a massive island with its own unique ecosystem, only its ghost remains in the form of a fringing coral reef, called an atoll.

As soon as the islands were born, a conspiracy of elements proceeded to dismantle them. Ocean waves unmercifully battered the fragile and fractured rock. Abundant rain, especially on the northeastern sides of the mountains, easily carved up the rock surface, seeking faults in the rock and forming rivers and streams. In forming these channels, the water carried away the rock and soil, robbing the islands of their very essence. Additionally, the weight of the islands ensured their doom. Lava flows on top of other lava, and the union of these flows is always weak. This lava also contains countless air pockets and is criss-crossed with hollow lava tubes, making it inherently unstable. As these massive amounts of rock accumulated, their bases were crushed under the weight of subsequent lava flows, causing their summits to sink back into the sea.

What we call the Hawaiian Islands are simply the latest creation from this island-making machine. Kaua'i and Ni'ihau are the oldest of the eight major islands. Lush and deeply eroded, the last of Kaua'i's fires died with its volcano a million years ago. O'ahu, Moloka'i, Lana'i, Kaho'olawe—their growing days are over as well. Maui is in its twilight days as a growing island. After growing vigorously, Hawaiian volcanoes usually go to sleep for a million years or so before sputtering back to life for one last fling. Maui's volcano, Haleakala, awakened from its long sleep and is in its final eruptive stage. It last erupted around 1790 and will continue with sporadic eruptions

for a (geologically) short time before drifting into eternal sleep.

The latest and newest star in this island chain is the Big Island of Hawai'i. Born less than a million years ago, this youngster is still vigorously growing. Though none of its five volcanic mountains is considered truly dead, these days Mauna Loa and Kilauea are doing most of the work in making the Big Island bigger. Mauna Loa, the most massive mountain on Earth, consists of 10,000 *cubic miles* of rock. The quieter of the two active volcanoes, it last erupted in 1984. Kilauea is the most boisterous of the volcanoes and is the most active volcano on the planet. Kilauea's most recent eruption began in 1983 and was still going strong as we went to press. Up and coming onto the world stage is Lo'ihi. This new volcano is still 3,200 feet below the ocean's surface, 20 miles off the southeastern coast of the island. Yet in a geologic heartbeat, the Hawaiian islands will be richer

Ancient forests dripping with life still abound on O'ahu.

with its ascension, sometime in the next 100,000 years.

These virgin islands were barren at birth. Consisting only of volcanic rock, the first life forms to appreciate these new islands were marine creatures. Fish, mammals and microscopic animals discovered this new underwater haven and made homes for themselves. Coral polyps attached themselves to the lava, and succeeding generations built upon these, creating what would become coral reefs.

Meanwhile, on land, seeds carried by the winds were struggling to colonize the rocky land, eking out a living and breaking down the lava rock. Storms brought the occasional bird, hopelessly blown off course. The lucky ones found the islands. The even luckier ones arrived with mates or were pregnant when they got here. Other animals, stranded on a piece of floating debris, washed ashore against all odds and went on to colonize the islands. These introductions of new species were rare events. It took an extraordinary set of circumstances for a new species to actually make it to the islands. Single specimens were destined to live out their lives in lonely solitude. On average, a new species was successfully deposited here only once every 20,000 years.

As with people, islands have a life cycle. After their violent birth, islands grow to their maximum size, get carved up by the elements, collapse in parts, and finally sink back into the sea. Someday, all the Hawaiian islands will be nothing more than geologic footnotes in the Earth's turbulent history. When a volcanic island is old, it is a sandy sliver called an atoll, devoid of mountains, merely a shadow of its former glory. When it's middle-aged, it can be a lush wonderland, a haven for anything green, like Kaua'i and O'ahu. And when it is

Hawai'i's First Tour Guide?

Given the remoteness of the Hawaiian Islands relative to the rest of Polynesia (or anywhere else for that matter), you'll be forgiven for wondering how the first settlers

found these islands in the first place. Many scientists think it might have been this little guy here. Called the

Before they leave for Alaska.

kolea, or golden plover, this tiny bird flies over 2,500 miles nonstop to Alaska every year for the summer, returning to Hawai'i after mating. Some of these birds continue past Hawai'i and fly another 2,500 miles to Samoa and other South Pacific islands. The early Polynesians surely must have noticed this commute and concluded that there must be land in the

direction that the bird was heading. They never would have dreamed that the birds leaving the South Pacific were head-

When they return.

ing to a land 5,000 miles away, and that Hawai'i was merely a stop in between, where the lazier birds wintered.

young, it is dynamic and unpredictable, like the Big Island of Hawai'i, but lacking the scars of experience from its short battle with the elements. The first people to occupy these islands were blessed with riches beyond their wildest dreams.

THE FIRST SETTLERS

Sometime around the fourth or fifth century A.D., a large double-hulled voyaging canoe, held together with flexible sennit lashings and propelled by sails made of woven pandanus, slid onto the sand on the Big Island of Hawai'i. These first intrepid adventurers, only a few dozen or so, encountered an island chain of unimaginable beauty.

They had left their home in the Marquesas Islands, 2,500 miles away, for reasons we will never know. Some say it was because of war, overpopulation, drought or just a sense of adventure. Whatever their reasons, these initial settlers took a big chance and surely must have been highly motivated. They left their homes and searched for a new world to colonize. Doubtless most of the first groups perished at sea. They could not have known that there were islands in these waters since Hawai'i is the most isolated island chain in the world. (Though some speculate that they were led here by the golden plover—see box on previous page.)

Those settlers who did arrive brought with them food staples from home: taro, breadfruit, pigs, dogs and several types of fowl. This was a pivotal decision. These first settlers found a land that contained almost no edible plants. With no land mammals other than the Hawaiian bat, the first settlers subsisted on fish until their crops matured. From then on, they lived on fish and taro. Although we associate throw-net fishing with Hawai'i, this practice was introduced by Japanese immigrants much later. The ancient Hawaiians used fishhooks and spears, for the most

The Last Battle for Supremacy

One of the more popular lookouts on O'ahu is the Pali Lookout on Hwy 61. The view from this precipice is simply glorious. As you soak in the beauty of the lookout, it's difficult to believe that this was the scene of one of O'ahu's bloodiest battles.

King Kamehameha was sweeping across the islands on his way to becoming the first man to conquer them all. When his fleet landed at Waikiki, he steadily drove the O'ahu army farther and farther up Nu'uanu Valley. Once they got to what is now the Pali Lookout, they had nowhere to go but down the cliffs. With the help of western arms and sailors (whom he had captured and then cunningly made into his advisors), Kamehameha's army was turning the battle into a rout. Once at this location some of the enemy tried to scramble down the cliffs. Around 400 others were driven off, their bodies smashing onto the rocks below. This would be the last major battle for conquest in Hawai'i. Kaua'i would eventually surrender, and Kamehameha would at last have his kingdom.

part, or drove fish into a net already placed in the water. They also had domesticated animals, which were used as ritual foods or reserved for chiefs.

Little is known about the initial culture. Archeologists speculate that a second wave of colonists, probably from Tahiti, may have subdued these initial inhabitants around 1000 A.D. Some may have resisted and fled into the forest, creating the legend of the Menehune.

Today Menehune are always thought of as being small in stature. The legend initially referred to their social stature but evolved to mean that they were physically short and lived in the jungle away from the Hawaiians. (The ancient Hawaiians avoided living in the jungle, fearing that they held evil spirits, and instead settled on the coastal plains.) The Menehune were purported to build fabulous struc-

It's hard to imagine, but 50 generations of Hawaiian royalty were born at these sacred rocks in central O'ahu.

tures, always in one night. Their numbers were said to be vast, as many as 500,000. It is interesting to note that in a census taken of Kaua'i around 1800, some 65 people from a remote valley identified themselves as Menehune.

The second wave of settlers probably swept through the islands from the south, pushing the first inhabitants ever north. On a tiny island northwest of Kaua'i, archeologists have found carvings, clearly not Hawaiian, that closely resemble Marquesan carvings, probably left by the doomed exiles.

This second culture was far more aggressive and developed into a highly class-conscious culture. The society was

If ancient Hawaiian legend is correct, this rock near Ka'ena Point called Leina-a-ka-'uhane—the leaping place for souls—is the last earthly sight that a Hawaiian soul will see before he joins his ancestors.

governed by chiefs, called ali'i, who established a long list of taboos called kapu. These kapu were designed to keep order, and the penalty for breaking one was usually death by strangulation, club or fire. If the violation was serious enough, the guilty party's family might also be killed. It was kapu, for instance, for your shadow to fall across the shadow of the ali'i. It was kapu to interrupt the chief if he was speaking. It was kapu to prepare men's food in the same container used for women's food. It was kapu for women to eat pork or bananas. It was kapu for men and women to eat together. It was kapu not to observe the days designated for the gods. Certain areas were kapu for fishing if stocks became depleted, allowing the area to replenish itself.

While harsh by our standards today, this system kept the order. Most ali'i were sensitive to the disturbance their presence caused and often ventured outside only at night, or a scout was sent ahead to warn people that an ali'i was on his way. All commoners were required to pay tribute to the ali'i in the form of food and other items. Human sacrifices were common, and war among rival chiefs the norm.

By the 1700s, the Hawaiians had lost all contact with Tahiti, and the Tahitians had lost all memory of Hawai'i. Hawaiian canoes had evolved into fishing and inter-island canoes and were no longer capable of long ocean voyages. The Hawaiians had forgotten how to explore the world.

OUTSIDE WORLD DISCOVERS HAWAI'I

In January 1778 an event occurred that would forever change Hawai'i. Captain James Cook, who usually had a genius for predicting where to find islands, stumbled upon Hawai'i. He had not expected the islands to be here. He was on his way to Alaska on his third great voyage of discovery, this time to search for the Northwest Passage linking the Atlantic and Pacific oceans. Cook approached the shores of Waimea, Kaua'i at night on January 19, 1778.

The next morning Kaua'i's inhabitants awoke to a wondrous sight and thought they were being visited by gods. Rushing aboard to greet their visitors, the Kauaians were fascinated by what they saw: pointy-headed beings (the British wore tricornered hats) breathing fire (smoking pipes) and possessing a death-dealing instrument identified as a water squirter (guns). The amount of iron on the ship was incredible. (They had seen iron before in the form of nails on driftwood but never knew where it originated.)

Cook left Kaua'i and briefly explored Ni'ihau before heading north for his mission on February 2, 1778. When Cook returned to the islands in November after failing to find the Northwest Passage, he visited the Big Island of Hawai'i.

The Hawaiians had probably seen white men before. Local legend indicates that strange white people washed ashore on the Big Island sometime around the 1520s and integrated into society. This coincides with Spanish records of two ships lost in this part of the world in 1528. But a few weird-looking stragglers couldn't compare to the arrival of Cook's great ships and instruments.

Despite some recent rewriting of history, all evidence indicates that Cook, unlike some other exploring sea captains of his era, was a thoroughly decent man. Individuals need to be evaluated in the context of their time. Cook knew that his mere presence would have a profound impact on the cultures he encountered,

but he also knew that change for these cultures was inevitable, with or without him. He tried, unsuccessfully, to keep the men known to be infected with venereal diseases from mixing with local women, and he frequently flogged infected men who tried to sneak ashore at night. He was greatly distressed when a party he sent to Ni'ihau was forced to stay overnight due to high surf, knowing that his men might transmit diseases to the women (which they did).

Cook arrived on the Big Island at a time of much upheaval. The mo'i, or king, of the Big Island had been militarily spanked during an earlier attempt to invade Maui and was now looting and raising hell throughout the islands as retribution. Cook's arrival and his physical appearance (at 6-foot-4 he couldn't even stand up straight in his own quarters) almost guaranteed that the Hawaiians would think he was the god Lono, who was responsible for land fertility. Every year the ruling chiefs and their war god Ku went into abeyance, removing their power so that Lono could return to the land and make it fertile again, bringing back the spring rains. During this time all public works stopped, and the land was left alone. At the end of this *makahiki* season mankind would again seize the land from Lono so they could grow crops and otherwise make a living upon it. Cook arrived at the beginning of the makahiki, and the Hawaiians naturally thought *he* was the god Lono coming to make the land fertile. Cook even sailed into the exact bay where the legend predicted Lono would arrive.

The Hawaiians went to great lengths to please their "god." All manner of supplies were made available. Eventually they became suspicious of the visitors. If they were gods, why did they accept the Hawaiian women? And if they were gods, why did one of them die?

Cook left at the right time. The British had used up the Hawaiians' hospitality (not to mention their supplies). But shortly after leaving the Big Island, the ship broke a mast, making it necessary to return to Kealakekua Bay for repairs. As they sailed back into the bay, the Hawaiians were nowhere to be seen. A chief had declared the area kapu to help replenish it. When Cook finally found the Hawaiians, they were polite but wary. Why are you back? Didn't we please you enough already? What do you want now?

As repair of the mast continued, things began to get tense. Eventually the Hawaiians stole a British rowboat (for the nails), and the normally calm Cook blew his cork. On the morning of February 14, 1779, he went ashore to trick the chief into coming aboard his ship where he would detain him until the rowboat was returned. As Cook and the chief were heading to the water, the chief's wife begged the chief not to go.

By now thousands of Hawaiians were crowding around Cook, and he ordered a retreat. A shot was heard from the other side of the bay, and someone shouted that the Englishmen had killed an important chief. A shielded warrior with a dagger came at Cook, who fired his pistol (loaded with small shot). The shield stopped the small shot, and the Hawaiians were emboldened. Other shots were fired. Standing in knee-deep water, Cook turned to call for a ceasefire and was struck in the head from behind with a club, then stabbed. Dozens of other Hawaiians pounced on him, stabbing his body repeatedly. The greatest explorer the world had ever known was dead at age 50 in a petty skirmish over a stolen rowboat.

KAMEHAMEHA THE GREAT

The most powerful and influential king in Hawaiian history lived during the time of Captain Cook and was born on the Big Island around 1758. Until his rule, the Hawaiian chain had never been ruled by a single person. He was the first to "unite" (i.e., conquer) all the islands.

Kamehameha was an extraordinary man by any standard. He possessed Herculean strength, a brilliant mind and boundless ambition. He was marked for death before he was even born. When Kamehameha's mother was pregnant with him, she developed a strange and overpowering craving—she wanted to *eat* the eyeball of a chief. The king of the Big Island, mindful of the rumor that the unborn child's real father was his bitter enemy, the king of Maui, asked his advisers to interpret. Their conclusion was unanimous: The child would grow to be a rebel, a killer of chiefs. The king decided that the child must die as soon as he was born, but the baby was instead whisked away to a remote valley to be raised.

In Hawaiian society, your role in life was governed by what class you were born into. The Hawaiians believed that breeding among family members produced superior offspring (except for the genetic misfortunates who were killed at birth), and the highest chiefs came from brother/sister combinations. Kamehameha was not of the highest class (his parents were merely cousins), so his future as a chief would not come easily.

As a young man, Kamehameha was impressed by his experience with Captain Cook. He was among the small group that stayed overnight on Cook's ship during Cook's first pass by of Maui.

(Kamehameha was on Maui valiantly fighting a battle in which his side was getting badly whooped.) Kamehameha recognized that his world had forever changed, and he shrewdly used the knowledge and technology of westerners to his advantage.

Kamehameha participated in numerous battles. His side lost many of the early ones, but he learned from his mistakes and developed into a cunning tactician. When he finally consolidated his rule over the Big Island (by luring his enemy to be the inaugural sacrifice of a new temple), he fixed his sights on the entire chain. In the 1790s his large company of troops, armed with some western armaments and advisors, swept across Maui, Moloka'i, Lana'i and O'ahu. After some delays with Kaua'i, the last of the holdouts, its king final-ly acquiesced to the inevitable, and Kamehameha became the first ruler of all the islands. He spent his final years governing the islands peacefully from his Big Island capital and died in 1819.

MODERN HAWAI'I

During the 19th century, Hawai'i's character changed dramatically. Businessmen from all over the world came here to exploit Hawai'i's sandalwood, whales, land and people. Hawai'i's leaders, for their part, actively participated in these ventures and took a piece of much of the action for themselves. Workers were brought from many parts of the world, changing the racial makeup of the islands. Government corruption became

O'ahu is blessed with more offshore islets than all the other Hawaiian islands combined.

the order of the day, and everyone seemed to be profiting, except the Hawaiian commoners. By the time Queen Lili'uokalani lost her throne to a group of American businessmen in 1893, Hawai'i had become directionless. It barely resembled the Hawai'i Captain Cook had encountered the in previous century. The kapu system had been abolished by the Hawaiians shortly after the death of Kamehameha the Great. The "Great Mahele," begun in 1848, had changed the relationship Hawaiians had with the land. Large tracts of land were sold by the Hawaiian government to royalty, government officials, commoners and foreigners, effectively stripping many Hawaiians of land they had lived on for generations.

The United States recognized the Republic of Hawai'i in 1894 with Sanford Dole as its president. It was annexed in 1898 and became an official territory in 1900. During the 19th and 20th centuries, sugar established itself as king. Pineapple was also heavily grown in the islands, with the island of Lana'i purchased in its entirety for the purpose of growing pineapples.

As the 20th century rolled on, Hawaiian sugar and pineapple workers found themselves in a lofty position— they became the highest paid workers for these crops in the world. As land prices rose and competition from other parts of the world increased, sugar and pineapple became less and less profitable. Today, these crops no longer hold the position they once had. The "pineapple island" of Lana'i has shifted away from pineapple growing and is focused on tourism. The sugar industry is now dead on the Big Island, O'ahu and Kaua'i, leaving only Maui to grow it commercially.

The story of Hawai'i is not a story of good versus evil. Nearly everyone shares in the blame for what happened to the Hawaiian people and their culture. Westerners certainly saw Hawai'i as a potential bonanza and easily exploitable. They knew what buttons to push and pushed them well. But the Hawaiians, for their part, were in a state of flux. The mere presence of westerners seemed to bring to the surface a discontent, or at least a weakness, with their system that had been lingering just below the surface.

In fact, in 1794, a mere 16 years after first encountering westerners and under no military duress from the West, Kamehameha the Great volunteered to cede his island over to Great Britain. He was hungry for western arms so he could defeat his neighbor-island opponents. He even declared that as of that day, they were no longer people of Hawai'i, but rather people of Britain. (Britain declined the offer.) And in 1819, immediately after the death of the strong-willed Kamehameha, the Hawaiians, of their own accord, overthrew their own religion, dumped the kapu system and denied their gods. This was *before* any western missionaries ever came to Hawai'i.

Nonetheless, Hawai'i today is once again seeking guidance from her heritage. The echoes of the past seem to be getting louder with time, rather than diminishing. Interest in the Hawaiian language and culture is at a level not seen in many decades. All of us who live here are very aware of the issues and the complexities involved, but there is little agreement about where it will lead. As a result, you will be exposed to a more "Hawaiian" Hawai'i than those who might have visited the state a generation ago. This is an interesting time in Hawai'i. Enjoy it as observers, and savor the flavor of the islands.

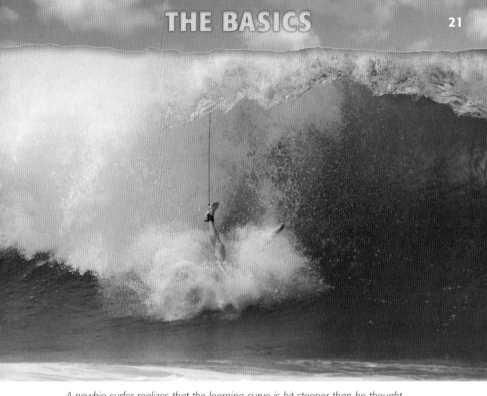

A newbie surfer realizes that the learning curve is bit steeper than he thought...

GETTING HERE

In order to get to Hawai'i, you've got to fly here. (You might be able to find a cruise to Hawai'i, but it's a pretty big and featureless piece of water to cross in a boat.)

When planning your trip, a travel agent can be helpful. Their commission has been paid directly by the travel industry, though that may change in the future. The Internet has sites such as Orbitz, Expedia, Cheaptickets, Cheapair, Pandaonline, Priceline, Travelocity, etc. If you don't want to or can't go through these sources, there are large wholesalers that can get you airfare, hotel and a rental car, often cheaper than you can get airfare on your own. The biggest one is **Pleasant Holidays** (800–742–9244), which provides complete package tours.

If you arrange airline tickets and hotel reservations yourself, you can often count on paying top dollar for each facet of your trip. The prices listed in the WHERE TO STAY section reflect the RACK rates, meaning the price you and I pay if we book direct. Rates can be significantly lower if you go through a wholesaler.

When you pick your travel source, shop around—the differences can be dramatic. A good package can make the difference between affording a *one-week* vacation and a *two-week* vacation. Also, look in the Sunday travel section of your local newspaper—the bigger the paper, the better.

All passengers arriving on O'ahu land at Honolulu International Airport. If you're going to any of the neighbor islands, interisland flights are done by **Hawaiian**

(800–367–5320), go! (888–435–9462) and Island Air (800–652–6541).

WHAT TO BRING

This list may assist you in planning what to bring. Obviously you might not bring everything on the list, but it might help you think of a few things you may otherwise overlook:

- Water-resistant sunscreen (SPF 15 or higher)
- Two bathing suits
- Shoes—flipflops, trashable sneakers, water shoes, hiking shoes
- Mask, snorkel and fins
- Camera with lots of storage

- Junk clothes for bikes, hiking, etc.
- Light rain jacket
- Mosquito repellent for some hikes. (*Lotions*—not liquids—with DEET seem to work the longest.)
- Shorts and other cool clothing
- Hiking sticks (carbide-tipped ones work best here)
- Cheap, simple backpack—handy even if you're not backpacking
- Hat or cap for sun protection

GETTING AROUND
Rental Cars

Rental car prices in Hawai'i *can be* (but aren't always) cheaper than almost anywhere else in the country, and the competition is ferocious. O'ahu is the only major Hawaiian island where a sizeable number of visitors stay *without* renting a car. (Waikiki is small and walk-

Even when they're crashing right in front of you, it's hard to appreciate the size of waves when no one's in the water to provide scale. This is what a four-story high wave looks like at Waimea Bay.

able, and many activity companies will shuttle you to their locations.) While it's true that you *might* not need one if you don't plan to leave Waikiki or intend to let activity companies shuttle you to their offerings, we think it's a big mistake if you don't have a rental car for at least *part* of your stay. Even if you're planning to take tour buses or the county bus, many of the glorious sights described in the driving tours will be unavailable to you. If you're trying to save money and spend much of your trip in Waikiki, get a rental car for at least some *part* of your trip. You won't regret it.

Avis, Hertz, National, Dollar, Enterprise and Budget are the most convenient rental car companies due to their return locations. Other companies, such as Alamo, are *outside* the airport. There's a gas station at the airport right before the car rental return, and they charge the usual confiscatory airport prices.

If you are between the ages of 21 and 25, most companies will rent to you. You'll pay about $25 extra for the crime of being young and reckless (except Enterprise, which has no surcharge). If you're under 21, **VIP** and **Paradise** will rent to those 18 and older.

Many hotels, condos and rental agents offer excellent room/car packages. Find out from your hotel or travel agent if one is available.

Here's a list of rental car companies. All the big companies have desks at the airport and in Waikiki.

The Big Guys
Alamo (877) 222-9075
Avis (800) 321-3712
Budget (800) 527-0700
Dollar (800) 800-4000
Enterprise (800) 261-7331

Hertz (800) 654-3131
National (877) 222-9058
Thrifty (800) 367-5238

The Little Guys
JN Rentals (808) 831-2726
Paradise Rent-a-Car (808) 946-7777
VIP (808) 922-4605

4-Wheel Drive
On Kaua'i and especially the Big Island we've strongly recommended getting a 4WD vehicle, but it isn't important on O'ahu. There aren't many off-road opportunities, and there are few places where access will require one. The dirt road leading part of the way to Ka'ena Point on the North Shore is just about the only area where it *might* be junky enough to require 4WD, but it's hard to justify the increased price just for that. Consider skipping the 4WD. If you want to splurge, spring for a convertible instead. They can be fun.

Taxis & Shuttles
If you don't want a rental car (or will be renting one in Waikiki later during your stay), there are plenty of taxi companies around the island. Their meter rates are set. They charge around $35 from the airport to Waikiki. If you call them in advance (instead of hailing them), you can usually get a cheaper rate. For instance, **O'ahu Airport Shuttle** (681–8000) charges about $30 to get you into Waikiki, **Akamai Cab Company** (377–1379) charges a similar price *for up to four people*. **Waikiki Shuttle** has workers lurking at baggage claim who will take you to Waikiki for $10. Once in Waikiki, cabs can easily be hailed.

Motorcycles
If you think riding a HOG is something you do at a lu'au, you may want to skip

this section. There's *something* about Harleys. Maybe it's the sound, or maybe the looks. But riding a Harley-Davidson around O'ahu is a blast. If you want to rent one to experience things on your own (freedom, after all, is what HOGS are all about), you can get them, and other motorcycles from:

Paradise Rent-a-Car (946–7777) located at 1835 Ala Moana Blvd. has Harleys for $179 per day.

Other two-wheeled options include:

Hawaiian Style Rentals (946–6733) at 2556 Lemon Rd. rents mopeds from $35–$50, depending on the model.

Big Kahuna (924–2736) at 407 Seaside Ave. rents motorcycles for $70–$190 per day. (The latter reflects their top end Harley.) Mopeds are $40 per day.

Adventure on 2 Wheels (944–3131) at 1946 Ala Moana has mopeds for $30 per day or $20 for 4 hours.

Check out the bike first. We've seen some pretty bald tires and snotty attitudes at some of these places. We've also had unhappy e-mails in the past from readers who've rented from Big Kahuna and Adventure on 2 Wheels. Small, single passenger scooter rentals don't require a motorcycle license.

Exotic Cars

O'ahu has lots of opportunities to rent a flashy ride. Ferraris, Vipers, 'Vettes, Porsches and other sexy autos can be had—for the right price. You're looking at around $500 for a Viper, $800 for a Ferrari, etc. That's *per day!* Bear in mind that there are no good opportunities to open them up—we have no empty straightaways to throttle these puppies—but if you just want to experience the thrill of driving a fantasy car, and you have a wad burning a hole in your pocket, give it a shot.

Hawai'i Luxury Car Rentals (222–2277) operates out of a not-so-luxurious booth on Beachwalk Ave. They require hefty credit card deposits. If you're 21–25 years old, it'll cost you more.

Driving Around O'ahu

O'ahu has some of the most confusing roads and highways you'll find anywhere in the United States. Roads change names randomly and with no warning, leaving you confused as to where you actually are. Let's use an example. Kamehameha Hwy (a major island highway) is also called Hwy 99...until it changes its name to Hwy 80 where Hwy 99 changes to Wilikina Drive, then Kamahanui Road. Then Kamehameha Hwy (also called Kam Hwy) becomes Hwy 99 again, then Hwy 83, then Hwy 830 (*if* you remember to turn left at the Hygienic Store in Kahalu'u), then Hwy 83 again. All this for *one* highway. Or consider Farrington Hwy. Look on a map, and Farrington Hwy wraps around the western tip. Oh, except for the 6 miles around the tip where it doesn't actually exist. You'll have to go around via Hwy 99...or is it Kamehameha Hwy?

Plus when you're on our freeways, you'll find it maddening when you discover that you can often get *off* a freeway...but not back *on* it. Or maybe you can only get on it by driving in the *opposite* direction you want to go.

While making our maps, we've repeatedly driven the roads with the computer files literally in our laps and tried to mark things as you're likely to see them, not necessarily by their official names. At times we've left off confusing and conflicting names. Nonetheless, though we've gone to considerable effort to make the maps as easy to read as possible, you *will* get confused and lost if you drive around long enough. Hey, don't blame us. We just make the maps; we didn't devise this embarrassing road system.

Remember, Honolulu is a big city, and you *won't* be the only one trying to get somewhere. Although traffic can be bad anywhere at any time, the **basic traffic pattern** is this: *Into* Waikiki and Honolulu from all points in the morning, and *away* from Waikiki and Honolulu to all points in the afternoon. H-1 is backed up pretty often, especially eastbound where H-1 and Hwy 78 meet (called the *Middle Street Merge*).

If you're heading west on H-1, locals call that being *'Ewa-bound*. If you're heading east, it's *Koko Head-bound*.

Seat belt and **child restraint** use are required by law, and the police will pull you over for this alone. It's also illegal for drivers to use a **cell phone** without a headset. Open roads and frequently changing speed limits make it easy to accidentally speed here. Sobriety checkpoints are not an uncommon police tactic on O'ahu.

It's best not to leave anything valuable in your car. **Car break-ins** can be a problem here. Thieving scum looking for anything of value regularly hit rental cars. When we park at a beach, hiking trail or any other place frequented by visitors, we take all valuables with us, leave the windows up, and leave the doors *unlocked*. (Just in case someone is curious enough about the inside to smash a window.) There are plenty of stories about people walking 100 feet to a beach, coming back to their car, and finding that their brand new video camera has walked away. And don't be gullible enough to think that trunks are safe. Someone who sees you put some-

Some of the things that we consider quintessentially Hawaiian, like coconut trees, were actually imported by Hawai'i's first settlers.

thing in your trunk can probably get at it faster than you can with your key.

Buses

O'ahu is the only Hawaiian island with a truly great bus system, cleverly called **The Bus** (848–5555). About 30% of visitors use the bus system, according to the state. You'll find bus schedules sprinkled in kiosks all around Waikiki. It's $2.50 for a one-way fare (includes one transfer), $60 for a monthly pass. Bus #8 is the one that circles Waikiki and Ala Moana Shopping Center (there's one every 10 minutes), and we've shown the route on the Waikiki map. Even if you have a rental car, it might be tempting to jump on the old #8 bus to take you to the other end of Waikiki instead of worrying about parking.

Carry-on baggage is allowed, but "Baggage or carry-on items that will not be admitted on the bus shall include any large, bulky, dangerous or offensive article that may cause harm or discomfort to any passenger." *So there*.

The **Waikiki Trolley** (926–7604), on the other hand, is ridiculously overpriced at $25 per person per day, but their *online* price of $49 *per week* is a pretty good deal and can be combined for discounts on some attractions.

GETTING MARRIED ON O'AHU

Hawai'i, with its exotic beauty and nearly perfect weather, is one of the most popular wedding and honeymoon destinations in the world. And sunsets along the leeward side can provide a breathtaking backdrop for your ceremony.

License requirements in Hawai'i are simple. You both must apply to the health department (online is OK) and pay the $60. Your license will be good for 30 days. You'll have to present ID in person to a marriage license agent. (Call 586–4544.)

All the major resorts can provide planners to assist you with the details. They have the facilities and sites on their properties along with experienced staff to make the day go smoothly. The resorts can provide chapels, gazebos, waterfalls and lush gardens for your ceremony. Some of more popular resorts in Waikiki are the Hilton Hawaiian Village, the Halekulani, the Royal Hawaiian and the Sheraton Moana. If you prefer a resort outside Waikiki, consider The Kahala, Turtle Bay Resort or the JW Marriott 'Ihilani at Ko Olina. Aulani Disney Resort has fairytale weddings that they claim will allow you to live happily ever after. (Prenups are extra.)

There are also many independent coordinators with years of experience helping couples with their wedding plans. Be sure you and you planner are clear about your budgetary limits and what you want during your wedding day. Also be certain about the amount of assistance you will receive before the ceremony, so you can relax and enjoy your wedding day.

Be aware of holidays, the popularity of Valentine's Day and the month of June for weddings. By booking far enough in advance, you should be able to arrange a wedding during one of these busy times.

Always be sure there is a backup plan in case it rains. Beaches are public, so you will have other beachgoers present during your ceremony. If you're considering using a state or county park, be sure you have met their permit requirements.

Looking for a different but very Hawaiian reception? Consider holding it on one of the dinner cruises or joining in with one of the island's lu'aus (remember

Rainfall Map

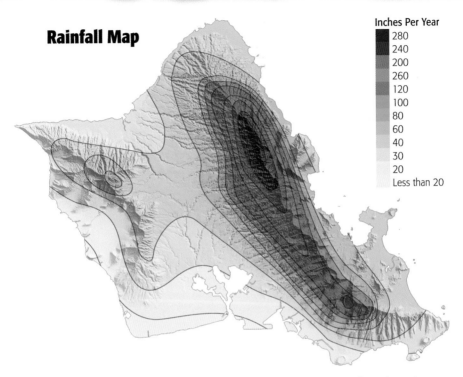

Inches Per Year
- 280
- 240
- 200
- 260
- 120
- 100
- 80
- 60
- 40
- 30
- 20
- Less than 20

that the Polynesian Cultural Center lu'au does not permit alcohol).

WEATHER

One of the biggest worries people have when planning their trip to the tropics is the weather. Will it rain? Is it going to be too hot? What about hurricanes? Let's deal with the last one first. There have been only three recorded hurricanes in Hawai'i in the past 200 years. One in the '50s, one in the '80s and *Iniki* on September 11, 1992, clobbering Kaua'i. None have hit O'ahu, so you should probably spend your precious worry energy elsewhere.

As for rain, it works like this: The prevailing winds (called trade winds) come from the northeast, bringing their moisture with them. As the air hits the Ko'olau mountains, it rises, cools and condenses into clouds and rain. So the mountains and shoreline facing the northeast, called the **windward side**, get the lion's share of the rain. Look at the rain graphic, and it will make more sense. Often by midmorning, the rising, cooling air causes clouds to form in the mountains, giving them an exotic, mystical look.

Once the air has had its moisture wrung out, it sinks and warms on the southwest side (called the **leeward side**) and often has minimal rain potential. So areas like Waikiki get little rain. The exception is when we get winds from the south or southwest—called Kona winds—where the rain pattern is reversed. These Kona winds only happen about 5%–10% of the time, most often in the winter.

Waikiki has an embarrassingly equable climate. The average high is 84°, and it has *never* gotten above 95° since thermometers have been in the islands. Waikiki gets only 20 inches of rain per year, and when it does rain, it's often in the form of short, intense showers.

Average **humidity** ranges from 65%–75%. And **ocean temperatures** go from 75° in February to about 80° in September.

GEOGRAPHY

The different Hawaiian islands have different geographic infrastructures. Kaua'i is made up of one giant extinct volcano. Maui has two (one of them still barely alive). The Big Island lives up to its name, consisting of a staggering five volcanoes, only one of which is extinct (though only two of them are active enough for us to see in our lifetime). On O'ahu, it took two now-extinct volcanos to create this para-

In the tropics, beautiful weather doesn't always mean sunny skies.

dise. (The second one is *probably* extinct. See page 60 for more.) **Wai'anae** in the west poked above the water 2.2 million years ago, followed a million years later by its younger sibling, **Ko'olau**, in the east. Ko'olau (called the Ko'olau Mountains locally, even though it's really only one long mountain) is shorter—peaking at 3,150 feet, but it's over 30 miles long. What's most impressive is that it's only half the original mountain. The other half has been erased by ceaseless erosion. The top of the older volcano, Wai'anae, is called Mount Ka'ala and towers 4,025 feet above the ocean.

HAZARDS
The Sun

The hazard that by far affects the most people (excluding the accommodations tax) is the sun. O'ahu, at 21° latitude, receives sunlight more directly than anywhere on the mainland. (The more overhead the sunlight, the less atmosphere it

filters through.) If you want to enjoy your *entire* vacation, make sure that you wear a strong sunblock. We recommend a water-resistant sunscreen with at least an SPF of 15. We use lotions when hiking, and the gel types like Bullfrog when going in the water (because they stay on better). Many visitors who get burned do so while snorkeling. You won't feel it coming because of the water. We *strongly* suggest you wear a T-shirt while snorkeling, or you may get a nasty surprise.

Try to avoid the sun between 11 a.m. and 2 p.m. when the sun's rays are particularly strong. If you are fair-skinned or unaccustomed to the sun and want to soak up some rays, 15–20 minutes per side is all you should consider the first day. You can increase it a bit each day. *Beware of the fact that our breezes will hide the symptoms of a burn until it's too late.* You might find that trying to get your tan as golden as possible isn't worth it. Tropical suntans are notoriously short-lived, whereas you are sure to remember a bad burn far longer. If, after all our warnings, you *still* get burned, aloe vera gel works well to relieve the pain. Some come with lidocaine in them. Some resorts even have aloe plants on the grounds. Peel the skin off a section and make several crisscross cuts in the meat, then rub the plant on your skin. *Oooo,* it'll feel so good!

Water Hazards

The most serious water hazard is the surf. Though more calm in the summer and on the leeward side, high surf can be found anywhere on the island at any time of the year. The sad fact is that more people drown in Hawai'i each year than anywhere else in the country. This isn't said to keep you from enjoying the ocean, but rather to instill in you a healthy respect for Hawaiian waters. See BEACHES for more information on this. And for a current surf report call 973–4383. Even hardened watermen call for a surf forecast before planning their day.

Ocean Critters

Hawaiian marine life, for the most part, is quite friendly. There are, however, a few notable exceptions. Below is a list of some critters that you should be aware of. This is not mentioned to frighten you out of the water. The odds are overwhelming that you won't have any trouble with any of the beasties listed below. But should you encounter one, this information should be of some help.

Sharks—Hawai'i does have sharks. Most are the essentially harmless white-tipped reef sharks, plus the occasional hammerhead or tiger shark. Contrary to what most people think, sharks are in every ocean and don't pose the level of danger people attribute to them. In the past 25 years there has been only a handful of documented shark attacks off O'ahu, mostly tigers attacking surfers. Considering the number of people who swam in our waters during that time, you are statistically more likely to get mauled by a hungry timeshare salesman than be bitten by a shark. If you do happen to come upon a shark, however, swim away slowly. This kind of movement doesn't interest them. *Don't* splash about rapidly. By doing this you are imitating a fish in distress, and you don't want to do that. The one kind of water you want to avoid is murky water, such as that found in river mouths. Most shark attacks occur in murky water at dawn or dusk since sharks are basically cowards who like to sneak up on their prey. In general, don't go around worrying about sharks. *Any* animal can be threatening.

Portuguese Man-of-War—These are related to jellyfish but are unable to

swim. They are instead propelled by a small sail and are at the mercy of the wind. Though small, they are capable of inflicting a painful sting. This occurs when the long, trailing tentacles are touched, triggering hundreds of thousands of spring-loaded stingers, called nematocysts, which inject venom. The resulting burning sensation is usually very unpleasant but not fatal. Fortunately, the Portuguese man-of-war is not a common visitor to most island beaches. When they *do* come ashore, however, they usually do so in large numbers, jostled by a strong onshore wind usually at northeast-facing beaches. If you see them on the beach, don't go in the water. If you do get stung, immediately remove the tentacles with a gloved hand, stick or whatever is handy. Rinse thoroughly with salt or fresh water to remove any adhering nematocysts. Then apply ice for pain control. If the condition worsens, see a doctor. The old treatments of vinegar or baking soda are no longer recommended. The folk cure is urine, and for half the population, it comes with a handy applicator, but you might look pretty silly applying it.

Box Jellyfish—O'ahu is the only island in the chain where these guys are a problem. Once a month, 9 or 10 days after the full moon, box jellyfish approach the shoreline, especially at leeward beaches, such as Ala Moana, Waikiki and Hanauma Bay, and will sting anything that comes in contact with them. These are *not* the same notorious box jellyfish that kill people in Australia. Although you're certainly *allowed* to swim during that time, we personally choose not to and suggest you do the same. Sting treatments are similar to those for man-of-war, but vinegar *is* recommended for box jellyfish stings.

Sea Urchins—These are like living pin cushions. If you step on one or accidentally grab one, remove as much of the spine as possible with tweezers. See a physician if necessary.

Coral—Coral skeletons are very sharp and, since the skeleton is overlaid by millions of living coral polyps, a scrape can leave proteinaceous matter in the wound, causing infection. This is why coral cuts are frustratingly slow to heal. Immediate cleaning and disinfecting of coral cuts should speed up healing time. We don't have fire coral around Hawai'i.

Sea Anemones—Related to the jellyfish, these also have stingers and are usually found attached to rocks or coral. It's best not to touch them with your bare hands. Treatment for a sting is similar to that for Portuguese man-of-war.

Bugs

Though we're devoid of the myriad hideous buggies found in other parts of the world, there are a few evil critters brought here from elsewhere that you should know about. The worst are **centipedes**. They can get to be six or more inches long and are aggressive predators. They shouldn't be messed with. You'll probably never see one, but if you get stung, even by a baby, the pain can range from a bad bee sting to a moderate gunshot blast. Some local doctors say the only cure is to stay drunk for three days. Others say to use meat tenderizer instead of a brain tenderizer.

Cane spiders are big, dark and look horrifying, but they're not poisonous. (But they seem to *think* they are. I've had *them* chase *me* across the room when *I* had the broom in my hand.) We *don't* have no-see-ums, those irritating sand fleas common in the South Pacific and Caribbean.

Mosquitoes were unknown in the islands until the first stowaways arrived on Maui on the *Wellington* in 1826. Since then they have thrived. A good mosquito repellent containing DEET will come in handy, especially if you plan to go hiking. *Lotions* (not thin liquids) with DEET seem to work and stick best. Forget the guidebooks that tell you to take vitamin B$_{12}$ to keep mosquitoes away; it just gives the little critters a healthier diet. If you find one dive-bombing you at night in your room and you have an overhead fan, turn it on to help keep them away. Bees and wasps are more common on the drier leeward side of the island. Usually, the only way you'll get stung is if you run *into* or step *onto* one. If you rent a motorcycle, beware; I received my first bee sting while singing *Come Sail Away* on a motorcycle. A bee sting in the mouth can definitely ruin one of your precious vacation days.

Regarding cockroaches, there's good news and bad news. The bad news is that here, some are bigger than your thumb and can fly. The good news is that you probably won't see one. One of their predators is the gecko. This small, lizard-like creature makes a surprisingly loud chirp at night. They are cute and considered good luck in the islands (probably 'cause they eat mosquitoes and roaches).

There are no snakes in Hawai'i (other than some reporters). There is concern that the brown tree snake *might* have made its way onto the islands from Guam. Although mostly harmless to humans, these snakes can spell extinction for native birds. Government officials aren't allowed to tell you this, but we will: If you ever see one anywhere in Hawai'i, please *kill it* and contact the Pest Hotline at 643–7378. At the very least, call them immediately. The entire bird population of Hawai'i will be grateful.

Swimming in Streams

There are opportunities on O'ahu to swim in streams and under waterfalls. It's the fulfillment of a fantasy for many people. But there are several hazards you need to know about.

Leptospirosis is a bacteria that is found in some of Hawai'i's freshwater. It is transmitted from animal urine and can enter the body through open cuts, eyes and by drinking. Numbers are hard to come by, but around 100 people a year in Hawai'i are diagnosed with the bacteria, which is treated with antibiotics if caught relatively early. You should avoid swimming in streams if you have open cuts, and treat all water found in nature with treatment pills before drinking. (Many filters are ineffective for lepto.)

While swimming in freshwater streams, try to use your arms as much as possible. Kicking an unseen rock is easier than you think. Also, consider wearing water shoes while in streams. These water-friendly wonders are available all over O'ahu and allow you to walk in water while still protecting your feet.

Though rare, **flash floods** can occur in any freshwater stream anywhere in the world, even paradise. Be alert for them.

Lastly, remember while lingering under waterfalls that not everything that comes over the top will be as soft as water. Rocks coming down from above could definitely shatter the moment—among other things.

Dehydration

Bring and drink lots of water when you are out and about, especially when you are hiking. Dehydration sneaks up on people. By the time you are thirsty, you're already dehydrated. It's a good idea to take water with you in the car at all times. Our weather is almost certainly different from what you left behind, and you will probably find yourself thirstier than usual. Just fill a bottle or two before you leave in the morning and *suck 'em up* (as we say here) all day.

Pigs

We're not referring to your dining choice. We mean the wild ones you may encounter on a hiking trail. Generally, pigs will avoid you before you ever see them. If you happen to come upon any piglets and accidentally get between them and their mother, immediately bark like a big dog. Wild pigs are conditioned to run from local dogs (and their hunter masters), and Momma will leave her kids faster than you can say, "Pass the bacon."

Traffic

Oh, yeah. Traffic can be a *big* problem here, especially in Honolulu. See Driving Around O'ahu on page 24 for more.

Grocery Stores

A decided hazard. Restaurants are expensive, but don't think you'll get off cheap in grocery stores. Though you'll certainly save money cooking your own food if your room has cooking facilities, a trip to the store here can be startling. Phrases like *they charge how much for milk?* echo throughout the stores. Even items such as pineapples—*grown on this island!*—may cost more here than the ones jetted to you on the mainland. Go figure. If you're stocking up, consider buying groceries at **Costco** (526–6103) west of Waikiki on Alakawa Street between Dillingham Blvd. and Nimitz Hwy, or the massive 300,000-square-foot, 24-hour **Walmart/Sam's Club** (955–8441) just

outside of Waikiki on Keeaumoku Street near Ala Moana Shopping Center.

In Waikiki, the only real grocery store is the **Food Pantry** (923–9831) on Kuhio Ave. at Walina St. Prices will obviously be higher than other grocery stores, but if you have access to a kitchen in your room, it's very convenient.

TRAVELING WITH CHILDREN (KEIKI)

Should we have put this under HAZARDS? If you're coming to Hawai'i and bringing the keiki (kids), O'ahu has more kid-oriented activities than any of the Hawaiian islands—some of 'em cheap, some of 'em at *hurt-me* prices.

Hawai'i Children's Discovery Center (524–5437) is at 111 Ohe St. It's $10 general admission. Basically, kids up to about 9 will love the interactive exhibits rich with costumes, international cultures, various occupations and science. Kids 10 and up might get antsy. They have an unusually good gift shop.

The ATTRACTIONS chapter is the best place to look for keiki-friendly places. Check out our reviews of **Wet 'n' Wild Hawai'i**, **Sea Life Park**, **Waikiki Aquar-**

From the air, Kane'ohe Bay's odd-looking reefs appear to be more like giant amoebas than coral.

A mom jumps for joy capturing the perfect shot of her keiki.

ium, Honolulu Zoo and Hawaiian Railway Society.

If you're looking for a place for lunch, the Oceanarium Restaurant at 921–6111 (see DINING on page 238) has a quarter-million gallon aquarium next to their tables, and at lunch they send in a SCUBA diver to feed the fish. Always a hit with kids.

The Dole Plantation (621–8408) has a 137,000-square-foot hedge maze that keeps kids occupied for $4 ($6 for adults). See page 97 for more.

Podium Raceway Hawai'i (see page 122) has cool electric race carts that can be a hit with older kids.

In the ADVENTURES chapter we have swimming with dolphins—the kind of adventure kids *dream* of. See page 223.

The accommodations reviews describe resorts with good keiki programs. By the way, if your objective was to get *away* from the kids, then maybe these resorts won't be at the top of *your* list. Many resorts have been cutting back on their kids' programs in recent years.

Lastly, you should know that it's a big fine plus a mandatory safety class if your keiki isn't buckled up.

THE PEOPLE

There's no doubt about it—people really *are* friendlier in Hawai'i, even in urban Honolulu. You will notice that people are quick to smile and wave at you here. (Those of us who live in Hawai'i have to remember to pack our "mainland face" when we journey there. Otherwise, we get undesired responses when we smile or wave at complete strangers.) It probably comes down to a matter of happiness. People are happy here, and happy people are friendly people.

Some Terms

A person of Hawaiian blood is Hawaiian. Only people of this race are called by this term. They are also called Kanaka Maoli, but only another Hawaiian can use this term. Anybody who was born here, regardless of race (except whites), is called a local. If you were born elsewhere but have lived here long enough to get a drivers license, you are called a **kamaʻaina**. If you are white, you are a **haole**. It doesn't matter if you have been here a day, or your family has been here for over a century—you will always be a haole. The term comes from the time when westerners first encountered these islands. Its precise meaning has been lost, but it is thought to refer to people with no background (since westerners could not chant kanaenae—praise—of their ancestors).

The continental United States is called the **mainland**. If you are here and are returning, you are not "going back to the states" (we *are* a state). When somebody leaves the island, they are **off-island**.

Hawaiian Time

One aspect of Hawaiian culture you may have heard of is Hawaiian Time. The stereotype is that *everyone* in Hawaiʻi moves just a little bit slower than on the mainland. Supposedly, we are more laid-back and don't let things get to us as easily as people on the mainland. This is the stereotype…. OK, it's *not* a stereotype. It's real. Hopefully, during your visit, you will notice that this feeling infects *you,* as well. You may find yourself letting another driver cut in front of you in circumstances that would incur your wrath back home. You may find yourself willing to wait for a red light without feeling like you're going to explode. The whole reason for coming to Hawaiʻi is to experience beauty and a sense of peace, so let it happen. If someone else is moving a bit slower than you want, just go with it.

Shaka

One gesture you will see often—and should not be offended by—is the *shaka* sign. This is done by extending the pinkie and thumb while curling the three middle fingers. Sometimes visitors think it is some kind of local gesture indicating *up yours* or some similarly unfriendly message. Actually, it is a friendly act used as a sign of greeting, thanks or just to say, *Hey.* Its origin is thought to date back to the 1930s. A guard at the Kahuku Sugar Plantation used to patrol the plantation railroad to keep local kids from stealing cane from the slow moving trains. This guard had lost his middle fingers in an accident, and his manner of waving off the youths became well known. Kids began to warn other kids that he was around by waving their hands in a way that looked like the guard's, and the custom took off.

THE HAWAIIAN LANGUAGE

The Hawaiian language is a beautiful, gentle and melodic language that flows smoothly off the tongue. Just the sounds of the words conjure up trees gently blowing in the breeze and the sound of the surf. Most Polynesian languages share the same roots, and many have common words. Today, Hawaiian is spoken *as an everyday language* only on the privately owned island of Niʻihau. Visitors are often intimidated by Hawaiian. With a few ground rules you will come to realize that pronunciation is not as hard as you might think.

When missionaries discovered that the Hawaiians had no written language, they sat down and created an alphabet. This Hawaiian alphabet has only 12 letters. Five vowels: A, E, I, O and U, as well as seven consonants, H, K, L, M, N, P and W. The consonants are pronounced just as they are in English, with the exception of W. It is often pronounced as a V if it is in the middle of a word and comes after an E or I. Vowels are pronounced as follows:

A—pronounced as in *Ah* if stressed, or *above* if not stressed.

E—pronounced as in *say* if stressed, or *dent* if not stressed.

I—pronounced as in *bee*.

O—pronounced as in *no*.

U—pronounced as in *boo*.

One thing you will notice in this book are glottal stops. These are represented by an upside-down apostrophe ' and are meant to convey a hard stop in the pronunciation. So if we are talking about the type of lava called a'a, it is pronounced as two separate As (AH-AH).

Another feature you will encounter are diphthongs, where two letters glide together. They are ae, ai, ao, au, ei, eu, oi and ou. Unlike many English diphthongs, the second vowel is always pronounced. One word you will read in this book, referring to Hawaiian temples, is *heiau* (HEY-YOW). The e and i flow together as a single sound, then the a and u flow together as a single sound. The Y sound binds the two sounds, making the whole word flow together.

If you examine long Hawaiian words, you will see that most have repeating syllables, making them easier to remember and pronounce.

Let's take a word that might seem impossible to pronounce. When you see how easy this word is, the rest will seem like a snap. The Hawai'i state fish is the humuhumunukunukuapua'a. At first glance it seems like a nightmare. But if you read the word slowly, it is pronounced just like it looks and isn't nearly as horrifying as it appears. Try it. Humu (hoo-moo) is pronounced twice. Nuku (noo-koo) is pronounced twice. A (ah) is pronounced once. Pu (poo) is pronounced once. A'a (ah-ah) is the ah sound pronounced twice, the glottal stop indicating a hard stop between sounds.

Now, you can try to pronounce it again. Humuhumunukunukuapua'a. Now, wasn't that easy? OK, so it's not easy, but it's not impossible either.

Below are some words that you might hear during your visit:

'Aina (EYE-na)—Land.

Akamai (AH-ka-MY)—Wise or shrewd.

Ali'i (ah-LEE-ee)—A Hawaiian chief; a member of the chiefly class.

Aloha (ah-LO-ha)—Hello, goodbye, or a feeling or the spirit of love, affection or kindness.

Hala (HA-la)—Pandanus tree.

Hale (HA-leh)—House or building.

Hana (HA-na)—Work.

Hana hou (HA-na-HO)—To do again.

Haole (HOW-leh)—Originally foreigner, now means Caucasian.

Heiau (HEY-YOW)—Hawaiian temple.

Hula (HOO-la)—The storytelling dance of Hawai'i.

Imu (EE-moo)—An underground oven.

'Iniki (ee-NEE-key)—Sharp and piercing wind (as in Hurricane 'Iniki).

Kahuna (ka-HOO-na)—A priest or minister; someone who is an expert in a profession.

Kai (kigh)—The sea.

Kalua (KA-LOO-ah)—Cooking food underground.

Kama'aina (KA-ma-EYE-na)—Long-time Hawai'i resident.

Kane (KA-neh)—Boy or man.

Kapu (KA-poo)—Forbidden, taboo; keep out.

Keiki (KAY-key)—Child or children.

Kokua (KO-KOO-ah)—Help.

Kona (KO-na)—Leeward side of the island; wind blowing from the south, southwest direction.

Kuleana (KOO-leh-AH-na)—Concern, responsibility or jurisdiction.

Lanai (LA-NIGH)—Porch, veranda, patio.

Once endangered, green sea turtles are now much more common on O'ahu than they used to be.

Lani (LA-nee)—Sky or heaven.

Lei (lay)—Necklace of flowers, shells or feathers.

Liliko'i (LEE-lee-KO-ee)—Passion fruit.

Limu (LEE-moo)—Edible seaweed.

Lomi (LOW-me)—To rub or massage; lomi salmon is raw salmon rubbed with salt and spices.

Lu'au (LOO-OW)—Hawaiian feast; literally means taro leaves.

Mahalo (ma-HA-low)—Thank you.

Makai (ma-KIGH)—Toward the sea.

Malihini (MA-lee-HEE-nee)—A newcomer, visitor or guest.

Mauka (MOW-ka)—Toward the mountain.

Moana (mo-AH-na)—Ocean.

Mo'o (MO-oh)—Lizard.

Nani (NA-nee)—Beautiful, pretty.

Nui (NEW-ee)—Big, important, great.

'Ohana (oh-HA-na)—Family.

'Okole (OH-KO-leh)—Derrière.

'Ono (OH-no)—Delicious, the best.

Pakalolo (pa-ka-LO-LO)—Marijuana.

Pali (PA-lee)—A cliff.

Paniolo (PA-nee-OH-lo)—Hawaiian cowboy.

Pau (pow)—Finish, end; *pau hana* means quitting time from work.

Poi (poy)—Pounded kalo (taro) root that forms a paste.

Pono (PO-no)—Goodness, excellence, correct, proper.

Pua (POO-ah)—Flower.

Puka (POO-ka)—Hole.

Pupu (POO-POO)—Appetizer, snacks or finger food.

Wahine (vah-HEE-neh)—Woman.

Wai (why)—Fresh water.

Wikiwiki (WEE-kee-WEE-kee)—To hurry up, very quick.

Quick Pidgin Lesson

Hawaiian pidgin is fun to listen to. It's like ear candy. It's colorful, rhythmic and sways in the wind. Below is a list of some of the words and phrases you might hear on your visit. It's tempting to read some of these and try to use them. If you do, the odds are you will simply look foolish. These words and phrases are used in certain ways and with certain inflections. People who have spent years living in the islands still feel uncomfortable using them. Thick pidgin can be incomprehensible to the untrained ear (that's the idea). If you are someplace and hear two people engaged in a discussion in pidgin, stop and eavesdrop a bit. You won't forget it.

Pidgin Words & Phrases

An' den—And then? So?

Any kine—Anything; any kind.

Ass right—That's right.

Ass wy—That's why.

Beef—Fight.

Brah—Bruddah; friend; brother.

Brok' da mouf—Delicious.

Buggah—That's the one; it is difficult.

Bus laugh—To laugh out loud.

Bus nose—How one reacts to bad smell.

Chicken skin kine—Something that gives you goosebumps.

Choke—Plenty; lots.

Cockaroach—Steal; rip off.

Da kine—A noun or verb used in place of whatever the speaker wishes. Heard constantly.

Fo days—Plenty; "He got hair fo days."

Geevum—Go for it! Give 'em hell!

Grind—To eat.

Grinds—Food.

Hold ass—A close call when driving your new car.

How you figgah?—How do you figure that? It makes no sense.

Howzit?—How is it going? How are you? Also, Howzit o wot?

I owe you money or wot?—What to say when someone is staring at you.

Mek ass—Make a fool of yourself.

Mek house—Make yourself at home.

Mek plate—Grab some food.

Mo' bettah—This is better.

Moke—A large, tough local male. (Don't say it unless you *like beef*.)

No can—Cannot; I cannot do it.

No mek li dat—Stop doing that.

No, yeah?—No, or is "no" correct?

'Okole squeezer—Something that suddenly frightens you ('okole meaning derrière).

O wot?—Or what?

When you want to get away, but not too far away, how about visiting an offshore island?

Pau hana—Quit work. (A time of daily, intense celebration in the islands.)

Poi dog—A mutt.

Shahkbait—Shark bait, meaning pale, untanned people.

Shaka—Great! All right!

Shredding—Riding a gnarly wave.

Sleepahs—Flipflops, thongs, zoris.

Stink eye—Dirty looks; facial expression denoting displeasure.

Suck rocks—Buzz off, or pound sand.

Talk stink—Speak bad about somebody.

Talk story—Shooting the breeze; to rap.

Tanks eh?—Thank you.

Tita—A female moke. Same *beef* results.

Yeah?—Used at the end of sentences.

THE HULA

The hula evolved as a means of worship, later becoming a forum for telling a story with chants (called mele), hands and body movement. It can be fascinating to watch. When most people think of the hula, they picture a woman in a grass skirt swinging her hips to the beat of an 'ukulele. But in reality there are two types of hula. The modern hula, or hula 'auana, uses musical instruments and vocals to augment the dancer. It came about after westerners first encountered the Islands. Missionaries found the hula distasteful, and the old style was driven underground. The modern type came about as a form of entertainment and was practiced in places where missionaries had no influence. Ancient Hawaiians didn't even use grass skirts. These were brought later by Gilbert Islanders.

The old style of hula is called hula 'olapa or hula kahiko. It consists of chants and is accompanied by percussion only and takes years of training. It can be exciting to watch as performers work together in synchronous harmony. Both men and women participate, with women's hula

being softer (though no less disciplined) and men's hula being more active. This type of hula is physically demanding, requiring strong concentration. Keiki (children's) hula is charming to watch, as well.

BOOKS & MUSIC

There is an astonishing variety of books available about Hawai'i and O'ahu. Everything from history, legends, geology, children's stories and just plain ol' novels. **Barnes & Noble** (737–3323) in Kahala Mall has a great selection. Walk in and lose yourself in Hawai'i's richness.

Hawaiian music is far more diverse than most people think. Many people picture Hawaiian music as someone twanging away on an 'ukulele with his voice slipping and sliding all over the place like he has an ice cube down his back. In reality, the music here can be outstanding. There is the melodic sound of the more traditional music. There are young local bands putting out modern music with a Hawaiian beat. There is even Hawaiian reggae. Hawaiian Style Band, the late Israel Kamakawiwo'ole (known locally as Bruddah Iz) and Willie K are excellent examples of the local sound. Even if you don't always agree with the all the messages in the songs, there's no denying the talent of these entertainers.

THE INTERNET

We have recent updates on our website, **www.hawaiirevealed.com**, as well as links to cool sites, the latest satellite weather shots, a calendar of events and more. You can even check resort availability right from our site. We also show our own aerial photos of most places to stay on O'ahu, so you'll know if oceanfront *really* means oceanfront. It has links to every company listed in the book that has a site—both those we like and those we don't recommend. For the record we don't charge a cent for links (it would be a conflict of interest), and there are *no advertisements* on the site. (Well... except for our own products, of course.) We've been asked why we don't list websites and e-mail addresses in the book. Linking from the site makes more sense. Nothing is more mind-numbing than seeing URL addresses in print.

If you're on-island and need Web access (to check your mail, etc.), most of the big resorts have business services available for around $7 an hour.

If you brought your own computer or tablet, nearly all hotel rooms have hi-speed Internet access. If you're Wi-Fi enabled, you shouldn't find any difficulty picking up signals in Waikiki. The few places we found that have free access include: the food court at the International Marketplace, the Waikiki Marketplace at 2310 Kuhio Ave., and **Coconut Willy's** (921–9000) at 227 Lewers St. **Skywave** (866–374–7065) broadcasts wireless Internet throughout most of Waikiki for $9 a day (they may have a stronger signal than your hotel). They service a long list of hotels. Starbucks and McDonald's also have access for a small fee.

SHOPPING

Most of us long to return home with a smile, tan and gifts from Hawai'i for friends and family. Besides locally grown coffee, chocolate macadamia nuts, T-shirts, aloha wear and other reminders of your visit, there are some one-of-a-kind finds at nearby **Ala Moana Shopping Center**. Perhaps the million-dollar necklace from Cartier or the $200,000 ring from Tiffany will wow them back home. Or consider the $75,000 Hermes handbag or the $12,000 Montblanc pen for your boss. It's all there for you to choose from, and prices might even include a free gift box. (If the above shopping list seems reasonable to you, your humble author could use one of those Montblanc pens.) Ala Moana is the largest shopping center in Hawai'i and draws neighbor-island residents to its doors as well.

In Waikiki, **Kalakaua Avenue** has a multitude of shops from the very expensive to the affordable. The **International Marketplace** is well known as a bargain hunter's paradise—mostly inexpensive souvenirs from local vendors. And check out Lewers Street for some shopping opportunities.

Looking for a taste of local foods? Try one of many **farmers' markets** spread around the island. We've found that the markets sponsored by the Hawai'i Farm Bureau (below) have the best variety.

Saturday—Kapiolani Community College, 4303 Diamond Head Road. From 7:30 to 11 a.m.

Sunday—Mililani High School, 95-1200 Meheula Parkway. From 8 a.m. to 11 a.m. And in Hale'iwa from 9 a.m. to 1 p.m. Exact location in flux at press time.

Thursday—Longs Drugs in Kailua, 609 Kailua Road. From 5 to 7:30 p.m.

Friday—Kings Village Shopping Center (where Koa meets Kaiulani) in Waikiki has one from 4 to 9ish p.m.

The **Aloha Stadium Swap Meet** on Wednesdays, Saturdays and Sundays starts early and runs until 3 p.m. A good stop after visiting Pearl Harbor. It's where H-1, H-3, Hwy 78 and Hwy 99 converge.

Plan some time browsing in **Hale'iwa**. There are a number of shops filled with artwork, clothing and other unique items. The surfing theme is everywhere.

Another good stop is **Hilo Hattie**. Their main store is on 700 Nimitz Hwy (at Pacific Street), accessible by shuttle from Waikiki. They also have a smaller store at Ala Moana Shopping Center.

O'ahu's No. 1 cash crop—
after tourists, of course.

Plan on spending a half day browsing the shops in **Chinatown** and grabbing lunch there. This is a good place to purchase a beautiful lei, some fresh produce or a one-of-a-kind gift.

Finally, if you're out on the west side, there's the **Waikele Premium Outlet** stores near H-1 and Hwy 99 has a mixture of so-so deals and awesome deals.

MISCELLANEOUS INFORMATION

Traveler's checks are usually accepted, but you should be aware that some merchants might look at you like you just tried to offer them Mongolian money. You should also know that Discover Cards seem to be less welcome here than at other destinations. *Many* places will not accept them.

It is customary here for *everyone* to remove their shoes upon entering someone's house (sometimes their office).

If you are going to spend any time at the beach, woven bamboo beach mats can be found all over the island for about $3. Some roll up; some can be folded. The sand comes off these more easily than it comes off towels.

The **area code** for all of Hawai'i is (808).

Around the island you'll see signs saying VISITOR INFORMATION or something similar. Allow me to translate: That's usually code for WE WANT TO SELL YOU SOMETHING.

If you want to arrange a lei greeting for you or your honey when you get off the plane at the airport, **Kama'aina Leis** (800–563–4449), **Greeters of Hawai'i** (800–366–8559) and **Honolulu Lei Greetings** (800–665–7959) can make the arrangements for around $25 and up. Nice way to kick off a romantic trip, huh? Since they are made to order, arrange 48 hours in advance.

The waterfall at Waimea Valley is one of the few on the island that you can swim under.

A WORD ABOUT DRIVING TOURS

For directions, locals usually describe things as being on the *mauka* (mao-kah) side of the road—toward the mountains—or *makai* (mah-kigh)—toward the ocean.

Beaches, activities, attractions and adventures are mentioned briefly but described in detail in their own sections.

Sometimes it gets confusing trying to plan which attractions or activities are in the area you'll be exploring.

GETTING IN & OUT OF WAIKIKI

Though Waikiki is the main place where visitors stay, there is no dedicated on-ramp or off-ramp for it from the main highway, H-1. Leaving the airport, the most efficient way to Waikiki is H-1 East. Though the signs *won't* direct you this way, the quickest route is to drive past what they *call* the Waikiki exits, then take exit 24A (Bingham), right on Farrington, right on Beretania, left on McCully, which will take you into Waikiki. (See map on page 48.) Taking the so-called Waikiki exits (exits 22 and 23) is a less direct route. Most visitors erroneously take the Nimitz Hwy from the airport and are greeted by heavy traffic most of the way.

Leaving Waikiki to get onto H-1, take Ala Wai Blvd. to McCully, and follow the signs if you're heading west (toward the airport), or take McCully, right on Kapiolani and follow the signs if you're heading east on H-1.

A NOTE ABOUT ACCESS

If a lawful landowner posts a NO TRESPASSING sign on their land, you need to respect their wishes. That seems simple enough. But here's where it gets tricky.

It's common in Hawai'i for someone who doesn't own or control land to erect their own NO TRESPASSING, KEEP OUT and ROAD CLOSED signs. Picture a shoreline fisherman who doesn't want anyone else near his cherished spot, putting up a store-bought sign to protect his solitude. Or a neighbor on a dirt road who hates the dust from cars driving by, so he puts up a sign that he knows locals will ignore, but it might dissuade unwary visitors.

In the past we did our best to try to ferret out when NO TRESPASSING signs were valid, and when they were not, and we took *a lot* of heat from residents who thought we were encouraging trespassing when we weren't. But the current environment doesn't permit us to do that anymore. So if you're heading to one of the places we describe and you encounter a NO TRESPASSING sign, even if you think it's not authorized by the landowner (and even if it's on *public* land), we have to advise you to turn around and heed the sign. All descriptions in our book come with the explicit assumption that you have obtained the permission of the legal landowner, and unfortunately, it'll usually be up to you to determine who that is and how to get it. But please, under no circumstances are we suggesting that you trespass. Plain and clear. Don't trespass…ever…for any reason…period.

A NOTE ON PERSONAL RESPONSIBILITY

In past editions we've had the sad task of removing places that you can no longer visit. The reason, universally cited, is *liability*. Although Hawai'i has a statute indemnifying landowners, the mere threat is often enough to get something closed. Because we, more than any other publication, have exposed heretofore unknown attractions, we feel the need to pass this along.

You need to assess what kind of traveler you are. We've been accused of leaning a bit toward the adventurous side, so you should take that into account when deciding if something's right for you. To paraphrase from the movie *Top Gun*, "Don't let your ego write checks your body can't cash."

Please remember that this isn't Disneyland—it's nature. Mother Nature is hard, slippery, sharp and unpredictable. If you go exploring and get into trouble, whether it's your ego that's bruised or something more tangible, please remember that neither the state, the private land owner nor this publication *told* you to go. You *chose* to explore, which is what life, and this book, are all about. And if you complain to or threaten someone controlling land, they'll rarely fix the problem you identified. They'll simply close it… and it will be gone for good.

Sometimes even good intentions can lead to disaster. At one adventure, a trailhead led hikers to the base of a wonderful waterfall. There was only *one* trail, to the left at the parking lot, that a person could take. Neither we, other guides nor websites ever said, "stay on the trail to the left" because at the time there was only one trail to take. The state (in their zeal to protect themselves from liability at an unmaintained trail) came along and put up a DANGER KEEP OUT sign at the trailhead. Travelers encountering the sign assumed they were on the wrong trail and started to beat a path to the right instead. But that direction started sloping downward and ended abruptly at a 150-foot-high cliff. Hikers retreated and in a short time a previously non-existent trail to the right became as prominent as the correct (and heretofore *only*) path to the left. Not long after the state's well-intentioned sign went up, an unwitting pair of hikers took the new, incorrect trail to the right and fell to their deaths. They probably died because they had been dissuaded from taking the correct trail by a state sign theoretically erected to keep people safe.

Our point is that nothing is static and nothing can take the place of your own observations and good judgment. If you're doing one of the activities you read about in our book or someplace else and your instinct tells you something is wrong, *trust your judgment* and go do another activity. There are lots of wonderful things to do on the island, and we want you safe and happy.

The ultimate swimming pool slide in Kane'ohe Bay.

If the more crowded part of Waikiki gets you down, Fort DeRussy Beach is the widest part of Waikiki, and there are usually far fewer people.

Honolulu is the central hub of the Hawaiian Islands, and Waikiki is the center of tourism. Lots of people work, live and play in this part of the state, and odds are overwhelming that this is where *you'll* be staying. That's because there are around 90 resorts on the island of Oʻahu, and all but nine of them are in Waikiki. At any one time, 44% of visitors *in the entire state of Hawaiʻi* are spending the night in Waikiki.

WAIKIKI

Imagine an area of less than one square mile that has over 30,000 hotel rooms. Imagine that this area is blessed with one of the most user-friendly beaches in the world. Where just about anyone can take a surfing lesson and ride their first wave. A place with more restaurants than most decent-sized towns. A place with limitless shopping. Well, this place actually exists. Waikiki is the essence of carefree. Visitors here tend to feel safe, warm and happy.

Waikiki is about walking and gawking, eating and shopping, surfing and soaking up the sun. You don't come to Waikiki to get away from the action; you come here to get a *piece* of the action. This is the place where you and 4 million of your closest friends each year embrace the tropics and each other. If you're looking for a quiet, out-of-the-way destination, look elsewhere. Waikiki is a humming, happening visitor mecca.

There is almost nothing natural about Waikiki. A century ago the land behind the beach was a swampy sponge. Three rivers emptied into the ocean here, and the beach, though still a great place to swim, was hardly a must-see destination. Then in 1921 they started draining the swamp. People often wonder, *how do you drain a swamp?* Simple— you dig a canal to cut off the source of water and let nature dry it out. This they did by creating the Ala Wai Canal. And the rest is history. Waikiki, now backed by land suitable for development, was ready to take off. Throughout the 20th century, resort after resort sprang up, and visitors began coming here in droves.

Early evening is our favorite time to experience Waikiki, when the intensity of the sun is replaced by the joy of people-watching. Stroll along the sidewalks of Kalakaua Avenue (or Lewers, which is also pretty alive at night and considered part of the "Beachwalk" area) and shop, snack and enjoy the warm, secure feeling that dusk in the tropics provides. Incidentally, the main street, Kalakaua, has surprisingly few signs verifying that it's the street you're on.

If you want to stroll along the beach, you can walk from the Hilton at one end of Waikiki all the way to Kapiolani Park at the other. Those few areas that lack sand have other means of traversing the shoreline that will keep you dry. A sunset walk along Waikiki Beach is always a dreamy experience as you listen to music often spilling from the various resorts. If you walk from the Diamond Head side toward Honolulu, you'll be walking toward the sun. During part of the summer, the sun doesn't set over the ocean from most of Waikiki.

Though less than a square mile, it's one of those ironies of modern life that the smaller a place is, the more walking you're apt to do. *Forget the car, honey—we'll walk it.* That's the phrase you'll hear and say throughout your stay. Many people who come to O'ahu never even rent a car (which we think is a mistake—see BASICS on page 22). But for getting around this square mile of activity, odds are you'll either walk, take the bus, take a shuttle or rent a scooter. Driving your car around

The electric energy that you'll find at Waikiki doesn't end when the sun goes down.

Waikiki can be a pain because parking is such a problem.

The bus costs $2.50 one way, or you can get a monthly pass for $60. Number 8 is the main Waikiki route, so we've shown that one on our Waikiki map. The other bus, called the Waikiki Trolley, which has a walk-up rate of $30 *per person per day* but a great online rate of $49 *per week*.

Outrigger canoe rides have been a Waikiki staple for over a century. Aloha Beach Services (922–3111, ext. 2341) has rides for $10 (you get to ride two different waves), or you can charter the whole 8-passenger outrigger canoe (includes paddlers) for $300 per hour. Directly next door Waikiki Beach Services (388–1510) rides two waves in a private canoe for $75 per couple. Near the Duke statue, Star Beach Boys will give you three waves for $15 in a bigger canoe.

Picking where to stay in Waikiki is daunting. Price is presumably a factor, and generally, the closer you get to the water, the higher the price. Distance to the heart of Waikiki is also a consideration. If you don't want to walk great distances whenever you want to experience what Waikiki has to offer, the best location is on the ocean side of Kalakaua Avenue between Saratoga Avenue and the Waikiki Beach Center. The area around the Royal Hawaiian and the Moana Surfrider hotels is usually considered to be the center of Waikiki life.

Waikiki Beach

Although we have a dedicated chapter on beaches, we wanted to describe the beaches of Waikiki here instead of the BEACHES chapter because it's where nearly everyone stays on O'ahu, and

A REAL GEM

it's likely you'll stroll along them at various times throughout your stay.

Waikiki is a swimming and surfing beach, not a snorkeling site, and there are no great snorkeling conditions anywhere along here. If you insist, the best conditions are off the tip of Kapahulu Groin and the tip of the wall at the south end of Queen's Beach (both of these *only* if there are no surfers or boogie boarders in the area—they have little patience for snorkelers) and, ironically, offshore of the Waikiki Aquarium.

Also remember that although Waikiki Beach is very sandy, the nearshore waters often have lots of rocks and reef that con-

WAIKIKI RESORTS

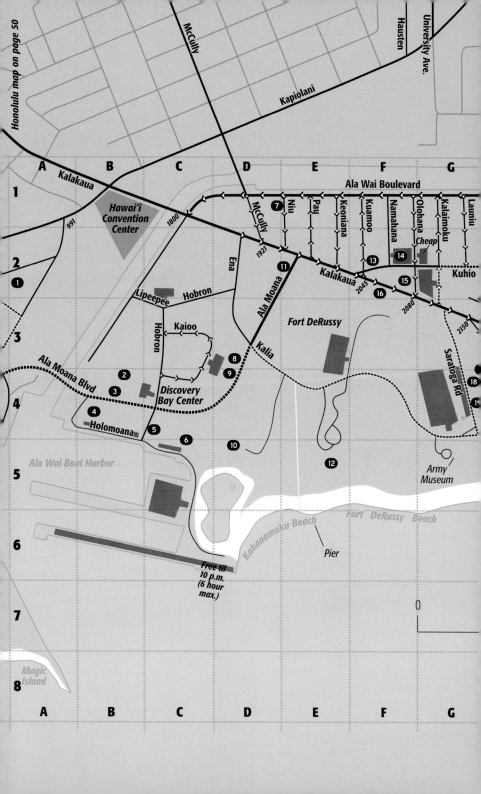

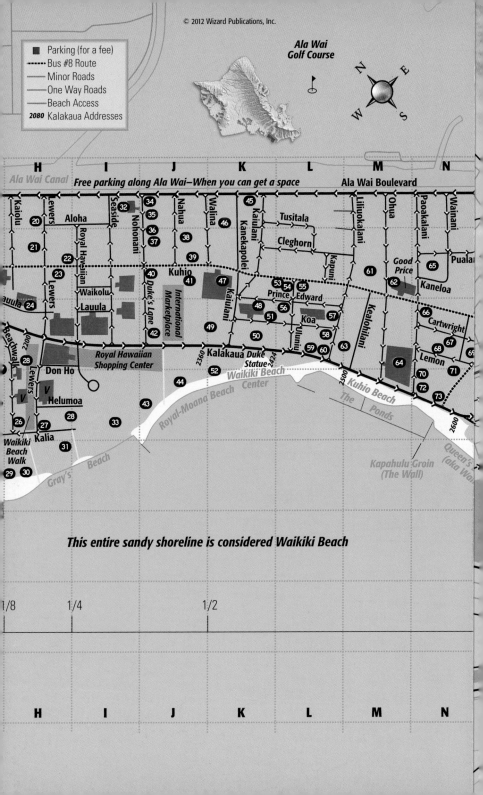

Honolulu

Map continued on page 68

Map continued on page 62

Tantalus Dr

Mott-Smith

Round Top

Makiki Heights

To Manoa Falls

University

Nehoa

Makiki

Metcalf

Wilder

Exit 24A

H-1

Isenberg

Wilder

Piikoi

Alexander

Dole

Farrington

Exit 24A

Exit 23 (Punahou) to Waikiki

Punahou

To H-1 West out of Waikiki

S. King

McCully

Waikiki map on page 48

S. Beretania

Kalakaua

Honolulu Academy of Arts

Piikoi

S. King

Keeaumoku

Rycroft

Kapiolani

Century Center

Pensacola

Walmart / Sam's Club

Makaloa

Hawai'i Convention Center

Ala Wai Blvd

Kalakaua

Waikiki

Neil S. Blaisdell Center

Kapiolani

Kona

Lipeepee Hobron

Ena

Ala Moana

Kaioo

Kalia

Ala Moana Shopping Center

92

Ala Wai Canal

Hobron

Queen

Kamakee

Ward Village Shops

Piikoi

Queen St.

Ala Moana Blvd

Ala Wai Yacht Harbor

Auahi

Warehouse

Ward Centre

Ala Moana Blvd

Ala Moana Beach Park

Kahanamoku Beach portion of Waikiki

Pier

Kewalo Basin

Magic Island

A peaceful morning on Waikiki Beach.

spire to attack your feet. Smart beachgoers wear reef or water shoes. The **sandiest patches** are off Waikiki Beach Center (for a little ways), in front of the ultra-pink Royal Hawaiian tower building (although the water there tends to be cloudy) and at the eastern (Diamond Head) side of Kahanamoku Beach up to the pier in front of the Hilton.

The entire beach is known as Waikiki Beach, but different stretches have different names. Starting in front of the massive Hilton Hawaiian Village, **Kahanamoku Beach** (named after Hawai'i's favorite son, surfing legend Duke Kahanamoku) is usually very crowded. It's considered a very safe swimming beach due to its protection from a breakwater on one side, a reef offshore and a jetty on the Diamond Head side. There's an easy-to-walk concrete beach path that runs from the Hilton to the far end of Fort DeRussy Beach. If you're looking for a snack, soda or adult beverage, grab one at the Hau Tree Beach Bar behind the beach, or, better yet, use the unexpectedly cheap Happy's Snack Bar at the Hale Koa. It's a military hotel, not normally open to the public, but a loophole allows you to wander in from the beach and eat at pool or beachside there. See DINING on page 235 for more.

Fort DeRussy Beach is the *widest* part of Waikiki Beach. The sand is also unusually firm (in case you brought your dune buggy from home). The southeast end occasionally gets balls of seaweed washing ashore, and the water along the wall—especially on the left side—has cold basal springs that drop the water temperature. But this is a fantastic part of Waikiki and is a bit less crowded compared to other parts of the beach.

much less padded in the nearshore waters than it used to be, so water or reef shoes are recommended in most parts of the beach.

At **Royal-Moana Beach**, the beach is at its sandiest, and beach use tends to be high. You won't find a lot of vacant sand here.

Next door is the **Waikiki Beach Center**. This is the spot for surf lessons and outrigger canoe rides. There are no resorts lining this part of the beach, and Kalakaua Avenue is right next to the park.

Past here is **Kuhio Beach**, also known as **The Ponds**. Kuhio has concrete walls forming two separate ponds—perfect for kids and those skittish about swimming in the open ocean.

Gray's Beach is the one part of Waikiki that has mostly washed away. Waikiki has been enhanced many times over the years with importations of sand, most recently in 2012. Officials tend to be hesitant to bring in more sand, fearing that they'll alter the shape of Waikiki's famous waves. But being bureaucrats, they're also fearful of making a wrong decision, so little has been done in recent years to stop the erosion of sand other than a small project at Kuhio Beach and the strip of beach between Waikiki Beach Center and the Royal Hawaiian. As a result, Waikiki is thin in areas like Gray's Beach. It's also

When you leave Kuhio Beach, you leave the resort towers of Waikiki behind. The **Kapahulu Groin** is the jetty extending into the sea where Kalakaua Avenue meets Kapahulu Avenue. This is our favorite place to be in Waikiki when the surf's up—usually in the summer. It extends out into the waves, so you'll feel like you're part of the action. Boogie boarders and body surfers cruise right up to you, then past you. You'll quickly gain

A slightly less peaceful afternoon.

a perspective of the waves that's not possible from the shore. Boogie boarders often surf right up to the shore, hop on the groin, run to the end and jump off to start over again. (By the way, *we* always thought a groin was something you pulled playing football. Actually, it's a wall that runs perpendicular to the beach to stop sand migration.)

Though the north end of the groin is usually swimming-pool calm, the south end sometimes provides some of the nicest and longest boogie board rides in South Oʻahu. Queen's Beach is named after a long-gone restaurant by that name. It's also a good place to stretch a towel and is usually less crowded than the beaches in front of the resorts. (The section of Queen's next to the groin wall is known locally as Walls.) The sand beach ends here. See BEACHES chapter on page 123 for descriptions of all other island beaches.

South of Waikiki

Behind you, Kapiolani Park is a giant, triangular-shaped lawn where people play soccer, fly kites, walk their dogs and jog to their hearts' content. Diamond Head seems to tower over this park. The north end is where you'll find the Waikiki Shell, a seashell-shaped outdoor amphitheater where live performances are occasionally held. And check out the gigantic banyan tree on the Paki Road side of the park. (Yeah, that's *one* tree.)

Kapiolani Park is also where you'll find the Natatorium and the Waikiki Aquarium. (Before you get too worked up over the aquarium, read the ATTRACTIONS chapter on page 112 to see if it's for you.)

The Natatorium is a WWI memorial built in 1927 to honor Hawaiʻi's casualties from the "great war." Its 100-meter pool was used by generations of residents for swim meets and recreation. The Natatorium fell into disrepair and was closed by the Department of Health in 1979. It has been partially renovated but is no longer used for swimming and has been stuck in political quicksand for years. It's now merely a place to park for

Part of Waikiki Beach at Kuhio Beach Park is ultra-protected by a breakwater for effortless swimming.

Meet the only royal residence in the United States—'Iolani Palace.

free and is used for its bathrooms by swimmers at Sans Souci Beach next door. At press time there was talk about tearing it down, but in the meantime, it's sort of a white elephant that Hawai'i residents, out of embarrassment, kind of hope you don't see.

Sans Souci Beach is a nice but small beach on the south end of the Natatorium. It's semi-protected by one wall of the Natatorium, has showers, restrooms (at the Natatorium) and lifeguards. The sand is fairly coarse and brushes off more easily than the fine stuff, and it extends far enough into the ocean to provide a cushion for your feet. Park at the Natatorium on Kalakaua Avenue.

International Marketplace

The International Marketplace is a 125,000-square-foot, brick-lined tropical bazaar with countless stalls of vendors and bartering customers, sprawling banyan trees and a hissing waterfall. Shop for pearls still in the oyster, tons of inexpensive jewelry, clothing, surfing gear, wood tikis and a billion things that you can put on your desk back home. Located between Kalakaua and Kuhio avenues next to Duke's Lane.

Cocktails in Waikiki

It's been our observation that adult beverages in Waikiki sold next to the beach tend to be a bit weak, especially when served by big resorts like the Hilton, and no amount of coaching seems to make a difference. Perhaps they're counting on multiple purchases. For the record, it's illegal to consume alcohol on the beach in Hawai'i. This rule comes as a complete surprise to anyone visiting since restaurants and barefoot bars next to the beach often serve their drinks in plastic cups and sort of wink and nod while they tell you about the law when you ask for a drink to go. The law seems to be little enforced on

Cruisin' up to the beach at Waikiki.

Waikiki Beach, and a visit to nearly any beach on the weekend will reveal locals with giant ice chests full of beer. From the Hau Tree at the Hilton to Rumfire at the Sheraton Waikiki, drinks in plastic cups are available. At Rumfire (no bathing suits allowed) their Hai-Maka Mai Tai (made with my favorite sipping rum, Ron Zacapa) is a pricey but unusual and *super-refreshing* mai tai with a hint of ginger. I review it every time I walk the beach, just to confirm consistency. (No thanks necessary. It's my job.) It's good about 70% of the time, but I'm trying to fine tune that percentage. Great rum selection, too.

Freebies in Waikiki

Waikiki is a great place to get rid of all that pesky money you've been earning throughout the year. Everywhere you turn, there are plenty of people and companies that will gladly take your hard-earned cash. If you need a breather, here are a few things that *won't* cost you dearly.

There's a nightly sunset torch lighting ceremony at Kuhi'o Beach, as well as a music and a hula show *some* nights. Under the banyan tree to the left of the bronze statue of Duke Kahanamoku. (By the way, don't linger under that tree near sunset. There are thousands of birds in its branches who would love to drop their special brand of aloha on you.)

Sunset on the Beach takes place sometimes weekly, sometimes less often (for "budget reasons") at Queen's Beach (AKA Queen's Surf Beach). Picture a 30-foot screen on the beach, food concessionaires selling the expected junk food, and movies equivalent to recent DVD releases being shown for free. It's lots of fun (although crowded). Call 923–1094 for listings and schedules. If there's no movie, you might catch a lively beach volleyball game there.

The Hilton Hawaiian Village (949–4321) has a Polynesian show near the pool at 7 p.m. every Friday. Afterward they have fireworks over the ocean. Some boat tours plan their sunset cruises around this event. There may be some exciting fire dancing after the pyrotechnics.

The Hyatt Regency Waikiki (923–1234) puts on a small Polynesian show every Friday at 4:30 p.m. Drummers, dancers and even a fire knife dancer perform on the ground floor between the two towers. They also have crafts and lei-making demonstrations.

Street performers are common along Kalakaua Avenue. The silver guys, in particular, range from talented to just plain lame.

Sunday Showcase at the Waikiki Beach Walk displays the talents of local entertainers from hula dancers to well-known 'ukulele player Jake Shimabukuro. Shows start at 5 p.m. on the Plaza Stage, third floor above the Yardhouse on Lewers Street.

HONOLULU

Honolulu is overrepresented when it comes to attractions you may want to visit. It's got so many, in fact, that we have a dedicated ATTRACTIONS chapter you should read. Check out places like 'Iolani Palace, Punchbowl National Cemetery, Chinatown, The Bishop Museum, Doris Duke's Shangri La and garden tours.

Driving around Honolulu and Waikiki can be maddening, and no matter how much effort we put into our maps, they can't cover up the fact that our road system was created by…well, morons. (Sorry, but it's true.) Having a navigator who's good at reading maps on the fly can help, (as can our smartphone app, so you can see where you are right on our maps), but you should count on getting lost, irritated and driving in the vicinity of something you're trying to get to only to curse in rage that you can't find it or maneuver to it. Hey…it's O'ahu. After a week or so you'll learn some of its tricks and shortcuts, but the learning curve can be steep. Even living here, we get frustrated at the unintuitive layout. And getting on and off the H-1 freeway can be a joke. We still find it incredible that the primary place where visitors stay—Waikiki—doesn't have a dedicated on-ramp to get back onto H-1

Friday night lights, island style.

Fifteen minutes from the asphalt jungle of Honolulu lies a different kind of jungle off Tantalus Drive.

west. From McCully, you're directed though a neighborhood until you wander onto an on-ramp. It's embarrassing, but it's part of our charm, right?

Tantalus

Regardless of how brief your stay in Honolulu, at some point you should take a drive along Tantalus and Round Top. This 10-mile-long road wiggles and winds up the mountains **NOT TO BE MISSED!** through a pretty forest above Honolulu to the 1,610-foot level, and in the process you'll gain an appreciation of Honolulu's beauty you never really expected.

As a loop road you'll start at one end and finish at another. Take Ala Wai Blvd. then a right on Kalakaua Ave., across the Ala Wai Canal and out of Waikiki, left onto Kapiolani, right onto Keeaumoku, up and over H-1, right on Wilder, left on Makiki. When you get to Makiki Heights Drive, take a left onto it (if it's the afternoon) and right when it dead ends onto

Tantalus to do the loop. If it's the morning, stay on Makiki and go past Makiki Heights Drive, then turn left onto Round Top to begin the loop, turning left onto Makiki Heights Drive when you're done. (This route takes best advantage of the lighting.) See maps on pages 50 and 68, which ought to help.

This is a great road to drive in a convertible. Leadfoots may be tempted to take the winding road fast, but you'll actually want to drive this road slowly, or it'll be over too soon and you'll miss some of the scenery. Keep an eye out for pullouts along the way. Several have fantastic views of the leeward side of O'ahu below you. No view, however, can compare to the pure majesty of the view from **Pu'u Ualaka'a State Wayside Park**. When you pull into this park, stay left at both intersections till the road ends, then walk out a hundred feet to the point. From one corner of the island at Barbers Point all the way past Diamond Head to Kahala, a giant 25-mile swath of O'ahu presents itself. We're only sorry that we don't have a camera lens wide enough to show it all to you. You'll

Bishop Estate and the Kamehameha Schools

Everyone who lives in Hawai'i knows what the Bishop Estate is. It is feared, admired, detested and loved. It is synonymous with absolute power—and absolute corruption. And it owns 9% of all the land in these islands.

The last descendant of King Kamehameha the Great was Princess Bernice Pauahi. She married an American named Charles Bishop and, when she died of cancer in 1884, left most of her assets—meaning 431,000 acres of Hawai'i—to a trust set up "to erect and maintain in the Hawaiian Islands' two schools, each for boarding and day scholars, one for boys and one for girls, to be known as, and called, the Kamehameha Schools."

The will stipulated that trustees were to be chosen by the Hawai'i Supreme Court and, over the years, becoming a trustee became the ultimate political plum job. Hawai'i's old boy political machine took care of its own. Trustees paid themselves almost $1 million a year each, even during years of mind-boggling losses of a hundred million dollars or more, and sweetheart deals were rampant and only minimally covered up. Some of the land was sold, but with so much land and power remaining, the trust grew to be worth over $10 billion. All this to pay for a central school that houses around 3,200 students, some preschools and two small neighbor-island campuses. (Ignoring the will's language, the trustees created a single co-ed O'ahu school in 1965.) Corruption, arrogance and mismanagement became the face that residents associated with Bishop Estate, but it was so intertwined with the political establishment that few challenged it.

Finally in the late 1990s, the stench of corruption reached such unbearable levels that the state and federal governments stepped in. (The spark that started it all was an op-ed piece in the local newspaper written by five very respected members of the local community.) Smelling blood from the heretofore untouchable estate, newspapers, prominent leaders and government agencies converged on the Bishop Estate from every direction. All the trustees resigned or were removed. Indictments, convictions, prison and even suicide resulted from this reckoning, and the IRS came perilously close to revoking the estate's tax-exempt status since so few dollars were being spent on the supposed object of the charity—the school.

Today Kamehameha Schools/Bishop Estate tries to keep a lower political profile in Hawai'i. Trustees are now chosen by a probate judge, not the Supreme Court, and trustee fees are less, though still generous. They're still the largest private landowner in the state, but they've come down a notch or two in the eyes of most residents.

have to see for yourself. It (and this road in general) is also a great place to come and observe the city lights at night.

Ala Moana Area

Just outside Waikiki is Ala Moana. If you'd been visiting Honolulu in the early 1900s, you'd never have wanted to visit the Ala Moana area. It was a nasty, swampy and smelly area of **A REAL GEM** mud flats that also housed the almost continuously burning Honolulu garbage dump. Everyone avoided the area except duck pond owners. Then in 1912 a dredging company owner named Dillingham bought this worthless land. His friends thought he was an idiot, but Dillingham was looking for a place to dispose of all of his dredged earth. In the 1950s a mile of sand was dumped at this park, creating the perfect swimming spot you see today. And in 1959, the year Hawai'i became a state, the state's most prestigious shopping center was built across the street, the 50-acre Ala Moana Shopping Center. Ala Moana went from uninviting wasteland to a beautiful and treasured beach park backed by the largest open-air shopping center in the world in less than 50 years.

WAIKIKI & HONOLULU BEST BETS

Best Former Swamp—Waikiki Beach

Best Sunset Walk—From Kapiolani Park to the Hilton Hawaiian Village

Best Place to View the Most O'ahu Real Estate—From Pu'u Ualaka'a State Wayside Park

Best View at Night—A hotel room in the Waikiki Sheraton above the 20th floor facing Diamond Head

Best Place to See How Royalty Lived—'Iolani Palace

Best Winding Road—Tantalus Drive

Best Place to See Weird Edible Sea Critters—Maunakea Market Place

Best Dining Deal on Waikiki Beach—Hale Koa Military Hotel

Best Place to Watch Boogie Boarders Close-up—Kapahulu Groin

Best Place to Hear a Crooner Sing Sad Music—Happy's Bar, Hale Koa

When Did the Last Eruption Take Place on O'ahu?

Surprisingly, nobody knows. Ask any geologist, and you might be told with complete confidence that it was 320,000 years ago...or over 100,000 years ago... or maybe as recently as 5,000 years ago. What we do know is that the most recent eruptions have been near the shoreline, from Diamond Head to Kaupo Beach Park. The land that looks the youngest is Kaohi-ka-ipu Island off Makapu'u Beach Park— it's mostly raw lava. These were explosive eruptions where seawater mixed with underground magma and burst to form the hills and craters so prominent along here. The wicked snorkeling at Hanauma Bay, the popular hike up Diamond Head and the massive Koko Crater we all owe to O'ahu's last gasp at island-making. The rejuvenated phase of a volcano can have very long gaps, and technically the island could still be in its final phase of lava flows, though most geologists consider it highly improbable that there will be another eruption here.

Part of Highway 72 was carved out of the cemented ash of Koko Crater.

Talk about an embarrassment of riches. You have several ways to get to Kailua on the windward side, all of them pretty. Odds are you'll want to take the coastal highway (72) because there are a number of not-to-be-missed sights along the way. But even if you take the coastal road this time, you should definitely find the time during your stay to take one of the highways that punch though the Ko'olau mountains—the best being the H-3, which is arguably the most beautiful stretch of freeway in the world.

THE COASTAL ROUTE TO KAILUA

Leave Waikiki behind by taking Kalakaua Avenue to Diamond Head Road to Kahala Avenue—more scenic than getting on H-1 East right away. You'll pass the lower part of Diamond Head where some pretty scenic lookouts await. Kahala Avenue is where some of O'ahu's richest residents live. There are some truly stupendous mansions along here. In addition, there are some obscenely expensive eyesores on this road, proof that money doesn't necessarily buy good taste.

Turn left on Pueo, right on Kilauea, right on Waialae, which'll turn into H-1 East. (Look for the signs.) The H-1 will become Hwy 72, known locally as the Kalanianaole Highway. (Don't try to pronounce that seven syllable word; you might strain your tongue.)

The beaches along this lower leeward stretch aren't very good, thanks to runoff from Hawai'i Kai, a giant housing subdivision. Don't worry—the beaches will get *much* nicer.

When an island like O'ahu is nearing the twilight of its volcanic life, the volcanoes usually go to sleep for up to a million years, then sputter back awake for a short time, often creating explosive eruptions near the shoreline instead of the typical drooling type that characterizes most of its eruptive life. Hawaiian volcanoes get hot-tempered in their old age. The results of the volcanoes' last gasp are often cone-shaped mountains of cemented ash called *tuff*, created when seawater seeps into the underground magma, flashing into steam and causing monstrous pressures that eventually explode. Diamond Head and the two giant hills in front of you—called **Koko Crater** (to your left) and **Koko Head** (to your right)—are examples of the volcanoes' final temper tantrums.

The populated section of Koko Head can be reached by taking Portlock Road or Lunalilo Home Road toward the ocean. If you drive to the end of Lumahai Road (see map below), there's a little-known hidden gem near a hard-to-see public access corridor that requires a 2-minute walk down a steep path to an unnervingly constant sloping bluff. But, ahh, what a sight. The **spitting cave of Portlock** is below a gorgeous layered shoreline. Even without the cave, the shoreline itself is mesmerizing. Each layer represents a different volcanic explosion, and the waters here are exceptionally clear and blue.

A REAL GEM

The spitting cave is where the ocean is chiseling its way inland, attempting to break the point in two. As the waves drive into the cave, they're repelled by its backside, causing the ground to tremble beneath your feet, and water and mist to explode out of the cave if the surf is right. Summer generally brings higher surf to south-facing shores, but even smaller winter waves can cause the effect. Standing right over the cave creates the best tremble; standing to the right of the cave (as you face the ocean) gives the best views. For generations, locals have come here on weekends to jump off the 65-foot cliff in front of the cave during calm seas, but the injury and death toll from this has been particularly high, and you'll probably want to refrain from it. (You'll see memorial plaques in the rock for those who perished.)

Back on Hwy 72 you'll start climbing Koko Head and come to one of the

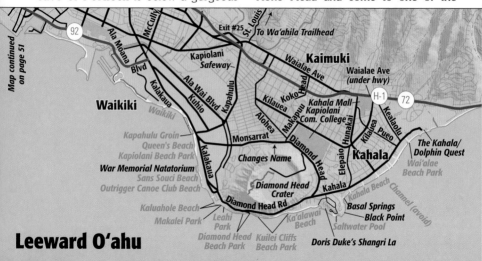

Map continued on page 51

Leeward O'ahu

island's biggest attractions. If you've heard *anything* about Oʻahu, you've heard about the snorkeling at **Hanauma Bay**. It's one of the most popular activities on the island. A lot of hype and misconceptions exist about this bay. Let's dispel some of them.

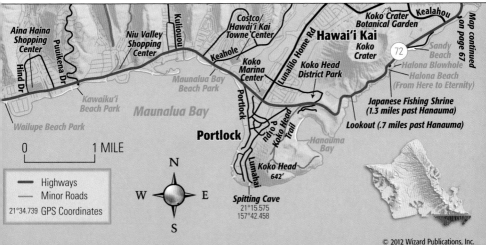

A REAL GEM

Hanauma Bay Nature Preserve (396–4229) is a crescent-shaped bay that's partially protected from the open ocean. In the past, people fed the fish, which actually resulted in fewer varieties of fish. (Bolder species did well, driving out meeker types.) Feeding is no longer allowed.

It's full of crystal clear water with tons of coral, right? 'Fraid not. The water tends to be a bit cloudy, and much of the reef is actually made from coralline algae, which *looks* like dead coral, but it's actually a stony material created by plants. It's *supposed* to look like that. And some of the real coral has been damaged over the years.

But what you *should* expect are fish...lots and lots of fish of many varieties that are so tame and used to people, they'll hang out near you. This is the perfect place to spend some quality

bonding time with the little (and not so little) buggers. You should also expect crowds, because you'll definitely get them here. Hanauma Bay is *not* a well-kept secret.

Hanauma Bay is safe most of the time. There are lifeguards, and the inner bay is pretty protected. That said, some years, this is the drowning capital of Oʻahu. After all, it *is* the ocean and anything can happen. Besides, if you invite over a million people a year to use *your bathtub*, odds are you'll lose one or two of them. Just remember not to go in the water 9–10 days after a full moon. (See box jellies under HAZARDS.) The bay is open from 6 a.m. to 6 p.m., closed Tuesdays.

It'll cost $1 per car and $7.50 per person to get in. You'll have to watch a 9-minute conservation video before you're allowed to walk down to the bay 150 feet below you. They also have a tram to the bottom for a couple of bucks. Good for hill-haters or those with lots of beach stuff or SCUBA gear. There's a food concession at the top and showers at the bottom. A $16 million "education center" is also at the top. (Though nice, it's hard to see how they spent *that* much on it.)

Map continued on page 67

© 2012 Wizard Publications, Inc.

Nearly everyone we've heard at the Lana'i Lookout speculates about which islands they're seeing. And nearly everyone gets it wrong. Here the islands are labeled as we saw them on this wickedly clear morning. Note that although Haleakala is twice as tall as East Moloka'i, it seems shorter due to its distance (100 miles). That's 1/250 of the circumference of the earth, so its bottom portion is below the planet's curvature.

East Moloka'i   West Moloka'i   Maui's Haleakala

Snorkel gear is available for rent at the bottom—convenient, though it's overpriced at $12 for cheap-o gear. They also have flotation gear. Lockers are $7.

The parking lot is often full by 9:30 a.m. As groups of cars leave, the park will let small groups of cars in, but basically you'll want to arrive by 9 a.m. if you want to be sure you get a parking spot.

An alternative is **Hawaiian Ocean Promotions** at 396–9199. For $21 they'll take you to and from some Waikiki hotels to Hanauma Bay. Includes snorkel gear. **Tommy's Tours** (373–5060) has a similar service for $18. Arrange a day in advance.

For the most part, Hanauma Bay lives up to its promise. It's a great place to spend the morning or afternoon, whether you're a novice or an experienced snorkeler.

Continuing on Hwy 72, there's a turnout ¾ mile past the entrance to Hanauma Bay. This is the **Lana'i Lookout**, which is oddly named because if you see an island offshore, odds are it *ain't* Lana'i, it's Moloka'i. (See photo caption for an explanation.)

About 1³⁄₁₀ miles past the Hanauma Bay entrance is a very narrow pullout.

There's a Japanese fishing shrine here with a carving of a Japanese guardian god that was said to preside over dangerous waterways. Originally, there was a stone statue installed by a Japanese fishing club, but during WWII it was demolished, and this carving took its place. Walk past the shrine along the ridge for a hundred feet or so, and you're treated to wonderful view of the **Halona Beach** below and Halona Blowhole. Though more distant, in some ways this vantage point is even better than the dedicated blowhole lookout 500 feet up the road. This perspective shows the size of the blowhole eruptions in relation to the people at the lookout platform above. Locals still call this beach *From Here to Eternity Beach* since they filmed what was then (in the '50s) a steamy love scene there with the actors kissing and rolling around in the surf.

Just past the shrine is the parking lot for the **Halona Blowhole**. This is where the ocean has undercut the lava and drilled a hole through to the top. It's fairly reliable, but if the surf is not high enough, it won't be erupting. High tide is best. The lookout hangs below the parking lot with heavy

NOT TO BE MISSED!

Lana'i

Those who do and have been knocked in the hole are nearly always killed. Frankly, when we have visitors, we usually take them to see the blowhole from below. But we never do it when the ocean's raging, and we're always aware that our safety depends on the ocean being in a good mood.

Sandy Beach is your first good beach along this stretch. That giant lawn is where hang gliders and paragliders land after soaring the cliffs of Makapu'u. It's not uncommon to have a hang glider pilot come up to you and ask you to drive him and his vehicle to the top of Makapu'u and return his car to Sandy Beach. (You can't drive up there on your own because permits are needed.) Sandy Beach is also where **ultralights** are launched. Some of the aerial photos in

railings to dissuade you from walking down to the blowhole itself. (Give yourself a pat on the back if you guessed that *liability* was the reason.) Of course, it's perfectly legal to walk down to Halona Beach on your right and walk along the lava bench for a few minutes if you really want to visit the blowhole from below. If you do, be very cautious of the ocean, and never get between the ocean and the blowhole.

Snorkelers rejoice—the pool is open at Hanauma Bay.

It's impossible to resist stopping at the overlook above Makapu'u Beach backed by its offshore islands.

this book were taken from our ultralight launched from here. Although the air along the windward coast tends to be smooth, the mountain toward the east causes nasty turbulence right over Sandy Beach, and ultralight landings here tend to look pretty ugly.

As you round the easternmost part of the island, giant **Makapu'u** defines the eastern tip. There's a parking lot and **scenic lookout** next to an abandoned road snaking up to the 647-foot summit. The road is hugely popular with locals who do their morning walks there. Sunrises are particularly nice from up top if you can motivate yourself to get up that early. During whale season the beasties

tend to come pretty close to the point and are amazingly visible from up there. If you're looking for a series of blow-holes that puts Halona Blowhole to shame and you don't mind hiking, check out the **Dragon's Nostrils** in ACTIVITIES on page 180.

Make sure you stop at the pullout above **Makapu'u Beach**. The vantage point is excellent. Although this beach is popular with locals who bodysurf here and at Sandy Beach, novice bodysurfers need to be leery since the shorebreak at these beaches tends to be pounding, which can drill you into the sand like a fencepost. Behind Makapu'u is **Sea Life Park**, east O'ahu's version of Sea World. See ATTRACTIONS on page 117 for more.

Those islands you see off Makapu'u were probably where the last eruptions took place on the island. The shorter island, called **Kaohi-ka-ipu** was made from a traditional lava flow when the ocean level was lower and the land there high and dry. It looks dark and burnt, a tribute to its relative youth. **Manana Island** behind it is a tuff cone like Diamond Head made from a steam explosion. Locals usually refer to it as **Rabbit Island** because a local resident used to raise rabbits there in the 1880s. They *say* that there are still rabbits there, but we've never seen any, only the thousands of seabirds that make their home there.

After Makapu'u you're driving through **Hawaiian Homelands** and the town of **Waimanalo**. In 1920 the government set aside over 200,000 acres of land to be used only by people of Hawaiian descent. Waimanalo is such a place.

The shoreline along here is almost uninterrupted sand beach consisting of Kaiona Beach, Waimanalo Beach, Bellows Beach and Waimanalo Bay State Recreation Area. The latter is backed by a thick forest of ironwood trees. To this day locals refer to this area as **Sherwood Forest**. That's because during the '60s the forest became a hot place to strip cars and rob beachgoers. The gang that was responsible called themselves Robin Hood and the Merry Men because they took from the rich and gave to...well, *themselves*, actually.

Though the leeward side's Wai'anae Range is taller, the **Ko'olau Range** on the windward side *looks* taller and much more dramatic. The sheer, fluted cliffs carpeted with every shade of green are among the most wondrous sights on the island and never fail to impress. The tallest peaks of the Ko'olaus, just south (to the left) of the

A REAL GEM

Pali tunnel and peaking at 3,150 and 3,105 feet, are called **Konahua-nui**, literally translated as the *big, fat testicles*. Hey, we don't make up the legends, we just report 'em. (Perhaps they're named in honor of the first Hawaiian who had enough guts to climb them?)

As you gaze at the splendid cliffs of the Ko'olaus, consider this. In old Hawai'i, when a particularly beloved chief died, it was customary to sacrifice several of his trusted servants, as well. (And you thought *you* sacrificed a lot for your boss.) When the servant heard about his chief's death, he would kiss his wife and children goodbye and, without

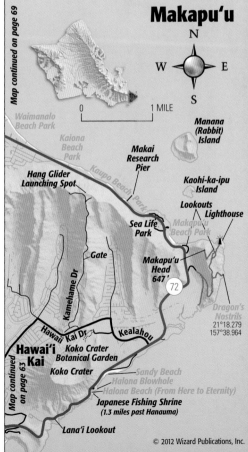

Makapu'u

Map continued on page 69

0   1 MILE

Waimanalo Beach Park

Kaiona Beach Park

Hang Glider Launching Spot

Kaupo Beach Park

Makai Research Pier

Manana (Rabbit) Island

Kaohi-ka-ipu Island

Lookouts

Lighthouse

Sea Life Park

Makapu'u Beach Park

Gate

Kamehame Dr

Makapu'u Head 647'

72

Dragon's Nostrils

21°18.279
157°38.964

Hawaii Kai Dr

Kealahou

Hawai'i Kai

Koko Crater Botanical Garden

Koko Crater

Map continued on page 63

Sandy Beach

Halona Blowhole

Halona Beach (From Here to Eternity)

Japanese Fishing Shrine
(1.3 miles past Hanauma)

Lana'i Lookout

© 2012 Wizard Publications, Inc.

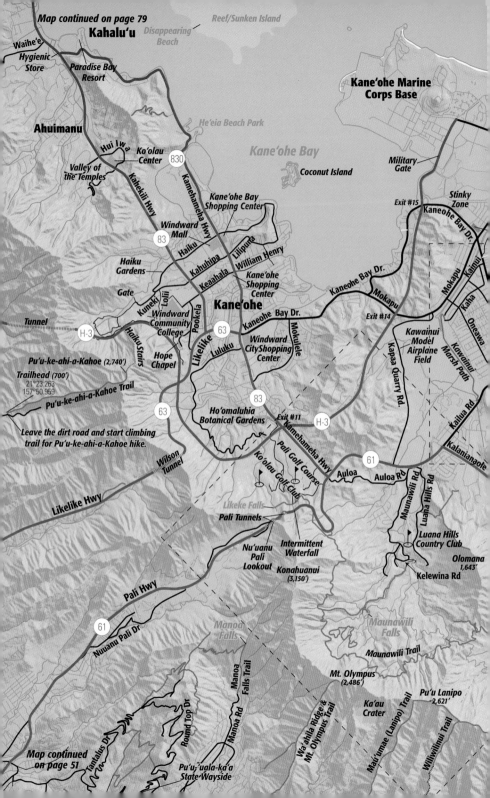

N
W   E
S

0   1 MILE

Highways
Beach Access
Minor Roads

Mokolea Island

Military Gate

Aikahi Park Shopping Center

Kailua Bay

Kalama Beach Park

Kailua

Kalaheo

Kailua Beach Park

Flat Island (Popo-i'a Island)

Kuulei

Kainalu

Kailua   Kailua   Kawailoa

Hamakua

Wanaao

Mokulua Rd

Lanikai Beach

Lanikai

Alala

Aalapapa

Moku-lua Islands

Enchanted Lake

Keolu

Kailua detail on page 70

Old Kalanianaole Rd/Norfolk Rd
(some nice mansions)

72

Gate

Bellows Beach (road access only open weekends)

Waimanalo Town Center

Kumuhau

Poalima

Tinker

Waimanalo

Aloiloi

Waimanalo Bay Recreation Area (Sherwood Forest)

Maunawili Trail
map on page 184

Pu'u o Kona 2,200'

Kuli'ou'ou Ridge Trail

Hawai'iloa Ridge Trail

Waimanalo Beach Park

Kiona Beach Park

Manana (Rabbit) Island

Kaohi-ka-ipu Island

Kaupo Beach Park

Map continued on page 67

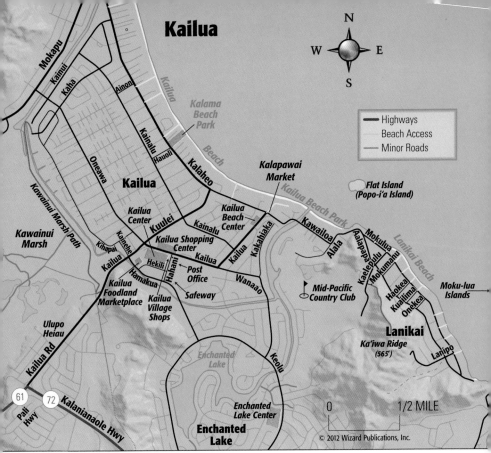

Kailua

telling them why, leave to become a *moepuʻu*, or companion in death. He would then enter the hut where the chief's body was being kept and lie down between the dead man's legs. The only way his life could be spared was if one of the heirs to the kingdom so decided. If none of the dead chief's servants came forward to sacrifice themselves, one of his officers or relatives might be called upon to do so. This is why the chief's health was *always* a topic of interest to those closest to him. They had a vested interest in keeping him healthy.

When it came time to bury the chief, the funeral procession often hiked to the top of the Koʻolaus from the leeward side. The chief's bones, having been separated from the valueless flesh, were lowered by rope along with a digger. Once the digger gouged out a cavity in the cliffs, the bones were placed inside and the digger would tug on the rope. Then the men at the top cut the rope, and the digger plunged to his death, taking with him the secret to where the chief's bones lay. In this way the sacred bones, which Hawaiians believed contained their *mana*, or spiritual power, could never be found and desecrated. And it was actually considered an *honor* to be the doomed digger.

KAILUA

Kailua is your classic beach town and, in our minds, one of the nicest places to stay if you're not going to stay in Waikiki. Though only 30 minutes from Honolulu via the Pali Highway, it's a world away from big city life. There are no resorts here, but vacation rentals and B&Bs are plentiful. Two of the finest beaches on the island bless this community, the kayaking in Kailua Bay to offshore islands is fantastic, and there are some excellent restaurants. If you're looking for a dreamy beach scene backed by offshore islands, **Lanikai** is a must. If you want a long, delicious beach to stroll along or want to kayak these waters to a nearby island, you gotta check out **Kailua Beach**. See BEACHES for more on these.

In addition to the beaches, scattered around Kailua are some things to keep an eye out for.

On Kapaa Quarry Road across from the *lovely* Kailua Dump is the **Kawainui Model Airplane Field** where people fly some surprisingly sophisticated model airplanes and helicopters. Well used on weekends and less so during the week. Avoid when it's real rainy as the road is prone to flooding.

On Hwy 61 (Kailua Road) between Hwy 72 and Hamakua Drive across from the Tesoro Gas Station, there's a short path leading to the **Ulupo Heiau**, which is little more than a pile of rocks. They have some signs describing the interesting geology of Kailua.

At a dirt turnout mauka (toward the mountain) of Kailua town is an access for a very nice walking path through the otherwise water-logged **Kawainui Marsh**.

The Direct Highways to Kailua

There are three highways that drill through the Ko'olaus directly to the

Acting as an acid bath, the ocean is slowly dissolving the sandstone that makes up Flat Island off Kailua Beach, creating a Swiss cheese landscape in the process. Here you can see a hole in the island and the morning light seeping in from underneath.

The Pali Lookout is one of the better reasons to take the Pali Highway to Kailua...

windward side, ending up in Kailua or Kane'ohe. Pali and Likelike are highways, not freeways, with traffic lights and intersections part of the way. H-3 is a classic elevated freeway.

Of all your non-coastal routes, H-3 is the most rewarding, especially going from Kailua to Honolulu. H-3 is an interstate highway. *Hey, wait a minute. Hawai'i's a bunch of islands. How can it be an interstate highway?* Simple. If we'd called it a *state* highway, *we'd* have to pay for it. I believe I speak for all Hawai'i residents when I say, thank you for your generous federal tax dollars.

Anyway, this 16-mile road cost almost $100 million *per mile* to build and took a mere *37 years* to complete. They spent *20 years* of that time doing environmental impact study after environ-

A REAL GEM

mental impact study. But the results are incredible. If you saw it in a movie, you'd dismiss it out of hand as too beautiful to believe. Elevated high above the ground while cruising toward and next to the fluted cliffs of the Ko'olaus, this is the next best thing to taking a helicopter ride along the mountains.

You'll often notice that as you pass through the H-3 tunnel, the weather might be different on each side. Weather on O'ahu is strongly affected by the mountains. Moist air from the northeast encounters the Ko'olau mountain range, rising and cooling. Cooler air can't hold as much moisture as warmer air, so the moisture condenses—in other words, forms a cloud. If it has more moisture than this now-cooler air can hold, it rains. With the air-deflecting mountain behind it, the traveling air sinks and gets warmer. Having already wrung out the moisture over the mountains, this drier air tends to be less prone to cloudiness. Hence, the leeward side's sunny days.

By the way, shortly before the H-3 tunnel (if you're coming from the windward side), look for a metal staircase on the side of the mountain on your left. It'll be winding its way up into the clouds. That's the **Haiku Stairs**, also called the **Stairway to Heaven**, and it's described in more detail on page 219.

As an alternate to H-3, you can also take the **Pali Highway** (61) from Honolulu. It heads straight into downtown Kailua. Until the Old Pali Road was built, leeward residents who wanted to visit friends and relatives on the windward side had to take a winding trail up Nu'uanu Valley, where it terminated at a sheer cliff. From there a nerve-wracking portion slithered down the cliffs to the plains below. With the completion of the Pali Road (later replaced by the Pali Highway), this place of fear became a place of wondrous beauty. Kane'ohe Bay, Mokapu Peninsula, the cliffs of Ko'olau and even Chinaman's Hat island off in the distance create a glorious expansive panorama at the **Pali Lookout**. The last major Hawaiian **A REAL GEM** battle took place here, and the results changed the political landscape. (See page 14.)

Bring the warmest clothes in your suitcase for the Pali Lookout. Yeah, sure, this is the tropics and the elevation is only 1,200 feet. But you're at a slit in a mountain that funnels the now-cooler trade winds piling up against the larger

...and this is the reason to take H-3.

mountain, and you'll freeze your 'okole off here if you're not prepared. (Of course, maybe we're just wimps who have lived here in Hawai'i too long.) To the right are the remains of the Old Pali Road, now a hike listed on page 178, which goes all the way to the Likelike Hwy and beyond. It's $3 to park at the Pali Lookout.

Got any bacon with you? Local custom says that if you take the Pali Hwy with any pork in your car, bad things will happen to you. This is because this area was said to be the home of Kamapua'a, a demigod who was half man, half pig. If you have any pork with you, it's an in-your-face gesture that Kamapua'a will take offense with—and perhaps respond to.

The third highway poking through the mountain, **Likelike Hwy** (63) is the least attractive of the trans-Ko'olau highways

The serene setting of the Byodo-In Temple exudes peacefulness.

and should be your last choice. By the way, if someone asks, it's pronounced LEE-KAY-LEE-KAY, not LIKE LIKE.

If you want to head back to Waikiki, take one of these highways. If you're gonna keep going to the North Shore, see the next chapter. We should probably have put Kane'ohe in the North Shore chapter, but it felt...weird, because it's contiguous to Kailua. So, before you head back to Waikiki, here's what you're missing in Kane'ohe.

KANE'OHE

If you're heading north, Kane'ohe is your next town, and there are different ways to get there. Orient yourself with the map on page 68. The most important landmark in Kane'ohe is the **Kane'ohe Marine Corps Base**. Forget your visions of row upon row of barracks with privates running around as sergeants bark out orders. This is a charming, self-contained city with all the com-

forts of home, sort of an island within an island. It has restaurants, a movie theater, gas stations, neighborhoods of beautiful houses, schools and school buses, car rental companies, stellar beaches and a very nice golf course called Klipper. Everything a growing marine and his/her family could want. The only thing you won't find here is…*you*. It's an active marine base and access is restricted.

The prominent **Ulu-pa'u Head** at Kane'ohe Base is the result of steam explosions offshore that formed a separate island. The world was warmer then and the sea level higher. As the world cooled, the sea level dropped, connecting the land via a peninsula.

Ironically, Kane'ohe Base's destiny as an island apart from the rest of O'ahu is assured, both politically and geologically. It's *barely* attached to the main island by a nearly flooded plain. With naturally rising sea levels (which have risen 180 feet over the past 12,000 years), it almost certainly will be cut off from O'ahu within a hundred years or so without human intervention.

By the way, contrary to popular belief, Pearl Harbor was not the first place attacked on December 7, 1941. Kane'ohe was, since there was an airfield here that the Japanese wanted to neutralize before they went after the fleet on the other side of the island.

Driving along, if you've been lusting after the Ko'olau mountains and want to drive a bit closer to them, you can take a detour to a free botanical garden that backs up to them. On Hwy 83 just north of its intersection with H-3 is Luluku Road. Up this road is the **Ho'omaluhia Park Botanical Garden** (233-7323). The drive through the gardens gets you more intimate with the mountains. If

you're interested in touring the gardens, see Land Tours on page 199.

The only thing more beautiful than the Ko'olaus on a clear morning is on those afternoons when the invisible trade winds cause the soft clouds to dance along the jagged summit in a scene that will surely cause you to think, *this must be what heaven looks like*.

If you take the Kahekili Hwy (83) through Kane'ohe, north of Kane'ohe town is the **Valley of the Temples**. This

A REAL GEM

is simply a large cemetery. Well, maybe not so simple. It's $3 (cash) per person to get in, and there are various temples scattered around the area. In the back is the greatest temple of them all. The **Byodo-In** is a grand replica of a 950-year-old Buddhist temple in Uji, Japan. Built in the 1960s to commemorate the 100th anniversary of the arrival of Japanese immigrant workers to Hawai'i, the temple is the absolute essence of serenity. It's like taking a mini-trip to Japan. Backed by the gorgeous Ko'olau mountain range and fronted by a large pond filled with koi fish and curious swans, it's impossible not to feel peaceful here. (The only distraction is the seemingly constant sound of gas-powered weed whackers. Of course, it's those same personnel who keep the grounds so flawlessly sculpted.) This temple is still used today by worshippers. If you visit, it's customary to ring the richly toned bell before entering. Morning light is best here.

In **Kane'ohe Bay**, **Moku-o-Lo'e** (usually called **Coconut Island**) was formerly owned by a Fleischmann's yeast heir. (Ironically enough, the island actually did "rise" while this yeast guy owned it. He doubled its size by dredging and planted the coconut trees.) The island went through a series of owners and is used today by the Hawai'i Institute of Marine Biology. It's barely recognizable from the time it was filmed to represent *Gilligan's Island* in the '60s.

Kane'ohe Bay's reputation among long-time locals is less than pristine. For 25 years the military base and the local community discharged untreated sewage into the south part of the bay, and the bay became known as the *last* place you'd want to go into the water. Although the practice stopped in 1978 (treated water is piped to a trench *way* offshore where currents carry it away), many locals from the leeward side still connect Kane'ohe Bay with bad water and avoid it, which pleases windward residents who get it all to themselves.

In fact, one of our favorite kayak trips on the island is in Kane'ohe Bay. It visits a 1,000-acre sunken island and two beaches that appear and disappear twice each day. See KAYAKING on page 194.

After driving through the town of Kane'ohe heading north, you're committed to the shoreline route that you'll be hugging for the next 40 miles.

EAST O'AHU BEST BETS

Best Sunrise—From the top of Makapu'u or Ka'iwi Ridge in Kailua for the motivated

Best Beach Stroll—Kailua Beach

Best *Empty* Beach Stroll—Bellows Beach *During the Week*

Best Place to Get Drilled into the Sand—Bodysurfing at Sandy Beach or Makapu'u Beach

Best Place to See Water Fly Out of a Cave—Spitting Cave of Portlock

Best Place to Lose Your Hat—Pali Lookout

Best Bodysurfing Waves—Flags at Kailua Beach

What could be more magical than greeting a new day from Kailua Beach?

Yeah, now that's what we call a highway.

The North Shore is the prettiest drive on the entire island. Forget the big city and its multi-lane highways. This is a place with only a few traffic lights and a two-lane road that hugs the shoreline, embracing the Hawai'i of yesteryear. Along the way you'll find yourself constantly drooling over the beaches and mountain scenery.

We've marked the following maps in terms of miles and time (without stops or traffic) from Windward Mall in Kane'ohe. You'll usually know when you've gone from one town to the next.

This is a long chapter because once you've driven past Kane'ohe, you're committed to the drive to Hale'iwa. So, although part of windward O'ahu is on this tour, we're sticking with the term NORTH SHORE SIGHTS. (NORTH SHORE AND THE NORTHERN PART OF WINDWARD SHORE SIGHTS wouldn't fit in the heading.)

KUALOA

As you approach the northern part of Kane'ohe Bay on Hwy 83, Tropical Farms is a mac nut farm with a very pretty garden area and gorgeous monkeypod trees providing shade. They're very generous with the flavored mac nut samples. (They can afford to be at these prices.) Watch out for the two hazards here: wasps flying around the sampling area and tour buses flying around the parking lot.

Kualoa Beach Park is at the very edge of Kane'ohe Bay. This gigantic beach park has an endless lawn, a long ribbon of sand fringing it and an *oh-so-tempting* offshore island called **Chinaman's Hat** (Hawaiian name Mokoli'i). This uninhabited island can be yours to rule. See ADVENTURES on page 226. The road into Kualoa Park was an airstrip during WWII and it extended *across* the Hwy (where the grass is today). When the P-38s (used here in WWII for photo recon) had to take off or land, they had someone stand at the Hwy to stop traffic. Instead of concrete, the entire 6,500-foot runway was paved with steel grates.

Past the park, **Kualoa Ranch** is a huge, breathtakingly beautiful windward ranch. It's also a giant visitor-processing machine that in some areas does a good job, but their prices are high. Many of their customers are tour groups from Japan. Some of their activities seem a bit over-hyped to us. For instance, on one of their tours, the "private beach" they take you to is a sandbar that anyone could walk to from the adjacent Kualoa Beach.

They also have horseback rides (nose-to-tail walks, but the mountain scenery is very pretty) and ATV tours (same description). See ACTIVITIES for more.

That old concrete chimney on the side of the road past Kualoa Park is all that remains of a short-lived, Civil War-era **sugar mill**. Shortly after it opened the co-owner's young son was accidentally bumped into a vat of boiling sugar syrup and died. The mill closed five years later when they realized that the area didn't get enough rain.

Soon the highway starts cozying up to the ocean in a dramatic way. It's heavenly to drive along so close to the sand and the breakers. In the town of **Ka'a'awa** (pronounced as if you were coughing up a furball) you'll find **Uncle Bobo's**, which has good BBQ and cheap food across from Swanzy Beach Park next to the Post Office (before the 7-Eleven).

At the north end of town after the 27 mile marker is the **Crouching Lion Inn**.

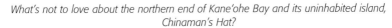

What's not to love about the northern end of Kane'ohe Bay and its uninhabited island, Chinaman's Hat?

Lava rocks on the mountain form the silhouette of a lion. Most people mistakenly look at the most obvious rocks near the road and think that's the lion. Actually, you'd have to be in the private driveway *before* (to the left of) the Crouching Lion Inn and look up past the cement driveway to see it from its best view. There you'll find the little bugger with his mouth slightly open, facing partially away from you. By the way, don't believe any stories about a Hawaiian legend of a crouching lion around here. The ancient Hawaiians would have had as much familiarity with lions as they'd have had with chainsaws. Lions ain't native to Hawai'i. Below the Crouching Lion restaurant they sell a tasty treat called **Donkey Balls**, an unusual chocolate mac nut. Available in any quantity (not just pairs).

KAHANA BAY

After the tongue-twisting Ka'a'awa is the easier-to-pronounce **Kahana Bay**. Although the bay's waters are never ultra-clear thanks to runoff from the Kahana River, the beach setting is **A REAL GEM** picturesque, and it's rare to find more than a few people here during the week. One of the easier kayak trips is up the jungly-looking river. (See KAYAKING on page 197 for more.) The state park behind the bay is the **Ahupua'a O Kahana State Park**.

Your drive along the North Shore won't be exactly *filled* with dining options. Forget what you may have heard about eating lunch at the Crouching Lion—it's a disappointing tourist trap. Your best bet is to eat at one of the shrimp vendors ahead in Kahuku, wait until you get to the North Shore around Sunset Beach or Sharks Cove,

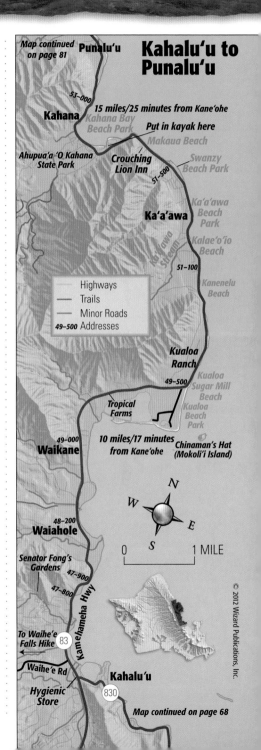

Kahalu'u to Punalu'u

Map continued on page 81

Punalu'u

53-000

15 miles/25 minutes from Kane'ohe

Kahana
Kahana Bay Beach Park
Put in kayak here
Makaua Beach

Ahupua'a 'O Kahana State Park
Crouching Lion Inn
51-500
Swanzy Beach Park

Ka'a'awa
Ka'a'awa Beach Park

Kalae'o'io Beach

51-100

Kanenelu Beach

Highways
Trails
Minor Roads
49-500 Addresses

Kualoa Ranch
49-500
Kualoa Sugar Mill Beach
Kualoa Beach Park

Tropical Farms

49-000
Waikane

10 miles/17 minutes from Kane'ohe

Chinaman's Hat (Mokoli'i Island)

N
W   E
S

48-200
Waiahole

Senator Fong's Gardens
47-900
47-800

0   1 MILE

© 2012 Wizard Publications, Inc.

Kamehameha Hwy

To Waihe'e Falls Hike   83

Waihe'e Rd

Hygienic Store

Kahalu'u
830

Map continued on page 68

Sometimes nature patiently chips away at things, and sometimes she's in a hurry. This sea arch off La'ie Point was created in one day when Mother Nature angrily put her fist through the island.

or hit Hale'iwa, which has a good restaurant selection.

In the town of Hau'ula, **Sacred Falls Park** *was* one of the most popular waterfall hikes on the island. A fatal landslide on Mother's Day in 1999 and subsequent lawsuits prompted its closure. The state has since passed a law immunizing itself from future lawsuits (isn't it cool to be able to pass a law immunizing yourself?), but at press time the falls and 1,300-acre park were still closed as bureaucrats pondered its future. The only thing they've been able to agree on is to change the name of this closed park to **Kaluanui State Park**. By the way, Kaluanui means *the big pit*.

LA'IE

The biggest town along this part of the island is La'ie. In terms of driving time, there is probably no place on the island that takes longer to get to from Waikiki than La'ie. It's also light years away in terms of the culture. La'ie is a town heavily dominated by the Latter Day Saints (often called Mormon) Church. Their university, **Brigham Young University**, has a campus and a beautiful temple here as well. Some of the businesses do things a bit differently in La'ie. For instance, the only grocery store is closed on Sunday and refuses to sell any alcohol. The Chinese restaurant in La'ie doesn't serve tea unless you ask for it.

One of the biggest attractions in all Hawai'i, the Polynesian Cultural Center, is in La'ie. This sprawling center was created to attract visitors, who help subsidize Brigham Young students from all over the Pacific. They do a particularly good job re-creating island life from around Polynesia. See ATTRACTIONS on page 109 for more.

Take a right at the stoplight at Anemoku, then right on Naupaka. This leads to La'ie Point. Oh, what a beautiful sight! This point is made up entirely of sandstone with several small islands offshore. The closest one is 432 feet offshore (looks closer, doesn't it?). It has a natural arch carved dead center that was created on April Fool's Day in 1946 when a tsunami literally punched a hole through the island. To the right are more islands, along with a view of Windward O'ahu itself. The 360° vantage from this point is grand, and if the surf is up, the symphony of crashing waves is a delight to listen to.

NOT TO BE MISSED!

Past the center of town, La'ie Beach is also known as Hukilau Beach. A hukilau is a fishing event where non-fishermen are able to catch fish. A net is laid out in a horseshoe shape with the open end toward the shore. While some people splash around, driving fish into the net, people on the shore slowly pull the net onto the land. After WWII, the LDS church performed a monthly hukilau here to help raise funds for the church. It got so popular that a state agency, the Hawaii Visitor's Bureau, asked them to continue performing it and promoted it to visitors. So why doesn't the church still do hukilaus there anymore? Because *another* state agency saw its popularity as a way to get money. The Hawai'i government decided it wanted to tax the event in 1970, so the

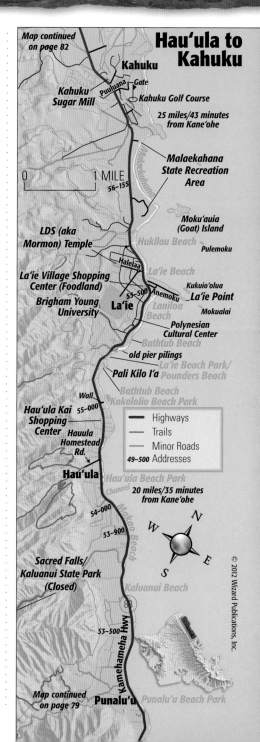

Map continued on page 82

Hau'ula to Kahuku

Kahuku
Kahuku Sugar Mill
Puuluana — Gate
Kahuku Golf Course
25 miles/43 minutes from Kane'ohe

0   1 MILE
56–155

Malaekahana State Recreation Area

Moku'auia (Goat) Island
Pulemoku

LDS (aka Mormon) Temple
Hukilau Beach

La'ie Village Shopping Center (Foodland)
Brigham Young University
Halelaa
La'ie Beach
55–500 Anemoku
Kukuio'olua
La'ie Point
La'ie
Laniloa Beach
Mokualai

Polynesian Cultural Center
Bathtub Beach
old pier pilings
La'ie Beach Park/ Pounders Beach
Pali Kilo I'a
Bathtub Beach
Kokololio Beach Park
Wall
Hau'ula Kai 55–000
Shopping Center
Hauula Homestead Rd.

Highways
Trails
Minor Roads
49–500 Addresses

Hau'ula
Hau'ula Beach Park
Channel
20 miles/35 minutes from Kane'ohe

54–000
Makao Beach
53–900

N
W   E
S

Sacred Falls/ Kaluanui State Park (Closed)
Kaluanui Beach

83

53–500

Kamehameha Hwy

Map continued on page 79
Punalu'u   Punalu'u Beach Park

© 2012 Wizard Publications, Inc.

Turtle Bay to Waimea

29 miles/50 minutes
from Kane'ohe

Kuilima Cove

Turtle Bay Resort

83

Turtle Bay

Stables

Kawela

Bunker

Kawela Bay

Regional Relay Facility

57–500

Waiale'e Beach
Park (unmarked)

58–300

Oopuola
Sunset Point 59–000

Sunset Beach
Support Park

Sunset Beach
59–200

Kammie Land

Gas Chambers

Pupukea
'Ehukai Beach Park

Banzai Pipeline
Back Doors
Off the Wall
Log Cabins

Cloud Break

59–500

Foodland

Pupukea Rd

Puula

Waimea

Shark's Cove
Tide-pool

Kapuhi

Pu'u o Mahuka Heiau

Pupukea Beach Park

Three Tables

Waimea Valley

Waimea
Bay

36 miles/60 minutes
from Kane'ohe

Iliohu Pl

61–200

Uppers

© 2012 Wizard Publications, Inc.

Map continued on page 81

Highways
Minor Roads
49–500 **Addresses**
Lost Filming Site

0   1 MILE

Map continued on page 84

Mormons simply stopped doing them. Incidentally, as with other things in La'ie, Hukilau Beach (or at least the access to it) is closed on Sundays.

After La'ie is a large state beach park called **Malaekahana**. If you're looking for a beach that takes a bit more to get to than simply walking up and falling into the sand, **Moku'auia Island** (also called **Goat Island**) is 240 yards offshore from the park. You can usually wade to it, and those who put in the effort are rewarded with a picture-perfect crescent sand beach often deserted in the morning.

A REAL GEM

The notable thing about Malaekahana are the **cabins** for rent. They're old private beach houses that were taken over by the state when this area was converted into a park. Although pretty run down, they can be yours if you make arrangements in advance. See CAMPING on page 163 for more.

KAHUKU

After La'ie on Hwy 83, the town of Kahuku is famous for its shrimp trucks and shacks. Although shrimp is commercially grown nearby, some of the trucks get their shrimp from off-island sources. It's easy to look at businesses like these "sleepy little shrimp trucks" and assume that they're struggling little mom and pop enterprises. Sometimes they're much more. **Giovanni's Aloha Shrimp Wagon** is a case in point.

The current owner bought the business for $120,000. Four years later, in 2001, the previous owner said she wanted it back. Apparently, she *really* wanted it back. According to prosecutors, she met with the owner and demanded he sell her the business back for the price he paid. He replied that it was now worth much more—$700,000, to be precise. (If you've ever seen the long lines at Giovanni's during lunch, that sounds reasonable.) When he refused to sign a contract for $120,000, two large gunmen walked in, threatened his family on the mainland, stuck a gun in his left eye and politely asked him to sign the contract (which he did). He later went to the police, and the woman was convicted of robbery, extortion and kidnapping. Sleepy little businesses, indeed.

You're nearing the northernmost part of the island. Past the shrimp vendors, there's a vast area on your right belonging to the James Campbell Company. Formerly an estate trust with 176 heirs worth *$2 billion*, it was broken up in 2007. Although they occasionally offer tours when it's not nesting season, don't bother. Except for the wild, windy shoreline (for which we have a hike listed on page 187), the land you're not seeing is probably the ugliest part of the island. The land looks stressed, beaten up and tired. Every region has to have an ugly side, and this is O'ahu's, in our opinion. So don't be concerned that you're missing something special.

After Kahuku is a store on the ocean side called S. Tanaka Store Antique & Bottles. This place sure lives up to its name. It's positively *packed* with very old bottles from early Hawaiian bottlers, endless Coca-Cola antiques, Japanese glass fishing floats and more. Worth stopping for if you like antiques and *if* they're open.

TURTLE BAY

O'ahu has been amazingly successful at containing resorts in a single area. Outside of Waikiki there are only nine resorts. Turtle Bay is one of them.

As an aside, we always include aerial photos of all the resorts in our WHERE TO STAY section. This resort and beach are always the hardest to photograph. Their location at the end of the Ko'olau Mountains is where different types of winds converge, and the air above this resort is almost always turbulent to the point of being violent. Trying to hold the camera steady and flying the pitching aircraft while screaming and crying for mama is a bit awkward, so if our aerial shots of this area are a bit blurry, you'll understand why. You'll also notice wind turbines along here and closer to Hale'iwa. Between them there are 42 turbines cranking out 81 megawatts of power to feed O'ahu's thirsty power grid.

THE NORTH SHORE

When surfers talk about the North Shore, they generally mean the 7 miles of surf breaks from Sunset Point to Pua'ena Point near Hale'iwa town. Other islanders consider the North Shore to be everything from Sunset Point all the way out to the westernmost tip of the island at Ka'ena Point.

The population of the North Shore doubles during the winter surf season, and traffic often backs up near beaches visible from the road as rubbernecking drivers find wave-watching irresistible. (Residents are the *worst* offenders.) During those times when the waves don't materialize during the winter, you'll see them *bumming hard core, brah*. The pulse rate of the North Shore slows considerably when the surfing season dies down in the spring. Laid back and casual become the order of the day.

Just before Sunset Beach you'll see Ted's Bakery on the left. You should know that their chocolate/haupia (made from coconut) pie is legendary on the

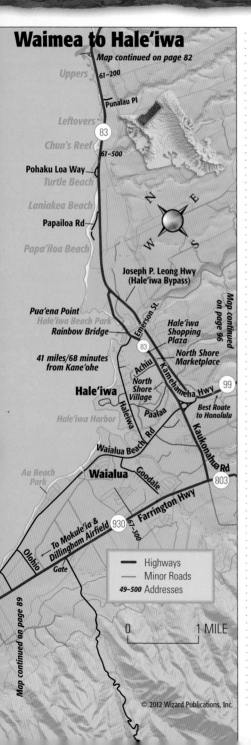

Waimea to Hale'iwa

Map continued on page 82

Uppers
61–200

Punalau Pl

Leftovers
83

Chun's Reef
61–500

Pohaku Loa Way
Turtle Beach

Laniakea Beach

Papailoa Rd
Papa'iloa Beach

N
E
W
S

Joseph P. Leong Hwy
(Hale'iwa Bypass)

Pua'ena Point
Hale'iwa Beach Park
Rainbow Bridge

Emerson St.

Hale'iwa
Shopping
Plaza

Map continued on page 96

83

North Shore
Marketplace

41 miles/68 minutes
from Kane'ohe

Achiu

North
Shore
Village

Kamehameha Hwy

99

Hale'iwa

Haleiwa

Paalaa

Best Route
to Honolulu

Hale'iwa Harbor

Waialua Beach Rd

Kaukonahua Rd

Au Beach
Park

Waialua

Goodale

803

Farrington Hwy

To Mokule'ia &
Dillingham Airfield

930

67–300

Olohio

Gate

Map continued on page 89

— Highways
— Minor Roads
49–500 Addresses

0   1 MILE

© 2012 Wizard Publications, Inc.

island. Frankly, to us it tastes pretty unremarkable, but some island residents and many of our readers get downright teary-eyed over it. If you try it, please let us know if we're off the mark on this one.

The Sunset Beach area was known to ancient Hawaiians as Pau-malu. According to lore, there was once a local woman renowned for her ability to catch octopus. One day as she was preparing to go hunting here, an old man stopped her and told her to limit her catch to a certain number. She agreed but, while hunting, she got carried away and caught more than the allotment. Just then a giant shark came and bit off both her legs. Locals concluded that she had angered the shark god that watched over the reef and named the area Pau-malu, meaning *taken by surprise*.

Today Sunset Beach is a dreamy beach that brings fantastic waves in the winter and placid, warm waters in the summer.

Imagine owning a beachfront house along here. Then imagine this: The stretch of shoreline from Sunset Point almost to Shark's Cove is all sandy beach. In 1919 a developer broke the entire 2 miles into individual parcels for beachfront homes. He sold them all in less than two months and pocketed—are you ready for this?—a whopping $46,000 *for all the parcels combined*. Today it would cost at least 50 times that amount for a *single* parcel.

Surf sites vary in their fame. But in all Hawai'i there is no more famous surf break than the Banzai Pipeline. During large (but not giant) surf, swells coming from the northwest form perfect barrels at this site. It's hard to find prettier waves anywhere in the world than on a good day at the pipe. Yet there are no signs telling you where it is, and there's no beach named

A REAL GEM

The jumping rock at Waimea Bay...and the sound of a belly-flop heard round the world.

Who the Heck is Eddie…and Why Would He Go?

Drive around O'ahu and you'll see bumper stickers that say, "Eddie Would Go." The biggest big-wave surf contest in the world is the Quicksilver in Memory of Eddie Aikau contest. It's held every few years—only when waves on the North Shore are 20 feet high or more. (A 20-foot wave, measured from the back as many Hawaiian surfers do, has a 40-foot face!)

So who's this Eddie guy?

Eddie Aikau was a pure-blood Hawaiian big-wave surfer from O'ahu who, as a lifeguard at Waimea Bay, literally saved hundreds of lives by braving monster winter surf to rescue people who'd gotten into trouble. Long-time locals have memories of Eddie charging into waves three or four stories high to pull helpless visitors back in. Often a helicopter would be called to raise the swimmer in a basket. Then Eddie would swim back though the surf to the shore.

In the '70s a voyaging canoe called the Hokule'a was built to prove that Polynesians had navigated to and from Hawai'i using only the stars. For the first trip to Tahiti, the crew brought along a navigator from Micronesia to teach them how to navigate using only the heavens. But tensions were so high that the navigator refused to return to Hawai'i on the boat after fistfights erupted. The Hawaiian crew resented the rules and regulations set by the science-minded white leaders, and the white leaders resented the Hawaiians who only seemed to want to smoke their pakalolo (marijuana) and listen to their taped music.

In 1978 a second voyage was planned to Tahiti, and Eddie Aikau was accepted as a volunteer crewman. On March 16th a crowd of 10,000 gathered at Magic Island to see them off. Even though the weather was turning foul, the great turnout created pressure to leave anyway. That night, after some hatches had been improperly shut, the hulls filled with water and the canoe capsized. Their radio was flooded, and their emergency beacon was lost. Almost immediately Eddie volunteered to take his surfboard through the 15-foot swells and 35 mph winds to Lana'i. The captain refused. Cold, wet and scared, the crew spent the dark night calling to each other to make sure no one had been washed away. The next day Eddie again asked to go. Although Lana'i was now 20 miles away through angry seas, the captain and his officers reluctantly agreed. "Eddie was godlike," one of his crewmembers said. If anybody could do it, it was Eddie.

The crew gathered around to say a prayer, and then Eddie started paddling his 12-foot surfboard. When he was 50 feet from the boat, he took off his life jacket (so he could paddle better) and continued on his way. Eddie Aikau was never seen again. Later that evening the crew shot a flare into the air as the last inter-island flight flew by and, miraculously, the pilot saw and responded to the flare. The remaining crew members were rescued by a Coast Guard helicopter.

Today the name Eddie is synonymous in Hawai'i with trying…going for it…risking it all for your friends. Hey, brah, Eddie would go.

after it. So here's how to find it. The Banzai Pipeline is 100 yards to the left of 'Ehukai Beach Park and 185 yards offshore. (The park—often missing a sign—is across the street from Sunset Beach Elementary School.) From the road you'll know if it's going off. Not because you can see the waves (which you can't), but because the small parking lot at 'Ehukai will be *filled* with local cars. (During calm summer months the amount of sand at the beach increases exponentially when truckloads of sand are transported here by the ocean.)

Past 'Ehukai is Shark's Cove. During summer months (May to September or October) this is one of the best places on the island to snorkel. Clear water, lots of fish and a fair number of turtles make this an inviting body of water. To the left

A REAL GEM

of the cove is a giant tide pool that kids love splashing in. See BEACHES on page 153 for more on Shark's Cove.

Just past Shark's Cove at the Foodland is Pupukea Road. About ⅔ mile up this road, turn right and drive another ¾ mile (over 10 speed bumps) to come to the Pu'u o Mahuka Heiau. These remnants of a Hawaiian temple, perched 250 feet above Waimea Bay on a ridge, possess a peaceful and serene view from the top of Mt. Ka'ala all the way out to Ka'ena Point. It's worth the detour for the view alone. One of the plaques says they could communicate with Wailua on Kaua'i by fire, but that's probably a Hawaiian wives' tale since Wailua is 86 miles away. (It's doubtful even a monstrously large fire could be seen that far away, even on a crystal clear day.) All that remains of this heiau is a lava stone foundation. While it's tempting to think of a temple as a spiritu-

The simple life on a North Shore beach...

al place, this was a *luakini* heiau, where human sacrifices took place. Countless Hawaiians and possibly some westerners were murdered here to feed the hungry gods. When the Hawaiians overthrew their religious kapu system in 1819 (by their own hand and with no outside intervention or pressure—this was *before* any missionaries ever came to the island), few Hawaiians of that day shed a tear that this particular temple was being dismantled. Although the ali'i (chiefs) revered it, to the common man of that time *luakini* heiau were places of oppression and fear.

WAIMEA BAY

Hwy 83 soon takes you to Waimea Bay, the place to be when the winter surf is *really* high—say 20-foot waves and higher. Surf of this height causes other surf sites to close out and simply look **A REAL GEM** messy and frothy. (See page 214 to learn more about waves and what surfers look for.)

Most people observe big surf from the beach, but finding a parking spot at Waimea Bay Beach Park can be difficult. We prefer a spot from the left side of the bay. There's a dedicated public access from the end of Iliohu Place, though at press time locals were parking at the end of Iliohu *Way* and taking a short trail through the brush. Either way it leads to a wicked vantage point.

Behind Waimea Bay is the entrance to **Waimea Valley**. If you've read about **Waimea Falls Park** and are jonesin' for some of the adventure activities there, you're in for a disappointment. It's been converted to a low-key botanical garden and cultural center that also happens to have a waterfall you can swim to when it's flowing. See LAND TOURS in ACTIVITIES chapter on page 198 for more.

In 1792 George Vancouver (as in Vancouver, Canada), was visiting the islands. He had been on Captain Cook's fatal voyage to Hawai'i 13 years earlier. Vancouver was exceptionally skilled at diplomacy and was well regarded by Hawaiian chiefs. While he was on Kaua'i, his sister ship stopped here at Waimea to secure water. The armed captain of that other ship and crew members were directed by the Hawaiians to travel farther up the stream (to avoid the saltier brackish water at the mouth). Then the Hawaiians further enticed the captain, the astronomer and two crewmen to come see some hogs

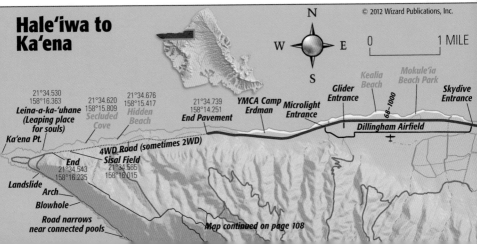

Hale'iwa to Ka'ena

© 2012 Wizard Publications, Inc.

N
W — E
S

0   1 MILE

21°34.530
158°16.363
Leina-a-ka-'uhane (Leaping place for souls)
Ka'ena Pt.

21°34.620
158°15.809
Secluded Cove

21°34.676
158°15.417
Hidden Beach

21°34.739
158°14.251
End Pavement

YMCA Camp Erdman

Microlight Entrance

Glider Entrance

Kealia Beach

Mokule'ia Beach Park

Skydive Entrance

68-1000

Dillingham Airfield

4WD Road (sometimes 2WD)

End
21°34.543
158°16.235

Sisal Field
21°34.565
158°16.015

Landslide
Arch
Blowhole
Road narrows near connected pools

Map continued on page 108

Innocent swimmers were minding their own business when this rude turtle just cut them off. Some turtles at Turtle Beach simply don't have any manners.

and bananas they wanted to sell them. Once the men were away from their party, the Hawaiians stoned then stabbed them to death (one crewman escaped) and took their arms. In the 1800s the renowned Hawaiian historian *Kamakau* interviewed one of the aging killers, who told him, "We killed the men to get the guns," and that chiefs had ordered that "if a ship came into the area, they were to kill the foreigners and get the guns" (which had that magical power to kill a man from a distance).

Unfortunately, this would be only one example of Hawaiians killing westerners and vice versa in the early years of western contact.

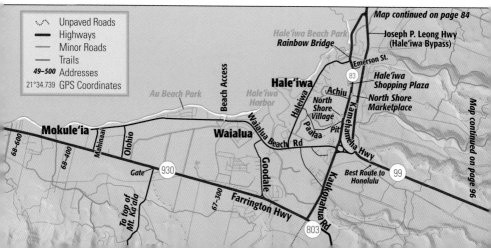

Map continued on page 84

Map continued on page 96

Halfway between Waimea Bay and Hale'iwa town (and at the south end of a loop road called Pohaku Loa Way) is a small beach known locally as Turtle Beach. Residents request that you park on the mauka side of the highway

NOT TO BE MISSED!

and avoid their quiet street. This is the only place in Hawai'i where the turtles are so gregarious, we've seen them actually swim after beachgoers who have gotten bored from turtle-watching. (We suspect that some nearby resident might be secretly feeding them to create this kind of behavior.) Anyway, they're not *always* there, but when they are, it's a joy to see turtles so close to the shore (sometimes *on* the shore) and so accepting of people nearby. Remember that it's illegal to touch or handle them, and beware that, right at the shoreline, waves might send them crashing into your shin. (Got the scar to prove it.)

SURFING LIFE

There are two seasons on the North Shore—surfing season (during winter months) and the agonizing waiting season when the fickle waves pound the southern hemisphere. Winter waves usually start rolling in around November, and North Shore towns such as Hale'iwa and Waimea instantly transform from sleepy summer towns to jam-packed surfing meccas.

Strewn along this stretch of the island are numerous surfing houses, many with notorious names known to surfers throughout the country. Each night during surfing season, throngs of surfers and those attracted to the lifestyle gather in these houses where BBQs are smoking, someone is always lifting weights, beer is being consumed *at all times*, surfing videos or surfing video games are being

played, and talk is about waves and those who ride them. Some have outside jobs, some don't. All share a passion for waves that non-surfers find baffling. You can listen to surfers talk for hours about how the waves are breaking and how they did or would respond. It's more than a lifestyle; it's closer to a religion.

Though O'ahu's North Shore is known around the world as home of the planet's best surfing, it's surprising to learn that until the 1950s nobody surfed any of the sites here. The waves were considered too big and too powerful, so Makaha in West O'ahu was the home to serious surfing. The first few hardy pioneers to surf the North Shore's waves got ground into dust by the breakers, but by the 1960s word got out, and the North Shore was "discovered" by the outside world. The big change occurred when the old heavy redwood boards were replaced by new, lightweight (and more maneuverable) balsa wood boards, and a radical invention allowed surfers to tackle taller waves that would have turned their boards sideways. The invention? The surfboard fin. Now surfers had a chance. By the time fiberglass boards came along, North Shore waves were being shredded by riders lured from all over the world.

HALE'IWA

Hale'iwa is the biggest town on the North Shore. It's a quaint town that centers around surfing in the winter. (Summers are pretty mellow.) There aren't any resorts up here, but B&Bs aren't hard to find. Several good restaurants and some pretty good shopping are available. If you're looking for a treat, consider the shave ice at Aoki's or Matsumoto's on Kamehameha Highway. (The latter often has unjustifiably long lines, so don't hesitate to go to Aoki's—see page 267.)

What could possibly motivate you to walk a mile and a quarter from your car?
How about Hidden Beach?

If you drive west on Hwy 930 (Farrington Hwy), there are stretches of sand beach past **Mokuleʻia Beach Park** that are usually deserted. See BEACHES on page 157 for more.

PAST THE PAVEMENT

Although we generally don't recommend 4WDs on Oʻahu the way we do on Kauaʻi or the Big Island, this is the *one* occasion when you *might* wish you had one, because the last 2¼ miles are an unpaved road (sometimes nice, sometimes junky), and there are a couple of sights worth seeing—enough so that you might want to walk to them. (Bring water since it's shadeless.)

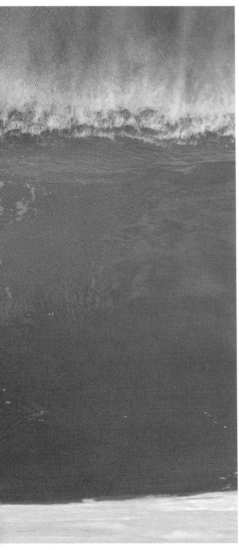

little snorkeling when the ocean's not pounding too hard.

At 1¾ miles into the dirt road (³⁄₁₀ mile before the end of the dirt road) is a secluded cove that we're cleverly calling…secluded cove. (It has no actual name.) You can see it from the dirt road. The wind is almost always blowing in this area, and the seas are nearly always choppy. This cove is a wonderful exception. Except when the seas are very heavy, it's usually protected and calm with great swimming and a ruggedly beautiful, contoured shoreline patiently chiseled out of solid sandstone by the relentless sea.

The snorkeling is the best you'll find along the Mokule'ia shoreline. (Granted, this isn't an area renowned for its snorkeling—like being the best hockey player in all of Ecuador.) Though the visibility is a bit cloudy, there's a nice variety of little fish. (Shoreline fishermen tend to snag their bigger family members.) Until around 2 p.m. on weekdays this area tends to be unoccupied. Late afternoons sometime bring 4WD-equipped fishermen.

To the right of the cove is a Jacuzzi-sized pool in the reef that makes a great swimming hole when the seas cooperate. You can't see it—or its occupants—from the shoreline; you have to know it's there.

Now that you've gone 2¼ miles on the unpaved road, there's a rock vehicle barricade. Less than a five-minute walk past the rock barricade at the end of the dirt road is a layered sandstone rock on the ocean side of the path. This rock was absolutely sacred to the ancient Hawaiians. The word "sacred" can be overused, but in this case it can't be overstated. This area is called *Leina-a-ka-'uhane*—the leaping place for souls. The ancients believed that while you were

About 1¼ miles into the dirt road, 16 telephone poles past the metal gate you went around, and possiblly marked by a sign that points to a road called C-1, is a hidden beach. You can't really see it well from the dirt road. Imagine having a small, sandy cove to yourself. Might happen, might not. But you've got a chance here. There's even a

A REAL GEM

on your deathbed, your soul left your body and wandered about. For those Hawaiians who lived on O'ahu, the soul eventually ended up here where it would climb this sandstone rock, face the ocean and leap into the company of its ancestors—and at that exact moment, the person died. If a soul had no ancestors who cared enough to greet it, the soul fell into the *po pau 'ole o milu,* the endless night, or wandered about the island for eternity as a ghost, known in the islands as a night marcher.

From Hale'iwa take Hwy 99 for your journey back to Waikiki.

AIN'T TECHNOLOGY GRAND?

Above Ka'ena Point is a satellite tracking station. That title implies that it was built to track satellites, but space technology wasn't always so advanced. Throughout the '60s, until 1972, a supersecret "black" group called the *Corona Project* carried out one of America's most important reconnaissance tasks here.

Spy satellites launched about once a month took photographs of America's enemies during that part of the Cold War. But the images were just that—*photographs...on film*. The resolution of film was so much greater than beamable television cameras of that era that they had to take film-based snapshots. So how did they get the photos from the satellites to the spies who needed them? As strange as it sounds, canisters full of film were jettisoned from the satellites, small rockets guided the capsules to the appropriate drop zone 600 miles from O'ahu, and parachutes were deployed to slow the film's descent. Air Force cargo planes were guided to the parachutes from Ka'ena Point Tracking Station, and they snagged the parachutes *in mid-air*. The films were then taken back and analyzed.

Imagine how hard it would be to fly a bulky cargo plane just *barely* over the top of a rapidly sinking parachute and snag it with a loop dragged behind you. If the plane missed, the capsules landed in the ocean and were designed to float for 1–3 days before sinking. That's long enough for a U.S. ship to locate it, but not long enough to fall into the wrong hands if lost. They accomplished this time-critical float with a method that would make Betty Crocker proud—they simply drilled a hole in the capsule and plugged it with compacted brown sugar that would dissolve in the seawater at a known rate.

Of all the U.S. space programs, this one had by far, the highest failure rate. Of the first 25 satellites launched, *only three* returned usable photos. But they learned from their mistakes, ultimately launching 145 satellites and discovering that the dreaded '60s "missile gap" with the Soviet Union was a hollow bluff on the part of its leader, Nikita Khrushchev.

NORTH SHORE BEST BETS

Best Shoreline Drive—From Kualoa Beach Park to Hale'iwa

Best Place to Watch Turtles—Turtle Beach

Best Snorkeling—Shark's Cove (when it's calm)

Best Beach That You Can't Drive a Car to—Hidden Beach

Best Place to Stay Out of the Water— Anywhere on the North Shore when the surf's up

Best Photo Op of You Under a Waterfall—Waimea Valley

Best Surf Spot That's Not Marked— Banzai Pipeline

Best Use of a Cargo Plane—Snaring parachutes containing spy film

What a shame that few visitors will ever see some of the fantastic sights that Wai'anae has to offer, like Makua Beach.

Wai'anae in the west and Central O'ahu are the least visited parts of the island. Central O'ahu is dominated by vast fields of pineapple while Wai'anae is dominated by exceptionally clear water and an bad reputation among island residents.

If you're heading out to Wai'anae, skip to page 103.

CENTRAL O'AHU

This may be a little disorienting, but we're going to describe Central O'ahu from the north to the south. That's because we're assuming that most people will first see it *after* having driven around the North Shore, when they're on their way back toward Waikiki. Even if you bolted straight to the North Shore from Waiki-ki on a mission, this is how you'll tour it on the way back.

Taking Hwy 99 leaving Hale'iwa, you'll pass through a 155-acre **Waialua Estate Coffee and Chocolate Plantation** on the other side of Cook Island pine trees (used as a wind break). The coffee was abandoned for years and the trees got pretty sickly. Now they've added chocolate (who's harvesting season is the opposite of coffee so workers can stay employed year-round).

Soon you'll notice that most of this area is dominated by one crop—**pineapple**. James Dole started planting the fruit here in 1900 and then bought the entire island of Lana'i in 1922, converting it to a gigantic pineapple farm. (They stopped grow-

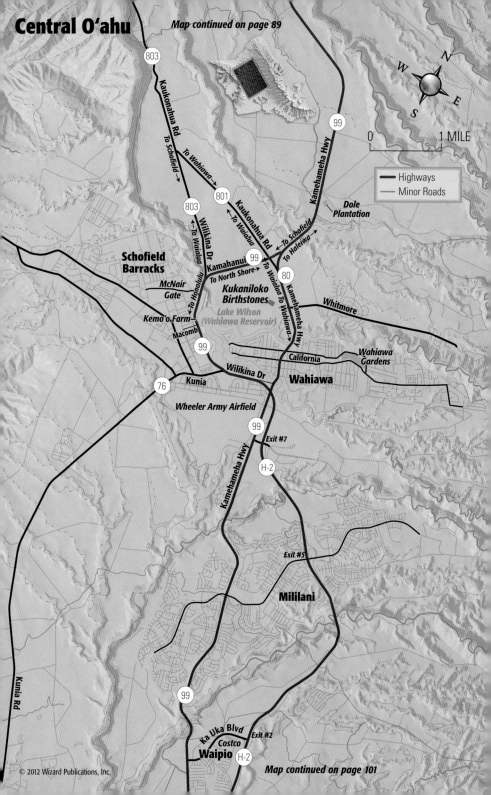

Central O'ahu

Map continued on page 89

803

Kaukonahua Rd

To Schofield

To Wahiawa →

801

803

Wiliknia Dr

To Waialua

Kaukonahua Rd

To Wahula

99

Kamehameha Hwy

Dole Plantation

To Schofield →

To Haleiwa →

To Waialua To Wahiawa

80

Kamahanui

To North Shore

Schofield Barracks

McNair Gate

Kukaniloko Birthstones

Lake Wilson (Wahiawa Reservoir)

Kemo'o Farm

Whitmore

Macomb

99

Wahiawa Gardens

California

Wiliknia Dr

Wahiawa

76

Kunia

Wheeler Army Airfield

99

Exit #7

99

H-2

Kamehameha Hwy

Exit #5

Mililani

99

Ka Uka Blvd

Exit #2

Costco

Waipio   H-2

Kunia Rd

Map continued on page 101

ing it commercially on Lana'i in 1990 in favor of a more profitable crop—*visitors*.)

Pineapple likes to be warm during the day and cool at night. This plateau is at 1,000 feet and cooler than the shoreline. Dole Pineapple has 11,500 acres under cultivation. At 27,000–33,000 low-to-the-ground pineapple plants per acre, there could be as many as *350 million* plants out here. It takes 20 months for a new plant to mature. When they harvest the fruit, they twist the top off and replant it where it'll make more pineapples in a little more than a year. You might notice that the area is littered with tattered black plastic. They put it down during planting to reduce the amount of water and pesticides needed. (Kind of ironic, isn't it? The area is littered with black plastic *to protect the environment*.)

The shape of the individual fields is no accident. They're laid out so that the arm of the harvesting machine can reach exactly halfway across the field while pineapple workers walk behind picking the fruit. It's tough, hot work, and walking through a pineapple field is a horrible affair. If you're curious to see what it's like, try practicing at home by walking through a giant pile of razor blades—same effect.

By the way, you'll hear lots of wives' tales regarding how to check a pineapple for ripeness and sweetness. Pulling leaves from the crown, measuring the buds on the skin, looking for golden color, looking for smooth and flattened eyes—there are plenty of ways, and everyone seems to swear by their method. Living in Hawai'i and having purchased countless pineapples, we can say authoritatively that the secret to getting a sweet pineapple is…pure luck. None of these tricks seems to work for us. And despite Dole's contention that "they're all picked ripe," we've certainly gotten some pretty sour

pineapples over the years. One thing that does seem to help is to put them in the fridge for a day upside down to let the sugar even out instead of pooling at the bottom. (Otherwise, the bottom's sweet and the top is sour.)

As an aside, excessive consumption of pineapple cores can cause "fiber balls" to form in your digestive tract. (You'll need instructions from your cat on how to cough them up.) And old-timers use pineapple juice to clean machetes and knife blades and will mix it with sand to clean boat decks.

On Hwy 99 just north of Hwy 80 and Wahiawa town is **Dole Plantation** (621–8408). While undeniably your classic "tourist trap," there are a couple of reasons some might want to stop here. They have a hedge maze that covers 137,000 square feet. According to the *Guinness Book of World Records,* it's the largest in the world. (They expanded it after they were beaten by the Irish a few years back.) The idea is to wander through the maze and locate eight hidden stations before exiting. It'll take up to an hour and costs $6. The hedge is 8 feet tall. (If you want to take a photo of it, the only way *we* could do it was to put the camera on a timer and hoist it up on a stick.) They also have a garden area that's $5 (and possibly overpriced at that unless you're a certified garden junkie) and a train ride tour for $8 ($6 for kids). A pineapple field is not exactly the most thrilling place to take a 20-minute tour, but kids seem to like riding the train. (Adults get antsy in about 5 minutes.) You'll learn everything you ever wanted to know about pineapple…but were afraid to ask.

Dole also has a gift shop with food in the form of locally grown coffee, hot dogs, chili and all things pineapple, including flavors of frozen Dole whip. (We'll boldly predict that "pineapple" will be featured as their "flavor of the day.") You can drop a lot of money quickly at Dole, but the gift shop's not bad. Also at Dole is a farmer's market with fresh local produce.

After Dole, heading south, you'll have a choice of taking Hwy 99 through Schofield Barracks or Hwy 80 through Wahiawa, which has a mainland feel due to heavy presence of the military base here. Take Hwy 80. Just before Wahiawa on Hwy 80 you'll come upon a short dirt road on the right at the intersection of Hwy 80 and Whitmore. In the middle of a pineapple field is one of O'ahu's less-visited yet oddly peaceful sites. The **Kukaniloko birthing stones** (shown on page 15) are where royalty of yesteryear came to give birth to future rulers. The rocks in this area are strangely weathered and look out of place, yet legend states that the patterns are natural, not manmade.

Royal birthing procedures were different from what commoners went through. When the time came, the woman would arrive at what was then a secret spot, and in the presence of 36 male chiefs she would position herself at certain stones and in certain ways to give birth while they watched. (Gee, *that* must have created quite the awkward moment...) Within minutes of birth the child was taken away, and the mother would not see her child again until it was grown. This was to ensure that the child would not be murdered. Infanticide in high-ranking families was common among rival chiefs.

The sign indicating the sacredness of this site to Hawaiians is correct. We've seen entire Hawaiian families making pilgrimages to this site, chanting and praying for hours.

In ancient Hawai'i, parenting was a much different affair than what we're used to. The rights of the grandparents superseded the rights of the parents. Parents could not raise their own child without the consent of the grandparents. First-born children were whisked away from the mother at birth and raised by the husband's relatives if it was a boy or the mother's relatives if it was a girl. And every boy, first-born or not, was taken from the woman's hut when old enough to be weaned and raised in the men's hut. Never again in his lifetime would the man be allowed to eat with women, even his mother *or his wife*. The punishment for any man caught eating with women was death.

Some children were designated at birth never to do any kind of physical labor for their entire lives. This extended to feeding themselves. Poi or fish would be dropped into their mouths and water poured directly into them. These people were required to sit around all day long on tapa mats being attended to, bringing laziness to a fine art. The 17th-century Hawaiian historian Kamakau referred to them as "human pets." (Today we simply call them *teenagers*.)

Youths raised by kahuna professionals, such as omen readers, deep sea fishermen, tapa cloth makers or star readers, were consecrated at birth, and everything associated with them was kapu—off limits to others. Their food calabash, their clothes, their houses—even their hair couldn't be touched or trimmed and grew tangled and snarled. Only when their training was complete were the kapus lifted, and they could live a more normal and less sacred life.

WAHIAWA

Wahiawa, along with Wai'anae, often has the cheapest gas on the island after Costco, so gas up there.

In Wahiawa there's a garden called **Wahiawa Botanical Garden** off Cali-

A visitor getting lost in the world's biggest maze at the Dole Plantation.

fornia Street. See LAND TOURS on page 198 if you're interested.

After Wahiawa or Schofield you'll take H-2 south to H-1.

Of course, there's more to this area than meets the eye. There are large military bases out here, which you can only glimpse from the road. What you *won't* see, however, can be more interesting. There are miles and miles of tunnels carved underground. There's also a massive underground complex called the KUNIA REGIONAL SIGNALS INTELLIGENCE OPERATIONS CENTER buried near the pineapple fields. This is where intercepted messages from around the world are decrypted and analyzed.

From here, you have several places you could head to besides back to Waikiki.

MT. KA'ALA

Wai'anae and Central O'ahu are separated by the tallest mountain on the island. The top, called Mt. Ka'ala, is a flat plateau of swampy ground dominat-

ed by mosses and lichen. At 4,025 feet, it's usually cloud-covered, and trees at the top are stunted. Fully grown 'ohi'a trees—normally growing to over 20 feet tall—top out at only 2–3 feet, creating a natural bonsai garden. Unlike the similarly soggy summit of Wai'ale'ale on Kaua'i, which the Hawaiians considered sacred, Ka'ala was held in slightly less regard by the Hawaiians of yesteryear. Nearly every recorded chant referring to Mt. Ka'ala seems to focus on the "cold dews of Ka'ala," and little affection for the place percolated down to the common man.

At the summit today are radar towers that your Hawai'i-bound pilot communicated with when you got within 200 miles of Hawai'i. Although there is a paved road to the top, it's gated and you're not very welcome up there. There's a separate trail to the top, but it's insanely difficult and not particularly rewarding in the views department. While not as tall, the top of the Ko'olaus presents better views.

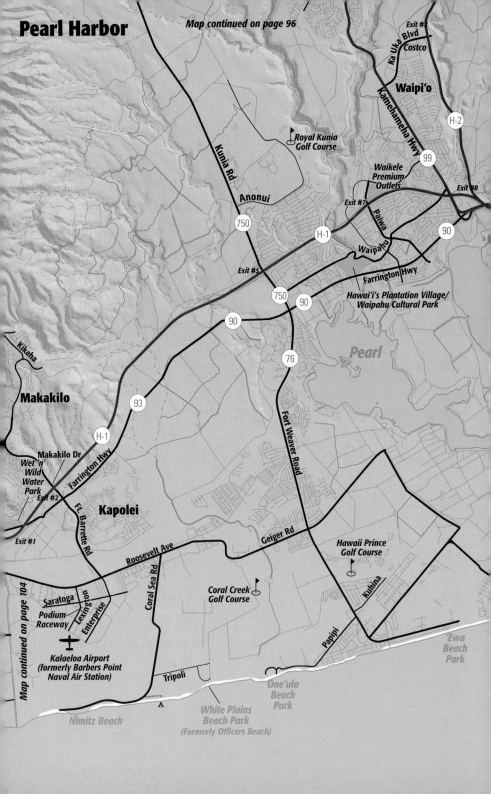

Pearl Harbor

Map continued on page 96

Exit #1
Ka Uka Blvd
Costco

Waipi'o

Kamehameha Hwy

H-2

99

Royal Kunia
Golf Course

Kunia Rd

Anonui

Waikele
Premium
Outlets

Exit #7

Exit #8

750

Paiwa

90

H-1

Waipahu

Exit #5

Farrington Hwy

750   90

Hawai'i's Plantation Village/
Waipahu Cultural Park

90

Pearl

Kikaha

76

Makakilo

Fort Weaver Road

93

H-1

Makakilo Dr

Wet 'n'
Wild
Water
Park

Farrington Hwy

Exit #2

Ft. Barrette Rd

Kapolei

Geiger Rd

Hawaii Prince
Golf Course

Exit #1

Roosevelt Ave

Coral Sea Rd

Coral Creek
Golf Course

Kuhina

Map continued on page 104

Saratoga
Podium
Raceway

Lexington

Enterprise

Papipi

Ewa
Beach
Park

Kalaeloa Airport
(formerly Barbers Point
Naval Air Station)

Tripoli

One'ula
Beach
Park

Nimitz Beach

White Plains
Beach Park
(Formerly Officers Beach)

Sam's Club

Kuala

Waimano Home Rd

Moanalua

Hoomalu

Pearl City

Exit #10

H-1

99

Kaonohi

Kea'iwa Heiau

Halawa Valley

Pearl Country Club
Golf Course

Moanalua Rd

Aiea Heights Dr

H-1

Aiea

Kamehameha Hwy

Pearlridge
Shopping
Center

H-3

Arizona Memorial Dr
*(parking for Memorial,
Bowfin & Missouri)*

Aloha
Stadium

Exit #13

H-201

Red Hill

Ala Aolani Rd

Map continued on page 50

Harbor

Military Bridge

U.S.S. Bowfin Submarine

Arizona St
Halawa Dr

Ice Palace

Formerly Hwy 78

Moanalua Fwy

Exit #2

Tripler Army
Medical Center
(Pink Bldg.)

Ford
Island

*U.S.S. Arizona
Memorial*

99

H-1

*U.S.S. Missouri
Battleship*

North

Salt Lake Blvd

Salt Lake

Fort Shafter

Radford

Exit #15

Exit #15A
(For USS Arizona,
USS Bowfin
& USS Missouri)

Puuloa

H-201

Exit
#19B

Exit #15B
(Don't Take)

Nimitz Hwy (under H-1 along here)

H-1

H-1

Inter-Island
Terminal

Airport Exit #16

Aolele

92

Ke'ehi
Lagoon
Park

92

Nimitz
Hwy

Hickam Air Force Base

Main Terminal

Rental Car Return
& Gas Station

Sand Island Rd

Honolulu Airport

Lagoon Dr

Sand Island State
Recreation Area

Seaplane
Departures

0   1 MILE

N
W   E
S

Highways
Minor Roads

© 2012 Wizard Publications, Inc.

While it's tempting to assume the top of the mountain must have been the summit of the volcano that created the mountain, it's not. The actual summit was to the west. The peak of Mt. Ka'ala is simply the only remaining remnant of the original gently-sloping shield volcano that was once here. The rest has worn away from erosion, leaving this unusually hardened lava relic of the volcano's youth.

PEARL HARBOR

Pearl Harbor is named after the many pipi (Hawaiian oysters) that used to live here. Visiting ships from the late 1700s described abundant pearls from this harbor. A visitor in 1810 wrote that the king had discovered their value to the outside world and employed numerous divers to pluck the oysters from their shallow bed. By the end of the 1800s overharvesting and runoff from nearby cattle operations had virtually eliminated the pearl oysters, but the name Pearl Harbor lives on, and its Hawaiian name, Pu'u-loa (long hill), is scarcely known, even among Hawaiians.

The large island inside the harbor is called **Ford Island**. It is owned by the U.S. military and houses some of the officers and crewmen stationed at Pearl Harbor.

In ancient times, Ford Island had an entirely different purpose. It was called Moku-'ume'ume, meaning *island of the sexual game*. In those days, if a commoner couple had trouble conceiving a child, they came here. Large groups gathered around a fire, couples sitting apart. A master of ceremonies would go up to a man, tap him with a maile wand, then tap a randomly selected woman, and together they went off into the darkness to share the night. If a child was conceived, it was regarded as the offspring of the husband, not the biological father. If no child was

conceived, they'd head back to this island to give it a whirl again.

You can't do a driving tour of Pearl Harbor—it's still an active Navy base, and access is restricted. But the most popular visitor attractions on the island—the **USS Arizona Memorial** and the **Battleship Missouri**—are available for touring. See ATTRACTIONS on page 117.

'EWA

'Ewa is the area below H-1 on your way out to Wai'anae. This is where the

county wants to direct future growth. It's hot, dry and not particularly pretty, so there's really not much for the visitor out here other than **Hawai'i's Plantation Village, Hawaiian Railway Society** and **Wet 'n' Wild Hawaii**. See ATTRACTIONS for more on these.

KALAELOA/BARBERS POINT

The Navy purchased the land at Barbers Point a century ago for their aircraft. Not planes, however. It was for *blimps*. (Yes, the Navy was a major blimp opera-tor.) When the Navy got out of the blimp business in the 1930s, they converted it to an airfield. At the end of the 20th century, the Navy handed the land to the state of Hawai'i, which now controls it. The area is very industrial, though there are a few decent beaches. See BEACHES chapter for more.

WAI'ANAE

Wai'anae is the name of a town, but it's also the name generally used to describe the western coastline leading all the way to

With the USS Arizona Memorial in the distance, symbolizing the day America was caught by surprise, sailors on the USS Nimitz aircraft carrier stand guard with machine guns ready, ensuring that a surprise won't happen again on their watch.

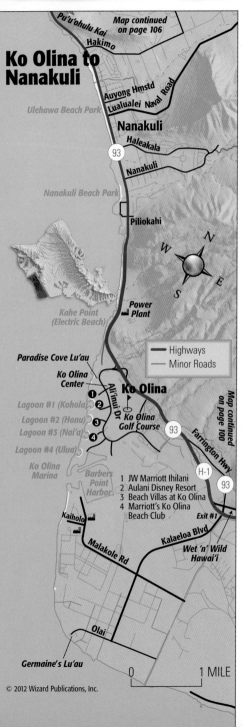

Ko Olina to Nanakuli

Map continued on page 106

Pu'u'ohulu Kai

Hakimo

Auyong Hmstd

Lualualei Naval Road

Ulehawa Beach Park

Nanakuli

Haleakala

93

Nanakuli

Nanakuli Beach Park

Piliokahi

Kahe Point (Electric Beach)

Power Plant

Paradise Cove Lu'au

Ko Olina Center

Ko Olina

Ali'inui Dr

Lagoon #1 (Kohola) ❶

Lagoon #2 (Honu) ❷

Ko Olina Golf Course

Lagoon #3 (Nai'a) ❸

93

Lagoon #4 (Ulua) ❹

Map continued on page 100

Farrington Hwy

Ko Olina Marina

Barbers Point Harbor

1 JW Marriott Ihilani
2 Aulani Disney Resort
3 Beach Villas at Ko Olina
4 Marriott's Ko Olina Beach Club

H-1

93

Exit #1

Kaiholo

Kalaeloa Blvd

Malakole Rd

Wet 'n' Wild Hawai'i

Olai

Germaine's Lu'au

— Highways
— Minor Roads

0   1 MILE

© 2012 Wizard Publications, Inc.

Ka'ena Point. Wai'anae is one of the poorer sections of the island, and it has a reputation for being a rough place. In the '70s that was certainly true. A number of violent crimes against visitors created an image among island residents that persists to this day. *Don't go to Wai'anae*, they say. *You'll get beaten up.* Well, frankly, that's ridiculous, and those who espouse that attitude need to come out here more often. Because it's so dry, Wai'anae has some of the nicest ocean water on the island, and you shouldn't let its reputation dissuade you from partaking of its delights. For this edition we went to the police to confirm that today, violent crimes against visitors are extremely rare here. It's mainly petty theft—frankly, a lot of it. That means some dirtbag breaking into your car to steal your camera while you're at the beach, or even stealing your stuff right off your beach towel. In the past the beach parks here were often "taken over" by homeless encampments. A few years ago authorities enforced the NO CAMPING rules at all but one beach, creating nicer environments at most beach parks and a *dense* concentration of homeless farther north at Kea'au Beach Park. In 2012 they evicted the homeless even from this park.

When we're out in Wai'anae, we simply don't leave anything valuable in the car. (Frankly, we do that everywhere we go.) There's always a chance someone will break in anyway, but it has never happened to us anywhere in Hawai'i. (And we've left our car in a *lot* of places.) As for safety, common sense needs to be applied, no matter where you are. If you're at a beach park after dark, and the parking lot is filled with young toughs drinking copious amounts of beer, you don't need us to tell you that now is not the right time to go over and show them your fancy Rolex watch. The biggest problem we've found with Wai'anae isn't the people—it's the bad restaurants. There are a few decent places to eat, but many people may stick with fast food out here. And like all beaches on the island, avoid them on weekends when they're crowded with local residents.

When H-1 ends, it becomes Hwy 93. Before the towns start rolling by, the resort area of **Ko Olina** is the main resort out here. Their four man-made lagoons offer super-protected swimming and some surprisingly good snorkeling in lagoon #2 on occasion. By the way, the speed bumps at Ko Olina will *mess you up* if you don't respect 'em.

Past Ko Olina as you pass by the power plant, keep an eye out for **dolphins** here. You may get lucky. We've seen them more often here than just about any other place on the island.

The first town is **Nanakuli.** One explanation of how Nanakuli got its name is out of local embarrassment. In ancient times this was a dry, inhospitable place to grow food. Residents had little spare water or food. When travelers walked by, it was customary to give them nourishment. Residents here hid from approaching travelers, fearing shame if they had to refuse to be hospitable. When they couldn't avoid pass-

An Oversight Leads to a Spared Gas Station—and Victory in WWII

Say what you want about the Japanese attack on Pearl Harbor: Militarily, the plan was brilliantly conceived and executed. The level of surprise was only matched by the level of destruction, and Japanese losses were minimal. Although U.S. aircraft carriers weren't there (by chance, not design), the Japanese nonetheless achieved their goals and didn't make any mistakes...except for one—a mistake so giant, so glaring and so important that it possibly ended up costing Japan the war.

When the Japanese warplanes were swarming around during the attack, their pilots were so single-mindedly focused on destroying ships and planes that they totally ignored row after row of conspicuous white fuel tanks above the ground. In them was the fuel that powered all of America's Pacific Fleet. If a single bomb had been dropped on just one of the tanks, it could have set them all ablaze. It would have taken a year to replace that fuel. A year that our aircraft carriers would have sat idle without any gas. A year when the Japanese navy would have had free reign. A year that could have changed the outcome of WWII.

Having dodged that potentially fatal bullet, the Navy accelerated a plan that was already in the works—building giant gas tanks underground beneath Red Hill to hold the quarter billion gallons of fuel needed to power the Navy's Pacific Fleet. (Large naval ships can only travel a few feet per gallon.) To this day if you're near the H-3 and H-201 freeway intersection and look mauka (toward the mountain), you'll see Red Hill, the Pacific Fleet's gas station and the Navy's response to the Japanese's biggest blunder of the Pacific War.

Ma'ili to Makaha

Map continued on page 108

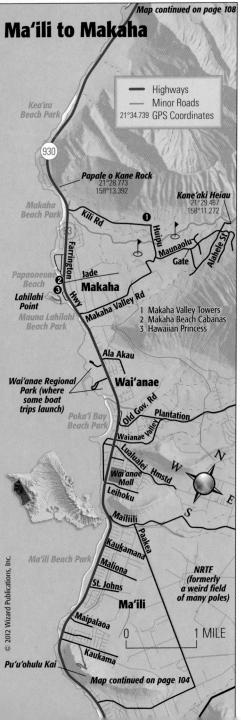

Highways
Minor Roads
21°34.739 **GPS Coordinates**

Kea'au
Beach Park

930

Papale o Kane Rock
21°28.773
158°13.392

Kane'aki Heiau
21°29.467
158°11.272

Makaha
Beach Park

Kili Rd

Huipu

Maunaolu

Gate

Alahele St

Papaoneone
Beach

Jade

Makaha

Lahilahi
Point

Mauna Lahilahi
Beach Park

Makaha Valley Rd

1 Makaha Valley Towers
2 Makaha Beach Cabanas
3 Hawaiian Princess

Ala Akau

Wai'anae Regional
Park (where
some boat
trips launch)

Wai'anae

Poka'i Bay
Beach Park

Old Gov. Rd

Plantation

Waianae Valley

Lualualei Hmstd

Wai'anae
Mall

Leihoku

N
W   E
S

Mailiili

Paakea

Kaukamana

Ma'ili Beach Park

Maliona

St. Johns

Ma'ili

NRTF
(formerly
a weird field
of many poles)

Maipalaoa

0   1 MILE

Kaukama

Pu'u'ohulu Kai

Map continued on page 104

ing travelers, residents pretended to be deaf so they'd be able to feign a lack of understanding. When puzzled travelers moved on, they'd comment on the strange village full of nothing but deaf people who just stared at them. Nanakuli means to *look deaf*.

Look mauka and you'll see **NRTF Lualualei** (the **Naval Radio Transmitter Facility**). Back in earlier editions we were mystified as to their purpose and simply referred to the area as a "weird field of many poles." Here's the real story: The two largest masts in this field are each 1,503 feet high, making them slightly taller than the twin Petronas Towers in Malaysia. The facility is one of five on the planet that communicates with *submerged* nuclear submarines using Very Low Frequency transmissions (3-30kHz). These radio waves can pass through solid rock and deep seas to send urgent messages to the subs while they're thousands of feet below the surface. In other words, if the order is given to commence global thermonuclear war, those joyous messages will pass through these massive antennas. Pretty wild stuff for sleepy Wai'anae.

Next, the town of **Wai'anae** is where some boat tours depart. The waters off the Wai'anae Coast can be particularly blue due to a lack of runoff and the steepness of the underwater terrain.

MAKAHA

Makaha is the last town along here. In talking about this part of the island and its rough reputation, you should realize that this is not a recent development. Even in ancient times Makaha—which means "savage" or "fierce"—was a place travelers feared. A notorious band of robbers and cutthroats lived up in the valley and ambushed groups passing by.

Tucked away in a quiet part of Makaha Valley, Kane'ahi Heiau is a nicely restored Hawaiian temple.

These robbers were skillful at a type of fighting called lua (bone-breaking). They plucked all the hair from their bodies and smeared themselves with oil so they'd be hard to grab in a fight. At the north end of Makaha Valley on the *mauka* (mountain) side of the road across the street from Makaha Shores Apartments, you'll see a tall, upright rock. The top of that very rock, called **Papale o Kane**, was where the gang's lookout waited. When an approaching group was within striking range, the lookout would yell *low tide,* which signaled that the group was beatable. If he yelled *high tide,* it meant the group was too big or too well-armed to take advantage of, so the robbers would let them pass.

Hawaiians of old created temples, called heiau, to worship their gods. Up in Makaha Valley is a somewhat mysterious heiau called **Kane'ahi**. This was built as an agricultural heiau—where

A REAL GEM

growers prayed for good conditions—but for some reason it was eventually converted to a heiau to the war god, Ku— where chiefs prayed for victory over their enemies. It's been nicely restored, and you can visit it Tue.–Sun. 10 a.m. to 2 p.m., unless it rains (which doesn't happen often in Makaha). You can call the guard shack at 695–8174 to see if it's open. Take a right on Makaha Valley Road; it'll turn onto Huipu Road. Then turn right on Maunaolu Road. You'll have to sign a waiver at the gate, show license and proof of insurance. After leaving the heiau on Alahale Street, if you were to accidentally turn left instead of right onto Maunaolu, the road goes a little higher and exposes pretty views of Makaha Valley from behind.

The least known resorts *on the entire island* are in Makaha. **Makaha Beach Cabanas** and **Hawaiian Princess** both have heavenly locations right on Papaoneone Beach, one of the lesser known beaches, and they're very reasonably priced for what you get. If you're not interested in staying in Waikiki, these resorts have an incredible beachfront setting. See WHERE TO STAY on page 294 for more.

THE END OF THE ROAD

The last 5 miles, before Farrington Highway ends at Yokohama Bay, and frankly, we're not sure *what* you're gonna see. Until 2012 there was an *enormous* homeless camp along the road in Keaʻau

Beach Park. It was the most visually shocking example of poverty and squalor in all Hawaiʻi and a gigantic embarrassment to people pitching Hawaiʻi as a paradise. During the eviction many vowed to return once authorities stopped focusing on the area. Authorities responded by stripping much of the vegetation people were using in their "camp." Time will tell.

Past Keʻeau Beach Park you're back in paradise, and you'll be amazed at how little use beaches like **Makua Beach** and **Yokohama Bay** get during the

A REAL GEM week.

Makua Cave is an old sea cave gouged out by the ocean during a time when the world was warmer and the oceans higher. Now high and dry, it's on the mauka side of Hwy 93 just past the 17 mile marker. Legend says that a shape-shifting shark god lives in the area and visits the cave via an underground tunnel to the ocean. If you're looking for a secluded beach or a short hike to a tortured sandstone bench, see ʻOhiki-lolo Beach on page 128 or the hike on page 188.

Once at Yokohama Bay, the road ends. The western tip of the island at Kaʻena Point is almost 2½ miles away. You can hike it; see ACTIVITIES on page 189.

WAIʻANAE & CENTRAL OʻAHU BEST BETS

Best Place to Impersonate a Rat in a Maze—Dole Plantation

Best Beach—Makua Beach

Best Hawaiian Relic—Kaneʻahi Heiau

Best Forgotten Resort—Hawaiian Princess

Best Frequency to Send a Text Message to a Submerged Nuclear Submarine—3-30kHz or use the NRTF

Best Place to Observe the Speed Limit—Ko Olina

Makua to Kaʻena

Kaʻena Point
Leina-a-ka-ʻuhane (Leaping place for souls)
21°34.530
158°16.363
Gate
Secluded Cove
21°34.620
158°15.809
Hidden Beach
21°34.676
158°15.417
Landslide Portion
Sisal Field
4WD Road
End of Pavement
930

Farrington Hwy

Yokohama Bay/ Keawaʻula Beach
Gate
930

Unpaved Roads
Highways
Minor Roads
21°34.739 GPS Coordinates

Makua Beach/ Kaʻena Point State Park

ʻOhiki-lolo Beach Park
Sandstone
21°30.958
158°13.786

Makua Valley (Under Military Control)
Makua Cave

0   1 MILE

© 2012 Wizard Publications, Inc.

Map continued on page 88
Map continued on page 106

Woe to any enemy that ever saw the business end of these USS Missouri guns, which could hurl a 2,700-pound projectile 23 miles.

You gotta drive there or take a bus there, and it's the only reason you're in that area. This is what the ATTRACTIONS chapter is all about. We don't have an ATTRACTIONS chapter in our neighbor island books because, frankly, we didn't need one before. But O'ahu has tons of attractions that you'll drive to. This chapter excludes lu'aus (covered at the end of DINING), but includes the Polynesian Cultural Center, Hawaiian Waters Adventure Park, Bishop Museum, 'Iolani Palace and more.

POLYNESIAN CULTURAL CENTER
(293–3333)

It's as far from Waikiki as you can get—both literally and figuratively. Be-cause the Polynesian Cultural Center (PCC) is *so* popular, a lot of preconceived misconceptions exist. This is not a Hawaiian Disneyland with rides and dolphins leaping out of the water. This is a laid-back collection of re-creations from various island villages from around Polynesia. They don't pretend to be completely authentic. Power outlets and plywood, electric lights and cell phones are ever-present. What they've attempted to do is to create a non-frantic environment where you can wander around at your leisure and see various styles of huts, lots of dancing demonstrations, education in all things Polynesian, spear-throwing and more. Coconuts, drums and palm fronds along with a meandering, cement-lined

The Polynesian Cultural Center has shows and demonstrations throughout the day.

lagoon create an island atmosphere that's certainly closer to reality than anything you'll find in Waikiki.

The LDS Church (often called Mormon) created and runs this place in association with Brigham Young Hawai'i University. Basically, your entrance fees help subsidize students from all around the Pacific. In exchange, those students work here at PCC, so it's likely you'll come in contact with many young people from the very countries represented in the faux villages. Hearing them sing in their various languages is a real treat.

Start by taking a canoe trip to the other side of PCC and walk your way back, stopping along the way whenever something strikes your fancy. You may find yourself playing drums in **A REAL GEM** Tonga or getting a fake tattoo in the Marquesas Islands. Wear a wide-brimmed hat since even on windy days there are areas where the winds are blocked, and it can get hot.

The PCC also has a lu'au and an excellent evening show called Ha: Breath of Life. (See Lu'au in ISLAND DINING on page 270 for more.)

The PCC is worth the time if you have any interest at all in learning about the Polynesian way of life. And although it's very popular with visitors, PCC has managed to keep a good and friendly attitude. It doesn't feel like a mob scene, and the staff is top-notch. You can tell they feel honored to be working here, showing you their way of life. We think the PCC is a class act through and through. There are many, many shops inside. Our only dig is that there are probably a few *too* many opportunities for you to buy your picture taken at various times during your stay.

Price is pretty steep at $74, but that includes a buffet dinner at one of their restaurants and unguided entrance to everything, including the on-site IMAX theater and the evening show. (It's $50 for the park only.) It's an extra $22 for bus transportation to and from Waikiki (a 60–90 minute drive away). It's $124 for guided tours, and the lu'au is included. On Hwy 83 in La'ie on the windward side of the island. They open at noon, but demonstrations are more numerous after 1:30 p.m. There's too much to see in one day, but if you're so inclined, you can come back free within three days. Closed Sundays.

WET 'N' WILD HAWAII (674–9283)

Waterslides and other ways to get wet. This place is usually packed on weekends but often uncrowded Monday–Friday. It's on the small side, but the rides are well-chosen to appeal to people of all ages, and it's an easy place to spend half a day or more sliding into various pools and getting hammered in the wave pool or simply floating along in the current-driven whirlpool. If it's sunny you will really appreciate this tip: Wear water shoes. Most people wear flip-flops and leave them at the bottom of the rides, then fry their feet on the endless ramps and steps.

You'll need a lanyard for your glasses. If you don't want to eat park food, they're good about letting you go in and out of the park.

It's $45 to get in, which includes most of the attractions. Kids 42 inches tall or below are $35. (Tots are free.) They have pay lockers to keep your junk, and a few things, such as *Da Flowrider* (a static, rideable wave), cost extra. Closed some days in non-summer periods, and expect them to close and rotate rides when it's slow.

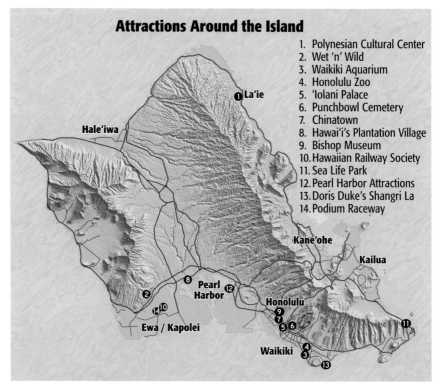

Attractions Around the Island

1. Polynesian Cultural Center
2. Wet 'n' Wild
3. Waikiki Aquarium
4. Honolulu Zoo
5. 'Iolani Palace
6. Punchbowl Cemetery
7. Chinatown
8. Hawai'i's Plantation Village
9. Bishop Museum
10. Hawaiian Railway Society
11. Sea Life Park
12. Pearl Harbor Attractions
13. Doris Duke's Shangri La
14. Podium Raceway

La'ie

Hale'iwa

Kane'ohe

Kailua

Pearl Harbor

Ewa / Kapolei

Honolulu

Waikiki

WAIKIKI AQUARIUM (923–9741)

You can walk to this from most Waikiki hotels. This is a tiny aquarium in Kapiolani Park on Kalakaua Ave. Entrance is a cheap $9. (13–17 year olds pay $4; 5–12 year olds pay $2; 4 and under are free.) But if you're an adult expecting the same kind of *ooh-ah* value you'd get at a bigger aquarium, you're likely to be disappointed. An hour or so is probably about enough to see this place. It's more geared toward smaller kids.

We don't mean to be disrespectful, but just about any aquarium built on the mainland in the past 20 years outshines the Waikiki Aquarium. There are no giant tanks with scuba divers feeding the fish, just a series of smaller tanks with colorful fish and coral (from around the Pacific—not just Hawai'i) and a spartan seal enclosure with one very bored monk seal. Kids will find it interesting here, but others may not, especially if you've seen nicer aquariums elsewhere. In fairness, the $9 entrance fee certainly doesn't imply opulence.

HONOLULU ZOO (971–7171)

We don't mean to sound negative after giving the nearby Waikiki Aquarium a lukewarm review, but the Honolulu Zoo is merely so-so. It's 42 acres of cages, and there are problems. For one, the mesh they use on some of the cages makes it difficult to see the exhibits. Too much metal, too little openings. This is especially a problem with the numerous bird exhibits. Also, the zoo doesn't exactly seem scrupulously well cared for. The hippo, tiger and Galapagos tortoise exhibits are a hit, however. Bottom line—adults without kids won't find it compelling. With kids? Hey, it's a place with animals; they'll be entertained for an hour or two. Avoid at midday due to heat. Entrance is on Kapahulu Ave. Cost is $14; kids 4–12 is $6. Open 9 a.m. to 4:30 p.m. daily.

'IOLANI PALACE & HISTORIC BUILDINGS

The United States has been a republic since it broke from England, so we don't

Getting sucked into the Tornado at Wet 'n' Wild.

Using howitzers, soldiers fire off a 21-gun salute during a ceremony at Punchbowl.

really have any examples of royal palaces—except for 'Iolani. These islands were a kingdom until 1893, and in 1882 Hawai'i's last king, David Kalakaua (who was actually elected by the Legislature), ordered this palace to be built to show all the world that Hawai'i had a monarchy just as grand as any other. There are many historic buildings downtown, but this is the finest of them all.

'Iolani Palace (522–0832) is as much a testament to the desire to restore as it is to the king who built it. It was only used as a royal palace for 11 years. For the next 75 years a series of gov- **A REAL GEM** ernments used it as government building and, frankly, let it deteriorate to the point that some wanted to bulldoze the building in the late '60s. Most of its artifacts were auctioned off over the years. Once the bureaucrats got their own Capitol building next door in 1969, local volunteers worked for years to retrieve many of the artifacts and restore the palace to the glo-

rious condition you see today. The beautiful woodwork, the grandness of design and the great info conveyed along the way make it a worthwhile diversion.

'Iolani is open Monday–Saturday 9 a.m. to 4 p.m. Reserve in advance since only 20 people are allowed per guided tour, which is $20 per person; no kids under 5. (Self-guided tours of the grounds are free, and there's a $12 self-guided tour inside.) The quality of your tour depends on the quality of the docent, which varies, but the ones we've seen were incredibly enthusiastic and—although it's a cliché—really made the building come alive. Park in the metered lot on the grounds and stuff at least two hours worth of quarters into the meter. At King and Richards. Take Ala Wai Boulevard right on Kalakaua to the end, left on Beretania, left on Richards, left on S. King and left into the parking lot. Closed Sundays.

After 'Iolani Palace, if you have some extra quarters for the meter, you can leave your car and check out some of the other historic buildings, though they aren't as compelling as the palace. See map on page 50.

Kawaiaha'o Church at King and Punchbowl was completed in 1842 and is made from 1,000-pound chunks of coral chiseled from reefs 10–20 feet deep. It is still used as a place of worship. On the grounds is the tomb containing the remains of a lesser-known king from the 1800s, Lunalilo, who wanted to be buried next to his people rather than in the Royal Mausoleum.

The **Hawai'i State Art Museum** (586–0900) is on Richards at Hotel Street. It has art from Hawai'i artists, as well as others from around the world. Entrance is free. If you're an art buff, it's worth your time. Others may not be so impressed. Closed Sunday and Monday.

At Beretania and Richards Street is **Washington Place**. This was the home of Hawai'i's last monarch, and they still use it for political functions. Tours are awkward to arrange but possible. Call 586–0248 and keep your fingers crossed.

At Punchbowl and King Street you'll find the **Mission Houses** (531–0481), some of the earliest living quarters built by missionaries upon their arrival in 1820. The 45-minute tours are a bit pricey at $10. Think of it as more of a lesson on early missionary life and their effort to create a written Hawaiian language. The whole experience is educational, if a bit dry.

PUNCHBOWL CEMETERY (532–3720)

National Memorial Cemetery of the Pacific at Punchbowl is an incredibly moving place. In ancient times Hawaiians buried their royalty here and also used it as a place of human sacrifice. The Hawaiian name for this crater is Pu'u-o-waina—hill of human sacrifices. It's eerily fitting that since 1949 it's been used as a cemetery for those in the military who sacrificed their lives in the Pacific.

Bustling Chinatown is the place to buy foods you won't find at Walmart.

Driving into the crater is an experience that is guaranteed to put a lump in your throat. At the far end is a giant statue of Columbia holding a laurel branch. Between you and her are the graves of over 45,000 men and women. No large tombstones or even crosses here—just simple slabs marking the final resting places. Drive up to the statue and look at the walls. In addition to these graves, you'll find over 28,000 names carved into the walls. During the wars of the mid-20th century, young men died in such vast numbers and so rapidly that there wasn't always time to keep track of them. These 28,778 names are of those "whose earthly resting place is known only to God." Under the sculpture of Columbia is a quote from Abraham Lincoln when he wrote to the mother of five sons lost in the Civil War: "The solemn pride that must be yours to have laid so costly a sacrifice on the altar of freedom."

There are some interesting displays of the various battles that claimed these lives. Look at them from the left side to the right. The cemetery is open from 8 a.m. to 5:30 p.m. Entrance is free.

The simplest way to get there from Waikiki is to take Ala Wai Blvd., right on Kalakaua, left onto Beretania, right onto Alakea which becomes Queen Emma. It'll pass under H-1 and then become Lusitana. Look for San Antonio angling back on your right. Take it, then go left on Puowaina, and it'll eventually fork into the cemetery. There should be signs pointing the way.

CHINATOWN

If you're expecting a made-for-tourist Chinatown, you ain't gonna get it. This is the real deal. Having worked in China for a few years, for me, going to the markets here was like going back to the

Far East. Stroll the aisles of the markets, and you come across raw chicken feet, tank after tank of various live fish, whole pig heads, more fruits and vegetables than you even knew existed, Asian orange soda (which is amazingly ubiquitous in China), salted duck eggs and more—all with the sound of Cantonese in the background and the ever-present haggling: *How much? Figh dallah!*

That guy you just bumped into might have been the star chef at the fancy restaurant where you ate last night. Chinatown is where many chefs get their fresh seafood and veggies. This is also where much of the Kahuku shrimp from the North Shore ends up—still live and wiggling in the early morning.

More than China is represented here, and you'll see stores that sell Vietnamese food next to their jewelry selections. Don't just hit the stores on the street. The real fun is in the Kekaulike Market (between King and Hotel on Kekaulike Street) and Maunakea Marketplace.

If you get hungry (and you will), check our Chinatown dining (page 250) for individual reviews.

You'll want to arrive in Chinatown by 10 a.m., before it gets too hot and when the merchants are still hungry. Park at the garage on Maunakea between King and Hotel streets if you can. Things sometimes get a bit unsavory near River Street.

HAWAI'I'S PLANTATION VILLAGE (677–0110)

I've lived in Hawai'i for a number of years now, but I got more of a feel for the essence of plantation life during this 1½-hour tour than in all the time I've lived here.

In the 1990s the county took this parkland and attempted to re-create a typical sugar plantation camp, and they did a pretty good job. In real life each plantation camp represented a single ethnic group. Here what they've done is create regions of camps representing Chinese, Portuguese, Puerto Rican, Japanese, Filipino, Okinawan and Korean camps. Don't hesitate to engage your guide because that's what makes the experience so cool—at least for us it was. It's $13. The last tour starts at 2 p.m. Located at the west end of Pearl Harbor. Take H-1 to exit 7, left on Paiwa toward the ocean, right on Waipahu. Look for it eventually on your left. Closed Sundays.

BISHOP MUSEUM (847–3511)

This is Hawai'i's most comprehensive museum. Established by the husband of Bernice Pauahi Bishop, the last descendant of King Kamehameha the Great, much of Hawai'i's culture and heritage is stored here. Priceless items such as the royal feathered cape worn by Kamehameha himself along with more common items like lava poi pounders sit side by side. Other examples include the feathered war god Kuka'ilimoku, combs made from coconut leaflet ribs, a grass hut, royal jewelry, kapa cloths, miniature representations of heiau (temples), leiomanu (shark's tooth-studded wooden weapons that were kept hidden and then used to disembowel unsuspecting enemies), a 55-foot sperm whale skeleton, scrimshaw, and a conch shell that's over 600 years old and wonderfully worn down from all the generations of Hawaiians who rubbed it while blowing through it like a bugle.

The museum also has displays from other parts of Polynesia, exhibits from cultures that immigrated to the islands, a hall of natural history, temporary exhibits, hula demonstrations and an awesome Kahili room that is especially regal—don't miss that one.

They also have a Science Adventure Center geared toward kids with lots of things to poke, pull and push. (Their $645,000 "erupting volcano" that simply spits orange water proves that even a high-brow museum can get snookered.)

Anyone with an interest in history or the Hawaiian culture will want to devote at least a couple of hours to this museum. $18 per person; kids 4–12 and seniors are $15. In Honolulu at 1525 Bernice Ave. From Waikiki get on H-1 West, take exit 20B, go right on Houghtailing, immediate left on Bernice Street. Open 9-5, Closed Tuesdays.

HAWAIIAN RAILWAY SOCIETY (681–5461)

For train junkies and those with kids, this is a sugar plantation railroad car and paraphernalia collection dating from 1888 to 1947. Their prized possession is a fully restored private parlor car used by Benjamin Dillingham to entertain royalty and foreign diplomats. On Sundays they have a 90-minute train ride through 'Ewa. ($12 for adults, $8 for kids.) Keiki might love the air horn and track rumble, but you'll be struggling to stay awake. No credit cards.

SEA LIFE PARK (259–7933)

This is O'ahu's version of Sea World, though it's *far* smaller than most mainland aquarium parks. And that's probably the thing you'll notice most. Even the tanks that the dolphins live in seem small. Though it costs $30 to get in ($20 for kids 3–11) plus $5 to park, you can see this whole park in a couple of hours. Things included with admission include a so-so dolphin show, a pretty good sea lion show and several feedings. (Though you pay extra if you want to be the one feeding them.) You'll notice *many* opportunities here to spend more money on additional attractions such as snorkeling with sting rays for $20 or participate in their dolphin programs for $105 to $235. (Though we recommend Dolphin Quest's program more—see page 223.) When you go to their activity booth to sign up for these things, it seems like they're usually pushing "specials" to make it cheaper.

Sea Life Park isn't usually too crowded and seems to be a hit with kids. More than half of their customers are Japanese tour groups, and some of the narrations are in Japanese first. You can drop a lot of money fast here, but it's not a bad attraction.

Near the easternmost tip of the island on Hwy 72 near Waimanalo. Open 10:30 a.m. to 5 p.m.

WWII VALOR IN THE PACIFIC NATIONAL MONUMENT

USS Arizona Memorial
USS Missouri Battleship
USS Bowfin Submarine
Pacific Aviation Museum

There are three historic Navy vessels all moored near each other. And, frankly, all

The dolphin show at Sea Life Park is their most popular attraction.

three are worth your time. The sunken USS Arizona is the most somber of the three, the USS Missouri the most impressive in its scale, and the Bowfin the most interesting for observing what it must have been like to live in a submerged vessel. The Pacific Aviation Museum has restored vintage aircraft from the war over the Pacific.

Directions to all are the same: From Waikiki, get on H-1 West. Take exit #15A *(not 15B)*, which says ARIZONA MEM./ STADIUM, and stay on Kamehameha Hwy (99) West, past Radford, past Arizona/ Halawa Road, then left on Arizona Memorial Place/Kalaloa. (If you get to the stadium, you went too far.) You'll see signs. (See map on page 101.)

If you're coming from the *other* way, take exit 10 off H-1 towards Pearlridge (right fork), merge onto Moanalua Rd. First right on Kaahumanu St., left on Kamehameha Hwy, right on Arizona Memorial Pl. (I can't help but wonder how often those Hawaiian words get hideously butchered by the navigator in the car.)

Parking can be difficult at peak times. If you don't see a spot, keep driving and there's often an opening or two in a parking lot on your right, next to a pool before the overpass.

Because of security (this is an active Navy base), you can't bring anything into these attractions other than a normal-sized camera—no purses, backpacks, camera bags, etc. They'll charge to store your stuff, so don't bring it along. Swimwear is not allowed.

The **USS Arizona Memorial** (422–3300) is the single most popular visitor attraction on O'ahu. When the Japanese attacked Pearl Harbor in 1941, 21 vessels were damaged or sunk. But it was the sinking of the USS Arizona that caused the most deaths—1,177

NOT TO BE MISSED!

young, promising lives were cut short when an armor-piercing bomb dropped from a Japanese plane drilled through her top deck and ignited the battleship's own ordnance. The vessel sank in 9 minutes, and only 337 were able to escape. In all, over 2,400 people were killed during the sneak attack here, a figure that would stand as an unwelcome record for six decades. It seemed like the kind of event that could only happen in the distant past, until today's generation experienced their own sneak attack. And like September 11th, America rode a roller coaster of emotion after Pearl Harbor—from shock to anger to resolve. For Pearl Harbor it took an empire's entire military might—a whole fleet of ships and subs, including six aircraft carriers, 353 planes and thousands of soldiers. September 11th required four planes and 19 men with boxcutters. But, whatever the source, it awakened a nation that had previously felt safe and insulated from the harshness of the world.

Sadly, though. In a poll taken a decade after the Sep. 11th attacks, 92% of people in Afghanistan had *never heard* of the World Trade Center attacks and didn't know that the attackers—led by Osama Bin Laden—were living in, and be protected by, their nation's leaders at the time of the attack. Instead, they thought that U.S. soldiers were in their country simply to destroy their nation and seize their resources.

Visiting the memorial is one of those must-dos on O'ahu, and for good reason. Since there are so few WWII vets left, it makes WWII real for the rest of us. *We* know how WWII ended because we've lived our lives *after* the attack. But those men still entombed under your feet

Paying respects at the USS Arizona Memorial.

at the memorial only knew the shock and awe of how they died. And it's not until you're standing on the memorial, perched over the sunken ship, that the echo of their lives can be heard. And when you see the massive marble wall with their names engraved, only then does the beginning of WWII turn from an event that happened as part of our history to an assault that stole the lives of people like you and me and galvanized a nation.

The memorial visit includes an excellent 23-minute film, a short boat ride and time at the memorial. (Sit on the starboard—right—side going out, port side coming back for the best photos.) It'll take 75 minutes *plus* whatever time you wait. And that wait could be anywhere from 1–3 hours, sometimes more. The Arizona museum and bookstore aren't enough to keep you occupied for *that* long, but you can grab your free tickets and leave for a while. See one of the other attractions mentioned below, or go have lunch. To minimize your wait, either get there first thing in the morning (7:15–8 a.m.) or around 1–2 p.m. A

much better and lesser known way is to book *in advance* at a government website called **www.recreation.gov** for a tiny fee.

The **USS Missouri Battleship** (877–644–4896) is a short distance from the sunken Arizona. When the Navy was looking for the final resting place for this proud warship, the symbolism of this location wasn't lost on them: placing the floating ship that ended WWII next to the sunken ship where the war began. Because it was on the Missouri's deck that the Japanese signed the surrender agreement, bringing the bloody fighting in the Pacific to a close.

The "Mighty Mo" was launched in 1944, near the end of the war. It was the last battleship ever built, and after only 11 years in service it was considered obsolete and mothballed in 1955. It seems hard to imagine how a state-of-the-art battleship—the toughest and most visually menacing ship ever built with guns that could fire a 2,700-pound projectile *23 miles*—could be considered obsolete. In essence it comes down to this: It's more effective to *drop* things on the enemy than to *throw* things at 'em. Once ship-based aircraft had matured, aircraft carriers were far more efficient at projecting power than the greatest battleship could ever be. Even though the ship was brought back to service in the mid-'80s for a short time and armed with Tomahawk missiles, the usefulness of battleships had long since passed, even for a giant that's 887 feet long and weighs over *100 million* pounds.

It costs $20 to self-tour, $10 for kids 4–12. (Make *sure* you have a photo ID for the Missouri and the Pacific Aviation Museum, or you won't be allowed to go.) Or you can take guided tours, which are much more interesting. They have several. We liked the $47 Battle Station's Tour (90 minutes) since it went into the firing rooms, engine room and other nuts and bolts areas that self-tours can't visit,

or the $65 Passport to Pearl Harbor which gives you access to nearly everything else. Ironically, at least half the ship is off limits, even to guided trips. The reason? It's dirty. And although conditions were good enough for sailors who were there on the ship's final tour, it's not clean enough for the EPA to sign off.

However you tour it, it's a real treat to peer into this symbol of America's might during the mid-20th century. The sheer scale of this vessel can only be appreciated in person. It's amazing to stand on its giant teak deck, under the massive guns capable of such destruction, and try to imagine the dread that must have been felt by any enemy that watched this warship coming at them in anger.

Just in front of the entrance to the Missouri is the **USS Oklahoma Memorial**.

For only $10 you'll get to see the USS Bowfin submarine the way her crew saw her— without the two-year stint.

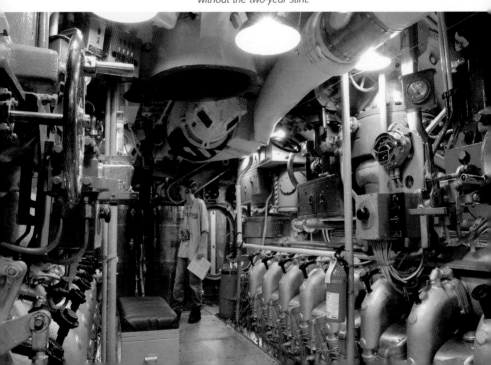

In all, 429 officers, sailors and marines were lost on the Oklahoma, second only to the Arizona. The men were recovered, the hull was patched and the ship was sold as scrap to a company in San Francisco. As it was being towed across the Pacific, a storm caused her to sink again, this time forever, just 540 miles east of Hawai'i.

The almost forgotten attraction here is the **USS Bowfin** (423–1341). Launched in 1942 (and nicknamed the Pearl Harbor Avenger), this submarine sank 44 enemy ships and now is available for self-guided tours for $10 ($4 for kids 4–12). The latest you can start the tour is 4:30 p.m., and it'll take about 30 minutes. They'll give you a narrative audio recorded by the ship's last WWII captain. And it's great to walk through this sub and see the instruments and experience how the sailors lived and fought. From the turrets to the torpedoes to the toilets—you'll see it all. When you're done, the nearby **Submarine Museum** (423–1341) is *excellent*—much better than the Arizona's museum. Kids under 4 are not allowed on the sub, but they can go into the museum.

Pearl Harbor is not just about boats. In the historic hangars at Ford Island the Navy opened in 2007 the **Pacific Aviation Museum** (441–1000). It houses a small but growing collection of vintage aircraft. You can follow the timeline of the attack on Pearl Harbor highlighted by a fully restored Japanese Zero and a private plane that was in the air and attacked by the first wave of fighters. The jewel of Hangar 37 is actually a rusty pile of steel found in a pasture on the island of Ni'ihau. On December 7, 1941, a Japanese Zero was hit with anti-aircraft fire and made an emergency landing on an island he had been told was uninhabited—Ni'ihau. Airman 1st Class Shigenori Nishikaichi had been instructed to wait for a submarine, but found the island was very much inhabited, mostly by Hawaiians. He quickly befriended the three people on the island who were of Japanese ancestry and escaped from his Hawaiian guards with their help. His freedom didn't last long as he was eventually overpowered and literally crushed by a local Hawaiian who had been shot *three times* by Nishikaichi. Over time the crashed Zero weathered away and was stripped by local farmers of its steel skin. But what remains is still an incredible physical piece of history. There are also displays about Midway, Guadalcanal, Doolittle's raid, and a Stearman biplane that President George H.W. Bush flew as a pilot in-training.

DORIS DUKE'S SHANGRI LA
(866–385–3849)

It's the 1930s, and one of the richest women in the world, the sole heir to a tobacco empire, buys a scrumptious oceanside piece of property at Black Point. **A REAL GEM** She has an obsession with Islamic art and architecture. This is a time before oil becomes synonymous with the Middle East. A time when someone, with enough money, could travel to Iran, Iraq and neighboring countries and buy what are now priceless art and architectural pieces for a relative pittance. And that's what Doris Duke did. Today, her 5-acre palace is what results when you mix 150 workmen, 50 years of effort, limitless money and a reverence for antiquities.

Three times a day, two groups of 12 people are guided through Doris Duke's estate for $25, and it's nearly always sold out a week or more in advance. You'll meet at the Honolulu Academy of Arts at the corner of Beretania and Ward Avenue and be driven to the estate. It'll take 2½ hours (1½ hours at the house). There's no a/c in the house, so try to get an early tour. No children under 12 allowed. Open Wednesday through Saturday.

We didn't expect to be so impressed. Though touted as Islamic, there are plenty of non-Islamic pieces, some as old as 1,000 years. And we're not talking about paintings on the walls, but rather a sensory overload of Middle Eastern history that is simply astounding. Forget what's happening in the world right now. These pieces predate the tensions that define our relationship with that part of the world today. The tour ends in the Turkish Room—an overwhelming experience for the eyes that'll make your heart beat faster.

You board the van at the **Honolulu Academy of Arts** (532–8701). At the

Stop doggin' me, man...

art academy you'll find a healthy mix of interesting 2,000-year-old artifacts and self-indulgent abstract junk that only an artist's mother can love.

PODIUM RACEWAY HAWAI'I
(682–7223)

It's tempting to think electric go-kart racing is a kid's attraction. But I assure you—adults won't walk out without a serious kid-like grin on their face. You and up to a dozen other drivers rip along an indoor track, squealing around corners, trying to beat everyone's time. I was surprised at how intense the racing felt. Spectators get to stand right next to the track. Food is restricted to vending machines between races. Avoid this place *like the plague* on weekends—super busy. All in all, a fun way to blow $20–$50. Located in Ewa near Kalaeloa Airport at 91-1085 Lexington St. See map on page 100.

Ask any local on O'ahu where Kawela Bay is, and they'll probably say Kaua'i.

The biggest surprise about O'ahu is how many beautiful beaches there are and how often they're utterly uncrowded. Residents and visitors alike tend to congregate at the same popular beaches, leaving beautiful stretches of sand lightly touched. So we gave ourselves the difficult and thankless job of visiting *every* sand beach on the island to swim, snorkel and frolic. (See, and you thought all we did was *frivolous* stuff.)

No matter what kind of beach experience you're looking for, O'ahu has something for everyone. In trying to pick a beach, you should consider the island's geography. The **windward** side has some of the most underutilized and lovely beaches on the island, but it didn't get the name *windward* for nothing. If the trade winds are smoking along at 15–30 MPH, these beaches tend to be windy. But if it's a 10–20 MPH day, the cool breezes might be just right.

Wai'anae has lots of beaches that are protected from the wind thanks to the mountain behind them, and the waters tend to be clean and clear. But some of their beaches, especially near the Wai'anae towns, might be more crowded. Keep driving past the towns toward Ka'ena Point for the best two Wai'anae beaches.

North Shore beaches can be a wonderful playground in the summer with calm waters and beautiful vistas along with breezes that tend to be slightly *offshore* until you get to Hale'iwa, keeping nearshore waters smooth. But winter can bring monstrous waves that would rip you to pieces if you got careless.

And finally the **leeward** side with Waikiki, Ala Moana and Hanauma Bay tends to have calmer and safer water than the rest of the island, but you sure ain't gonna have 'em to yourself.

BEACH SAFETY

The biggest danger you will face at the beach is the **surf**. Though it is calmer on the leeward side of the island (where Waikiki is), that's a relative term. Most mainlanders are unprepared for the strength of Hawai'i's surf. We're out in the middle of the biggest ocean in the world, and the surf has lots of room to build up. We have our calm days when the water is like glass. We often have days when the surf is moderate, calling for respect and diligence on the part of the swimmer. And we have the high surf days, perfect for sitting on the beach with a picnic or a mai-tai, watching the experienced and the audacious tempt the ocean's patience. Don't make the mistake of underestimating the ocean's power here. Hawai'i is the undisputed drowning capital of the United States, and we don't want you to join the statistics.

Other hazards include rip currents, which can form, cease and form again with no warning. Large "rogue waves" can come ashore with no warning. These usually occur when two or more waves fuse at sea, becoming a larger wave. Even calm seas are no guarantee of safety. Many people have been caught unaware by large waves during ostensibly "calm seas." We swam

There's a reason why we say never turn your back on the ocean...

and snorkeled most of the beaches described in this book on at least two occasions (usually more than two). But beaches change. The underwater topography changes throughout the year. Storms can take a very safe beach and rearrange the sand, turning it into a dangerous beach. Just because we describe a beach as being in a certain condition does not mean it will be in that same condition when *you* visit it.

Consequently, you should take the beach descriptions as a snapshot in calm times. If seas aren't calm, you probably shouldn't go in the water. If you observe a rip current, you probably shouldn't go in the water. If you aren't a comfortable swimmer, you should probably never go in the water, except at those beaches that have lifeguards. There is no way we can tell you that a certain beach will be swimmable on a certain day, and we claim no such prescience. There is no substitution for your own observations and judgment.

A few standard safety tips: Never turn your back on the ocean (even when you're in it). Never swim alone. Never swim in the mouth of a river. Never swim in murky water. Never swim when the seas are not calm. Don't walk too close to the shorebreak; a large wave can come and knock you over and pull you in. Observe ocean conditions carefully. Don't let small children play in the water unsupervised. Fins give you far more power and speed and are a good safety device in addition to being more fun. If you're comfortable in a mask and snorkel, they provide considerable peace of mind, as well as opening up the underwater world. Lastly, don't let Hawai'i's idyllic environment cloud your judgment. Recognize the ocean for what it is—a powerful force that needs to be respected. Call 973-4383 for a **surf report** before choosing your beach for the day.

If you're going to spend any time at the shoreline or beach, **water shoes** are the best investment you'll ever make. These water-friendly wonders accompany us whenever we go to any beach. You can get them at lots of places, including the ubiquitous ABC stores. Even on sandy beaches, rocks or sea life seem magnetically attracted to the bottoms of feet. With water shoes, you can frolic without the worry. (Though don't expect them to protect you from everything.)

The ocean here rarely smells fishy since the difference between high and low tide is so small. (In other words, it doesn't strand large amounts of smelly sea plants at low tide like other locations.)

Theft can be a problem when visiting beaches. Visitors like to lock their cars at all beaches, but piles of glass on the ground usually dissuade island residents from doing that at secluded beaches. We usually remove anything we can't bear to have stolen and leave the car with the windows rolled up but unlocked. (Though that may negate your rental car insurance.) That way, we're less likely to get our windows broken by a curious thief. Regardless, don't leave *anything* of value in your car. (Well...maybe the seats can stay.) While in the water, we use a waterproof pouch or box (which you can buy online) for our wallet and keys, and leave everything else on the beach. We don't take a camera to the beach unless we are willing to stay there on the sand and babysit it. This way, when we swim, snorkel or just walk, we don't have to constantly watch our things.

Use sunscreen early and often. Don't pay any attention to the claims from sunscreen makers that their product is waterproof, rubproof, sandblast proof, power-wash proof, etc. Reapply it every couple of hours and after you get out of the ocean. The ocean water will hide sunburn symptoms until after you're toast. Then you can look forward to agony for the rest of your trip. (And yes, you *can* get burned while in the water.) Gel-based sunscreens work best in the water. Lotions work best on land.

People tend to get fatigued while walking in sand. The trick to making it easier is to walk with a very gentle, relaxed stride while lightly striking the sand almost flat-footed.

The Hawai'i Supreme Court ruled in 2006 that *all* beaches are public to "the upper reaches of the wash of the waves...at high tide during the season of the year in which the highest wash of the waves occurs." This means that you can park yourself on any stretch of shoreline sand you like. The trick, sometimes, can be access. You might have to cross private land to get to a public beach. We've pointed out a legal way to every beach on the island, and some of the maps have access routes in yellow to show you the way.

In general, surf is higher and stronger during the winter, calmer in the summer, but there are exceptions during all seasons. When we mention that a beach has facilities, it usually includes restrooms, showers, picnic tables and drinking water.

You might want to pick up a cheap-o beach chair at an ABC store and donate it to your hotel when you leave the island.

Lastly, remember that just because *you* may be on vacation doesn't mean that residents are. Monday through Thursday is the best time to go to the beach. Local residents *love* their beaches, and they show their affection every weekend.

Beach conditions around the island are almost entirely determined by the direction they face, and the dividing lines around O'ahu are rather dramatic. From Makapu'u in the east to Kahuku in the north, you'll often find moderate, onshore winds and somewhat choppy seas year-round—being the *least* windy in the winter months—and wave sizes are rarely monstrous but often respectable. From Kahuku in the north to Ka'ena Point in the west, giant surf in the winter and calm seas in the summer are often combined with light winds at the shore or winds coming from right to left, with windier conditions just offshore. (But onshore winds increase if the trade winds become more northerly.) From Ka'ena Point in the west to Barbers Point in the south, much of the winds are blocked by the mountains, and the surf tends to be big when there's a westerly swell, usually in the winter. The south-facing shoreline, including Waikiki and Hanauma Bay, tends to get small to flat surf in the winter and somewhat larger surf in the summer, but rarely gets the towering waves that the North Shore is famous for.

But remember, these are generalities. We've seen huge surf from the north in June, and we've seen the North Shore flat in February. Nothing can substitute your own eyes and judgment. Ultimately, that's what'll keep you out of trouble.

We're going to start our beach descriptions from the westernmost tip of the island at Ka'ena Point on the left side of the main map and work our way around the island counter-clockwise. Beaches that are *supposed* to have **lifeguards** are highlighted with this ⊕ symbol.

WAI'ANAE BEACHES

⊕ Yokohama Bay/Keawa'ula Beach

This is as far as you can drive in Wai'anae, and it's a worthy destination. This long, glorious beach is lightly used during the week because local residents will usually congregate at beaches closer to the Wai'anae towns and because visitors are usually told to avoid the Wai'anae Coast.

A REAL GEM (Which we consider bad advice. See explanation on page 103.) The result is a heavenly stretch of sand with impossibly blue water, drop-dead gorgeous views and no weekday crowds. The offshore waters are clean and clear, and the beach is usually protected from strong winds by the mountain ridge behind you.

The beach tends to be wider in the summer and narrower in the winter, which can sometimes expose more sandstone beachrock, but this is always a sandy beach, never stripped bare by big surf. Large waves can, however, create strong currents, so avoid the water when the ocean's angry. There's no shade, but there are full park facilities, such as restrooms and showers.

Yokohama is really a nickname that has stuck to the point that few islanders even recognize its real name, Keawa'ula Beach. Early Japanese immigrants used to come here in large numbers to fish, and other immigrant groups began referring to the area as Yokohama Bay.

If you're in the mood for a hike, check out the Ka'ena Point hike on page 189.

❖ Makua Beach/ Ka'ena Point State Park

One of our favorite beaches on the island—and during the week it's *never* crowded. **A REAL GEM** Here's the story. The U.S. military trains in the valley *behind* the beach, though they rarely visit the beach itself. Because of this, and the fact that it's

You can't drive any farther along the Wai'anae coast than Yokohama Bay. Then again, why would you want to?

several miles from the nearest town, local residents rarely come here in numbers. And even fewer visitors come here. The south end has a super-convenient access via a dirt road ½ mile past Makua Cave (but before the tall observation tower on the mauka side of the road). This dirt road isn't easily noticeable, so most people drive right past it. Whether the ocean's calm or pounding, this beach stands apart as one of the most achingly beautiful on the island with clear blue waters, and it never fails to astonish us how lightly it's used during the week. Moderate to high surf can create currents and surge, so be cautious. Access to the northern end of the beach is from the pullout right next to the sand. No facilities, but there's some shade.

Makua is the second to last beach on Hwy 930 in Wai'anae several miles past the town of Makaha.

'Ohiki-lolo Beach is probably the least known beach in all of Wai'anae.

By the way, many residents refer to this beach as "pray for sex" beach in reference to the still-visible 1960s graffiti written on a rock at the south end of the beach.

❖ 'Ohiki-lolo Beach

Huh...where? Few locals and even fewer visitors have ever heard of this beach. It's a few miles from the end of the road in Wai'anae. Just before Makua Cave, a fence on the ocean side of the road causes most people to think the shoreline isn't accessible here. But many years ago the county set the shoreline aside as a beach park; they just never marked it or mentioned it. So although the land mauka of the beach is private, *the beach itself* is all yours. The lovely and secluded pocket of sand is mostly protected by a sandstone bench and is often deserted during the week. At high tide a large pool forms where fish and crab make a living.

A beachgoer battles the mid-week crowd at Makaha Beach Park.

There are plenty of turtles in the near-shore waters, but access to the open water is awkward and should only be attempted when the ocean's completely calm. Just past this beach is a peninsula composed of an intricate sandstone lattice. See HIKING on page 188 for more on that.

Access is via a 10-minute walk from your car. Park across from Makua Cave after the 17 mile marker on Hwy 93 in Wai'anae. Take the trail at the left end of the lot down to the shoreline, then walk left along the shore. Don't leave anything valuable in your car here.

By the way, 'Ohiki-lolo is Hawaiian for either *prying out your brains* or *crazy sand crab*. (It's commonly translated both ways.) Don't know why, but either way someone was having a pretty bad hair day when they named it.

❖ Kea'au Beach Park

This beach park had been used by the community as a giant homeless encampment until 2012. It was the most visually shocking example of poverty and squalor in all Hawai'i and a gigantic embarrassment to people pitching Hawai'i as a paradise. During the eviction many vowed to return once authorities stopped focusing on the area. Time will tell. In the meantime, it might be a good park to avoid. Although cleaned up, there isn't much to recommend here.

⊕ Makaha Beach Park

A REAL GEM A nice, wide beach that is rarely too crowded during the week. Summer is the best time to visit because the wide sand is usually complemented by gentle water. Sometimes small surf can make for some nice, long boogie board rides. If the surf's up, however, longshore currents converge in the center, then a rip current heads out to sea, so avoid if it's not calm. In the winter large waves create dangerous conditions, but that's also when you'll see

You'd think with all those houses around that Papaoneone Beach would be crowded—yet it never is during the week.

some of the prettiest waves on this part of the coast. Local expert surfers *love* Makaha's winter waves. (And photographers without a $10,000 telephoto lens will *love* how close the surfers get to the shore.) Full facilities. Snorkeling is good when seas are right. Kick out to the closest mooring buoy, and follow the reef ledge to the farther buoy. If you were to keep kicking, you'd come to a good SCUBA site called Makaha Caverns a few hundred feet offshore, and boat companies often take divers here.

Located across the street from Kili Road and Hwy 93 in Makaha. See map on page 106.

❖ Papaoneone Beach

A REAL GEM The beaches near the Wai-'anae towns tend to be more heavily used, but this one is visited less than most because it's backed by three resort buildings that seem to have the effect of discouraging non-residents (of the apart-

ments) from coming here. We've never seen it crowded during the week. The beach is excellent, and the shorebreak is steeper than most beaches, so decent-sized waves rip up and down the beach, which can be a blast to ride if you're careful. Even bodysurfers will enjoy them if the waves are not too big and powerful. Just beware of undertow here, and don't try riding waves that are too big for you. Winter brings big surf; summer usually has flat waters and excellent snorkeling. Easy access from the pullout across the street from Jade Street in Makaha, or take Moua Street and look for a *less* convenient public access next to 84-879 Moua St. No facilities and no shade except for the shadow of the apartments in the morning. Nearby locals sometimes call this beach **Turtle Beach**, not to be confused with a beach of the same name on the North Shore. If you take the trail from the south end of the beach, it goes to the top of the point. The view from 231-feet high Lahilahi Point is awesome. See map on page 106.

❖ Mauna Lahilahi Beach Park

Very pretty with Mauna Lahilahi hill standing guard at one end, picnic tables near the road and easy access. Water entry is awkward and difficult due to a rocky bench, so water activities aren't much to speak of. Park at Hwy 93 near Makaha Valley Road in Makaha.

➊ Poka'i Beach Park

This is one of the safest places to swim on the Wai'anae coast due to a protective breakwater. Even when the surf's high elsewhere, Poka'i may be relatively calm. For this reason, it's often packed, even during the week, with parents who bring their keiki to swim. Poka'i is also a popular canoe-launching location. Full facilities and some shade. One note—we've often seen reef sharks cruising inside the breakwater, though these animals, which rarely exceed 6 feet, are generally not considered dangerous to people.

In Wai'anae. Turn toward the ocean where Wai'anae Valley Road meets the highway (93). See map on page 106.

➊ Ma'ili Beach Park

This beach is over a mile long with a nearly mile-long grassy lawn lined in parts with palm trees. Camping is permitted. Although the facilities aren't in tip-top shape, this beach is lightly used during the week, and it's a short walk from your car. The south end across from Maipalaoa Street has some protected swimming most of the time. During the winter some of Ma'ili's sand erodes away, and high surf can bring strong rip currents.

In Ma'ili—can't miss it. See map on page 106.

❖ Ulehawa Beach Park

This one's also over a mile-long beach, but don't let that get you too excited. The beach park where Princess Kahanu Avenue meets the highway is the worst part of the beach. A sandstone bench makes the swimming poor. You're better off to the left (south) where the conditions are sandier, but overall, this isn't a great beach to spend some time. By the way, Ulehawa is Hawaiian for *filthy penis*, and was named in honor of a not-so-loved chief from the area.

➊ Nanakuli Beach

This is a small beach with a very steep shorebreak, which is lots of fun if you want to rake up and down the shoreline feeling the ocean's raw power. It's not so fun if the surf is too strong, or you're skittish about the ocean and don't want to feel the ocean's force unfiltered by more gently sloping shorelines elsewhere. High surf, especially in the winter, creates dangerous conditions. The right (north) end of the park has a lawn, ballfield and playground. At the extreme north end where the cyclone fence forms a 90° angle, you'll find a sandstone blowhole that snorts, gasps and spouts when the surf's up.

Camping is allowed with a free county permit. Located where Nanakuli Avenue meets the highway (93) in Nanakuli.

❖ Electric Beach/Tracks/ Kahe Point

Just before the impossible-to-miss power plant on Hwy 93 before Nanakuli is a tiny pocket of sand called Electric Beach. It's a popular SCUBA diving and snorkeling spot. Good snorkeling when calm, but visibility can be poor. The long beach just past the power plant is known by local surfers as Tracks (after the nearby, now-abandoned railroad tracks). The surf is often fairly gentle here, making the swimming good much of the time.

❖ Ko Olina Lagoons

A REAL GEM In the 1990s the developers of Ko Olina created four semicircular lagoons mostly protected from the open ocean. The swimming is excellent and ultra-protected near the beach. Swim from the sandy shoreline to the open end where the snorkeling can be outstanding around the rocks. Watch for currents flushing in and out of the openings. These lagoons are extremely pretty, and sunsets from here are fantastic. Lagoon #4 has the most parking spaces—about 100. Lagoons 1, 2 and 3 have only 18 parking spaces (plus another 18 at parking lot

Who cares if they're man-made? The lagoons of Ko Olina are exceptionally good beaches.

1B). Bottom line, whichever lagoon you choose, you should arrive before 10 a.m., or go in the late afternoon if you want to get a parking space. A concrete path connects them. Signs say you can't bring temporary shade (umbrellas) or Frisbees, but beaches in Hawai'i belong to the public, so we don't understand how Ko Olina can enforce such rules. Cabanas *might* be available at Lagoons 1 and 3.

Take H-1 west until it becomes Hwy 93 (*after* exit #1), and look for an road to Ko Olina on the *mauka* side of the highway. The roads to the lagoons are labeled. See map on page 104.

'EWA & LEEWARD BEACHES

❖ Nimitz Beach

Lining the south end of Kalaeloa Airport, the water's better than 'Ewa Beach (below), and in winter the seas can get

exceptionally calm, though swimming can be awkward due to reefs offshore. There's some shade, and it's not a bad place to stake your claim and stretch out on the sand. The beach park itself (where the facilities are) has beachrock at its shoreline, but it's sandier at the eastern end. The best portion of the beach is near the campsites. Where Coral Sea Road veers right, there's an unpaved road on the left. See map on page 100 and take exit 5.

❖ White Plains Beach Park
The best thing about this beach is the surfing break just offshore. Great novice surfing conditions—crumbling waves like Waikiki when conditions are right. But unless you bring your own board, you need a military ID to rent their surfboards. The beach is open to the public but *services* are only available to the military. Swimming isn't great due to

lots of reef and rocks in the nearshore waters. Same directions as Nimitz Beach, but turn left at Tripoli Road. Weekends are crowded when local families enjoy the waters and the full facilities. Stick to weekdays.

❖ One'ula Beach Park
There's even less reason to come here than 'Ewa Beach. It's lined with beachrock that's hard on your feet and anything else that comes in contact with it. In past editions we said that "this is also where the area's...less-than-savory characters tend to hang out, from what we've observed." Well, we heard from one of them, who said, "That would be me and my friends, dedicated surfers who keep trim and healthy by a daily dose of paddling and surfing." Fair enough. Consider us properly chastised.

❖ 'Ewa Beach
This beach doesn't really look very Hawaiian. If you were transported here, you might think you had ended up in Florida. With its long, yardstick-straight sand beach, no shade and a sandy lawn behind it, the beach is appreciated by nearby residents but doesn't attract much attention from visitors spoiled by better offerings elsewhere. The water is always less than clear since so much of it originates in mucky Pearl Harbor and gets carried here by currents. And the surrounding 'Ewa Plain is just what the name implies—plain and featureless except for the development. See map on page 100.

❖ Ke'ehi Beach Park
This park has tennis courts, a giant lawn and playgrounds and is adjacent to flat, calm water, though it's less than sparkly. Near the airport on Lagoon Drive, turn left onto Aolele.

❖ Sand Island

Sounds like a great place to go to the beach, but it's actually an industrial area (where much of our imported cargo comes in). The bottom half of the island is ringed with a beach park. The water's not the clearest and snorkeling is poor, but it's mostly dead calm. The west end is actually kind of pretty. The southern portion that faces the open ocean has a nice sand beach and large lawn area, but it's backed by cranes and shipping derricks. The north end near the entrance faces downtown Honolulu and is a good place to see giant boats pulling into and out of the harbor.

❖ Kaka'ako Beach Park

This park makes a rotten first impression when you're driving up past an industrial area and a boat graveyard. But the park itself is actually a nice place to sit at the shoreline and watch the sunset, because if there's any surf, it comes crashing into the lava rock wall. Watching it can be surprisingly relaxing. It'll be almost all local residents—this place is unknown to most visitors. Just west of Waikiki, take Ala Moana Boulevard to Ward Avenue to Ahui toward the ocean.

➊ Ala Moana Regional Park

A REAL GEM These beaches are the main nearby alternatives to Waikiki beachgoing. If Waikiki feels a little small to you, Ala Moana is an ultra-wide beach with endless sand and shallow, very protected water. The southeast end can be like a bathtub. Just be aware of where the sea-floor drops off to deeper water.

Behind Ala Moana is a gigantic lawn where locals bring their volleyballs, Frisbees, croquet and just about every other plaything you can imagine. The only shade on the beach is from the moving shadows of palm tree crowns. While visitors gravitate toward Waikiki, Honolulu residents tend to be the most frequent users of Ala Moana, and on weekends and holidays they pack the place.

Because it's so calm most of the time, it's popular with timid swimmers and families with kids. Of course, if the sound of screaming kids is what you're trying to get *away* from, you might want to go elsewhere. See map on page 51.

❖ Magic Island

This is that peninsula on the Diamond Head side of Ala Moana. It was created in 1964 and was slated to be a resort, but the developers ran into money problems, and it was eventually turned into parkland. Even fairly large waves are usually diffused here and at Ala Moana, creating another bathtub backed by sand, lawn, palm trees, the city skyline and finally the Ko'olau mountains. This is classic Honolulu. The only areas you want to stay away from are the breaks in the wall that allow ocean water in. Water shoes are a good idea here as the bottom is not entirely sand-lined. No snorkeling—just swimming. From the south end you can watch the small boats coming into Ala Wai Harbor.

Overall, we prefer Ala Moana over Magic Island due to its better water quality and sandier sea bottom.

➊ Waikiki

A REAL GEM Since this is the heart of where most people stay, we've put the description in the WAIKIKI AND HONOLULU SIGHTS chapter. The beach areas from Kahanamoku to Sans Souci are covered there on page 47.

Magic Island is close to Waikiki and has ultra-protected waters most of the time.

❖ Kaluahole/Makalei Beach

Not too many people staying in Waikiki come to this small pocket beach because it's a ¼ mile walk from the nearest parking at Kapiolani Park. It's used mostly by residents whose houses line the shore. If you're up for a walk (or you have someone to drop you off), the swimming is good, and you're likely to be the only non-resident there. See map on page 62.

❖ Diamond Head Beach Park & Kuilei Cliffs Beach Park

These two parks are at the shoreline of Diamond Head. There are only intermittent pockets of sand, and the surf is usually ridable here. Longshore currents heading toward Waikiki often form, meaning surfers might not be able to effortlessly bob in place. Swimming and snorkeling aren't very good. Consider these pretty to look at but not overly user-friendly for most water activities. Showers behind the beach.

❖ Ka'alawai Beach

A REAL GEM One of the least-appreciated beaches near Waikiki. The section of sand closest to Black Point (the far, eastern end) has excellent swimming that's fairly protected most of the time, with good snorkeling opportunities. The beach access is not well known, so it stays off the radar screen of most visitors. You get there either by walking along the shoreline from the easternmost Kuilei Cliffs Beach Park lookout, or take Kahala Avenue to Papu Circle. Right on Kulamanu Street, left on Kulamanu Place. No facilities. Some shade is available only in the summer due to the shifting sun. See map on page 62.

❖ Kahala Beach

A REAL GEM Kahala is where the rich and not-so-famous live on O'ahu. Huge oceanfront mansions line parts of the shoreline here. Kahala Beach is the intermittent sandy strip on the far side of Diamond Head, from Black Point to Wai'alae Beach. You access it by driving from Waikiki until Kalakaua Avenue turns into

If you're looking for a quieter beach experience than Waikiki, Ka'alawai Beach is a short drive away, and the pace is waaay calmer.

Diamond Head Road, then Kahala Avenue. Continue and park near the intersection of Kahala and Elepaio streets where the curb isn't painted red, and take the first beach access you see.

The snorkeling here is different than places like Hanauma Bay. Forget big fish eyeballing you. Most of them have been taken by resident fishermen. What's good about the snorkeling here are the small, intricate marine critters making a living over this flat, shallow reef. Most of the time you're swimming in only a couple feet of water, gliding just over the reef. Once away from the shore (and nearer the outer reef edge), the observant and patient snorkeler will notice tiny shrimp passing by, small blennies sticking their heads out of holes and a host of other small 1–2 inch fish going about their business. You'll want to wear a T-shirt to protect you when the water gets too shallow. Some cheap gloves wouldn't hurt either. The general flow of

Though this part of Wai'alae Beach is right next to The Kahala Hotel and Resort, it never seems crowded or frantic.

water is over the reef (it will resist your advances the closer you get to the edge), along the shore and out the channel at Hunakai Street. (So avoid the channel.) The closer to the reef edge, the more fish. (They're almost completely absent at the shoreline.) If the fish seem unusually skittish, remember: They've watched their bigger siblings get nabbed by critters that look *just like you*.

Near Black Point there's a small sand pocket where the point starts. As you approach it, you'll see lots of distortive perturbations in the water, and you'll notice rapid temperature changes. There are basal springs of brackish and fresh water percolating from the ground here. Fresh and saltwater don't like mixing, so you can literally see them rubbing against each other, and the lighter (and colder) freshwater tends to stay on top. Quickly push your flat hand through it, and you'll actually be able to *see* the normally invisible roiling turbulence you create as you pass through the water. Dig a hole in the sand just above the surf line and notice how it fills with water. The sand is saturated from

the spring, and your feet sink faster in the sand here. If you've taken the beach access we suggested, you can swim to this pocket, then out toward the reef edge, let the current take you along toward (but stop before!) the channel, then take another beach access from the beach to Kahala Avenue and walk back to your car.

❖ Wai'alae Beach Park

Calm, protected waters most of the time make this a very good swimming beach, but snorkelers need not apply since the water isn't very clear. The best part of the beach is a few minutes' walk to the left, near The Kahala Hotel and its tiny offshore island. It's very pretty, and though that area is a resort beach, it's got a much more relaxed atmosphere than most resort beaches, and they have beach toys for rent.

At the beach park itself, over the bridge to the right, the sandy shoreline is lightly used except by the beach house owners. (Remember, *you* own the beach, not the nearby homeowners.) Ironically, the worst part of the beach is the narrow, sandy stretch fronting the park itself due to stream runoff and the crumbling remains of an old sidewalk that occasionally poke through the sand. On Kahala Avenue near Kealaolu Avenue. Full facilities.

❖ Wailupe Beach Park

Very easy access off Hwy 72 near Aina Haina, but the uninviting water makes it a must-miss.

❖ Kawaiku'i Beach Park

A good place to launch a kayak if you just want to paddle the super-calm, protected water from here to Koko Head. The water quality for swimming is poor thanks to runoff from Hawai'i Kai. But it's pretty with lots of shade trees, picnic tables and facilities. At Hwy 72 and Puuikena Drive.

❖ Maunalua Bay Beach Park

At Hwy 72 and Keahole in Hawai'i Kai, this is a popular boat-launching place, and you can launch a kayak from here. Otherwise, there's not much for you.

◯ Hanauma Bay

A REAL GEM The snorkeling mecca of the island. We've described it in detail in the EAST O'AHU SIGHTS chapter on page 63.

Experienced bodysurfers only need apply at Sandy Beach. All others will be pounded into oblivion by the shorebreak.

❖ Halona Cove

A REAL GEM This is an idyllic Hawaiian sandy cove. So idyllic, in fact, that in 1953 they filmed it in the now-famous, roll-in-the-sand-while-kissing scene for the movie *From Here to Eternity*. When calm, the cove makes for great swimming. If there's a little surf, it provides good bodysurfing. And when the surf is stronger, it becomes a washing machine that will clean your clothes by banging them into the side rocks—with you in them.

You park at the Halona Blowhole Lookout 1⁴⁄₁₀ miles past (east of) the entrance to Hanauma Bay on Hwy 72. Walk down the short, natural boulder stair-step path near the road.

➊ Sandy Beach

Pretty obvious name, huh? Like identifying a "wooden tree." For years local residents called it the "sand beach near the blowhole," and it was eventually shortened to Sandy Beach. Some call it Sandys. Anyway, this beach is ultra-popular with locals for its bodysurfing. Note that we said *locals*. That's because the sandy shoreline is steep, and the waves have a wickedly powerful shorebreak. Anyone who isn't very experienced is likely to (and often does) get pile-driven into the sand, resulting in some terrible neck injuries. (Barack Obama bodysurfs here when he's on island but he's very experienced.) Unless you know what you're doing, consider bodysurfing elsewhere. We've often used the giant lawn next to the beach to launch our ultralight, and too many times we've seen ambulances here carting away injured bodysurfing visitors.

The park has full facilities and that same lawn is popular with kite fliers, hang gliders (for landing—they *launch* off the cliff above Kaupo Beach Park) and other lawn sports. On Hwy 72 just before the road reaches its easternmost point. By the way, it's not uncommon to be asked by hanggliding beggars to drive them up the mountain and drive their cars back to Sandys.

WINDWARD BEACHES

➊ Makapu'u Beach Park

This is the first beach on the windward side after you've rounded Makapu'u Head, and the boogie boarding and bodysurfing can be excellent here. Conditions are similar to those at Sandy Beach—fantastic, but only for the experienced or the lucky, unless the ocean's pretty calm. During high surf the waves can wash up the entire beach. At times like that, the raging surf scratches and claws at the cliffs to the right, producing quite a sight. Even during smaller seas, the waves will feel pretty powerful for their size due to the shape of the nearshore seabed, making it fun to get tossed around as long as you're aware of the ocean's potential to rough you up.

There's a great lookout above the beach, as well as a convenient access at the bottom of the hill across from Sea Life Park. The offshore islands of Manana (AKA Rabbit Island) and Kaohi-ka-ipu add to the scenery. Full facilities.

❖ Kaupo Beach Park

After Sea Life Park, across from the Oceanic Institute (they farm shrimp), is a beach access and a small lawn that is used as a hang glider landing spot (hence the windsock). This is mainly a surfing beach since the shoreline is pretty rocky, but there's a nice tide-pool here. To the left of the nearby pier is where some introductory SCUBA dives take place, but frankly the water conditions there are pretty poor, and you'd be wise to do your SCUBA diving somewhere else. Also known locally as Cockroach Bay.

❖ Kaiona Beach Park

Well known among residents as the home of the Waimano Canoe Club, it is indeed a good place to launch a canoe or kayak. A long reef offshore protects you from most of the ocean's force. Snorkeling can be good at times, but water visibility might be poor. Consider snorkeling about 700 feet off a house with a light green tile roof (which is far to the right of the park entrance) for fairly good fish life and reef structure. If you ever saw the TV show *Magnum PI,* walk along the beach to the right, and you'll see a house with a tennis court. That's the smaller-than-you-expected Robin Masters estate. (Of course, if you never saw the show, you couldn't care less.) Showers and restrooms available. Packed with local campers on weekends. If you drive past the park, a much less used part of the beach is easily accessible from the road just before it peels away from the shoreline. Just pull over and grab a spot. Gobs of nice sand, if not the clearest water.

❖ Waimanalo Beach Park

A long, very pretty strip of sand with great swimming much of the time. The ocean's usually clearer than Kaiona, though snorkeling is still pretty poor. There are picnic tables, facilities and some ironwood trees for shade. Weekends are particularly crowded, but on weekdays it's lightly used. Car break-ins can be a problem here, so don't leave anything valuable in your car.

The nearby baseball field attracts lots of BBQers on weekends. Camping is allowed, but you may not feel very welcome. Easy to find on Hwy 72 after the highway leads away from the Ko'olau Mountains in Waimanalo near a ball park.

➊ Waimanalo Bay Recreation Area

A REAL GEM The beach has a pretty thick pad of sand that drops to depth fairly quickly, making it fun to splash around in the water if you respect the fact that the waves will have a bit more force. Currents can form parallel to the shoreline (called longshore currents), but they're usually easy to get out of by swimming perpendicular to them back to shore. Full facilities. Very nice beach for a long walk. Heavily used on weekends. Located halfway between Kailua and Makapu'u (the easternmost point) off Hwy 72. Camping is allowed with free county permit. The REAL GEM designation refers to the super long beach walk available when you combine it with Bellows Beach.

➊ Bellows Beach

This is an unusual beach because it's only open to the public from noon Fridays to midnight Sundays. (It's a county park that fronts a closed military base.) As a result of the weeklong pent-up demand, weekend use tends to be unusually high.

The waters offer pretty good swimming most of the time (though not good snorkeling), and the forest of ironwood trees behind the beach gives it an undeveloped feel.

The beach has one historical high point. The first Japanese prisoner of war was taken here during WWII when a mini-submarine washed up on the

A future developer gets his first lesson on how close to build to the shoreline.

reef, and the officer straggled ashore. Camping is allowed on weekends with free county permit. Look for the entrance off Hwy 72 in Waimanalo town. There will be a military guard.

Here's the best part. Though access *from the road* is weekends only, Monday–Thursday you can usually walk from Waimanalo Bay Recreation Area north along the beach. Remember, all beaches are public, and they only seem to close the sand beach when they are doing military exercises. During the week, most the southern end of Bellows is a deserted beach walk.

❖ **Lanikai Beach**

A REAL GEM

Lanikai has that dreamy, tropical look that postcards and paintings are made of. Beautiful sand, stunning blue water and two idyllic offshore islands combine to create the quintessential island atmosphere. Lanikai's no secret, and one thing that you need to know is that many of the descriptions you read about this beach are outdated. The last 20 years haven't been kind to Lanikai. More than half of the beach that lives in the memory of residents—and those who created the paintings—is gone. It's ironic. House lots on the beach might sell for $6 million and up. These wealthy landowners built seawalls to protect their precious investments. According to many observers, seawalls cause the very kind of beach erosion that people try to prevent. The result? What was once a beach well over a mile long is now less

Kailua Beach goes on and on and on...

than half a mile long. (The beach accesses south of Onekea lead to a sandless shoreline.) Much of the generous sand that once defined Lanikai has now shifted over to Kailua Beach, whose residents, no doubt, thank the Lanikai community for inadvertently donating their sand.

It may be smaller now, but Lanikai is still a feast for the eyes. And the snorkeling along the stretch of water between Mokumanu Drive and Haokea Drive can be great, featuring a healthy community of coral and fish—mostly small fish, but lots of 'em. The only thing that keeps this area from having world-class snorkeling is a general cloudiness in the water. That shouldn't dissuade you; just don't expect it to be as crystal clear below the surface as it *appears* from above the surface.

By the way, the offshore islets are called Moku-lua, and the name applies to both. This is fitting since Moku-lua means *two islands*.

There are beach accesses all along Lanikai. If you have a kayak to launch, go to the far end at Lanipo Drive. If you're looking for a larger patch of sand, go to Kuailima Drive. There's usually enough parking along Mokulua Road and on the side streets. No facilities and no shade. In Kailua, take the Pali Highway until it ends (ignore name changes) and turn right onto Kalaheo, then check the map on page 70 to see which feeder street to take to Lanikai Beach.

➕ Kailua Beach

This lovely 2½-mile stretch of delicious sandy beach fits nearly everyone's profile of **A REAL GEM** a beautiful tropical paradise. This is one of the best beaches on the island to simply stroll along as the waves splash your legs. Four different offshore islands beckon the adventurous. And Kailua rarely gets the monstrous 30-foot surf that pounds the North Shore.

The swimming, boogie boarding and bodysurfing at Kailua are good when conditions cooperate—which is most of the time. Snorkeling isn't worth your time, thanks to the runoff from Enchanted Lake and the Kawainui Canal.

The kayaking here is particularly good, and you can rent kayaks right at Kailua Beach Park. See KAYAKING on page 196 for more.

This beach is your best opportunity to spot the elusive **mole crab**. These quarter-sized buggers live under the sand beneath the surf line and can only be pinpointed by subtle clusters of V-shaped water wakes as waves recede from their barely exposed eye-stalks. (They're different from the ghost crabs that live in holes above the surf line.) On those occasions that Portuguese man-o-wars drift in, mole crabs will snag a passing tentacle and pull it under the sand, munching away on it like spaghetti. Speaking of man-o-wars, they are unfortunately more common here, especially during summer months (April–October) than at most other beaches, one of the few dings to this otherwise great beach.

You can either park at Kailua Beach Park at Kalaheo and Kailua Road, or at Kalama Beach Park (less used) at Kalaheo and Kapaa, which gets you closer to the center of the beach. There are also several rights-of-way along Kalaheo (shown on map), but parking might be a problem with them.

As an aside, during WWII, the island's police chief, for some reason, set a rule that "prostitutes can swim only at Kailua Beach." He also banned them "from all golf courses."

🟠 Kualoa Beach Park

A truly kickin' windward beach park. Straddling the point at the north end of Kane'ohe Bay, the park features endless lawn, plenty of facilities, camping, shade, picnic tables and an uninterrupted sandy strip of shoreline with usually calm waters,

A REAL GEM a gorgeous mountain backdrop and a tempting and utterly picturesque island. Chinaman's Hat island is 614 yards offshore. About the only thing this park *doesn't* have is crystal clear waters. The ocean gets some runoff from nearby streams, so the water tends to be a bit cloudy. But the shoreline is usually so protected that swimming can be great here—just not the snorkeling.

If you walk along the beach to the right, the sand keeps going, leading to land fronted by Kualoa Ranch. Although they sell that as their "private beach," calling it a "secret island" that they'll take you to for $30, you can have it for free just by strolling onto it from Kualoa Beach. Remember, all beaches are *public*. Kualoa Ranch only owns the land *behind* the beach. (But don't tell that to any of the beachgoers who Kualoa charged to take them there—it'll just antagonize 'em.) Camping is allowed with free county permit.

❖ Kualoa Sugar Mill Beach/ Kanenelu Beach/Kalae'o'io Beach

As soon as you leave the entrance to Kualoa Park heading north, the road starts hugging the shoreline, and sandy beaches present themselves. Although they're tantalizing (heck, we even used a photo of one to start the NORTH SHORE SIGHTS chapter), they aren't the best beaches you'll find—they're just the *first* beaches lining the highway. Swimming is not bad but can be better elsewhere. Access is easy and totally obvious—just pull over when you want and dig in. These beaches tend to be fairly narrow.

❖ Ka'a'awa Beach Park

The sand is wider here than the beaches to the south, and the swimming's pretty good. Visibility is better, too, but often not good enough to encourage snorkeling. In Ka'a'awa. (We just love saying that word.) Access? Right next to the road.

❖ Swanzy Beach Park

There are unusually well-kept park facilities, and camping is allowed on weekends with free county permit. And although the waters are fairly protected and reefy, the fish count is pretty poor (probably overfished by local spearfishermen), and there's little sand here. A dozen miles north of Kane'ohe on Hwy 83 in Ka'a'awa. The BBQ across the street has good grinds.

❖ Makaua Beach

This beach is the easy-to-access strip of sand just before the Crouching Lion between Ka'a'awa and Kahana on your way to the North Shore from Kane'ohe. One of those beaches along the windward coast where you can just stop your car and hop right in, but it doesn't offer much, other than an easy presence to sand. The nearshore waters are rocky and pretty shallow. Sometimes the sand disappears completely.

❖ Kahana Bay Beach Park

Kahana is a pretty arc of sand fronting Kahana Valley. The water is never pristine due to runoff from the **A REAL GEM** Kahana Stream, but if you don't care about snorkeling, it's a nice place. There are trees for shade and picnic tables, and there's rarely more than a handful of people during the week. And if you want to kayak, the river feeding the bay makes for a very enjoyable kayak trip. See KAYAKING on page 197. Can't miss it in south Kahana 15 miles north of Kane'ohe on Hwy 83.

❖ Punalu'u Beach Park

Here's the perfect beach for the lazy beachgoer. You drive up and...well, that's it. **A REAL GEM** The beach literally touches the road. No muss, no fuss. And what a beauty it is. Long, inviting stretch of sand, lots of shade, full facilities, partial protection from an offshore reef and surprisingly few visitors during the week. In the winter the beach narrows during periods of high surf, but overall, this is an underappreciated windward beach. The snorkeling isn't world class, but the swimming much of the time is over a sandy bottom. Just stay away from the channel to the left (north) where currents can form. North of the facilities (and a bridge where the channel is) the beach gets even better and less used. In Punalu'u on Hwy 83; can't miss it. See map on page 81.

❖ Kaluanui Beach

Ya see the sign, ya pull over. Walk 50 feet and jump onto the sand. It's that easy, and it's usually empty during the week. Lots of sand here and thickly padded offshore. But don't venture too far out since channel currents could get strong.

❖ Makao Beach

Another one of those ridiculously easy beaches to access. The road's right next to the sand beach. Just find a place to pull over. The sand is narrow and almost disappears at high tide. The water is very protected by an offshore reef. Only at the extreme north end does current start to form as the water exits through

Kahana Beach doesn't have the clearest water on the island thanks to the nearby river, but if you're looking for delicious scenery or good kayaking, you've found your destination for the day.

the channel. Snorkeling can be good, though wintertime brings cloudy water, and overall, the area seems to have been overfished by local residents. On Hwy 83 just south of Ha'aula.

❖ Hau'ula Beach Park

The good news is that access is easy and convenient, and the park has full facilities. Camping is allowed with free county permit. The bad news is that the water tends to be cloudy and it's overfished. Overall, not a must-see beach. On Hwy 83 in Hau'ula across from 7-Eleven.

❖ Kokololio Beach Park

There are a few beach estates just north of the park. In case you're wondering what kind of people can afford an estate on a lovely beach like this, here's one example: The estate just south of the stream near Pali Kilo I'a is owned by the local electric company and used as a perk for its executives. (Apparently, we lowly rate-payers aren't invited.) Anyway, the beach is very pretty and there are full facilities. There's a small area with good snorkeling some of the time for adventurous snorkelers. If you follow the large wall that bisects the park to where it *would have* touched the water, and enter slightly to the right and paddle out a short way, longshore currents will carry you to the left along a short reefy wall that sometimes has an impressive number of fish. It's like being on a conveyer belt. Then in a hundred feet or so, swim perpendicular to the current (toward the shore), and walk back to where you started. (This is the typical current—we imagine that stronger currents could prove problematic if the surf's raging.) Sometimes, inexplicably, we've seen the fish almost completely absent. Other times they're everywhere. The far north end has a protected area sometimes called Bathtub Beach. (Not to be confused with the Bathtub Beach below.)

Camping is allowed here, but you may be happier elsewhere. See map on page 81.

❖ La'ie Beach Park/Pounders

A REAL GEM In La'ie, 1 mile past (north of) Hau'ula Kai Shopping Center, is an unmarked park called La'ie Beach Park. (It's also known locally as Pounders.) This is an attractive beach with a sandstone cliff defining the right (south) end. It's the waves at that end that inspired the name *Pounders*. When the surf's decent, the pounding waves can make for some good bodysurfing. But if you're not careful, they can also pound the living daylights out of you. Better and safer swimming is at the north end near the old pier pilings.

If you walk to the left along the beach for a few minutes, past the old pier pilings and around the corner, a wonderful treat awaits. Except during high tide and high

Instructions for Punalu'u Beach: Drive up, open door, fall out onto the sand... repeat if necessary.

Pounders Beach when it's not too pounding.

surf, a wonderfully protected set of ponds creates bathtub-smooth water, hence its nickname—**Bathtub Beach**. (Separate from the other Bathtub Beach at Kokololio Beach.) This is a fantastic place to splash about in the ocean while still feeling protected. (Of course, you're still in the ocean, so anything can happen, and high surf means that all bets are off, so you might not even be able to reach it by walking along the shoreline.) And the mountain views from here are *da kine*.

❖ Laniloa Beach

In La'ie town there's an easy-to-miss public access ²⁄₁₀ mile past McDonald's (toward Kahuku) just before the road curves left. We usually park on the other side of the street. The 60-second path takes you to a lovely ribbon of sand that overlooks impressive La'ie Point. Though the waters have a mostly reefy bottom, the swimming is usually safe due to a protective reef. There is a sandy patch in the water to the left of the shoreline access point. That, along with its mostly forgotten status, makes this a great beach to spend an afternoon. A few trees provide shade. See map on page 81.

❖ Hukilau Beach/La'ie Beach

A REAL GEM

If you go to a lu'au or listen to anyone play Hawaiian music for very long, you'll hear it. *Oh, we're going / to a hukilau / a huki huki huki huki hukilau...* This refers to the age-old practice of circling a portion of the ocean with a net and driving the fish in. Then a group of people hauls out the fish-laden net. That's what used to happen at this beach, and it was quite a sight to see—until the taxman heard about it. See page 81 for more.

Anyway, Hukilau Beach is yet another beautiful windward beach with fantastic views of Goat Island to the left, Pulemoku Rock directly offshore, and La'ie Point on the right. There's not much shade here. The right side of the beach is partially protected by reef and is often safe to swim. That end also has its own beach access at the end of Halelaa Street, but the NO PARKING sign usually convinces people to park at Hukilau Park. If you feel like walking, you could stroll ⅔ mile along the beach to the point nearest Goat Island, then wade to its offshore beach. Or park closer—see Malaekahana Beach. Most of the beach users here are students from nearby Brigham Young University. Showers available. Closed Sundays.

It's not hard to see why this hidden stretch of shoreline, which you can't see from the road or from nearby La'ie Beach Park, is affectionately called Bathtub Beach.

❖ Goat Island/Moku'auia Island

A REAL GEM This island is 720 feet off Malaekahana Beach. It has two beaches of its own, and the one to the left is fantastic. It's a classic, curving sandy beach with awesome swimming most of the time, thanks to the protection offered from the two points and an offshore reef. And since you need to swim to it (really, wade to it up to your chest unless the ocean's raging—you'll need water shoes since the bottom's uneven and sharp), it's never crowded. What a *great* getaway. See directions to Malaekahana Beach below. Some-

What makes the beach on Goat Island so special? 'Cause ya gotta earn it, brah...

times, especially in winter, waves can wrap around Goat Island and slap each other right where you'll be wading. You may get bumped around a bit if that's happening. Huge surf means you don't go.

In the mid-1800s, this small island was the home of a Hawaiian lawyer who kept two mistresses here. When the king of Hawai'i learned of this, he ordered the lawyer arrested. You know what they say...never mess with a lawyer, even if you're a king. The attorney did some research and found out that his offshore island wasn't recorded on any of the king's maps. So he declared that it wasn't part of Hawai'i, and that he was now king of his own island. (Even in the 1800s, lawyers will be lawyers.) The ploy worked, and the Hawaiian king left him alone.

❖ Malaekahana Beach

One of the less-appreciated beach parks near the northern tip of the island. The beach is a mile long and has pretty good swimming if you wear water shoes (since the nearshore waters are rocky). Near the northern (left) end there are several beach cabins. You can actually rent these—see CAMPING on page 163. Malaekahana seems to be one of those beaches that stays unknown to most visitors, so odds are you'll be sharing it with mostly residents. Offshore is Goat Island (see above) with its exclusive beach that you need to wade to.

Between the towns of Laʻie and Kahuku on Hwy 83. There are two entrances. The first (southern) one is closest to Goat Island and has more facilities. The second one leads to the cabins. See map on page 81.

❖ Kahuku Golf Course Beach

Think of it as a rose with thorns; look, but don't touch. More specifically, don't swim. That's because there's a pretty impressive rip current that's usually present here. But the good news is that the beach is often empty and exhibits a certain wildness. Sand and sandstone beachrock are the ingredients topped off by ever-present wind. You can walk along the shoreline for miles here—so much so that we've detailed it as a hike on page 187 since access to it is a bit awkward. At the northern tip of the island.

❖ Kuilima Cove

The snorkeling off the middle/right behind the semi-protective reef can be exceptional, even Hanauma Bay-like in terms of fish count, although this bay is much smaller and not as protected, so the snorkeling isn't as reliable. Stay away from the channel at the right end where the reef ends, and avoid the left side where the bay empties into the open ocean. Visibility won't be stellar—it's often somewhat cloudy. But the fish life can be extraordinary at times.

A REAL GEM

To get here, drive past the northern tip of the island and Kahuku, and turn into the impossible-to-miss Turtle Bay Resort. The cove is to the right of the hotel. See map on page 82.

❖ Turtle Bay

Past the Turtle Bay Resort, the western part is lightly used and beautiful. There's even an island to wade to when it's super-calm (which sometimes happens during summer months). The snorkeling around that island can be good, but currents can be a problem here, so be cautious. Much of the beach is fronted by beachrock, so swimming is often awkward. Winter waves make swimming impossible.

The name Turtle Bay comes from years ago when green sea turtles used to lay eggs on the beach. They don't do that anymore, and the bay is not necessarily more turtle-infested than any other beach. (Just so you don't get your hopes up.) Don't confuse Turtle Bay with Turtle Beach, described on page 156.

❖ Kawela Bay

There aren't many places like this on Oʻahu: a beach so little known that it's essentially a secret. If you don't live nearby, you probably don't know about this one. We first saw this beach from the air in an ultralight and wished there was a way to get to it other than a 30-minute walk from the Turtle Bay Resort. One end of the beach has a few houses on it, but it's a gated community—can't go there. From Hwy 83 it's not visible. The trailhead is 1 mile past (toward Haleʻiwa) the prominent Turtle Bay Resort entrance near the northern tip of the island. See map on page 82. (Another trailhead is further down at a small bridge.) Park at the end of a long chain link fence, and there may be a produce stand across the street. Walk around the fence, and when you get to some

A REAL GEM

incredible banyan trees, go straight to the beach and head to the right along the sand. Kawela Bay rarely, especially during the week, has more than a handful of people on it.

The middle/right portion has the best swimming with its sandy patches. (Bring polarized sunglasses to see through the surface better.) The left (west) end, where the houses are, has some weak basal springs that gurgle out of the sand above the ocean line. But it's the far *right* end that you want. It has your best snorkeling, though overall, the bay isn't a great snorkeling spot due to some sediment that comes out of the river. That side also has calm, lapping waves, abundant shade and striking beauty, along with a serenity that you'll remember for years. In the winter, big rains often cloud up the water for days at a time, but it never keeps this beach from being lovely.

❖ Waiale'e Beach Park

Unmarked at press time, this pretty little park has a small island 153 feet offshore. (Standing at the point, you'd *swear* it was closer.) When it's calm (and *only* when it's calm), the snorkeling to the right of the island can be exceptional. Lots of big and small fish and even occasional barracuda and octopus swim around this tiny area. If it's flat calm, consider swimming around the back side of **Kukaimanini**

It may be next to Turtle Bay, but we see more monk seals in this area than anything else.

Island, which is intricate and lattice-like and very different-looking than the front of the island. See if you can find the basal spring barely percolating from the beach sand area closest to the island. Located on Hwy 83 almost 2 miles southwest (toward Hale'iwa) of the entrance to Turtle Bay Resort (but northeast of Sunset Beach). See map on page 82.

NORTH SHORE BEACHES

These beaches are quintessential dual-personality beaches. During the winter (October–April) they can produce staggering waves that keep all but expert surfers out of the water—classic *look, but don't touch* beaches. During

Do I really need to say why this is called Sunset Beach Park?

the rest of the year, seas are *usually* small to calm.

✪ Sunset Beach Support Park/ Pau-malu

A REAL GEM

During summer months (May–September or October) this is an exquisitely beautiful beach that is irresistibly inviting. You won't find a better-looking beach to frolic on than Sunset on a calm day. Though mostly sand-bottomed, there are some reef areas near the lifeguard station and on the right (north) side that can offer downright kickin' snorkeling, very clear water and lots of fish. Otherwise, just wade in the crystalline water till you're waterlogged. The sand drops quickly, so you can be in chest-high water only a few feet from shore. Check with the lifeguard for conditions. Restrooms

across the street, as well as showers (which are unusually cold—we wonder if the pipes are ensconced in a chilly basal spring).

This steepness, along with fairly coarse sand, creates good conditions for Monastery Tag (named after a beach in California where we accidentally invented it one day after a SCUBA dive). Now bear with me, it'll sound a bit strange, but we've shown this to others and they *love* it. The three ingredients you need are unchecked waves, a steep beach and a padded (sandy) bottom. Basically, you lie in the water at the surf's edge, and zip up and down the beach up to 30 feet each way on a thin cushion of water, digging feet and hands into the sand to control your ascent and descent. Like a low-to-the-ground sports car, the sensation of speed is greater. Here, you're only inches above the sand, and the trick is to go as far up the shore as possible without getting stranded. To people on the beach it looks like you're mindlessly scraping along the sand, but actually you're unscathed as you orient the shape of your body for maximum efficiency. A mask and snorkel make it much easier. As with all *worthwhile* and important endeavors, it takes years of practice and dedication. On your back, front, head first, feet first—it's important to master them all. You really feel the power of the ocean this way. Obviously, you can't do this when the ocean's flat, and you'd be crazy to do it when the ocean's raging. Only during those in-between times.

⊙ 'Ehukai Beach Park

Few locals refer to this beach by this name, but that's what's on the sign out front. During summer months the ocean transports mountains of sand here, making the beach wide and thick with good swimming.

But it's the winter when this spot occupies its special place in the world of surfing. Because 'Ehukai is the home of the most famous surf site in all Hawai'i—the **Banzai Pipeline**. Classic tube-shaped waves roll ashore from the surf break to the left of the beach park, and experienced surfers and boogie boarders ride them with undisguised glee. If you're looking for a great surfing photo and the area is getting a west/northwest swell, Pipeline is the place to be. Just sit on the beach and watch *da buggahs shred 'em*.

Between Sunset Beach Park and Waimea Bay on Hwy 83 across the street from Sunset Beach Elementary School. (See map on page 82.)

❖ Pupukea Beach Park

This park is divided into two main areas: Shark's Cove and Three Tables.

❖ Shark's Cove

A REAL GEM

First of all, it ain't overly sharky. It was so named by divers years ago because it sounded more exciting than "the area to the right of the tide-pool at Pupukea." This tiny cove offers fantastic snorkeling and SCUBA much of the time during the summer (May–September) months. Yeah, it's popular and sometimes crowded with people. But it's also crowded with fish since this area is a preserve. You may find gobs of fish and the occasional turtle, hard-to-find octopus and even bait balls at times. Entry can be awkward over the slippery rocks. Most people enter from the left side, so if you want some wiggle room, consider entering from the right side of the cove. Snorkelers should stay inside the cove.

During calm days (usually from May to October) Shark's Cove can offer insanely good snorkeling opportunities.

SCUBA divers will love the shallow but interesting diving inside the cove. It's very relaxing since you don't need to kick far too see good stuff. Just slowly meander around the clear water, looking under rock shelves. Good for underwater photos. The more adventurous will wander out of the cove, staying to the right where walls, small caves and chasms await. Even inside the cove, experienced divers will enjoy the relief of big ol' boulders, overhangs and sandy patches. And since it's so shallow (under 30 feet), even heavy breathers will have staying power. Consider getting 63s instead of 80s to make it easier. One caveat: The cove is not at all tolerant of swells. Even a 2-foot swell, if aimed straight into the cove, can stir up the shallow water and make conditions annoyingly cloudy and surgy.

During high tide the tide-pool to the left gets deep enough to become a giant swimming pool when seas are calm. Visitors mistakenly think *this* is where they're supposed to snorkel. Granted, it looks interesting from the shore. But there are relatively few fish in there. Stick with the cove unless you hate the thought of venturing into deeper water. Big surf makes this tide-pool area dangerous and, of course, ruins the cove itself for swimming.

The rock defining the left side of the cove is often used as a place to jump into the water. Remember to look before you leap.

Across from an old gas station next to Puula Road. Snorkel gear can be rented across the street near Foodland. See map on page 82.

❖ **Three Tables**

A REAL GEM

Good snorkeling when calm around the little table islands (there are more than three at low tide). It can be a little surgy, and you'll want to avoid this place when the surf's up. SCUBA intros take place here. It's shallow (35 feet max) but has interesting underwater terrain with lots of overhangs, crevices and boulders off to the left, though divers are still better off over at Shark's Cove. Overall, a nice sandy beach with no facilities or lifeguard. Unmarked, it's where tiny Kapuhi Street meets Kamehameha Hwy (83) just north of Waimea Bay.

⊕ Waimea Bay Beach Park

A REAL GEM

Say the words "Waimea Bay" to any surfer, and his eyes will light up. This is the most famous *big wave* surf site in the world. In the winter, waves 20–40 feet high are not uncommon. Visitors and locals alike delight in coming here during these swells, lining the shoreline and road, and watching the best surfers in the world take their chances sliding down these four-story walls of water. A collapsing wave can snap boards, snap people, or hold 'em underwater for minutes at a time. If you're on O'ahu in the winter and the surf is giant, *this* is where you want to go. (Other surf sites close out with big surf—see box on page 214.) Needless to say, you don't want to get anywhere near the water during big winter surf. You'll die…period…no kidding.

What a shock to come here in the summer and find placid, lake-like water. The area around the southern end (left side) of the bay offers utterly magnificent snorkeling when calm. The entire area leading to the off-shore islets is studded with fish, interesting terrain and turtles. In fact, turtles are plentiful from here all the way to Turtle Beach, but the water gets cloudy after you leave the bay— from Uppers to Chun's Reef—due to intruding basal springs. Stay in Waimea Bay and around the islands for the best snorkeling during calm seas.

This lovely part of Pupukea Beach Park, called Three Tables, is named after the offshore reefs.

Waimea Bay in the summer when the swimming is peaceful.

The giant rock near the left end of the beach is a popular cliff-diving spot. People often climb up from the shore-facing side and leap off the back/right end. It's a pretty far drop, and you're on your own in evaluating it. Jumpers have to walk past the NO JUMPING sign to get to the top.

Waimea Bay Beach Park has full facilities. It's 5 miles north of Hale'iwa or 36 miles from Kane'ohe on Hwy 83.

❖ Chun's Reef

Most drive right by this park without noticing it. This is a decent place for beginner surfers when surf is light, because the ideally shaped reef creates waves in nearly any size swell. Or park there and walk to the right along the sand to rarely visited **Kawailoa Beach**, AKA **Leftovers**. Although there are houses on it, you'll almost never see many visitors here. Chun's Reef Park is near the 61-500 address across from Ashley Road between Waimea Beach Park and Hale'iwa.

❖ Turtle Beach/Laniakea Beach

This beach is famous. Not among people, but apparently in the turtle community. **A REAL GEM** Because the buggers sometimes congregate here in impressive numbers and seem so tolerant of people that we've seen swimmers get bored and swim away, only to have the turtle swim after them. This is the only place we've ever seen in Hawai'i where the turtles do this. (We suspect that some nearby resident might be feeding them to get this result.) Naturally, the turtles aren't *always* here (turtles *hate* to get into a predictable rut), but they're here *most* of the time. And when they are, it's great. Water visibility here is often poor. On Hwy 83 between Waimea Bay and Hale'iwa, at the south (toward Hale'iwa) end of a loop road called Pohaku Loa Way. Residents request that you do not drive on their quiet street but instead park on the mauka side of the highway. Tour buses stop here often.

Although the beach keeps going south, the swimming is not very good due to currents and the beachrock that lines much of the nearshore waters. Go for the turtles, not for the swimming. South of here is **Papa'iloa Beach**.

By the way, Turtle Beach is a modern name. It sure beats the ancient Hawaiian name for this beach, which was Kukae-'ohiki meaning *excrement of the ghost crabs*. (Just doesn't have the same ring to it, does it?)

◯ Hale'iwa Beach Park

Nice big lawn and usually a calm, protected shoreline, but the proximity to the river and harbor creates less than pristine water. It's popular with the local community. On Kamehameha Highway (83) in the heart of Hale'iwa.

❖ Mokule'ia Beach Park/Kealia Beach

Across from Dillingham Airfield near the northwestern tip of the island, this is a

Waimea Bay in the winter, when the swimming is a tad more challenging.

great place for kite surfing (or watching it). Near-constant winds and a sandy shoreline create excellent conditions. Mokule'ia stretches for miles in both directions.

Just past (west of) the beach park you'll find a series of usually deserted beaches. Even when other North Shore beaches are packed, you may be shocked to find these beaches completely empty. Sure, it tends to be windy here, and the swimming is dicey in the winter due to longshore currents, perhaps a bit better in calmer seas. But if the idea of an empty, sandy beach is appealing, you have a good shot here, and access is a snap. These are O'ahu's forgotten beaches, and it's ironic since you can drive right up to them. Some of the stretches have sandy nearshore waters;

others have waters lined with sandstone beachrock. Biggest downside here is that litter from local weekend use seems to occur more often than at most beaches.

Camping is allowed with free county permit.

❖ Hidden Beach

A REAL GEM

How fitting that we end the BEACHES chapter with this beach. Few people on the island even know about it. It's past the end of the pavement on Farrington Highway (930) on the North Shore, about 1¼ miles into the dirt road, 16 telephone poles past the metal gate you went around, at a road that *might* me marked with a sign saying C-1. You may even have this small, sandy cove to yourself. Snorkeling is possible when the ocean's not too pounding. Otherwise, just enjoy the remoteness, our reason for giving it a GEM.

Although locals drive their 4WDs to it on weekends and afternoons, Hidden Beach is often deserted during weekday mornings.

In a sudden burst of clarity, the boogie boarder realized that the guy at the rental counter was only kidding when he suggested the Banzai Pipeline would be the perfect place to ride his first wave.

If you want more from your Hawaiian vacation than a suntan, O'ahu offers a multitude of activities that will keep you happy and busy. Among the more popular activities are glider rides, ocean tours, golfing, hiking, SCUBA diving and kayaking.

We've listed the activities here in alphabetical order. Beware of false claims on brochures. We've seen many fake scenes in brochure racks. Computers have allowed photo manipulation to create realities that don't exist (which, by the way, we don't do).

Activities can be booked directly with the companies themselves. Ask them if they have any coupons floating around in the free publications, or if there is a discount for booking direct. You can also book through **activity brokers** and **booths**, which are numerous and usually have signs such as FREE MAPS or ISLAND INFORMATION. Allow me to translate: The word FREE usually means I WANT TO SELL YOU SOMETHING.

What we're about to tell you has gotten our other books pulled from some shops and badmouthed in some circles, but the truth's the truth. The objective at activity booths, as is the case with many concierges, is to sell you activities for a commission. *Occasionally,* you can get better deals through activity booths or your concierge, but not often, because 25–35 percent of what you're paying is their commission (which they call a "deposit") for making the phone call. That's why calling direct can sometimes save money. Companies are so happy they don't have to give away ¼ to ⅓ of their fee to activity booths, they'll sometimes give you a discount.

Here's an example: A friend of ours was coming to the island, and before he even arrived, the concierge from his hotel called him *on the mainland* to ask if there was anything they could do before his arrival to make things better. Specifically, "Are there any activities you'll want to do, such as SCUBA or helicopters we can book before you get here? The good ones tend to fill up early." My friend was impressed at their thoughtfulness, but declined, saying he knew the person who wrote this guidebook and would use that. The concierge proceeded to badmouth the book and strongly suggested he use the concierge's advice.

Telling our friend Peter what had *really* happened was like telling a kid that there's no Santa Claus. "Peter, they weren't calling you as a *courtesy* before your trip. They were salespeople, pushing activities on you and directing you *not* to the best companies, but to the ones who give them the *highest commission*. They were hoping to collect 35% or more from everything you did on the island." By the way, our explanation is also why the concierge didn't like our books. They'd rather be perceived as helpful than as salespeople. The reality is they're a bit of both.

Many of the activity booths strewn about the island are actually forums for selling timeshares. We are not taking a shot at timeshares. It's just that you need to know the real purpose of some of these booths. They can be very aggressive. (To use a wilderness analogy—they are the hunters; you are the hunted. Don't let them see the fear in your eyes.)

Selling activities is a *big* business on O'ahu, and it's important to know *why* they're pitching a certain company. If an activity booth or desk steers you to XYZ snorkel cruise and assures you that it's the best, that's fine, but consider the source. That's usually the company that the booth gets the *biggest commission*

from. We frequently check up on these booths. Some are reputable and honest, and some are outrageous liars. Few activity sellers have ever done any of the activities unless they got it *free* and the company *knew* who they were. On the other hand, we *pay* for everything we do and review activities *anonymously*. We have no stake in *any* company we recommend, and we receive *no* commission. We just want to steer you in the best direction we can. If you know who you want to go with (because you read our reviews and decided for yourself), call them direct first.

A warning: Many of the companies listed have a 24-hour (or more) cancellation policy. Even if the weather causes you (not them) to cancel the morning of your activity, *you will be charged.* Some credit card companies will back you in a dispute if the 24-hour policy is posted, some won't. Fair? Maybe not. But that's the way it is.

Consider booking on the Internet before you come. Good companies can fill up in advance, and the Web can pave the way for your activities. Our site at **www.hawaiirevealed.com** has links to *every* company listed here that has a site, even the ones we recommend *against*.

If you've read many travel books, you're familiar with the grumpy and pretentious travel writer, the kind who's impressed by very little because he's so much more advanced than peons like you and me. Well, we pride ourselves in not being like that. We're all here to have fun! But having written our neighbor island books before *O'ahu Revealed*, we've noticed that, relative to the outer islands, there's a complacency that permeates many of the Waikiki activity providers. A constant influx of potential customers has bred a less-than-hungry attitude. That doesn't mean you won't get good service—it's just that you might need to look harder for it.

These are those four-wheeled things that look like Tonka Toys on steroids with knobby tires. They're pretty fun to ride, though at press time there was only one company giving tours on these.

Kualoa Ranch (237–7321) on the windward side north of Kane'ohe has rides on their ranch. Though the ranch is pretty, they use relatively small 400cc bikes and take up to 16 riders per group, keeping them in single file. It's $69 for a one-hour tour, $99 for 2 hours. You must be at least 16 years old.

BOAT TOURS

See OCEAN TOURS on page 200.

Your choices are surprisingly limited if you want a bike tour of O'ahu. We could only find one company, **Bike Hawai'i** (734–4214). But they do a pretty good job. They have a tour of Kualoa Ranch (a gorgeous, private valley on the windward side) for $119 that includes lunch and pickup at your hotel. You'll see more of the valley than most other tours without the repetitive drone of a bus driver/tour guide. They have decent bikes with good components, and the guides show you how to ride them properly. If you're looking for a hardcore ride, look elsewhere. This tour is strenuous, but you make lots of stops for natural and cultural interpretation. Your guide can take you on more challenging trails if you ask. They also have a downhill trip down Tantalus Drive that includes a hike to a waterfall for $105. Overall, a good outfit.

Boogie Boarding

Boogie boarding (riders are derisively referred to as *spongers* by surfers) is

Catching a wave isn't the biggest challenge. The hardest part is holding onto the board and your pants at the same time.

Maleakahana State Rec. Area

Kaiaka Bay Beach Park

Kokololio Beach Park
Hau'ula Beach Park

Mokule'ia Beach Park

Ahupua'a O Kahana State Park

Swanzy Beach Park *(weekends only)*

Kualoa Beach Park

Kea'au Beach Park

Ho'omaluhia Botanical Gardens

Kea'iwa Heiau
State Rec. Area

Lualualei Beach Park
(summers only)

Bellows Field Beach Park
(weekends only)

Nanakuli Beach Park

Waimanalo Bay Beach Park
Waimanalo Beach Park

Sand Island State Rec. Area

where you ride a wave on what is essentially a sawed-off surfboard. It can be a real blast. You need short, stubby fins to catch bigger waves (which break in deeper water), but you can snare small waves by simply standing in shallow water and lurching forward as the wave is breaking. If you've never done it before, stay away from big waves; they can drill you. Smooth-bottom boards work best. If you're not going to boogie board with boogie fins (which some consider difficult to learn), then you should boogie board with water shoes or some other kind of water footwear. This allows you to scramble around in the water without fear of tearing up your feet on a rock or sea urchin. Shirts or rashguards are very important, especially for men. (Women already have this problem covered.) Sand and the board itself can rub you so raw your *da kines* will glow in the dark.

Boards can be rented just about anywhere for $10–$18 per day. See the BEACHES section for descriptions of specific beaches. Popular boogie boarding spots for visitors include the **Kapahulu Groin** in Waikiki and **Ala Moana Beach Park**. Those with experience should check out **Makapu'u Beach** and sometimes **Sandy Beach**. Many of the **Wai'anae** beaches offer great boogie boarding when the

ocean's cooperating. **Kailua Beach Park** on the windward side is good, and they rent boards there from **Hawaiian Watersports** (262–5483) and **Kailua Sailboards & Kayaks** (262–2555).

CAMPING

The ultimate in low-price lodging is offered by Mother Nature herself. O'ahu is a great place to camp with 16 different areas—four state camping areas and 12 county campsites. See map above.

County sites require a *free* county permit from the **Division of Parks & Recreation, Permit Section**, 650 South King St., Honolulu (768–2267). You can also get permits online at camping.honolulu.gov.

For state sites the rules are more complicated and the system more rigid. (We fell asleep halfway through the process description.) Apply in person at the **Division of State Parks** (587–0300), 1151 Punchbowl St., Room 310, Honolulu, or use the link from our website to apply online. You cannot apply more than 30 days in advance. It's $18 per night per campsite.

At all campsites you can only camp Friday through Tuesday (unless otherwise noted on map).

The cheapest place to buy your camping gear and supplies is the **Walmart/ Sam's Club Superblock** just outside of Waikiki on Keeaumoku and Makaloa. There's also a **Sports Authority** at the corner of Auahi and Ward.

One of the more interesting camping opportunities is the **cabins at Malaekahana** near the northern tip of the island in La'ie. These were private beach "cabins" run by a church as a substance abuse location until the mid '90s. The concessionaire now is called **Friends of Malaekahana** (293–1736). These are highly sought after, so call as far in advance as possible. Rates range from $50–$150 per night (more for big groups), depending on the cabin, yurt or grass shack you choose. Ask for a near the beach. At press time they were wrangling with the state for a lease and didn't appear to be putting much if any money into the dwellings, so expect to rough it.

Deep sea fishing is synonymous with Hawai'i. Reeling in a massive marlin, tuna or tough-fighting ono is a dream for many fishermen. When there's a strike, the adrenaline level of everyone on board shoots through the roof. Most talked about are the marlin (very hard fighters known for multiple runs). These goliaths can tip the scales at over 1,000 pounds. Also in abundance are ono, also called wahoo (one of the fastest fish in the ocean and indescribably delicious), mahimahi (vigorous fighters—excellent on light tackle), ahi (tasty yellowfin tuna) and billfish.

Most boats troll nonstop since the lure darting out of the water simulates a panicky bait fish—the favored meal for large game fish. On some boats, each person is assigned a certain reel. Experienced anglers usually vie for the corner poles with the assumption that strikes coming from the sides are more likely to hit corners first.

You should know in advance that in Hawai'i, the fish belongs to the boat. What happens to the fish is entirely up to the captain, and he usually keeps it. You could catch a 1,000-pound marlin and be told that you can't have as much as a steak from it. If this bothers you, you're out of luck. If the ono or other small fish are striking a lot and there is a glut of them, or if your fish is under 100 pounds, you might be allowed to keep part of it. You *may* be able to make arrangements in advance to the contrary.

You'll never please the captain if you bring bananas on a boat. They are forbidden by tradition on fishing boats. The superstition dates back to when cargo was unloaded by hand. Bananas often carried deadly spiders, so workers had good reason to consider them unlucky.

Most charters leave Kewalo Basin near Waikiki with some departing from Wai'anae and Hale'iwa on the North Shore in the summer. Most have 4-, 6- and 8-hour charters. Mornings offer best conditions. Prices are about $155–$200 per person for a shared charter. 8-hour private charters go for $900–$1,000 or more for the big boats. Usually, the bigger the boat, the higher the price since most are licensed to take only 6 passengers. Individual boat rates can change often depending on the season, fishing conditions and whims of the owners. Consequently, we'll forgo listing some of the individual boat rates since this information is so perishable and instead list a few companies that we recommend. Call them directly to get current rates. If you have 4 or more people, make it private so you can exercise more control.

If you're easy-queasy, take an anti-sea-sickness medication. There are people who never get sick regardless of conditions, and those who turn green just watching *A Perfect Storm* on DVD. Nothing can ruin an ocean outing quicker than being hunched over the stern feeding the fish. Scopolamine patches prescribed by doctors can have side effects including (occasionally) blurred vision that can last a week. Dramamine II or Bonine taken the night before and the morning of a trip also seem to work well for many, though some drowsiness may occur. Ginger is a mild preventative. Try powdered ginger, ginger pills or even *real* ginger ale—can't hurt, right?

Tipping: 10–15% split between the captain and deck hand is customary if you are pleased with their performance. If the captain is a jerk and the deck hand throws up on you, you're not obligated to give 'em diddly.

Because boat slips are so hard to get near Waikiki (Kewalo Basin), companies share boats or swap customers constantly. (They like you to charter the whole boat.) **Maggie Joe** (591–8888) has 4 nice boats. Also consider **Wild Bunch** (596–4709), **Magic Sportfishing** (596–2998) and **Kuu Huapala** (596–0918).

Sashimi Fun Fishing (955–3474) has several boats at Kewalo Basin. They do some exclusive charters and some shared. They use a *less-than-pristine* 65-foot Delta, and they do shark hunts at night. Nearby **Blue Nun Sportfishing** (596–2443) has a rusty boat and a salty crew. Even when nothing's biting, they'll keep going, and going, and going...

Out of Ko Olina there's **Boom Boom** (306–4162) and their 50-foot Sportfisher.

In Hale'iwa call **Chupu Charters** (637–3474) with a 42-foot Uniflite. **Go Fishing Hawai'i** (637–9737) uses a tiny "banana boat," but it's cheaper if you've only got 4 people.

GLIDERS

Gliders, sailplanes, skysurfing—whatever you call it, these engine-less aircraft offer a fun way to see the western tip of the island. You get towed up by airplane,

Soaring in a glider is fun, but it's not as quiet as most people think.

then during typical trade winds, ridge lift from the nearby mountains provides the buoyancy necessary to keep you aloft. Most people assume that glider rides are nearly silent. Sorry to burst your bubble, but most of these are 30-year-old gliders, and the wind noise can be so loud that it might be hard to hear some of the things your pilot is saying to you. (Newer, quiet 3-passenger gliders are obscenely expensive, and companies are hesitant to invest in them.) One thing we strongly suggest is that you spend the extra $20 to sit in front and take control if you want. (Don't worry, the pilot can control it from the back seat, too.) Another consideration is size. Although these are 3-person crafts, the back bench is crowded with two people unless you're *real* small. If there are two of you, consider tacking on another $10–$16 (per person) and taking separate rides.

Three companies are out at Dillingham Airfield on the North Shore. **Original Glider Rides** (637–0207) and **Hana Hou** (222–4235) provide similar rides for $98–$150 per person, plus the extras listed above, and you're in the air for about 15–20 minutes. (If these prices seem especially fluid, it's because both companies *seem* to charge different prices depending on how they feel. Frankly, we're not sure *what* you'll pay.) They want you there long before your flight (assuming you'll be late). Ask them what time you'll *actually be flying*. It's not an aerobatic ride (that's extra, too), but it's lots of fun and it's gentle. Generally, the earlier in the day you go, the smoother the air. By the way, neither company requires a credit card for a reservation.

The third company at Dillingham is **Acroflight International** (221–4480). They use a motorglider. It's no exaggeration to say that they literally scared us out of the sky, on multiple levels, and we absolutely, positively wouldn't recommend them for any reason. We'd love to say more, but let's leave it at that.

GOLFING

With its balmy trade winds, sunny skies and rich soil, O'ahu is an absolutely ideal place to build a golf course. And we're not the only ones who think so. More than *three dozen* courses carpet this tropical island. No matter what kind of golfing animal you are, O'ahu surely has a course that'll fulfill your dreams.

The one area where O'ahu courses come up short compared to their neighbor island brethren is with oceanside courses. There are only four: one's a military course, one's a private club, the third—Turtle Bay—inexplicably lets a thick grove of trees block your view most of the time. Only at a crusty 9-hole municipal course—Kahuku—does the promise of playing near the ocean come true. But don't fret. With *so* many courses on such a beautiful island, golfing on O'ahu will keep you smiling.

It's impossible to review all the courses—hey, we've only got so much space here. So below are some of the more notable courses.

Royal Hawaiian (262–2139)

Formerly called Luana Hills. In a state filled with pretty golf courses, this one stands apart as one of the loveliest. Simply put, it's achingly beautiful. Set in the center of Maunawili Valley behind Olomana Peak near Kailua, the back *ten* (yes, they have a real 19th hole, and it ain't a bar) in particular are draped in such a verdant setting that its nickname of Jurassic Park seems totally appropriate. Even the golf paths are so mouth-wateringly lush, you expect dinosaurs to come strolling by.

But this is also a hard course. Make that humiliatingly hard. There isn't a flat piece of ground on any of the narrow fairways. It's the perfect course to accidentally lose your scorecard on the first hole so you can enjoy the course for the purity of the play and the serenity of the scenery. Then you can exercise selective memory to convince yourself that you did well. The only evidence to the contrary will be a much lighter supply of balls at the end. (Bring *plenty*.)

One downside is that it does rain more here than on leeward courses, though not as much as other course-keepers might lead you to believe. Having lived in Kailua, we can tell you that its reputation among leeward residents as being too rainy is way overstated.

Bring your laser-guided ball for number 3. It requires the precision of a smart bomb to drive it onto the isolated green. Eleven is their signature hole—a drive across water onto an island green fronted by fountains. They close it several days a week since the island green gets

unusually soft. If you drive up to sneak a peek during its closure, smack a ball onto the green if you want. They don't mind. It's so striking that they often use it for weddings. (You'll be penalized a stroke if you hit the bride.)

Number 13 is a cruel joke. Try to launch it into the gully, then drop on the other side and take your punishment like a grown-up.

You'll put a lot of miles on your cart at this flawlessly maintained course, and you'll love every minute of it. The course is relatively short but calls for extreme accuracy. The front nine are the most open and forgiving. It's the back ten where egos are smashed and memories are made. Rates are $125, including cart. See map on page 68. The turn onto Auloa Road from Hwy 61 is easy to miss. Then immediate left onto Luana Hills Rd.

Turtle Bay (293–8574)

Way out near the northernmost tip of O'ahu off Hwy 83, two resort courses provide an amazingly uncrowded golf

Golf Course	Par	Yards	Rating	Fees
Royal Hawaiian	72	6595	70.9	$125*
Turtle Bay/Palmer	72	7088	74.4	$195*
Turtle Bay/Fazio	72	6535	71.2	$160*
Pali Golf Course	72	6524	70.4	$49
Pearl Country Club	72	6232	72.2	$130*
Kahuku Municipal	70	5398	65.2	$13.50
Coral Creek	72	6347	72.2	$140*
Ko Olina	72	6815	73.3	$189*
Royal Kunia	72	6507	73.5	$150*
Ala Wai Municipal	70	5861	66.8	$49
Ko'olau Golf Club	72	6406	71.7	$145*

* indicates carts are included and mandatory.
Yards and ratings are from the blue tees.

experience. During the week, tee times before noon often result in a nearly private golf game. There's often no one behind or in front of you. (Weekends are busy, and afternoons, especially Fridays, also bring locals who cut work early.) The **Palmer Course** (also called The Links at Kuilima—it was designed by Arnold Palmer) is the better of the two. It's well marked, pretty wide open and not a wickedly challenging links-style course. Check out the giant ficus trees before the 9th green. This is not an overly sandy course, but at 17 it's as if they needed to use up their supply. It's bunker city.

The other course, called the **Fazio Course** (designed by George Fazio), gets less respect—and seemingly less maintenance. Play this one only after you've played Palmer. It's extremely open and pretty easy on the ego. At 6 and 7 you *finally* get to see the ocean. In fact, both courses suffer the same shortcoming. With so much splendid oceanfront real estate to work with, they make surprisingly little use of it. Throughout the bulk of your play, you're totally detached from, and unaware of, the glorious Pacific Ocean so near and yet so far.

Turtle Bay ain't cheap, but it's a real treat to play courses of this caliber and maybe feel like you've rented the fairways for yourself. It won't happen every weekday, but it's more the norm than the exception.

Palmer is $175 for off-property players, $140 for Turtle Bay guests. Fazio is $115 and $100. This includes cart (walking is allowed) and some range balls.

Pali Golf Course (266–7612)

A municipal course that often has fairly mangy fairways but nice views. Lots of uneven lies here, and it's not real sandy, but it's a fun course, nonetheless. Par threes tend to have pretty big dips before the green. Hole 9 is one of the most beautiful municipal holes you'll ever see—right toward a pali pinnacle with H-3 terraced on the slopes. Otherwise, it's pretty overpriced for what you get. $49. No driving range. Off Hwy 83 near Hwy 61 in Kailua. See map on page 68.

Ko'olau Golf Club (263–4653)

This course is as difficult as it is beautiful. Lined with a continual backdrop of the towering Ko'olau mountains, this course will challenge your skills and overload your visual cortex. With a tournament rating of 153, four par 5 holes and multiple holes that are double carries from blind tees, this course has been humbling golfers of all skill levels since 1992. The pro shop has clubs if you need 'em for $40 or $45 as well as shoes for a few bucks extra. Stop at the 15th and drive up to the lookout point for panoramic views of Kaneohe Bay, the nearby military base and beyond. Spend a few minutes here gathering whatever strength you have left in preparation for the 18th—you'll need it. This mountainous course closes out with a 432 yard, double carry par 4. If you choke, you can tell the rest of your group that you were overwhelmed by the beauty of the views. And if you're feeling overly adventurous, they'll let you play a second round for just cart fees. This is the course to bring your "A Game." Rates are $145; it's $110 after noon. Carts are included and mandatory. From Waikiki, take Pali Hwy (61) through the tunnel, left onto Kamehameha Hwy, left onto Kionaole Road.

Pearl Country Club (487–3802)

Some courses excel at views; this course excels at staying in tip-top shape. Conditions are fantastic. (The fact that your cart has to stay on the path—not even a 90° rule here—helps keep the fairways in awesome condition.) The course is owned by the Honda family—as in Honda automobiles—and they obviously spend a great deal on maintenance. It's been here since 1967, so the trees are mature. Rolling hills and a surprisingly varied layout keep it interesting. Hole 4 is a tough par 4—uphill and into the wind for 411 yards. Swing for your life here. And at hole 5, don't aim for the fairway—aim for those coconut trees to the left to cut your distance.

Although you won't get those classic Hawai'i views, this is the course to play if you want to get pampered by the grounds-keepers. Most of your fellow golfers will be residents since this course isn't on most visitors' radars. Fees are $130. Carts included and mandatory. Near Aiea. From H-1 going west, take exit 13A, stay left onto Hwy 99. Then turn right onto Kaonohi; you'll see their driveway. See map on page 101.

Kahuku Municipal Course (293–5842)

Bad news and good news at this municipal course. The nine fairways are more like one big stressed-out lawn with some greens and a smattering of sand traps. The grass is only as green as the last rain (no sprinkler system). Now the good news: It's *right on the ocean,* and the views of the water are relaxing. Plus it's dirt cheap. $14 per 9 holes and rental clubs for $12. No power carts—pull carts only for $4. It's virtually never crowded during the week. If you can get over the skanky greens that only a groundskeeper's mother could love, it's a cheap way to walk and whack at an oceanside course. In Kahuku on Hwy 83 *waaay* up at the northern tip of the island. See map on page 81. Theft can be a problem here, so don't leave anything valuable in your car.

Coral Creek (441–4653)

An awesome O'ahu course nestled between housing tracts. Some of the roughs are stiff enough to snap your club, but the fairways are pretty wide open and well cared for, and greens tend to be fast and not too flat.

You'll start at either the front or back nine. Don't get greedy on hole 3; lay up or curse yourself afterward when you dump into that gully on the right or roll into an easy-to-miss hole.

At signature hole 10, a 3 par over water with a manmade waterfall behind the green makes for a pretty scene. As with most of the harder holes, it faces into the trade winds, so you'll want to account for that in your club selection.

Fees are $140 ($80 after noon). Carts are included. Walking is not allowed.

Take H-1 West past the airport, exit 5A to Kunia Road, which becomes Fort Weaver Road, then right on Geiger Road, and look for course on your left. See map on page 100.

Ko Olina (676–5300)

Waterfalls and black swans are the hall-marks of this beautiful course (though their symbol is a ladybug). The course is a big draw for lady golfers due to the wide open fairways and placement of the ladies tee boxes, and the pro shop has an enormous ladies selection. Nice touches abound like the GPS in the cart, which also allows you to order lunch so it's waiting for you after the 9th and 18th holes. (Way cool.) But that same GPS system finks on you if you slow down. They want you in and out in 4½ hours, and the marshals aren't shy about it.

The course is extremely well maintained, and they have nice (though pricey) graphite rental clubs.

At hole 12 you'll drive your cart behind a waterfall. (Hold out your club, and you can actually rinse it off.) It's a 3 par overlooking a pond with three waterfalls—very beautiful. At 18 there's a lake—lay up before it, then shoot to the back of the green; otherwise, you'll be putting uphill.

O'ahu may have fewer oceanfront courses than the neighbor islands, but the beauty of the tropics is never far away.

In all, this is an easy course to recommend. Fees are $189. Carts are included and mandatory. Ko Olina guests pay $169. Take H-1 West past the airport. When it becomes Hwy 93, take Alinui Drive into Ko Olina.

Royal Kunia (688–9222)

If the hallmark of Ko Olina is swans and waterfalls, this course can be described as the land of sweeping vistas and limitless bunkers. The developer must have owned an atoll somewhere in the South Pacific because he used enough sand to create his own island. We're talking 101 bunkers. And that's just the bunkers *above* the ground. This area used to be controlled by the military, and beneath your feet are numerous old naval *ammo* bunkers.

Opened in April 2003, the course might seem more mature. That's because it was built almost 10 years earlier, but they weren't allowed to open because they didn't pay a county demand of $25 million in the form of an "impact fee." (When the developer went bankrupt and then their *lender* went bankrupt, the county *graciously* shaved $10 million off their shakedown demand.) So ironically, for a decade the only people who could play this course were the very politicians who wouldn't let it open.

Overall, it's an awesome course with some glaring shortcomings. Let's get the downside out of the way. The clubhouse is very unimpressive. (But at least their rental clubs are nice.) And the driving range is far enough away that you can't walk to it. But they won't let you take a cart. So they'll drive you to the range, but there's no way to tell them when you want to come back. You'll have to wait until they bring someone else. And oddly, you buy your tokens back at the clubhouse, so if you hit all your balls, you'll either putt or sit and twiddle your thumbs until they return.

Once on the course, the views are particularly expansive. Don't be fooled by your eyes at hole 16. Sure, you can see the green. But you can't see a water hazard on the right side. Don't slice or you'll either get wet, or you'll be playing at the beach bunker next to it.

At the 18th, your long journey to the flag leads to a green backed by a waterfall pretty enough to stop and picnic at. What a way to end the game.

Fees are $150. It's $100 after 1 p.m. Carts are included and mandatory.

Take H-1 east past the airport, exit 5B to go right onto Kunia Road then right on Anonui. The course is on the right. See map on page 100.

Ala Wai Municipal Course
(733–7387)

We mention this 18-hole course because it's right across the Ala Wai Canal from Waikiki, and as a result it's the busiest course in the state, *by far*. They get an average of 400–500 players *a day*. It's also one of the least impressive courses. It's like one big lawn with its wide fairways, flat ground and lack of personality. Unless you're set on playing as close to Waikiki as possible, consider playing elsewhere. Rates are $49; carts are $20 extra.

First, I need to get something out of the way. Flying a powered hang glider (known as a trike) is different than any other type of aircraft. When I was growing up, I used to have a recurring dream that I could flap my arms and fly like a bird. My father flew little Cessnas, which, though fun, felt more to me like a car in the air than flying like a bird. I had forgotten my flying dreams until I reviewed a company on Kaua'i that gave lessons in this odd little craft. As soon as my instructor and I took off, I realized that a person *really could* fly like a bird. *This* was what the flying bug felt like! I was so smitten with the craft that I eventually hired the instructor on Kaua'i to teach me, and now I fly trikes myself. So although I have no personal interest in any company teaching trikes in Hawai'i, my perspective

isn't as remote as it is for most activities. After all, it's not possible to anonymously review some companies, like Paradise Air, because I know the pilots. (We're all members of the small triking community.)

With that explanation, powered hang gliding is an activity I recommend. Don't confuse this with hang gliding. This craft has an engine, it's bigger and more stable, and some even have a powered parachute attached to the craft...just in case (a safety feature boasted by only a small number of pricey traditional airplanes). Trikes take off and land on regular runways, and the ease and grace of the craft are glorious. (Rent the movie *Fly Away Home* if you want to see what they're like.) It's as close to flying like a bird as any form of flight I know. Trikes are what I have come to love so much and, in my opinion, are incredibly safe in properly trained hands. (I'm not a daredevil and wouldn't fly them myself if I felt unsafe in them, though any time you're in the air you're potentially at risk, even on the airlines.) I grin like a fool every time I fly and have never reviewed an activity that generates more enthusiastic responses from other participants. It seems that whenever I see people coming off a trike, its passengers are frothing at the mouth with excitement, proclaiming that it's the best thing they've ever done on vacation. (Unless they're on their honeymoon, of course; then it's the *second* best thing.)

The local company is **Paradise Air** (497–6033) out of Dillingham Airfield on the North Shore. The pilots, Denise and Tom Sanders, are very methodical in their approach to giving lessons in their high-end aircraft and maximizing your time in the air. With two trikes operating, couples can fly at the same time. They charge $165 per half-hour, $265 per hour. They have cameras mounted on the aircraft (still and video) to get shots of you that no one back home will believe,

Rock your world by flying along the coast in a powered hang glider.

and they can burn DVDs of your flight on the spot. (Pretty cool.) They primarily fly mornings when conditions are best and it's best to book in advance.

HELICOPTERS

We've been unabashedly enthusiastic in our recommendation of helicopter tours of Kaua'i and the Big Island and lukewarm about them on Maui. Consider us lukewarm about these tours on O'ahu as well. Compared to the other Hawaiian islands, O'ahu helicopter tours are a bit less compelling. Kaua'i, the Big Island and even Maui all have more nooks and crannies to explore than O'ahu due to the physical structure of the mountain ranges here. Although the Ko'olaus are beautifully sculpted and corrugated, they don't lend themselves to aerial exploration as well—they just don't *feel* as mysterious from the air—at least the way companies do tours here. They're incredibly beautiful, but a drive along H-3 from Kailua to Honolulu can give you a view that rivals some of what you'll get from a helicopter. For the money, it's hard to recommend a helicopter flight on O'ahu.

That said, if you want one anyway, the company we prefer is **Paradise Helicopter** (293–2570). They use 4-seater Hughes 500s and leave from the Turtle Bay Resort on the North Shore. They're *totally* flexible and will pretty much fly where the passengers want. Call in advance since they need 4 people to book the 60-minute flight (which is $235) or the 45-minute doors-off adventure (which is $214). Unlike others, they'll visit the Wai'anae Coast. You can also charter it for $1,112 an hour, which can be split four ways. (They charge $57 extra to take the doors off.)

Other companies, which leave from Honolulu Airport, include **Makani Kai** (834–5813). They use 6-passenger A-Stars for their 60-minute tours for around $300, plus some shorter flights. An example of a great trip on paper and yet horrible execution. Their manager wrote to us because he disagreed with our review. He also questioned whether I had ever flown with them because they couldn't find my name in their records. (Inside scoop to

If you opt for a helicopter flight, get one that showcases more than just Waikiki. The Ko'olau Mountain range is the star of any aerial tour.

readers—I rarely use my real name when reviewing because I don't want to be treated different.) Anyway, we are constantly rereviewing. For this edition things went downhill as soon as the tour started. The safety video says you have a mic to talk to the pilot, but onboard, we were told that they had been "banned over a decade ago because they could be used as a weapon." (Even the FAA laughed when we fact-checked *that* one.) And although the pilot's narration was pretty accurate, it was so hideously boring that he might as well have been reading from a map. This was the first tour in all the years I have been doing this that I saw a passenger *doze off* multiple times.

Blue Hawaiian (831–8800) has *very* nice Eco-Star birds and are preferable over Makani Kai.

Airplane Tours

If helicopters aren't your thing, a surprisingly good air tour is **Island Seaplane** (836–6273). They have a float plane—a de Havilland Beaver, which holds 6 passengers. Although some of the facts are a bit shaky, the pilot does a pretty good job on the narration. They try to fly their route so that both sides get good views, but overall, the left side is the best due to the counter-clockwise direction of the tour. They have a 30-minute flight for $149 and a pretty good 60-minute flight for $269. (We just wish they'd do Wai'anae, too, since central O'ahu is uninteresting.) Co-pilot seat available upon request. Earlier flights are usually smoother. Most of the time the pilot stays at about 1,500 feet.

You can also take an open cockpit flight in a **Stearman Biplane** (637–4461) at Dillingham Airport on the North Shore. One passenger per flight. Stearmans are known as capable aerobatic planes, but these tours are handled pretty conservatively—not much wildness, just a standard 40-minute tour including Pearl Harbor for $265 as well as shorter flights. If you want them to do any aerobatics during the flight, you have to cough up (if you'll pardon the expression) an additional $50 or do the 15-minute aerobatic-only flight for $170.

Because O'ahu has such a large and active population, hikers will find the island *filled* with good hiking trails. This presented a problem for us. Which ones do we include? What we ended up doing was including a few of the more popular trails (Diamond Head and Manoa Falls, for example) along with some lightly used trails, some of them never seen in any book. If you're an ultra-serious hiker who wants more options than our hiking section allows, there are a number of hiking books for O'ahu. Probably the best one is *The Hiker's Guide to O'ahu*.

Hiking Near Honolulu

Diamond Head (2 mi round trip)

Many vacation destinations have that *one* thing that you're practically *required* to do. In New York, you're supposed to visit the Statue of Liberty. In San Francisco, you've gotta see the Golden Gate Bridge. And in Honolulu, you're supposed to climb to the top of that ultra-prominent circular landmark that dominates Waikiki, Diamond Head. You're *supposed* to do this because from up top, the view is *da kine, brah!* (They close before sunset, which is a shame.)

Though you'll read that Diamond Head Crater was created 300,000 years ago, that's no longer accepted as correct. The truth is, we don't know how old da buggah is. Scientists debate whether the last eruption on O'ahu took place 400,000 years ago...or

Hiking some of O'ahu's less-trampled trails, like the Maunawili Trail, can reward you with tropical visions that will stay with you for a lifetime.

From the top of Diamond Head, Waikiki and Honolulu take on a whole new perspective.

5,000 years ago, as some of the radicals suggest. Most think it's been about 100,000 years, but that's a stab in the dark.

There are two great reasons to do this hike early—avoiding heat and assuring yourself a parking space. It's $5 per car. If the parking lot's full, they'll allow five cars at a whack to circle like vultures looking for a space. Otherwise, you'll have to park outside at Kapiolani Community College and walk an additional 1¼ uninteresting miles up the road. Bus riders will also have that additional walk.

The buildings inside the crater—shaped like a fluted bowl—belong to the FAA and until 2001 housed their air traffic controllers for Honolulu Center. (Doesn't it seem odd that the government agency in charge of the sky would choose to put its main office in a hole?)

On the trail you'll gain 560 feet over 1 mile (according to the GPS), and it'll take most people about 1½ hours. That's 30 to 40 minutes to go up, 20 minutes at the top, then the return. On this trail we've seen everyone from Ironman triathletes to people literally using walkers (though they didn't exactly hike it at the same speed, and the walker-users probably didn't go all the way to the top). The trail has sections of unevenness, so wear shoes instead of flipflops. Short marching steps work best along the constant incline. Near the end, it's the 99 steps plus a spiral staircase followed by more steps—or take the wheelchair access—that tucker most people out. (Ignore advice to bring a flashlight—the interior portions are lit.)

Once at the 761-foot summit it's all worth it. What a grand view. Waikiki is such a beautiful place from up here. From Barbers Point almost 20 miles to the west to Koko Crater 9 miles behind you, it's easy to see why the military bought this landmark in 1904—it's the perfect place to watch over all of leeward O'ahu. Look down on the ocean side, and you'll probably see lots of hats piled up below the lookout. We see somebody lose one almost every time we come up here, so hang on to yours.

It's crowded at the top—this wasn't designed to accommodate 1,500 hikers per day; it was designed for a few eagle-eyed lookouts.

To get here, take Kalakaua down to Monsarrat and head up that street for over a mile to the entrance on the right. (Monsarrat changes to Diamond Head Road.)

Top of the World Hiking

The Koʻolau Range is the long mountain that stretches 36 miles, effectively defining the windward side. (See fold-out back map to orient you.) From its meandering summit you'll find some of the best views on the island. Look one way, and most of the windward side stretches before you. Turn around, and the leeward side from Honolulu to Makapuʻu Point is all yours.

The leeward side of this range gently slopes toward the sea, so that's where all the trails to the summit are. (The wind-ward side of the ridge is cliffy.) Erosion has created a repeating pattern of ridges and valleys. What does this mean for the hiker lusting after the views up there? It means you'll be walking up one of the many ridges until you get to the summit.

Weather is the big question mark. More specifically, cloud cover, which would turn your grand, expansive view at the summit into a whiteout. Mornings are usually your best chance for cloud-free conditions, but sometimes it's best in the afternoon. Bottom line: You need to look to the summit before you go and, if it's clear, cross your fingers and hope that it'll stay that way.

Knowing that you don't have the time or desire to hike all the trails to the summit, we've spent considerable effort viewing the windward side from *all* the summit trails. Some, such as the Hawaiʻiloa Ridge Trail, have access issues. Fortunately, one of the best, **Kuliʻouʻou Ridge Trail**, is accessible and offers great views. That's because it's far enough north to get the wicked views of the windward side without being so far

The Kuliʻouʻou Ridge Trail (lower right side) ends at the razorback ridge of the Koʻolau range. The optional Puʻu o Kona slithers up to the left from the end of the trail.

north that your sweeping vistas begin to get clipped by a peak called Konahuanui.

Kuli'ou'ou Ridge Trail (4 mi round trip)

Unlike most ridge trails that service the Ko'olau Range, this one begins at the bottom of a valley. Despite its low beginnings, the trail climbs 1,800 feet to the top in only 2 miles. Most other trails in the Ko'olau Range climb more than 2,000 feet and can be almost twice as long. Because of the summit's lower elevation, you're more likely to see the view at the top of this regularly cloudy vista. If it's a really clear day, you'll be able to see Moloka'i, Lana'i and Maui.

Heading east of Honolulu, H-1 ends and becomes Kalanianaole Highway (72), adding streetlights and pedestrians to the eight lanes of automobiles. A little over 4 miles after this, look for Kuli'ou'ou Street on your left. Follow this street into the valley as it jogs left at a stop sign, then right again at the next intersection. From the highway, it's exactly 1 mile to your final right turn on Kala'au Street. Park your car near the cul de sac at the end of this road. The trailhead is down the access road blocked by a gate. This is a heavily used trailhead, so there are plenty of signs marking the way.

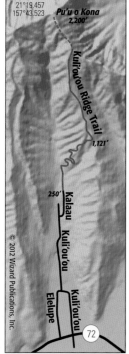

You'll begin on the Kuli'ou'ou Valley Trail. It intersects with the ridge trail after ²/₁₀ of a mile. Turn right.

A dozen or so switchbacks will carry you up 800 feet without getting seriously steep compared to what's ahead. Take your time and save your energy. Once on top of the ridge, you'll have entered the Kuli'ou'ou Forest Reserve. This area might make you forget that you're in the tropics. The ironwood trees and Cook Island pines are so thick that you'll see very few other trees. It reminded us of a Rocky Mountain pine forest. This is a good area to stop and smell the pinesap.

Shortly after reaching the ridge, you'll find a pair of covered picnic tables. Not only is this a great place to take a break, it's also the halfway point. From here, the trail gets steep and unrelenting. Exposed roots make the climb slippery in many places. At times the trail will disappear under the carpet of pines needles. Just keep marching upward, and the trail will show its face again.

When you leave the forest, you'll get your first views from high up on the ridge. Once on top, your view goes from Kailua, Waimanalo Beach and Rabbit Island on the windward side to Koko Crater and Diamond Head on the leeward side. It can be really windy up here, making it chilly after a sweaty hike. If you plan on staying up top for a while, you might want to bring some long sleeves.

The view from here is nice, but it could be better. To the left of the summit is a higher peak called Pu'u o Kona. Only advanced hikers and people with no fear of death should attempt this. Going left from the summit, you would traverse the Ko'olau Ridge Trail along the narrow edge of these mountains. Take your time maneuvering around rocks and climbing up fixed ropes, as it would be difficult to recover from a fall up here. You'll know when you've reached Pu'u o Kona when you get a clear view of the entire windward side from Chinaman's Hat to Rabbit Island. On a clear day, add Moloka'i,

Lana'i and Maui to that view for one of the best vistas the island has to offer.

Manoa Falls Trail (2 mi round trip)

Though this is generally considered the second most popular hike on the island (after Diamond Head), we haven't seen nearly as many people on it as its reputation suggests. It's popular for good reason. The surrounding forest is staggeringly beautiful and it's only a mile (each way), though you gain 800 feet in the process, and it rewards you with a very pretty 160-foot-high waterfall.

Right from the get-go, it's obvious that this is an impossibly lush area. Giant trees with luxuriant clinging vines, elephant-eared ape (pronounced AH-PAY) plants and every shade of green you could want along with a soundtrack of tropical birds create an Eden-like atmosphere. The stream is always nearby, and the verdant growth is ever present. Once at the falls, there's a bench to sit on and listen to the hissing water. All in all, a very rewarding hike for relatively little effort.

To get there, either take McCully out of Waikiki, past H-1 and onto Metcalf then left on University Avenue, or if you're on H-1, take the University Avenue exit (24B) and head mauka (toward the mountains). University Ave. will become O'ahu Ave. Then take the right fork—not the right *turn*—at a confusing 5-way intesection onto Manoa Road and drive until you see a paid parking lot ($5). Bring mosqui-

It's only a mile walk to Manoa Falls—long enough to dissuade casual visitors, but close enough for almost any hiker to visit.

to repellent, and expect some muddiness if it's been raining lately. (Which it probably has—that's why it's so lush here.)

Pali Trail & Likeke Falls (4¹⁄₁₀ mi round trip)

Who'd have thought an abandoned highway filled with the traffic noise of its newer replacement road below could make such a pleasant hike? And better yet, when you ventured off through a world of old graffiti and trash that you'd be rewarded with such a pretty jungly waterfall? From the Nu'uanu Pali Lookout, the Old Pali Road snakes its way to the right. It meanders downhill 600 feet over a span of 1¹⁄₃ miles and, in the process, shows you a side of Kane'ohe and especially Kailua you won't see from the lookout. You could go all the way to the end and turn around and come back. But we prefer to add a more natural slice of paradise to the hike.

To get here, take Kalakaua Avenue west out of Waikiki. Left onto Beretania, right onto Bishop/Pali Highway. Take Pali (61) toward Kailua and look for the NU'UANU PALI LOOKOUT sign toward the top. See maps on pages 50 and 68.

After paying $3 to park (preferable to the old *car break-in roulette* you used to have to play), start the hike by walking past to the right of the lookout down what's left of the old Pali Road. It appears that the old paved road linking the windward side and Honolulu was only one lane. It's hard to imagine road planners, even back in the day, sitting down and saying, *Yeah, one lane should be plenty...* About ½ mile into the trail is an intermittent stream flowing under the old bridge that you're walking on. Look straight down from the curved bridge, and you may see a waterfall beneath you *if* Mother Nature is cooperating. Note how plants such as banyan trees are reclaiming the old road-bed and guard-rails.

About ⁸⁄₁₀ mile into the hike you've lost 450 feet of elevation. You'll come to a point on the road covered with giant boulders, and it's almost level with the Pali Hwy. This is where we like to leave the Pali Trail for something more natural.

Likeke Falls Side Trip

To the left of the bouldery area is a short trail to the elevated Pali Hwy, and this is the trickiest part of the whole hike. You need to hop down under the highway, and the only way is via some rickety wood below you or a short cement drainway to the right. If you can safely navigate down the 5 feet or so, stay to the left. Do your best to ignore the trash and graffiti. Duck under the

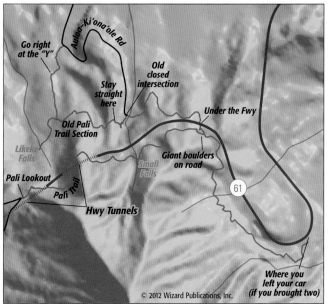

Go right at the "Y"

Aulaa-Ki'ona'ole Rd

Old closed intersection

Stay straight here

Old Pali Trail Section

Under the Fwy

Likeke Falls

Pali Lookout

Pali Trail

Giant boulders on road

Small Falls

61

Hwy Tunnels

Where you left your car (if you brought two)

© 2012 Wizard Publications, Inc.

road and stay to the left as you cross the median and walk under the Honolulu-bound lanes.

You'll notice that once again you're on an abandoned road, and there's only one way to go—down the narrow road remains. Eventually this road will intersect with Auloa–Ki'ona'ole Road. Forget what Mamma said about looking both ways when you cross this street. It's been closed since 1994. So much illegal activity occurred along the hidden bends of this road that the county had to block it off. There's a loop trail you can take starting at this intersection. We'll start you on the trail and bring you back on the road to this same spot. All of this land is government land, not private, according to local TMK maps.

At the intersection on your left is a concrete wall (and a wooden telephone pole inland) that's hiding stone steps leading into the vegetation. This becomes a trail that switchbacks up the ridge. In five minutes, once on top of the ridge, continue straight, and descend and ignore the power pole access trail you will be bisecting. You'll dip in and out of gulches until the trail starts to widen. Soon you'll be walking on an old stone road that's actually a remnant of

the original hand-laid Pali Trail. This was once the main thoroughfare for farmers bringing produce to the growing port of Honolulu.

Not long after reaching the old stone road, a separate spur trail will appear on your left. Follow this path for 200 yards to reach **Likeke Falls**. It's about 30 feet high with two *small* pools below. You can take a cold shower if you climb above the high pool to a ledge under the

Meet Likeke Falls, your goal for today on the Pahi Hwy hike.

main stream. If you were to continue down this trail (Likeke Trail), you'd eventually end up near the Likelike Highway, just before the Wilson Tunnel. (You don't want to do that today.)

Retrace the 200 yards and back at the old stone road, turn right to return the way you came, or go left to complete the loop. Going left, the stones soon disappear, and the old road becomes a trail again. When the trail splits at a Y, stay to the right, or you'll end up in a golf course parking lot. Then take another right when the trail ends on the abandoned Ki'ona'ole Road. Follow this back to the beginning of the loop at the intersection of the Old Pali Road. It's around 3–4 hours roundtrip if you go to the falls.

If Going to Likeke Falls Wasn't for You...

Ignoring the side trip to Likeke Falls, past the bouldery area this becomes a real trail. You'll have to get to the right side of a protective cyclone fence and walk along the mauka side. (If you're interested in a small waterfall, read the end of this description.)

Soon the forest has completely paved over the old road, and it'll veer inland. The traditional shades of every green adorn the scenery. If you haven't gotten used to the traffic noise below you, it may seem a bit more annoying here because, after all, this is a forest and the noise seems out of place. A sometimes-babbling brook will soon alleviate some of the noise.

When you come to an intersection, to the right is the Maunawili Trail described on page 183. To the left is a short trail to a highway turnout where the lazy (and well-funded) hiker could have left a second rental car. And behind you is where the rest of us poor slobs will have to walk to regain that 600 feet we just lost.

East O'ahu Hiking

Makapu'u Walk to the Dragon's Nostrils (2½ mi round trip)

There's an old abandoned road (called **Ka'iwi**) that heads to the top of Makapu'u Head, the easternmost point of the island. Over its 1¼ mile distance (each way) it gains 520 feet at a reasonably constant pace. This is a very popular hike with locals and visitors alike due to the sweeping views from up top and good whalewatching. What's less known is what lies at the foot of Makapu'u Head.

It gets hot by late morning here, so start this hike early. We like to walk up for the sunrise with flashlights, though it might be hard to motivate yourself to get up *that* early. (The vehicle gate doesn't open until 7 a.m., so the walk is slightly longer.) Take McCully out of Waikiki, then right on Kapiolani and up to H-1 east. Drive till you're past the 9 mile marker on Hwy 72, east of Waikiki. Drive past the gate to the parking lot. The abandoned road ascends the back side of the hill first, then slithers around to the windward side halfway up. Stop at an information plaque about whales and look for the buggers below if it's whale season (December–April). Remember that plaque on your way down.

Near the top, a lookout presents an unexpectedly dreamy view of Manana (AKA Rabbit Island) and Kaohi-ka-ipu islands and Waimanalo beyond. *Wow!* The vista is fantastic. All around you are reminders of the military significance of this hill during WWII. Old bunkers and gun emplacements lie all over this mountain. Wild cactus dot the mountain-top. The Makapu'u Lighthouse is below you on a bluff, but it's off limits.

The actual summit is another 10-minute hike past old bunkers and up the ridge. Walking away from the lookout, a short-lived stretch of blacktop heads

The Dragon's Nostrils aren't as reliable as the Halona Blowhole, but when they're going off, they're far more interesting. Here a visitor from Kauaʻi gets exposed to the dragon's fury.

toward the summit and quickly becomes a trail. Follow this up to the ridge and past the highest pillbox. From here you can add Diamond Head and Koko Head to your view.

Now here's the surprise. On your way back down toward your car, before you get to that whale plaque we talked about, keep an eye out below you. There's a lava bench that's only partially visible in spots. Do you see any mist? How about water shooting into the air? Maybe, maybe not. The hill blocks most of the view of it. But from the whale plaque, a faint trail works its way down the mountain to the lava bench below. And there you will find, *some* of the time (though not *all* of the time), a cluster of blowholes.

We've seen lots of blowholes in the islands. But these stand out as the most numerous in one spot, and they successfully convey a feeling of barely contained violence. It's as if there is a giant, furious beast pounding at his confines to get out. Sit a while, and you'll realize that there may be as many as seven blowholes down here on a good day. Some go off only occasionally. The snorting twin nostrils sound frightening and dangerous, and you can feel the ocean several feet below the

lava shelf you're standing on, pounding away at the lava. This great beast will escape someday; you can feel the inevitability in the air. Take your time here, but never take your eye off the violent ocean. Unlike many blowholes around Hawaiʻi, the opening is probably too small for someone to fall into. One of the twin nostrils separates the spray on the way out, creating three eruptions.

There's a good chance that the ocean may be too calm for the blowholes to work. Probably 60% of the time they're *not* going off. East swells and long period swells work best, but it'll be hard for you to know if that's what's hitting the island. Low tide seems to *diminish* the blowholes, but that's when the waves may smash against the shoreline the most dramatically, creating explosions of water shooting well over 100 feet into the air when the surf is really high. What we're saying is you won't really know what to expect until you start going down the trail. If the ocean's calm, there *is* a nice consolation prize. Some deep tide-pools make wonderful bathing. But only use the tide-pools if the ocean's calm. Pounding seas would make them hazardous.

The trail can be a little slippery going down and faint going back up—try to make a mental note of it. Also, don't tempt fate by getting too chummy with the ocean down here. Keep your distance unless you're *sure* you're in a safe place. Bring water for that climb back up to the 400-foot level. And wear closed-toed shoes.

Koko Crater Trail (1½ mi round trip)

This is the most prominent landmark in East Oahu. You can see it from Waikiki, and it towers over Hawai'i Kai. At 1,207 feet, it's the tallest tuff cone in the state. (See page 61 for a description of this volcanic remnant.)

During WWII, the summit of Koko Crater was a radar facility. Since it was too steep for a road, a funicular (tramway) was built to carry men and supplies to the station on top. Today the radar is gone, but the railroad track remains. Hiking to the top is straightforward—literally. The old rails make a beeline up the steep side with no consideration for your lungs' capacity. It's only ⁷⁄₁₀ mile to the summit, but it takes 30 to 90 minutes, depending on you fitness level and determination. Push yourself and gallop to the top, or take breaks along the way and make it easier. As the railroad ties get steeper, they become more like stairs, but they're spread out and you'll have to take a step between them. Many locals climb up for a workout, and we've found it busy any time we go.

Just over halfway, the rails cross a ravine on a bridge. There's nothing between the ties and the ground below, so if you're leery about crossing it, find the trail on the right to bypass it. After this, the rails are at their steepest until you reach the top. Up here you'll find some old equipment and short walls that make perfect seats to rest and catch your breath. The view overlooks Hanauma Bay, Koko Marina and out to Diamond Head and part of Waikiki. To see the other side, climb the short trail to the summit for views of the Ko'olaus and into the crater, which hosts an unimpressive botanical garden.

From here you can turn around and march back down the tracks to your car, or if you're feeling adventurous (and left a second car at Koko Crater Botanical Garden), you can hike along the rim of the crater. From the summit, follow the rim to the right (toward the ocean). The path is narrow but not too difficult. From the rim see the Halona Blowhole and a full view of Sandy Beach.

See map on page 63. To get to the trailhead, follow H-1 east until it turns into Kalanianaole Hwy (72). Turn left on Lunalilo Home Road in Hawai'i Kai, then right on Anapalau Street. It ends at the entrance to Koko Head District Park. Drive to the back and park in the farthest lot. Behind and above the baseball field is a paved road that heads toward the beginning of the tracks. The trail connecting the two is just opposite a rock wall. You can't hike this without hearing the constant sounds of gunfire from a nearby gun range. Avoid mid-day heat, and bring lots of water—you're gonna need it.

Maunawili Falls Hike (2½ mi round trip)

This is a small but pretty and user-friendly waterfall on the windward side, and the hiking is straightforward. It's 1³⁄₁₀ miles each way and will involve 500 feet of climb round-trip. Most people will take 40–60 minutes each way. You'll have to cross the Maunawili Stream four times, though during normal flow you'll *probably* be able to boulder-hop and keep your feet dry. See map on page 68.

The trailhead starts at the intersection of Maunawili Road and Kelewina Road in Kailua. From the Pali Highway (61) turn onto the *second* Auloa Road (the one

O'ahu has fewer waterfalls than Kaua'i and Maui,
and it's a treat to find one with no visitors.
Maunawili Falls is occasionally deserted for short stretches.

that's *not* across from Kamehameha Hwy), and stay on the left fork to veer onto Maunawili Road. Take that to the end to Kelewina Road, and park around the corner on Lola Road.

The trail is beautiful, jungly and easy to follow. (Bring bug spray.) It's a fairly constant incline upward for the first mile. Ginger, heliconia and banana are sprinkled along the way. Some of the trees have exotic vines all over them. Note the wild coffee trees after the second stream crossing. They have dark, slightly wrinkled leaves and small white blossoms at times. On the Big Island, where coffee is grown commercially, the blossoms are so numerous when blooming it's sometimes called Kona snow.

Before the third stream crossing you'll see a small concrete channel. This was built long ago to harness spring water from Api Spring, which you'll see coming out of the mountain.

After a bench, the trail goes down to the river 110 feet below. Turn left at the fork, cross and then parallel the stream for a couple of minutes to claim your prize— a waterfall that you can wade under. Since there aren't a huge number of accessible waterfalls on O'ahu, you probably *won't* have it to yourself. We've seen it empty for 20 minutes at a stretch *at most*, and we've seen it packed with locals on weekends. There's a trail on the far side of the falls that leads up to a platform that locals jump off, but it's steep and treacherous, and we don't recommend it. If you do it anyway, check where you'll be jumping *before* you jump.

Maunawili Trail (9½ mi one way)

There's a bowl-shaped valley called Maunawili tucked into the Ko'olau Mountain range that's mauka (toward the mountains) of Kailua town. The northeastern tip of this valley is defined by Olomana Peak. The northwestern tip is what the Pali Highway punches through. In between is a wonderland containing one of O'ahu's finest hikes.

Now there are several ways to skin this cat. The best way, *by far*, is as a shuttle hike—starting from the west and ending in the east. Now, we realize that renting a separate cheap-o car for the day and leaving it at the other end is a burden that many won't bear. Fair enough. We'll describe it from one end to the other and,

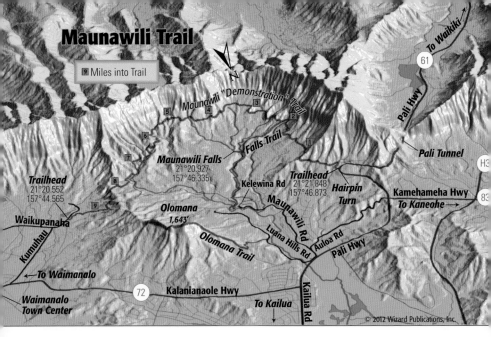

Maunawili "Demonstration" Trail

To Waikiki

61

Pali Hwy

Pali Tunnel

H3

Falls Trail

Maunawili Falls
21°20.927
157°46.335

Trailhead
21°21.848
157°46.873

Kelewina Rd

Hairpin
Turn

Kamehameha Hwy
To Kaneohe →

83

Trailhead
21°20.552
157°44.565

Maunawili Rd

Olomana
1,643'

Luana Hills Rd

Auloa Rd

Pali Hwy

Waikupanaha

Olomana Trail

Kumuhau

← To Waimanalo

72

Kalanianaole Hwy

Kailua Rd

Waimanalo
Town Center

To Kailua

© 2012 Wizard Publications, Inc.

---

if you only use one car, you can hike it one way until you're halfway to satisfied, then turn around and go back. But consider springing for the extra car or a taxi; this one's worth it.

You may read elsewhere that this hike only climbs a few hundred feet. Don't you believe it. That false notion is obtained by casually looking at topographic maps, noting that the trail starts at 600 feet, tops out at 1,000 or so (it's actually 1,120), never deviates from the contour lines *too much*, and guessing. Sounds good. But when we used a GPS with a built-in altimeter to keep track of all the "little hills and dales," we got very different results. You may only climb a hundred or so feet with each wiggle on a map—which barely shows up on a topo. But do that 25 times or so, and together those little climbs add up to 2,460 feet of climbing over 9½ miles. And that's *without* the side trip to the falls. It's not until the second half of the trail that those climbs start to get tiring.

Read these two paragraphs slowly—there's a lot of meat in them. The hike starts at the long, hairpin-turn pullout on the Kailua side of the Pali Tunnel. From H-1 near Waikiki, you'll go 7 miles up the Pali Hwy, through the second tunnel, and pull over at the marked lookout after the runaway truck ramp. The trailhead starts here toward the right of the pullout.

If you're leaving a car at the other end, take Kalanianaole Highway (72) to Waimanalo. Go mauka (toward the mountain) at Kumuhau Street, right when it ends at Waikupanaha, then go ¼ mile until you see a turnout on the right side at the trailhead. Driving back with your *other* car to that hairpin turn from here, you'll get back on the Pali Highway going mauka, drive past the hairpin (which you can't turn into from that side) through the tunnels, eventually turn right at the exit for the wayside park, back up the mountain, around through the wayside, back onto the highway going toward Kailua, and back through the tunnels again to the hairpin turn. (Phew!) See map on page 182.

After a couple minutes on the trail you'll continue straight at the intersection of the Pali Trail. As you start to leave the traffic noise behind, the trail begins to wind through lush forest, and the views can change rapidly. In one moment you're overlooking Kailua and the coast, then turn a corner and you're looking at a wild and lush valley. Around another corner is a mountain carpeted with lush ferns, another and you're overlooking a pretty banana farm. Many hikes on O'ahu require a long climb, culminating in a grand view at the top. This hike rewards you incrementally along the way. You never have to go too long without a treat.

About 2 miles into the trail, you'll come to an intersection…and a decision. Up until now you've had it fairly easy in the elevation department—somewhat gradual climbs. About 8/10 mile down that optional ridge is **Maunawili Falls** (see page 182 for more), a small but pleasant falls to spend some time. (Parts of this trail can be a bit overgrown.) But it means giving up (and then reclaiming) 500 feet of elevation quickly. If you're doing an out-and-back hike, it's worth a stop. If you're going all the way to

Waimanalo, you may not have the time or juice to go to the falls. Either way, at least go down the trail about 5 minutes, then turn around. The perspective of the fluted cliffs of Ko'olau is mind-boggling.

Staying on the Maunawili "Demonstration" Trail (as it's called), the variety of plants is amazing. Ti plants, tree ferns, kukui trees, wild orchids, 'ohi'a trees, koa trees—such a nice mixture in this valley. And the birds are more numerous than at almost any other place on the island. Especially delightful are the shamas, with their beautifully complex song. In places the bird life is intense enough, depending on the time of day, to drown out conversation.

Mile after mile, the views and forest just keep getting better and better. About halfway in, you've now left nearly all traces of civilization behind. The trail zigzags over and over again into Eden-like

A pack-laden hiker marvels at the fluted walls of Maunawili Valley.

lushness. You may even come across a small waterfall or two along the way, if it's been raining recently.

After 8 miles or so the visions of beauty might start getting supplanted by visions of cold beer. At least they did with us. You'll arrive at an intersection underneath powerlines. Go to the right here and at the other two intersections ahead, and you'll eventually reach your car—and soon those cold beers.

This 9⅓-mile trail is on the side of a mountain much of the time, giving opportunities to take a tumble if you are particularly clumsy. Also, keep track of the time it's taking. You want to leave early enough to take your time and to ensure you're not on the trail in the dark. Hiking shoes are best as several areas may be muddy, especially the second half. But overall, this is a well-cared-for and easy-to-follow trail.

Ka'iwa Ridge Hike (1 mi round trip)

It's short—only about ½ mile each way. And over that distance you'll gain almost 500 feet, so expect to puff and pant and wheeze and whine. But the views of the Moku-lua Islands 1¼ miles away and dreamy Lanikai Beach make it worth the sweat. Best times are either sunrise (if you're so motivated) or late afternoon. Don't hike it in the midday heat—there's not enough air in all Kailua to fill your lungs.

In Kailua—see directions to Lanikai Beach Park in BEACHES and the map on page 70. Then take a right on Kaelepulu Drive. Just before it ends at a private gate, look to the left for a cyclone fence. The trail is at the top of that unnamed road along the fence. At the top are a couple of former military pillboxes (concrete dug-in guard posts).

Kawainui Marsh Path (3 mi round trip)

This is a 1⁴⁄₁₀-mile (each way) dead flat cemented path through the Kawainui Marsh—sort of Hawai'i's version of the Everglades on a tinier scale. It's not much of an exaggeration to say that once you've seen the first 60 seconds or so, you've seen it all. Swamps are not exactly a hotbed of variety when it comes to scenery. Nonetheless, it's popular with walkers and joggers, and the views of the distant mountains are pleasing in the morning or afternoon. There are two places to park. The north end is the better of the two. In Kailua, take Oneawa to Kaha. See map on page 70. The path hooks from the right side.

Waihe'e Falls Hike (3 mi round trip)

This moderately easy, 1½-mile hike on a dirt, road gains 750 feet and takes you through lush rainforest before placing you at the base of the 30-foot Waihe'e Falls. To get to the trailhead, drive north of Kane'ohe where Hwy 830 merges into Hwy 83 (See maps on page 68 or 79). Take your first left *after* the Hygienic Store onto Waihe'e Road, and follow it until it ends at a gate. Parking near the gate is tight, so leave your car by the street curb.

The sign on the gate reads KEEP OUT, but that's apparently outdated since we *confirmed* from the state and the Board of Water Supply that you're now allowed to hike into Waihe'e Valley. After passing through the gap in the fence on the left, a gravel road stretches into the forest. This will take you all the way to the falls with a few interesting stops along the way. After a half-mile (15 minutes) you'll reach a popular swimming hole in the stream on the left. We've seen kids jumping off the spillway, but check the depth of the pool first and then decide if you're comfortable with it. Just after this, there will be a small clearing backed by an ominous concrete façade with a locked metal door at its base. This is one of only a few *dike tunnels* on the island.

It's like a horizontal well cut into the water table of the mountain. (Notice the water flowing from under the door.) The Board of Water Supply used to give tours here until 9/11 caused them to heighten security. Now they only schedule tours for grade school kids.

From here the road is less maintained, and it gets much steeper. Look for openings in the trees along the road for views of the valley walls. Continue climbing to the end where two colossal banyan trees reside under Waihe'e Falls. There is no pool to swim in, but you can easily take a refreshing shower under these cascading waters.

North Shore Hiking

Northern Tip Empty Beach Walk
(mileage varies)

Although the beaches on O'ahu are rarely deserted, here's an exception. The northern tip from the Kahuku Golf Course almost to the Turtle Bay Resort (about 5 miles) is beach and beachrock (sandstone). And since there's no convenient access (except for a club that has the keys to the James Campbell Estate locks), it's nearly always deserted during the week. Though not technically a public access, for years locals (mainly surfers) have been parking at the public golf course at the end of Puu-

The wild, windy beach near the northern tip of the island makes an ideal secluded beach walk.

luana Road (see map on page 81) and discreetly walking to the left of the parking lot along a dirt road to the shoreline. And although the county has their typical NO TRESPASSING signs at the golf course, the wink and nod system seems to be in effect, from what we've observed. (Theft can be a problem here, so don't leave anything valuable in your car.) Although the land *behind* the beach is private, all beaches are public in Hawai'i, so stay at the shoreline to stay in a public area.

Winds are virtually always blowing along here, and the frothing whitecaps, smell of the sea spray and the empty shoreline all combine to make a memorable walk. Remember the trick to walking in sand—gentle, relaxed strides while lightly striking the sand almost flat-footed. You probably won't want to swim here since rip currents are common. One downside is that this location seems to attraction more flotsam and jetsam.

Wai'anae Coast Hiking

'Ohiki-lolo Point (7/10 mi round trip)
    This is a short hike—only 10–15 minutes out to it. But it leads to one of the most interesting lattice-like sandstone benches we've seen in Hawai'i. Once you get to the stony peninsula, walk out as far as the ocean safely allows toward the water. This is all lithified sand, and the ocean is dissolving this former sand dune, creating sharp, awkward footing. Think of it as a large rocky bench that's been bathed in acid. Many of the places at the outer edge have holes and tiny arches eaten into the sandstone.

    Farther back you'll see lots of salt in the depressions. During the winter, giant surf sometimes washes over the entire bench. If that's the case when you're visiting, there won't be much to see here (other than your own demise if you were foolish enough to walk out onto the

Slabs of beautiful sandstone litter the crystal clear pools at 'Ohiki-lolo Point.

bench when it's being pounded). Those large boulders that lined the trail on your way out were tossed there during such periods, which gives you an idea how strong the surf can be at times.

To get here, drive to Wai'anae to near the end of the road. After the 17 mile marker is Makua Cave on the right. Park across the street from the cave, and take the trail on the left toward the shoreline, then walk left along the shore. The point is just after 'Ohiki-lolo Beach. Don't leave anything valuable in your car here.

Ka'ena Point (5 mi round trip)

There are two ways to hike out to the westernmost tip of the island at Ka'ena Point—the long way and the short way (if you have a 4WD). We prefer this long way, which is from the Wai'anae side. Drive along Hwy 93/930 until it ends at Yokohama Bay (see map on page 108). Nearly every map out there shows a 4WD road wrapping around Ka'ena Point. And nearly every map is wrong. The "road" soon becomes a trail, and it's not possible—nor would it be legal—to drive a car all the way.

Almost immediately into the hike there are opportunities via short paths from the road to amble over to the shoreline, which is dominated by sandstone lovingly sculpted by nature into a series of chasms, arches and holes. It's fun to look down into them as the ocean snakes its way through the maze.

Be aware that, although the wind may be calm here, you're in what pilots call a rotor from the mountain behind you, and wind gusts can strike from any direction at any time. (That's why pilots *hate* rotors.) Look up and you'll probably see clouds racing by in the *opposite* direction from the wind that's blowing on you.

In several areas the road exposes itself for what it really is—a former railroad track, and some of the trestles are still visible. In the old days this was how sugar cane was transported from Hale'iwa to Honolulu.

At ⁷⁄₁₀ mile from your car, after a rare wide spot in the road, look for a series of interconnected tide-pools below, one suitable for swimming if the ocean isn't raging. (Vague directions, we know, but there's little to reference along here.) It's an interesting place to watch the way the ocean exchanges water into various pools.

Be alert to opportunities to walk along the shoreline or along one of the many trail segments that are on the berm next to the road. It'll take longer, but it's more interesting, and you can always take the faster dirt road on the way back.

At 1²⁄₁₀ miles from your car, just below some old railroad ties hanging over the edge of the trail, you may hear a sharp-pitched gasping sound. Throughout Hawai'i, blowholes are relatively common, where the ocean undercuts the lava bench, shooting water and sometimes loud air though a hole. Though this one is man-made (probably drilled by the railroad), it produces the loudest horn we've ever heard when the ocean's cooperating. There's also a nice sea arch just past the blowhole.

From here on, a couple of narrow stretches convert the road to a trail. Riding a mountain bike here can be fun.

After 2 miles you'll see a landslide from 2006 that took out part of the trail. Rather than fix it, the state simply erected a now-faded TRAIL CLOSED sign. Most hikers, so close to the point, scramble up above or down below the landslide (both are hairy, the upper less so) and require the trail/road.

As you approach the point, things start to change. During normal trade wind weather you and the nearby ocean have been protected from the wind by the mountain next to you. Near Ka'ena Point a line of demarcation in the form of a distinct wind line abruptly transports you from a protected world to a windy one. Look for the transition line offshore. The ocean is often a white-capped frothy mess, and you'll feel instantly cool.

Ka'ena Point Natural Area Reserve is where many of the island's albatrosses live. They burrow holes in the sand here. Stay on the trails so you don't disturb them if it's nesting season. At Ka'ena Point itself there's a rock offshore which marks the westernmost point on O'ahu. This is called *Pohaku o Kaua'i*. According to legend, a demigod named Maui tried to bring together O'ahu and Kaua'i. Casting his magical hook across the channel, he snagged Kaua'i and gave a huge tug. Unfortunately, the hook came loose (landing inland and creating Ka'au Crater), and only a huge boulder from Kaua'i was pulled ashore here—the rock that you see in front of you. Hawaiians so believed in their legends that the channel to this day is called the Ka'ie'ie Waho Channel, named after the towline made from the 'ie'ie root that Maui used in his attempt.

This is a great place to be if the island is getting big surf from both the north and the south. The rocks at this point are getting slammed from north swells that may have originated in Alaska. The south side of the rocks may be assaulted by New Zealand-born swells.

You're 2⁴⁄₁₀ miles from your car back at Yokohama Bay. If you really want to make it to Ka'ena Point but don't want to walk as far, drivers can come from the *North Shore* end. The 4WD (sometimes 2WD) road past Dillingham Airfield gets to within ⁶⁄₁₀ miles of the point. You'll have to hoof it from there, and it'll be windier. See page 92 for more.

HORSEBACK RIDING

When people envision riding a horse in Hawai'i, they often picture themselves riding along a beach. **Turtle Bay** (293–8811 comes closest to that image. Sure, it's a nose-to-tail experience. You won't be galloping along with sand and salt flying everywhere. But *some* portions are along the fabulous North Shore at Turtle Bay, and there's something inextricably charming about that scene. It's $65 for a 45-minute ride, $105 for a 75-minute version in the late afternoon. Near the northern tip of the island at Turtle Bay Resort on Hwy 83. They can be bad about returning phone calls.

A better product is **Kahuku Kai** (293–8081). They have a very relaxed and laid-back attitude (unless you're late). They'll run the horses if you like, and it's along the shoreline. Kids are fine with them; their restrictions seem nonexistent. Call in advance to make reservations because they usually only go out with four people. Near the northern tip of the island in Kahuku behind the golf course. $75 (cash) for around an hour.

Kualoa Ranch (237–7321) has 1-hour rides for $69; 2 hours for $99. It's totally nose-to-tail walking, but the mountain scenery is *gorgeous*. On the windward side 10 miles north of Kane'ohe on Hwy 83. Good for novices, but Kualoa is sort of a visitor-processing machine

Hawai'i Polo Trail Rides, formerly Oceanfront Trail Rides (220–5153) has the same ponies used by the Hawai'i Polo Club. They go out every other day, using them for polo the other days. You'll notice that your steed will neck rein very well. Of your options for horsemanship on Oahʻu, this is your opportunity to test drive a Ferrari. These mounts are quick, ultra-responsive and inherently competitive. The trail itself leaves a little to be desired though. You'll head across the polo field and down the beach a short distance, circle through a paddock and head back the way you came. $95 for the 1-hour group ride.

Happy Trails (638–7433) has hourlong rides in the hills above Waimea Bay on the North Shore for $75 for 90 minutes. The ride itself is entirely nose to tail with no passing permitted as the horses are inherently competitive, and you could cause an unintended race. The trail is in a forest almost the whole time with limited views. Bring bug spray.

Yeah, this is our kind of riding!

'Cause I'm a rocketman...

It's our observation that those with little to no experience and maybe a bit skittish will enjoy Kualoa the most. Riders with the most experience will probably like Hawai'i Polo the most. The rest will likely fall somewhere in between. If you've never (or rarely) ridden horses, remember that horses respect strength. They can smell fear a mile away. Be confident. And if you're not confident…fake it. Don't ever let them feel that they're in charge.

Jet Skiing

Call them Jet Skis or Wave Runners (which are brand names), these motorcycles of the sea can be rented at several locations around the island. Sometimes you'll be restricted to a small area usually set off by buoys.

Early morning is usually the most smooth. Late afternoons can be choppy from the wind. Late morning seems to offer a good balance of smooth water seasoned by a little texture. Most people get tuckered out after 30–45 minutes, especially if you're like me and you drive it like it's stolen.

Companies like to encourage riders to double up, claiming it's "more fun." Hardly. Of course, having two people on one jet ski brings more revenue to the company while only using one machine. (Hmm, pretty cynical, aren't we?) Regardless, doubling up increases the chance of someone falling off, from what we've observed.

One thing you might want to consider is wearing goggles. Frankly, riding jet skis without them can be annoying if there's any wind. Companies that won't provide goggles should be avoided.

The best one is **Watercraft Connection** (637–8006) in Hale'iwa on the North Shore. They rent them for $65 per 30 minutes, and you can ride them in the open ocean, not on a circular track like the other two. Goggles available for $3.

Aloha Jet Ski (521–2446) operates out of Ke'ehi Lagoon, a very sheltered body of water near the airport. Goggles available for $5. $75 (1 person) or $90 for 2 people (cash only) for 45 minutes on a circular track.

Sea Breeze (396–0100) is at Maunalua Bay near Hawai'i Kai, 20 minutes east of Waikiki. They charge $69 for only 30 minutes on a circular track. No goggles available.

Rocketman

Not really a jet ski—technically an *ultra-modified* jet ski—but we didn't know where else to put it. This is where a picture is worth a thousand words. (And the experience costs over $25 per minute.) If you look at the photo and say, "Man, that's cool," read on, fellow pilot. Imagine a couple of fire hoses shooting you up into the air, powered by a jet ski engine in a raft you drag behind you. *You* do the steering with guidance from your instructor, courtesy of a speaker in your helmet. They only thing they control on your first "flight" is the throttle via a remote control. After some instruction, they strap you tightly to this jet pack and start you out slowly as you drag yourself through the water. If you take to it well, you'll eventually find yourself 10–15 feet above the water, steering slow circles next to a fixed water platform that holds your instructor and any witness (for an extra $25) you want to watch your first jet pack flight. You'll get about 15 minutes, and it will zip by faster than you wish.

All this can be yours for a mere *$400*. Expensive? *Insanely*, so look for discounts. (I bought a Groupon special for 50% off.) And if you don't catch on, you'll merely flop around in the ocean like an idiot with everyone on the water platform watching. (But you'll do fine. I have faith.) Either way, this is one unique ride, and as soon as I was done, I wanted to do it again. These $100,000 contraptions—called **Jetlev**—ain't exactly common, and chances like this don't come around often. **Sea Breeze** (396–0100) does this offshore Hawai'i Kai in Maunalua Bay. Photos and video are extra, and when you're done with the jet pack, you gotta wait for them to take you back to shore when they are good and ready.

Ocean kayaking O'ahu's nearshore waters can be heavenly. There's something unmistakably exotic about watching

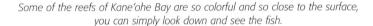

Some of the reefs of Kane'ohe Bay are so colorful and so close to the surface, you can simply look down and see the fish.

your kayak shadow slide over coral reef systems on your way to an offshore island.

The two best places to kayak are **Kane'ohe Bay** and **Kailua Bay**. Although many of the resorts rent kayaks for use off Waikiki, this is a relatively dull paddle. Do it for the novelty of kayaking, but not for the sights.

Kane'ohe Bay

One of the most dramatic kayak trips you can take—and the one with the smoothest waters—is one that almost no one does for a simple reason—it's to a sunken island of over 1,000 acres that you can't see from shore. It's Hawai'i's version of Atlantis.

The central part of Kane'ohe Bay has a *huge* barrier-type reef. (Technically, it's not a true barrier reef, but it has the same effect.) Unlike most reefs around Hawai'i, however, this one is nearly as broad as it is wide and is covered in most areas by sand. During the ice age 12,000 years ago this area was part of O'ahu, 180 feet above sea level. When the earth warmed and the seas rose, it became separated from O'ahu as an island, then vanished, transforming itself into the fringing reef we know today. At low tide part of it is still exposed as a football field-sized beach rising from the sea. At its farthest edge, a stranded sandstone island, the "summit" of this Atlantis forms the only visible remnant, towering a mere 14 feet above sea level.

See Kailua Bay (below) for details about **renting a kayak**. There's also a company at the bay called **Kama'aina Kids** (235–6509) for similar prices. Convenient location. They contacted us and implied that they were the only game in town for kayak rentals because "the pier no longer allows kayaks to launch at the pier." Uh, with all due respect, the state confirmed that you can effortlessly put your kayak in at the pier just north of He'eia State Park next to the Kane'ohe Canoe Club. (See map on page 68.) You don't have to rent from them. When you launch, look behind you at the mountain peak with a powerline pole on it—that's what you'll be paddling toward when you return. The edge of the reef is just over a mile to the north. Look for Kapapa Island—the only part of this Atlantis you can see—and paddle toward it. The waters are almost always smooth here. You may have a headwind going out—which should increase later and help you coming back. Almost immediately you'll go over shallow coral and fish. It's like snorkeling without the mask. Polarized sunglasses help you see through the glare.

Approaching the sunken island is otherworldly. Suddenly there's a sand beach 2–3 feet beneath your kayak, and you seem magically suspended above it as you glide along. To the left, if the tide is cooperating, a short paddle will bring you to the disappearing beach. On weekends locals bring their boats and their BBQs out and make a day of it. Weekdays you may have it to yourself. Even if the island is submerged, get out and walk along the shallows of this "beach." It's a surreal experience. Then look toward Kapapa Island. If you want to visit, head straight toward it from the south.

As you approach Kapapa, a strange phenomenon occurs. East shore surf, if it's up, is pounding at the outer edge of the shoal, but Kapapa Island is protecting you from it, creating a corridor of calmness except for the wraparound swells that are literally colliding with each other right under your kayak as you get nearer. Stay in the center to stay in the corridor. Once near Kapapa, the colliding wraparounds may start to become annoying, and you may want to hop out in the shallow water and walk your kayak ashore. (Water shoes are necessary as the ground is reefy here.)

The sandstone island is a good place to have your lunch under the shade of trees and gaze back at O'ahu and the shoal you just passed over. You're now 2⁴⁄10 miles from where you launched

One of our favorite kayak destinations is the 1,000-acre sunken island in Kane'ohe Bay, lightly used during the week but enjoyed by locals on weekends, like the day this photo was shot.

If the ocean's not your thing, the Kahana River makes a short but sweet jungle paddle.

your kayak. Exploring the island reveals lots of sandstone overhangs. Unfortunately, it might also reveal litter left by thoughtless fishermen who are too lazy to haul out what they hauled in.

Return the way you came.

Kailua Bay

A second ocean kayak trip is inside **Kailua Bay**. You can pick up a kayak at Kailua Beach Park and kayak to **Flat Island** or one of the **Moku-lua Islands** off Lanikai Beach. (Only the left of these twin islands is landable—the other is a bird sanctuary.) Waters are usually fairly protected (but not nearly as protected as Kane'ohe Bay), and these offshore islands, while popular with other kayakers, still make a great destination. The northern Moku-lua Island has a beach to sprawl onto. And Flat Island, or Popo'ia, has lots of pukas (holes) along its outer edge.

If you want a shorter paddle to the Moku-lua and are transporting your kayak, start from the far end of Lanikai Beach less than a mile from the islands.

For Kailua paddling, you can rent from companies nearby. Expect to pay $59 for a single, $69 for a double for a *half* day. **Hawaiian Watersports** (262–5483) will deliver the kayak to the canal near the beach, but you can't pay for it there. (Regulations—but they *can* take a credit card number over the phone.) At **Kailua Sailboards & Kayaks** (262–2555) you'll have to wheel the kayak to the beach yourself from their shop on Kailua Road. They also have soft racks for your car if you're heading to Kane'ohe Bay. **Twogood Kayaks** (262–5656) rents and will deliver to Kailua Bay. **Windward Watersports** (261–7873) is right at Kailua Beach Park. Kayak rentals are not available on Sundays. (And there was a move afoot at press time to limit them further.)

Other Kayaking Destinations

The **North Shore** has winds that are usually a kayaker's best friend—along the shore from north to south. If you can handle a shuttle paddle (kayak one way, and one of you takes the bus back to your car), put in at Waimea Bay and take out at Hale'iwa for a nice wind-at-your-back-most-days, 5-mile tour of some of the island's prettiest beaches. Only paddle here when the ocean is calm, usually during the summer months (May–September).

The waters off **Hawai'i Kai** tend to be pretty placid most of the time, so paddling is less challenging, but water quality and views aren't as impressive.

The kayaking along the **Wai'anae Coast**, especially toward the end of the highway near Yokohama Bay can be good. You probably won't have the same favorable following winds as the North Shore paddle, but the water tends to be wickedly clear.

Kahana River

This is the only river on the island that's worth kayaking, and it's super-relaxing. (Some would point to Hale'iwa Stream as well, but it's not as compelling.) Kahana is a mile each way down a tropical, dripping-with-life river with pretty mountain views in the distance and trees overhanging the banks for shade.

You put in at Kahana Bay—look for the easy-to-miss Huilua Fishpond access road at the east end of the bay where you can literally drive right to the river mouth. This bay is 15 miles (25 minutes) north of Kane'ohe on Hwy 83. Then paddle up the river under the highway bridge (on weekends, locals fishing off it might not appreciate your presence—we prefer to do this on weekdays). Since it's only 2 miles round-trip, don't dig in and paddle too furiously—it'll be over too quickly. Instead, paddle and glide and soak in the environment for a relaxing 1½–2 hour cruise. In 2011 they filmed a TV show here called *The River* because it had good scenery. Make sure you bring lunch and repellent for mosquitoes. (If you forget the latter, then you thoughtfully brought *their* lunch.) When you're done, you can also paddle around normally protected Kahana

Bay. Though the bay is reported to be a spawning area for hammerhead sharks, they ain't interested in you in your kayak.

Renting a Kayak

For renting *outside of Waikiki or Kailua Beach*, the biggest (and the most knowledgeable) kayak shop on the island is **Go Bananas** (737–9514) just outside of Waikiki at 799 Kapahulu. They'll strap the kayak(s) to your car, and you're off. They're cheaper than the Kailua companies. They also have a great selection of waterproof items. $30 per full day for a single, $45 for a double, add $10 for a 24-hour rental (which most of the other companies do as well).

In Hale'iwa on the North Shore, **Surf N' Sea** (637–9887) rents kayaks by the hour. Convenient for the area, but pricier than Go Bananas.

Also called kitesurfing. Imagine a modified wakeboard with fins at both ends. Then let a special, controllable four-line kite drag you along. As with windsurfing, you don't have to go the direction the wind takes you—you have control. Despite what some instructors tell you when they want to sign you up, it's harder to get up on the board than windsurfing and will take lots of lessons. But *oh, what fun it is!* More fun than windsurfing once you're comfortable on the board. One way you can prepare before you get here is to buy a two-string kite and master it so that you can instinctively maneuver the kite. It's not that hard, but it helps if you can steer the kite without thinking.

Lessons are *expensive* and seem to change with the whims of the company.

Windward Watersports (261–7873) and **Kailua Sailboards & Kayaks** (262–2555) are the cheapest with 3-hour group lessons for $150, private for $249. **Hawaiian Watersports** (262–5483) gives lessons at Kailua Beach for $229 ($279 for private) for 3 hours per person. Call for more options and prices. Transportation to and from Waikiki available.

The learning curve is steep. First you need to learn how to operate the kite (which is a hoot). Next comes body dragging. Though it sounds like something they do to you if your credit card is declined, it's actually when you let the kite drag you through the ocean while you manipulate it. Then comes the good part—*riding the board*—which may or may not happen during this first lesson.

Segway Tours

Remember Segway scooters? Those odd, upright people transporters that were gonna revolutionize the world and the way cities were built, but instead just became an expensive way for security to patrol airports and such. There are a couple of companies doing tours on these, and if you've never ridden one, it's a cool novelty the first time.

We much prefer **Segway Tours of Turtle Bay** (293–6024). Their off-road versions allow you to cruise on trails, partially along the north shore Kahuku shoreline, through a somewhat beat-up forest and along a golf course. The "tour" part is not especially compelling—we wish they'd do less talking and more scooter-

ing—but overall, it's a fairly cool way to spend 90 minutes for $99. During the stopping time you'll find yourself always in motion, wiggling and leaning and twitching the scooter constantly because…well, *'cause you can*.

In Waikiki there's **Segway of Hawai'i** (941–3151). You'll feel much more restricted on this tour because of the urban environment. But they're cheaper, starting at $49 for a half hour tour up to $130 for a 2½-hour trip. They also do tours of Kailua.

Garden Tours

There are several gardens on the island and they are by no means equal. The best are the **Waimea Valley** and **Foster Botanical Garden**.

Longtime visitors will be puzzled to see **Waimea Valley** (638–7766) listed under gardens. It used to be called **Waimea Falls Adventure Park** with lots of adventure activities. After years of legal wrangling, the Office of Hawaiian Affairs now controls the valley with a mindset of preservation plus the notion of cultural education. Think of it as a botanical garden with a waterfall and a lifeguard.

The giant garden itself (1,875 acres) is beautiful, and the setting on the Waimea River is tranquil. Take the opportunities to veer from the main road and walk along the river. (If you don't bring mosquito repellent down near the river trail, you'll donate more blood than you ever knew you had.) Most people make a beeline to the falls ¾ mile away (and slightly uphill) and take their time coming back. There are changing rooms at the falls if you brought your suit. The 40-foot-high falls dries up at times, especially in the summer. $15 to get in, $7.50 for kids 4–12. At the mouth of Waimea Bay north of Hale'iwa on Hwy 83. You'll probably spend about 1½ hours here. Tours are self-guided only.

Waimea Valley, once a well-known adventure park, is now the island's prettiest botanical garden.

Foster Botanical Garden (522–7065) is small—only 13½ acres. But it's pretty, has some of the largest trees we've seen in Hawai'i—one with a diameter of 10 feet—and their hybrid orchid collection is particularly nice. It's $5 to get in, $1 for kids 6–12. At 50 N. Vineyard Blvd. From Waikiki, take Kalakaua out, left on Kapiolani, right on Ward, left on Beretania, right on Nuuanu, left on Vineyard.

Nearby is the almost useless **Lili'uokalani Botanical Garden** (522–7060). It's a pretty poor excuse for a garden, and normally we'd steer you away from it. But it has one thing going for it—a small waterfall. (Of the four major Hawaiian islands, O'ahu is the poorest when it comes to accessible waterfalls, so beggars can't be choosers.) From Foster, make a U-turn on Vineyard, left on Nuuanu, left on School, right on Waikahalulu and park at the end of the street. Visit the falls and then leave—there ain't much else here for you. Admission is free, as it should be.

Another option is the **Ho'omaluhia Park Botanical Garden** (233–7323) in Kane'ohe on Luluku Road. It's off Hwy 83 (Kamehameha Hwy) just north of H-3. This 400-acre garden (built by the U.S. Army Corps of Engineers as a flood protection tool to protect Kane'ohe) backs up against the Ko'olau Mountains, which are simply gorgeous in the morning light, and even has a 32-acre lake. It's run by the county, and admission is free. You don't need to do a lot of walking here since you can drive to the many parking lots, each of which is devoted to areas featuring plants from different parts of the world. Even if gardens aren't your thing, it might be worth a quick drive along the main road to get a vantage point of the mountains that is hard to achieve otherwise, and the health of the plants in this area is impressive. They used to allow you to bring your own *horse*, but stopped that practice. So if you were thinking about bringing your stallion from home, might as well nix that idea.

In central O'ahu is the **Wahiawa Botanical Garden** (621–5463). Most of the 27 acres are in a ravine with marked plants along a primitive trail. The best part is the upper terrace near the entrance. It's more of a lush park with small, landscaped gardens throughout. Open areas are covered in groomed lawns, surrounded by stained concrete paths, ornate lampposts and benches. The garden started as an arboretum experiment in the 1950s, and they put more effort into maintaining the upper level than the ravine. See map on page 96.

The last two gardens are must-misses. In Kahalu'u is **Senator Fong's Plantation & Gardens** (239–6775). The tour seems more geared toward Japanese tour groups and at $15 isn't worth it.

And last (in every way) is **Koko Crater Botanical Garden** (522–7060). Government literature stresses their "long-term plans of continuing to grow plants." In the short term it's 60 acres of unremarkable, unmarked plants in the hot, dry, dusty Koko Crater. It's free (and worth every penny). See map on page 63.

Ocean Tours

What's not to love about spending the day on the water? The ocean off the leeward side of the island (meaning near Waikiki) tends to be fairly calm and somewhat protected. Whether you want to do a snorkel tour, whale watch or a sunset cocktail or dinner cruise, there are lots of boating opportunities off O'ahu.

Ocean tours off Waikiki tend to be on giant boats. (It's simple economics—getting a boat slip in Kewelo Basin is so valuable that anyone with a permit tends to use it for a big boat.) The exceptions are some of the boats that come right ashore at Waikiki.

From Waikiki Beach

Let's start with the most convenient ocean tours. Some boats slide right onto the beach at Waikiki. The best one we've seen is **Waikiki Rigger** (922–2210). They have a good 45-foot sailing cat. (Winds permitting, they won't just motorsail. They'll kill the engines and sail in quiet.) The 2½-hour snorkel trips are $47. The sailing and sunset trips are $40 for 90 minutes and include a free open bar and sometimes a slightly more raucous atmosphere. It's a hoot to ride the net (from one of their forward trampolines), though you might get wet. And their snorkel spot is a bit better than some of the other outfits that snorkel near here. They can hold up to 49 but usually go with less. They land in front of the Outrigger Reef Hotel.

We also like **Spirit of Aloha** (234–7245) that leaves from the Hilton Hawaiian Village pier. It's $99 for 2½ hours and includes lunch (deli only), snorkel and sail. You'll get a brand new snorkel, which you can keep. They'll motor out and sail back from Diamond Head. Really good crews. Their sunset sail isn't a booze cruise. (Two free drink coupons, but we predict that if you want more, you'll hear *I'm buying* from one of the crew.) $79 also includes hot appetizers.

At the other end of the spectrum **Maita'i** (922–5665) will put 47 people on their 44-foot catamaran for $28. (No food, and beverages are extra.) No snorkeling on this 90-minute trip. The sunset trip is $39 and includes beverages. They offer a 2-hour snorkel tour for $45. Not pricey but not impressive either. They pull ashore between the Sheraton Waikiki and the Halekulani.

The **Manu Kai** has 1-hour sails for $25 aboard their catamaran. No reserving for this one—you just show up in front of Duke's (next to Waikiki Beach Center), and if they have room, they'll take you. A no-muss, no-fuss way of getting on the water, but it's a no-frills trip. No food, and beverages are extra.

Nearby is a similar $20 walk-up hour-long trip on the **Kepoikai II**. They'll usually cut the motor and sail awhile offshore. Kids under 5 years old ride free. Popular with large Japanese groups. Beer and wine available but extra. Often a more subdued boat experience.

Na Hoku II is yet another walk-up situation on a catamaran (though they also take walk-up reservations). $30 for a 90-minute sail with beer and a free bar. The yellow boat is near the Royal Hawaiian Hotel.

Outrigger Canoe Rides off Waikiki

These rides are available from **Aloha Beach Services** (922–3111, ext. 2341). It's $10 (you get to ride two waves), or you can charter the whole 8-passenger outrigger canoe (includes paddlers) for $300 per hour. Directly next door **Waikiki Beach Services** (338–1510) rides two waves in a private canoe for $75 per couple. Near the Duke statue, **Star Beach Boys** will give you three waves for $15 in a bigger canoe.

It's hard to believe that a boat trip so close to Waikiki can still transport you to another world.

From Kewalo Basin

If you're looking to sail, **Makani Catamaran** (591–9000) is a great choice. Makani literally means *wind*, which is very appropriate for this ultra fast, top-of-the-line 64-foot sailing cat. No expense was spared on this catamaran. They claim that the carbon fiber mast alone cost $400,000. The boat's sleek design lets it rip through the waves faster and steadier than any other cat we've seen. There's a head on board and trampolines at the bow to relax in (though you might get wet). They offer three cruising tours a day; no snorkeling. Each 2-hour tour comes with a light meal, but only the sunset sail has two complimentary drinks, poured heavy. No one pressures you to dance or sing on this sail. Just kick back and enjoy the ride. Morning sail is $42, afternoon is $38, and the sunset trip is $53, except Friday, when they stay out an extra 30 minutes for the Hilton fireworks for $64. Sometimes hard to get ahold of on the phone.

If you're looking for a roller coaster in the sea, **Honolulu Screamer** (597–8669) lives up to its name. For just $36, you get thrown about and soaking wet in their 1,420 horsepower jet boat that does 180° turns at full speed. The best seats are in the first three rows (the ones with seatbelts), but no matter where you sit, you're getting wet. No pregnant women, people with back problems or children under 40 inches tall. They go out once a day, every day. Call for times.

For Kewalo Basin trips, bring quarters for the parking meter—50¢ per hour—or park across the street at Ward Warehouse.

From Honolulu Harbor at Aloha Tower Marketplace

Star of Honolulu (983–7827) has a whale watch cruise from December–May. You ride up and down the leeward coast, make leis, take hula lessons, etc. You won't get in the water (unless you fall overboard); you'll just *see* the water. $63 for the 2½-hour cruise includes lunch.

From Wai'anae

If you don't mind driving out to **Ko Olina** (35–45 minutes west of Waikiki *barring traffic*), the waters off the Wai'anae Coast can be delightful during summer months (April–October).

An impressive boat trip is the **Honi Olani** at Hawai'i Nautical (234–7245). They have a nice 53-foot catamaran. (Though it's a sailing cat, they'll mostly motorsail.) Good boat—they feed you well, the crew is good, and they give you a new snorkel that you can keep. We weren't impressed with their snorkel spot and were disappointed that they *made* you wear a flotation device, even if you're an Olympic swimmer, but you don't have to inflate it. Three-hour morning trips are $109, plus $30 if you need transportation from Waikiki, and includes light breakfast, lunch deli and two alcoholic beverages. Cash bar available. They leave from Barber's Point Harbor off Malakole Road.

Their smaller power cat, **Sea Dreams II** is better for whale watching as well as SCUBA.

There's also the less impressive **Ko Olina Ocean Adventures** (396–2068). They have 3½-hour trips for $119 in their cramped-feeling 37-foot power boat (called the Pacific Passion) and a nicer 53-foot sailing catamaran. Not a good deal.

Ocean Joy Cruises (677–1277) has a nice 61-foot power cat that isn't too crowded with the maximum 49 passengers. Their snorkel instruction on the boat may be thorough, but they fail to help the aqua-phobic masses into the water. Instead they point to the ocean and say, "go for it." This causes a traffic jam every time. They also require everyone to wear flotation devices whether you want to or not. Even if you're an Ironmn swimmer, you can't escape that rule. The buffet's just OK, and the mai tais are worse. It's hardly worth the $139.

Wai'anae Regional Park in Wai'anae is a farther drive. **Wild Side Specialty Tours** (306–7273) has a nice 42-foot power catamaran. They take 16 people max, so it's not too crowded on board the 3-hour tour for $115.

Dolphin Excursions (239–5579) is a 32-foot rigid hull inflatable. 20 people max. No shade, no toilet. Their goal is to locate dolphins, then let you slip into the water with them, and they claim an 90% success rate. (We've also seen them claim 70% success, so you decide…) $120, which includes a light lunch. Snorkeling also when surf permits. Save 10% if you provide your own transportation to Wai'anae.

Hoku Nai'a (983–7827) is the newest ship in Star of Honolulu's fleet. Since it's docked in Wai'anae, you might find it less crowded than their ships in Honolulu. The boat is a 65-foot double decker that holds 149 passengers. It was built in 2007 and only runs dolphin watch cruises. The area on the bow is great for photographers, and you get a fun ride if the boat is heading into a swell. The service is super friendly, and kids will enjoy it. Their gourmet burger buffet would be better if they kept the patties warm after they're cooked. *One* drink included (gee, thanks). Cost is $89 ($54 for kids) for the 2-hour dolphin watch or $106 for the half day tour that includes snorkeling. Leaves from the Waianae Boat Harbor.

A boat cruise off Waikiki can feel so relaxing, you'll think somebody has stolen your bones.

Hawaiian Reefs—*Why is it that...?*

What is that crackling sound, like bacon frying, I always hear while snorkeling or diving?
For years this baffled people. In the early days of submarines, the sound interfered
with sonar operations. Finally we know the answer. It's hidden snapping shrimp
defining their territory. One variety is even responsible for all the dark cracks and
channels you see in smooth lobe coral. A pair creates the channels, then "farms" the
algae inside.

Why are there so few shellfish in Hawai'i? It's too warm for some of the more familiar
shellfish (which tend to be filter-feeders, and Hawai'i waters don't have as much stuff to
filter). But Hawai'i has more shellfish than most people are aware of. They hide well
under rocks and in sand. Also, people tend to collect shells (which is illegal), and that
depletes the numbers.

Why do coral cuts take so long to heal? Coral contains a live animal. When you scrape
coral, it leaves proteinaceous matter in your body, which takes much longer for your
body to dispatch.

Why do some of the reefs appear dead? Much of the "coral" you see around O'ahu isn't
the kind of coral you're used to. It's called coralline algae, which secretes calcium
carbonate. It's not dead; it's *supposed* to look like that.

What do turtles eat? Dolphins. (Just teasing.) They primarily eat plants growing on rocks,
as well as jellyfish when they are lucky enough to encounter them. Unfortunately for
turtles and lucky for us, jellyfish aren't numerous here.

Is it harmful when people play with an octopus? Yes, if the octopus gets harmed while
trying to get it out of its hole. Best to leave them alone.

Why does the ocean rarely smell fishy here in Hawai'i? Two reasons. We have relatively
small tide changes, so the ocean doesn't strand large amounts of smelly seaweed at
low tide. Also, the water is fairly sterile compared to mainland water, which owes much
of its smell to algae and seaweed that thrives in the bacteria-rich runoff from industrial
sources.

Why is the water so clear here? Because relatively little junk is poured into our water
compared to the mainland. Also, natural currents tend to flush the water with a
continuous supply of fresh, clean ocean water.

Why do my ears hurt when I dive deep, and how are SCUBA divers able to get over it?
Because the increasing weight of the ocean is pressing on your ears the farther down
you go. Divers alleviate this by equalizing their ears. Sounds high tech, but that simply
means holding your nose while trying to blow out of it. This forces air into the
eustachian tubes, creating equal pressures with the outside ocean. (It doesn't work if
your sinuses are clogged.) Anything with air between it gets compressed. So if you
know someone who gets a headache whenever he goes under water...well, he must be
an airhead.

From Hale'iwa

North Shore Catamaran (351–9371) does summer (meaning May–September) 4-hour snorkel trips for $95 in their 40-foot sailing cat. (Includes lunch.) It's $80 in the afternoon with no lunch.

In Kane'ohe Bay

All Hawai'i Cruises—AKA Captain Bob—(942–5077) has a 42-foot catamaran (they mostly motor or motorsail). Four hours and a burger lunch at the offshore sunken island (sand bar) for $95, which includes pick-up from Waikiki. The sand bar is a cool place to hang out, and there's some (mediocre) snorkeling available. Overall, a reasonably good deal.

Dinner Cruises

Navatek I (973–1311) can be summed up like this—great boat, mediocre food and show. The boat is amazingly smooth using swath technology—where the craft floats on two torpedoes that ride below the surface. The buoyancy of the torpedo is constantly adjusted, resulting in a very cushy ride. The buffet has scant choices. The mashed potatoes had no gravy (we cringed at how many people mistakenly covered their potatoes with tartar sauce). The background music is weird for a tropical cruise—elevator versions of *Strangers in the Night*, etc. But when the live music starts, you may long for the canned music you were listening to. If you wander around the boat, you might discover a deck full of passengers you didn't know about. Most will be Japanese, and your first thought is, "Who *are* these people I never saw board—and why are they eating steak and lobster as opposed to my bad chicken and fish?" Well, they paid $126 for their cruise (plus an extra $22 to guarantee a window seat), and it's not worth

it. (Though their music is less lame than yours, your hula show is slightly better.) In all, Navatek has the potential to be a really great product—if only they'd try harder. $94, only 1 drink included. They leave from Pier 6 near the Aloha Tower Marketplace.

Star of Honolulu (983–7827) is a huge, 232-foot, rock-steady (most of the time) ship with 4 decks that can hold 1,500 passengers. (Don't worry, it won't have that many, and it doesn't feel as crowded as some smaller boats.) The fourth deck is where the fancy French food is served in a formal, air-conditioned atmosphere by fancily dressed waiters. But $179 makes the food hard to swallow.

Decks 2 and 3 have the steak and lobster for $133. No A/C (which is fine once the ship leaves the stuffy harbor).

The bottom deck is steak and crab for $93 in an A/C room.

Overall, they do a good job, and the crew is professional. The food's OK—not great, not bad. Some drinks are included, then you're on your own. There's also a quasi-Polynesian show, which is kind of cheesy but fun nonetheless. Our only complaint is that they come in too early and finish the show dockside.

Leaves from Honolulu Harbor next to the Aloha Tower Marketplace. If you park in the lot, *make sure* you buy something at a store there and get validated, or the parking fee can be hefty.

Last and certainly least is the **Ali'i Kai** (539–9400). This is a what happens when a bus tour company runs a dinner show. Pay attention when they try to upsell you to a boat window seat from the bus, because you're not allowed to wander over to take a sunset photo from your non-window seat during the buffet. Your *single* complementary drink ticket buys you any drink $6 or less, meaning perhaps a beer, but decreases in value if you try to upgrade to a pricier drink. And those drinks are hideous, anemic and infuriatingly overpriced. Add bad food, bad show and ambivilent staff and you gotta must-miss trip. $75.

Parasailing is where you become a human kite, attached to a parachute and pulled by a boat via a long line. It's an 8-minute ride, though, which includes reeling in and reeling out. It's been our experience that parasailing *looks* more fun and thrilling than it really is and doesn't seem worth the money. Think of it as a $50 amusement ride. (People afraid of heights, however, will no doubt be properly terrified.)

One tip (*especially* for guys): Don't wear any slippery shorts, or you may cinch forward in your harness resulting in...the *longest* 8 minutes of your life.

The companies (except Sea Breeze) operate out of Kewalo Basin a few minutes west of Waikiki.

X-treme Parasail (330–8308) has traditionally been your best bet. They have 3 trips—$47 for 8 minutes on a 700-foot line, $70 for 9 minutes at 850 feet, or $79 and they'll reel out almost a quarter mile—1,000 feet—for 12 minutes. But a fatal accident in 2012 certainly blemished their safety record.

Hawaiian Parasail (591–1280) charges $50 for 8 minutes (though they want 1–2 hours of your time from start to finish) at 600 feet.

Sea Breeze (396–0100) is out of Maunalua Bay 20 minutes east of Waikiki. It's $49 for 8 minutes on a relatively short 300-foot line, $59 for 10 minutes on a 500-foot leash.

You'd think that the most populous island in Hawai'i would have marginal SCUBA diving, but you'd be wrong. The diving here is incredible, and this is the shipwreck capital of Hawai'i.

Where to Dive

Although diving takes place all over the island, there are five main areas that most dive companies use. **Wai'anae** in the west, the wrecks off **Waikiki**, **Hanauma Bay**, near **Hawai'i Kai** and the **North Shore** in the summer.

Overall, **Wai'anae** offers the best dive conditions. It's calm most of the year, and visibility is often 100 feet or more. We don't recommend late afternoon dives there since you'll be fighting traffic the whole way. (Morning trips there go *against* the traffic.) One of the more interesting Wai'anae dives is the **Mahi**. You'll get an idea of what happens to a ship after a quarter century underwater with two hurricanes and an embarrassing incident involving a Navy anchor. The ship's collapsing and you can only *partially* enter it, but it's a fun dive, and it's often accompanied by patrols of spotted eagle rays flying in formation.

The wrecks off **Waikiki** are probably our second choice, because divers *love* shipwrecks, even if it's a simple sunken fishing trawler, and the visibility once you're away from the shoreline tends to be 100-foot plus with diverse fish life. Waikiki dives are super convenient since the boats leave from Kewalo Basin a few minutes away on Ala Moana Boulevard. Describing the individual Waikiki companies seems pointless since there are only a half dozen or so big boats and about 50 companies that charter space on them. (You probably won't have any say as to which boat you're on.) In general, dive operators off Waikiki are diver processing machines, and we found little difference between them. Get 'em in; get 'em out. You'll probably dive one of the three wrecks offshore for one dive, and a shallow dive the second. The Waikiki shipwrecks are the **Sea Tiger**, **YO-257** and the **San Pedro** right next to it. At these latter two wrecks you might see the Atlantis Submarine ambling about. Wave at 'em—some of their customers are probably wishing they were you.

Hanauma Bay is a shore dive, and though shallow (mostly 35 feet or less), it tends to be protected and calm and, though visibility isn't as good as other parts of the island, the fish life is excellent. Hauling heavy SCUBA gear to the shore (even using the trolley service to the bottom) is a bit daunting, so guided trips are recommended. **Breeze Hawai'i** (735–1857) does guided shore dives here, introductory dives. $115 (which is pricey for a 1-tank dive). See page 63 for more on Hanauma Bay.

Although the **Hawai'i Kai** area has some good dives (including an old Corsair airplane), it comes in fourth for us because the visibility tends to be less, and the terrain of most of their sites is a bit less interesting. (Though some of the sites are fantastic, we're playing the odds here.)

The **North Shore** has a fairly short window. **Deep Ecology** (637–7946) out of Hale'iwa is the shop to go to. When the surf starts pumping, they move their boat to the west side at Wai'anae.

If You've Never Dived Before

Nearly every diver starts their diving life with a supervised intro dive. And,

like us, you might be motivated to continue diving and become certified. You'll get instructions on land, then your instructor will take you and a few others down and should stay with you the whole time. Some companies do intro dives off boats, but we recommend shore dives for your first time. It'll seem less rushed, and new divers can get intimidated jumping into water over their heads from a boat. Introductory dives cost $100–$135. Some companies, like **Diamond Head Divers** (224–2770), will take you on their 2-tank boat dives for $125, and while the certified divers are sucking their first tank, you'll be learning the basics on the boat, then hopping into the water, but you still get a 2-tank dive. Not a bad plan if you don't mind having your first dive off a boat.

For shore dives you'll have to travel away from Waikiki (because shore diving there is poor). **Ocean Concepts** (677–7975) in Wai'anae does 2-tank intros for $150.

Surf N' Sea (637–9887) in Hale'iwa does intro shore dives in summer months at Shark's Cove, in winter usually at Electric Beach in Wai'anae. One tank is $95; two tanks is $120.

The Companies

Most of the dive outfits feed you little if anything between dives. (Note to dive companies: The quickest way to a diver's heart is to have simple cookies between dives. Over the years we've been reviewing dive companies around the state, it's *amazing* how a $6 bucket of cookies from Costco can turn a boat full of hungry divers into raving fans.)

There are *tons* of SCUBA operators on O'ahu, and compared to the neighbor island SCUBA companies, they don't seem to put as much effort into differentiating themselves from each other, especially the Waikiki operators.

Prices are higher in Waikiki, cheaper in Wai'anae and Hawai'i Kai, so it'll range from $99–$140 for a 2-tank boat dive depending on where you dive.

In Wai'anae, **Ocean Concepts** (677–7975) is one of the biggest SCUBA players on the island. Although large SCUBA operators often turn into cattle boats, these guys do an impressive job at keeping the quality up. They feed you well (but cookies after the dive would have made it better), they pace the dives well once you're in the water, and their guides are pretty good. Their boats leave from Wai'anae and Ke'ehi Lagoon near the airport. (We prefer the Wai'anae dives.) There are usually about 20 divers onboard broken into 3 groups. $115 for 2 tanks, plus $25 for gear.

Also in Wai'anae is **Captain Bruce's Extreme Comfort Diving** (373–3590). A misnamed company if we ever saw one. They pack their small boat with their own divers and rent out space to other companies, the food is mediocre, and the boat needs cleaning. Underwater guides were more aggressive with sea life than we prefer. *(Here, look at all this sea life we're willing to tear out of their homes to show you.)* Not worth your time.

If you prefer 6-pack vessels, **Aaron's Dive Shop** (262–2333) out of Kailua leases various 6-pack boats operating from multiple locations around the island, including Wai'anae. Although their shop personnel seem to slide into that arrogant dive shop attitude pretty easily, we've had good luck with their boat crews. Water *only* on board and some granola bars. Our biggest complaint is that rental gear doesn't include computers (unless you pay $20 extra), so the dive profiles will be set by the divemaster, not your actual dive. If you

have your own, bring it along and tell them you'll follow your own profile. $115 for 2 tanks plus $10 for gear.

Other companies include **Island Divers** (423–8222), **Hawai'i Water Sports Center** (395–3773), and **Waikiki Diving Center** (922–2121).

Skydiving is available on the North Shore at Dillingham Airport. You don't need us to tell you whether you should try this or not. It's either *Yeah, cool, where do I sign?* or *Yeah, right. Are you out of your mind?* Either way, it's around $175 (they may quote higher, but most discount or direct you to coupons) for one of the most scenic tandem jumps available in the United States.

I put off doing this activity for the first couple editions. I had done a solo jump on a static line some years previously (where an attached rope pulls your chute for you) but was a bit chicken to do it at Dillingham and said so in the write-up. Once I gave in and took the plunge (so to speak), I kicked myself for waiting so long. Jumping out 2 miles above the ocean over the North Shore was absolutely incredible. (One tip—*don't* wear a collared shirt or your one-minute free fall will feel like a non-stop bee sting on your neck.) The trade winds push you back onshore during your time under the canopy. You'll have the option of buying photos or video of your dive and will probably look at them more often in the years to come than most of the other shots from your trip.

It takes about 90 minutes for the whole process (half of that time is signing an endless string of waivers). You'll

be strapped to an instructor, and both of you will be dropped from 7,000–14,000 feet, freefalling for up to a minute. Companies to consider are **Skydive Hawai'i** (637-9700) and **Pacific Skydiving Center** (637-7472). Skydive Hawai'i has a tendency to do their beginner tandems from 7,000–8,000 feet, whereas Pacific usually goes all the way to 14,000 feet. So if a longer freefall is what you want, *definitely* go with Pacific.

If you've ever gazed into an aquarium and wondered what it was like to see colorful fish in their *natural* environment, complete with coral and strange ocean creatures, you've come to the right place. Hawai'i features a dazzling variety of fish. Over 600 species are found in our waters. We can't conceive of a trip to Hawai'i without snorkeling at least once. We got the

A first time—and last time—skydiver gets her much coveted bragging rights.

reef, we got the water, and we got the fish. What more do you need?

We'll admit that we're snorkeling junkies and never tire of experiencing the water here. If you snorkel often, you can go right to our list below of recommended areas. But if you're completely or relatively inexperienced, you should read on.

For identifying ocean critters, the best books we've seen are *Shore Fishes of Hawai'i* by John Randall and *Hawaiian Reef Fish* by Casey Mahaney. They're what we use. You should see plenty of butterflyfish, wrasse, convict tang, achilles tang, parrotfish, angelfish, damselfish, Moorish idol, pufferfish, trumpetfish, moray eel, and humuhumunukunukuapua'a or Picasso triggerfish—a beautiful but very skittish fish. (It's as if they somehow *know* how good they look in aquariums.)

We know people who have a fear of putting on a mask and snorkel. Gives 'em the willies. For them, we recommend

Snorkeling at Shark's Cove offers some of the best conditions on the island—when the surf's calm.

boogie boards with clear windows on them to observe the life below.

A Few Tips

- Feeding the fish is generally not recommended since it introduces unnatural behavior to the reef, and it actually causes the variety of fish to dwindle since bolder species do well and soon crowd out meeker species. It has been officially banned at Hanauma Bay.
- Use *Sea Drops* or another brand of anti-fog goop. Spread it *thinly* on the inside of a dry mask, then do a quick rinse.
- Most damage to coral comes when people grab it or stand on it. Even touching the coral lightly can transfer your oils to the polyps, killing them. If your mask starts to leak or you get water in your snorkel, be careful not to stand on the coral to clear them. Find a spot where you won't damage coral or drift into it. Fish, future snorkelers and the coral will thank you.
- Don't use your arms much, or you will spook the fish—just gentle fin motion. Any rapid motion can cause the little critters to scatter.
- If you have a mustache and have trouble with a leaking mask, try a little Vaseline. Don't get any on the glass— it can get *really* ugly.
- We prefer using divers' fins (the kind that slip over water shoes) so that we can walk easily into and out of the water without tearing up our feet. (If you wear socks or nylons under the shoes, they'll keep you from rubbing the tops of your toes raw.)
- Try to snorkel in calm areas. If you're in rougher water and a large wave comes and churns up the water with bubbles, put your arms in front of you to protect your head. You won't sense motion, and may get slammed into a rock before you know it.

Where to Snorkel

The BEACHES section describes the snorkeling potential of the various beaches around the island. Pay special attention to these:

North Shore

During summer months (meaning April–September):

Shark's Cove—Outstanding snorkeling during calm seas but can be crowded.

Three Tables—Not as good as Shark's Cove but nice around the separate reef areas.

Waimea Bay—The south end (the end closest to Hale'iwa) is *fantastic* when calm and lightly snorkeled.

Kuilima Cove—Protected most of the time and often has an excellent fish count. Next to Turtle Bay near the northern tip of the island.

Sunset Beach—One small stretch can be nice when calm.

Turtle Beach—Usually cloudy water but often lives up to its name and has the friendliest turtles we've seen anywhere in the state—somebody *must* be feeding 'em.

Leeward Side

From Waikiki—which has lousy near-shore snorkeling—to the eastern tip:

Ka'alawai Beach—The nearest place to Waikiki where you can snorkel decent waters.

Hanauma Bay—Legendary. Described in detail on page 63.

Kahala Beach—Not as dramatic but nice life on a small scale.

Wai'anae Coast

Papaoneone Beach—During calm (usually summer) months, turtles are often plentiful.

Ko Olina—Protected man-made lagoons have good snorkeling near the openings to the open ocean.

As for **snorkeling gear**, it can be rented just about anywhere. If you're going to snorkel more than once, it's nice to rent it for the week and keep it in your car so you can head to the water any time your little heart desires. If you want to buy your own, the cheapest prices will be at the Walmart/Sam's Club Superblock outside of Waikiki on Keeaumoku. Also consider Costco if you're a member.

Snorkel Boat Tours

These can be fun, though many of the boats moor close enough to Waikiki Beach to be influenced by its poor visibility. See OCEAN TOURS for more.

Now that's a window view!

submarine

You won't *Run Silent, Run Deep.* You won't hear the sound of sonar pinging away in the background. And it's rare that anyone shoots torpedoes at you. But if you want to see the undersea world and *refuse* to get wet, *dis is da buggah.* **Atlantis Submarine** (973–9811) operates two subs offshore, leaving by boat from the pier at the Hilton Hawaiian Village. Although they also have subs on Maui and the Big Island, we think their Oʻahu tour is the best because it visits sunken ships, a plane and some artificial reefs. In

fact, their dive site, which goes deeper than 100 feet, is a popular SCUBA site, so if you go in the morning, you might see SCUBA divers out your porthole, climbing over the shipwrecks.

This is the opposite of an aquarium—this world belongs to the fish, and *you* are the oddity. It's $119 (usually cheaper after noon) for the 64-passenger sub (slightly larger windows and seats), $99 for the 48-passenger sub. This 40-minute ride is a kick. Kids like it, adults like it, and even certified divers like us enjoy it. Claustrophobics will probably be too busy staring through the windows to be nervous. Photographers will want to turn *off* the flash and consider manual focus as cameras seem to have a hard time on auto. Wear a bright red shirt, and watch what happens to its color on the way down. Also, you have to descend (and later ascend) a ladder with a line of people behind you to get into the sub. Why am I mentioning this? Let's just say that ladies may want to leave their skirts back at the hotel.

Make *sure* you validate your parking slip, or the parking fee might be nearly as much as the sub ride.

O'ahu is the center of surfing in the islands, some say the world. And that's as it should be. This is where it was invented, this is where it was exported from, this is where so many great surf sites are, this is where the surfing culture thrives, and this is where you'll find one of the easiest beginner surf sites the planet has to offer—right where you're staying in Waikiki. That's no exaggeration. Having lived on all the major Hawaiian islands,

we can tell you that no other beach has the ideal combination of ingredients like Waikiki has. Perfectly shaped and sloped, waves at Waikiki crumble and push, spending their energy slowly. (Experts like breaking waves that curl and spend their energy faster, but those would kick your 'okole in the beginning.) Concessionaires give lessons right from the Waikiki Beach Center. It's about $40 for an hour lesson—five people max per group. You'll usually be allowed to keep the board an extra hour, but first-timers are usually so exhausted from paddling short distances (it's more tiring than it looks) that you'll probably pass on that extra hour—for now. Private lessons aren't as desirable as you may think for one reason: You'll be grateful for the rest as your fellow shredders take their turns.

Despite your preconceptions, odds are you *will* be able to ride a wave during your very first—and probably only necessary—lesson. Instructors come and go at these concessionaires, and although some of them can be pushy jerks, most are fine and it's incidental to your objective—riding your first wave. And oh, what a water god you'll feel like when you snag that first ride. The beginner boards are big and floaty, not like the small sticks you see the experts using.

Simply head to the Waikiki Beach Center in the heart of Waikiki and sign up. You don't need reservations, and classes are usually given on the hour. They also do lessons off the Hilton Hawaiian Village at a break called Kaisers, but beware that its waves aren't as reliable as the smaller swells off Waikiki Beach Center.

Although Waikiki is the optimal choice, if the south shore is too flat (or too big) during your stay, you can also try these companies that teach elsewhere:

Sunset Suratt (783–8657), locally known as Uncle Bryan, does a good job

Waves 101

Waves are mesmerizing to watch, and people can spend countless hours gazing at them. But most people don't realize that what they are seeing is the shock wave of an event that occurred far over the horizon.

Ocean swells are created by winds, usually hundreds or even thousands of miles away from us, that blow in the same direction long and hard enough to push the surface of the water away from what's beneath, forming ripples, then chop, then swells. These swells can travel quite efficiently over vast distances, carrying the spent energy of those localized winds with them. Think of the swell as a type of rolling battery, having been charged by winds from another part of the globe. South swells usually come from New Zealand storms; north or west swells often come from Alaska or Japan.

Near the shoreline, an ocean swell becomes a wave when it starts to feel the bottom, slowing it down. The surface water slows later than the deeper water, and the swell essentially gets ahead of itself, forming a wave. What kind of wave it will be depends on many factors, the most important being the slope of the ocean bottom. Gradually sloping bottoms like those at Waikiki form spilling waves that crumble—perfect for beginner surfers. Nearly all the energy is used up horizontally, pushing you forward. Ground that becomes shallow suddenly, like a reef ledge, form breaking waves called tubes or barrels—much lusted after by the big boys and girls. Lots of energy is directed downward in addition to the horizontal push.

The angle of the reef ledge relative to the swell is also important. If the swell hits the ledge head-on, the wave breaks everywhere at once, all across the shore—beautiful, but ultimately useless to surfers who prefer to ride more parallel to the shoreline, or down the line of a wave that's breaking over a longer period of time.

Now it might be tempting to think that the bigger the swells, the better the wave will look, but that's not the case. Each surf site has its optimal swell size. If it gets too big, the waves either break everywhere at once or break in large, irregular sections, becoming an unsurfable mess. Strong wind, either sideshore or onshore, also can close out a surf site by making it too bumpy. That's why surfers, when deciding where to surf, care about the swell direction, size and the winds. If they're hoping to surf at a prized site such as the Banzai Pipeline, the size of the swell might be perfect and winds might be light, but the direction it's coming from might be perpendicular to the ledge there, making it break all at once rather than at an angle. If the swell gets bigger, it might trigger the break at Waimea Bay (with its deeper ledge), but will close out Pipeline.

So when you see surfers gazing upon the ocean, they're looking at it from a perspective of beauty, physics and a little geometry. If you a chance, look for an excellent locally made movie called Fiberglass and Megapixels about big wave surfing and the incredible process of filming them in the water.

What your first wave feels like...   *...what it looks like.*

up on the north shore. Their 2-hour lessons for $80 are a great way to learn outside of Waikiki. In Hale'iwa.

Kailua Sailboards & Kayaks (262–2555) gives 90-minute lessons at Kailua Beach for $89.

Hawaiian Watersports (739–5483) takes you to the less crowded beaches of Diamond Head for $99 for 2 hours.

Girls Who Surf (772–4583) has an intriguing name if you envision a bikini-clad hottie teaching you to surf. The bad news is we got a guy instructor. The good news is he did a great job for $99.

Once you've had a lesson, you might want to return and rent a board to practice. Waves will seem a bit harder to catch because you don't have an instructor placing you in the perfect location and giving you a shove. Spend a few minutes on shore looking at the surf, and choose the location that seems to be breaking the way you want. As for not getting that shove off from the instructor, you'll simply have

to paddle harder when you want to catch a wave. Stick with big, floaty boards. One way to cheat is to buy a pair of webbed gloves. (You might want to buy them on the Internet before you arrive as they're hard to find, or try **Sports Authority** at 596–0166 at 333 Ward Ave. near Auahi Street.) With these you don't need to paddle as many strokes because each stroke is so much more powerful. It might look a bit weird, but it'll give you an edge, and it's much less tiring. Also make *sure* you wear a rash guard or simple T-shirt, or you'll get rubbed raw from the board in two spots you *don't* want rubbed raw.

And be aware of the territorial feelings residents have of their precious surf sites, especially on O'ahu. Respect gets respect. If you don't feel welcome at a surf site, then you're not. Be nice and find another spot.

Stand Up Paddling, or **SUP**, is the latest craze in the surfing world. The hardest part about learning to surf is standing up on the board while it's moving. This sport has made things easier by giving you a board big enough to dance on. SUP boards are wider, thicker and longer than the biggest long boards people commonly learn to surf on. SUP instruction focuses on keeping your balance while using a tall paddle to move you into the waves. (This provides an excellent central core workout, with your feet—of all things—hurting the worst.) The sight of people standing and dipping long paddles in the water has earned SUP surfers the subversive title "janitors" or "moppers" from traditional surfers. The size of the board as well as the fact that you are already standing up gives you an advantage in catching waves early. You don't have to drop in exactly where the wave is breaking. Moppers can catch waves behind the lineup, but all surfing rules apply once you've caught the wave. Traditional surfers will be more inclined to drop in on your wave since they'll feel that you didn't work as hard to get it as they did.

As for prices, it's cheaper in Waikiki than Kailua. Because it's a relatively new sport, rates are unpredictable but usually pricier than surfing lessons. Call the surfing guys listed above.

You can waterski in the ultra-protected waters of Hawai'i Kai. You should know in advance that the water there often has *lots* of moon jellyfish, but they don't seem to be a problem as

Professional surfers love to be photographed...most of the time.

far as we've observed. **Hawai'i Water Sports Center** (395–3773) does this for $49 for 20 minutes. They also have other things, such as wakeboards, they can drag you on behind the boat. (If you've never waterskied before, it's more tiring than it looks). Ride-alongs are $20 extra. They tend to be pretty rude here.

Whale Watching

Though they're not the only whales here, **humpbacks** are the stars of whale watching. They work in Alaska during the summer, building up fat, then vacation here from December to March or April when the females bear their young and the males sing the blues. More than 1,000 whales come to the islands each year, and the mothers and calves stay close to shore. Only the males sing, and they all sing the same song, usually with their heads pointed down. No air bubbles come out while singing, and scientists aren't sure how they do it. Humpbacks don't eat while they're here and may lose ⅓ of their body weight during their stay in Hawai'i. (I doubt that very many *human* visitors can make that claim.)

There's no question that the whale watching varies from year to year. Some years the humpbacks are boisterous and raising hell, constantly breaching, blowing and generally having a good time. Other years they seem strangely subdued, as if hung over from their Alaska trip. What's really going on is that some years O'ahu's whales visit other Hawaiian islands. Perhaps whales, too, want to avoid getting into a rut.

Few industries in Hawai'i bring as much shameless, phony advertising as whale watching. Computers allow fake scenes with relative ease. (For the record, we don't use computers to doctor our photos.) Some show whales leaping so close to boats you think they're going to get swamped. Just so you know, boats are forbidden by federal law from getting closer than 100 yards. The fine for violating a whale's personal space is obscene. The whales themselves are allowed to initiate closer contact (and they're rarely fined), but in general, count on staying a football field away. That's OK, because these oversized buggahs are so big that at that distance they're still incredibly impressive.

See OCEAN TOURS on page 195 for a description of the different boats. In addition, **North Shore Catamaran** (351–9371) has 2½–3 hour trips for $80 in their 40-foot sailing cat from Dec.–April. (They motor sail unless they have stiff winds.) Leave from Hale'iwa. Beverages only; bring your own food. This is probably your best bet. *However*, winter is the time of big swells on the North Shore, so if you're a cookie-tosser, you may want to avoid these guys.

Star of Honolulu (983–7827) is more like a ship than a boat. Dec.–April they do 2½-hour whale watching tours for $63 with buffet lunch, $47 without lunch. A vessel this big won't be the most responsive to whale sightings, but they'll generally go where they see the action, and their super-high deck lets you see more action.

In general, we've been less impressed with whale knowledge and facts from O'ahu companies that other islands, especially Maui where there's more professionalism. On O'ahu, especially off Waikiki, whale watching seems more like an afterthought for many of the boating companies.

Don't bother bringing bait on this fishing trip—you're the bait.

Some of the activities described below are for the serious adventurer. They can be experiences of a lifetime. We are assuming that if you consider any of them, that you are a person of sound judgment, capable of assessing risks. All adventures carry risks of one kind or another. Our descriptions below do not attempt to convey all risks associated with an activity. These activities are not for everyone. Good preparation is essential. In the end, it comes down to your own good judgment.

SWIMMING WITH SHARKS

One of the things that's available on O'ahu is swimming with dolphins. But if swimming with dolphins is a little too tame for you (after all, how many people ever get eaten by mere mammals?), how about swimming with sharks? (We wanted to say something about lawyers here, but thought better of it.) This is where you hop into a cage protruding just above the surface of the ocean. For 15 minutes you watch as sand bar sharks and possibly some Galapagos sharks circle menacingly. Two, three, ten, maybe fifteen sharks. Watching these predators just inches from you is fantastic. They're amazingly graceful and stealthy. We've SCUBA dived for years, but it wasn't until we did this simple *snorkel* trip that we were able to spend this much quality time with these animals. The cage keeps them out, and the biggest openings are covered with Plexiglas, which is appreciated when the big sharks bang into it. All in all, we thought it was an incredible adventure.

It all started decades ago with crab fishermen 3 miles off the coast of Hale'iwa. They'd pull their traps from the sandy bottom 400 feet below and throw the remaining bait overboard. Sharks became accustomed to this buffet and started hanging around. **North Shore Shark Adventures** (228–5900) started taking people out in the early part of this century. (You know, it *still* feels kind of funny saying that phrase.) **Hawai'i Shark Encounters** (351–9373) also does this. But for this edition we called *five times* throughout the week to reserve and didn't get a *single* call back. The next week we tried again and *finally* got our call returned, only to have them reschedule it the day before the trip. After all that, when a nasty case of food poisoning a few hours later caused us to cancel, they charged us anyway because of their cancellation policy. So we were not able to review them for this edition.

The boat ride is short and there's no food onboard, unless you like chum—think of it as sushi without the craftsmanship. (Actually they're not supposed to chum anymore, but we have no way of knowing if anyone does between trips.) North Shore Shark Adventures carries 24 people per boat, 8 in the cage at a time. Hawai'i Shark Encounter also put 8 people in their cage, and pack 16 people on their boat. Cost is $105–$120 per person. With North Shore you get less cramped cages; with Hawai'i Shark you get a hot shower after your experience. Ride-alongs with the former are $60.

Some people say shark cage tours are a bad idea and that it unnaturally brings sharks closer to shore. Others say it's harmless and that these types of sharks don't come near the shore and never attack beachgoers. We aren't smart enough to know which is correct; we'll just tell you what it's like and let you decide for yourself.

Consider wearing a tucked-in shirt to help keep you warmer in the water, especially in the winter, and take Dramamine or the equivalent if you're prone to seasickness, since the boat will be bobbing the whole time. It can take 2 hours from showing up at the Hale'iwa Boat Harbor to being on your way to lunch after your adventure. They go out year-round, only dissuaded if the North Shore surf is big enough to close Hale'iwa Harbor. They claim that shark no-shows are very rare. Snorkel gear provided. And remember, this brings new meaning to the phrase, "Keep your arms and legs inside the cage at all times."

PADDLE, HIKE & JUMP

The first two aren't particularly adventurous, but the last one is. You'll need to get a kayak (see KAYAKS for more on this) at Kailua Bay and make a beeline to Mokulua Nui Island. (It's the island to the left off Lanikai Beach. See map on page 69.)

Once at the beach, you'll need to hike to the left along the shoreline for about 10 minutes. The footing is a bit awkward, and you'll want to wear water shoes (like water socks). You'll come to what looks like a channel that cuts off a large piece of the island. If you're a jumper and want to try your luck, there's a lava pedestal overlooking a pool at the back of the channel. People sometimes jump into the surgy water below and climb back out to repeat the feat. Don't try it if the ocean is too strong, and certainly don't consider this if you're not a confident swimmer. You could hit a rock, drown, get swept out or get eaten by a shark. (Hey, just trying to convey that *this* part of it is the adventure.)

PU'U-KE-AHI-A-KAHOE (MOANALUA VALLEY TO HAIKU STAIRS)

One of the coolest places on O'ahu is the Haiku Stairs. Wooden ladders were

Leaping off the rarely seen back side of Moku-lua Nui Island.

originally strung up the ridge of Haiku Valley during WWII to facilitate the creation of a tower anchoring part of a *mile-long* ultra-powerful radio antenna stretching across the valley. The military would use this antenna to communicate with their ships throughout the Pacific and supposedly into the Indian Ocean. (Their goal was to have a transmitter so powerful that it could transmit to *submerged submarines in Tokyo Bay*.) Those access ladders were replaced by wooden stairs and finally a metal staircase. The 3,922 stairs climbing 2,200 feet became one of the coolest hikes on the island until vandals damaged part of the staircase in 1987. The local government was all set to reopen these stairs in 2005, going so far as spending almost $1 million to fix them up for hikers. But then intra-government squabbles and intransigence took hold, and today there is a *guard* posted at the base of the stairs to keep hikers out while the politicians point fingers at each other. (Sorry to sound so preachy, but it *really* is a crying shame.)

So if you can't climb 'em, how do you get to 'em? Well, there just so happens to be a beautiful hike up the ridge from the *Honolulu* side. It's state land, and hikers are permitted to cross. There's a pass-through at the start of the 3-mile dirt road.

The trail is in Moanalua Valley, one of Oahu's best-kept secrets. This area is home to many endangered species of plants, birds and snails, and contains historic sites from ancient Hawaiians and the

Damon family (who sold this land to the state in 2007). It culminates at the top of the Koʻolaus with the Haiku Stairs draped down the other side of the mountain.

The views from the top and along the way are amazing. Expect to see Pearl Harbor and the entire Waiʻanae Range during the climb and a towering view of Kaneʻohe Bay from the summit. The trail has two parts, a 3-mile road walk that hardly climbs, and a 2-mile ridge trail that's as hard to find as it is to hike. Be sure to bring a lunch and lots of water.

To get there (see map on page 101), take H-1 west from Waikiki and take exit 19B (a 2-lane, left exit) onto H-201. This is the shortcut that bypasses the airport. Next take Exit 2 and follow the signs for Moanalua Valley, taking a quick right to the off-ramp. Stay on Ala Aolani Road until it ends at Moanalua Valley Park. You'll want to start this hike *early* for two

reasons: The 10-mile round trip trail will take at least 7 to 8 hours to complete, and the Moanalua Valley Park closes its gate at 7 p.m., locking your vehicle inside if you don't make it back in time. We like to park *on the street* just before the gate. That way you can return late and still drive home.

The trail begins on the dirt road in the back of the park and rises to a gate. Go past the gate and stay on the road until you see a sign warning about rodent control systems. The sign is close to where the ridge trail begins. Immediately you'll notice how lush this valley is. Along the road, ginger and ferns are abundant. There are markers by the side of road that point out some of the important sites in the area. At marker 3, a trail leads into the woods past a gigantic monkey pod tree to one of the Damon homesteads. It's now

When you get to the radar dish (at left) you're treated to the ultra-grand view of the windward coast, as well as the forbidden Haiku Stairs below you.

merely a stone staircase and a foundation, but it's in striking contrast to the encroaching jungle.

Back on the road, this is where things get complicated. To find the trail that climbs the *correct* ridge, you have to count how many times you cross the (usually dry) stream. The road crosses the stream seven times on seven stone bridges. After the final bridge, at marker 10, a large boulder covered with petroglyphs sits under a mango tree. Next you'll cross the stream 10 more times (no bridges). Not all crossings are paved, so try to pay close attention. After the tenth crossing, as the road bends right, you'll see another rodent control sign. The well-beaten path closest to the sign is the *wrong* trail. Fifty feet *beyond* the sign, a shallow drainage ditch pours from the road into the stream. This is your trail. Follow it across the stream and up the other side.

Right away, you ascend steeply up the middle ridge of Moanalua Valley. The next 2 miles are straightforward: climb, climb, then climb some more. Unlike other Ko'olau ridge hikes, this one has no ropes, no steps and no descents along the way. This doesn't make it any easier (which is why it's in the ADVENTURE section). The trail is overgrown in places and non-existent in others. The ridge gets narrower and more exposed as you near the summit. Staring down at the trail, your peripheral vision looks down a thousand feet in both directions. When it seems like you're on a razor's edge, take your time and concentrate. There's no rush—you parked your car on the street, right?

Be sure to turn around for the views of Honolulu and Pearl Harbor. Eventually, you can see the entire Wai'anae

Snorkeling at night adds an adventurous twist to a classic Hawai'i activity.

range to your left. Nearing the summit, the trail levels out, allowing it to hold more water. Expect to march through ankle-deep mud, and don't be surprised to see or hear feral pigs roaming around—you're on their turf now. From the top, the view sweeps from Chinaman's Hat across Kane'ohe Bay, and the Moku-lua islands off Lanikai to Waimanalo. In all, you've gained 2,500 feet in elevation from the trailhead. That's 500 feet in 3 miles on the road and 2,000 feet in 2 miles on the ridge. (Yeah, it's steep.)

Muddy trails diverge in every direction from the top of Pu'u-ke-ahi-a-Kahoe. The 10-minute path on the left (nearest the leftmost USGS benchmark) will take you to the concrete structure with the large dish antennas on top, the terminus of the closed Haiku Stairs. You now have a perfectly legal way to see the stairs from the top. Starting super early maximizes your chances of not having clouds obscure your hard-won summit quest.

NIGHT SNORKELING

There you are, swimming in the ocean with an inky black sky full of stars. The only source of light is your waterproof flashlight slicing through the ocean like a light saber from *Star Wars*. Your beam cuts across a school of needlefish attracted to your light, then rests on a parrotfish snoozing in its nightly made cocoon. While it's true that snorkeling wouldn't normally be considered an adventure, doing it at night is an entirely different matter.

Make sure you read the snorkeling section, including the part on box jellies

On the leeward side we like **Ala Moana Regional Park** because it's relatively safe for the novice night snorkeler and offers better snorkeling than people would expect. This is a heavily used beach park during the day, and beachgoers certainly tend to scare the fish away. But when the sun goes down, some of those fish return. Visibility won't be good—and the swim out to the reef can be spooky through the suspended particles in the water. But at the reef's edge a hundred yards or so from the shoreline you'll see lots of shrimp, small fish and crabs, and if you're observant, octopus. (They are hard to see at night, even when you're looking right at them.) Park at the part closest to Waikiki, paddle out to the reef, and work your way to the right, slowly, along the inside of the reef. Make a mental note of your position when you start so you can return to the same place. And don't leave anything valuable in your car for any dirtbags to grab. The park is open until 10 p.m.

On the North Shore, your best and safest bet is often **Kuilima Cove** at the Turtle Bay Resort near the northern tip of the island. (See beach write-up on page 150.) The bay is usually fairly well protected. During the day it's not the best snorkeling you'll find, but we like it for night snorkeling because as long as you stay on the right side of the cove, you don't run the risk of getting pounded by the ocean unless seas are raging. And that's super important when you don't have daylight to keep you oriented.

SWIMMING WITH DOLPHINS

Although it's not exactly a nail-biting event, we couldn't call *hanging with dolphins* anything but an adventure. And although it's marketed toward kids, when we've been there, the majority of customers have been adults.

Two companies offer this—**Dolphin Quest** (739–8918) and **Sea Life Park** (259–7933)—creating two radically different experiences. We brought along our 15-year-old nephew as a "consultant," and the verdict from all of us was unanimous—Dolphin Quest is a *far* better experience.

This is an up-close-and-personal dolphin experience. You'll even don masks to watch underwater as they swim by you. And you'll touch them to your heart's content. The only thing you won't do is get pulled through the water by them (our nephew's only complaint with Dolphin Quest since they do that at Sea Life Park). The trainers' love and affection for these animals is obvious. Dolphin Quest's dolphins live in a much nicer world than they do at Sea Life Park. Dolphin Quest is located at The Kahala Hotel and Resort, 15

minutes east of Waikiki. The same outfit does this on the Big Island and Bermuda, and for most of the year it's a good idea to reserve this a month in advance. For $225, you'll spend about 25 minutes in the water with these mammals. For $295 you get the same amount of water time plus a half-hour on the dock learning more about them. Kids 5–10 years old have a 1½-hour program for $275—20 minutes with the dolphins in the water and the rest at the beach, with some stingrays and other education experiences.

Sea Life Park has three programs—a $105 short program where interaction is minimal, a $185 program where you'll get pulled through the water by them, and for $235 you get all of the above *and* will have two dolphins push you around by your feet. For what it's worth, the dolphins didn't seem as

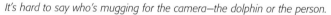

It's hard to say who's mugging for the camera—the dolphin or the person.

Though your legs may still be shaking, stop on your way down from Mt. Olympus to admire the view of Honolulu.

healthy or happy here. (Granted, that's a super-subjective observation and only our admittedly untrained opinion.) And the swimming pool-like enclosures were smaller. The experience didn't feel as intimate as it did at Dolphin Quest—more like being processed. Park admission is included with the prices.

WA'AHILA RIDGE TO MT. OLYMPUS

Why put another ridge hike in the Adventures section? Simple. It's fairly tough (2,600 feet of climbing and 5¾ miles round trip), there are steep areas where you can slip, and there are numerous places where a wrong step could be fatal. Yup, that'll do it. But it also rewards you with a dramatic view of the windward side—from Coconut Island in Kane'ohe Bay to Bellows Beach south of Kailua—if the clouds are cooperating.

You'll start at an elevation of 1,030 feet, and your objective is at 2,486 feet.

Therefore, you'll read in other places that there's about 1,500 feet of climbing. Yeah, you wish! What people seem to forget is that when a climbing-type trail undulates up and down, every downhill section on the way up to your goal means you have to gain that elevation three times. Once initially, once to regain it after a downhill, and again climbing *up* that downhill on the way back.

Right after the trailhead the trail splits—you'll take the left fork. The trail is hot and windless in the beginning, and vegetation blocks all views. You'll start climbing right away, then promptly lose much of the elevation you just sweated for. Get used to it. There will be some super steep sections followed by infuriating descents.

Keep an eye out on the left for some awesome views behind you of Honolulu. If you're afraid of heights, you'll hate some of the stretches where a narrow ridge trail straddles a horrible fall on both sides. You'll probably also dislike some of the rockface scrambles. A couple of side trails merely lead to power poles.

Unfortunately, you can't often see the summit you're striving for, so you'll start to silently threaten it. *Those clouds better not be surrounding that summit, grumble, grumble...*

The intersection of the Kolowalo Trail (which goes left; you'll go right) has a warning sign saying the trail is unmaintained from this point. Ironically, it was *more* maintained on our last hike than it has been in years. Some steep climbing stretches make having a rope a good idea (for the return). You can loop it around a tree to help you down, then pull on one side at the bottom. The last part is especially steep, slippery, and there's not much to grab. If it's raining, you may be screwed—simple as that. Either way you may choose to slide back down on your 'okole during your return. Long pants aren't a bad idea as they'll also protect your legs from the ferns that sometimes scratch at you during the second half of the trail.

Once at the top you'll have a truly Olympian view. Keep heading to your right along the ridge for a better opening. Then ponder whether you want to scramble that last little saddle to the actual summit, or simply drink in the view from this part of the Ko'olaus while remembering all those downhill sections (which are now *uphill* sections) that now await.

It'll take most people at least 6 hours to complete this trip. To get to the trailhead from H-1 going east, take the King Street exit (25A), turn left under the highway onto Waialae Avenue, then turn left onto St. Louis Drive. After lots of winding, just before St. Louis ends, turn right onto Peter Street, then turn left onto Ruth Place and head into the Wa'ahila Ridge State Recreation Area. Park in the lot and look for the trailhead. See driving map on page 62. If you're coming from Waikiki, take McCully out of Waikiki, right on Kapiolani, which becomes Waialae, left on St. Louis and follow the directions above.

RULE YOUR OWN ISLAND

If you ever wanted to be the master of your own island kingdom, you can either start a revolution here in Hawai'i (hey, if you plan to lower our state taxes, we may join you), or you can simply do it this way: There's an island called Mokoli'i (AKA Chinaman's Hat) that's 614 yards offshore from Kualoa Beach Park near Kane'ohe. (We were in a particularly precise mood that day, so we measured it with a golfing rangefinder—*definitely* a par 5.) Anyway, this island can be yours—just bring your mask, fins, and make sure you eat your Wheaties that day.

During the swim over, we've never experienced any particularly strong currents, though we don't fully understand the tidal mechanics at this part of the bay, so it's possible it could happen. Your trip over should be *partially* protected by an offshore reef. If the seas are calm, there's a small sandy beach on the back side of the island around the left (north) point. Otherwise, just come ashore at the nearest point and scramble up the rocks. Once on your island you can wander around the bottom portion along faint trails. You'll need shoes; either water shoes or you can stuff your regular shoes in a garbage bag and hope it doesn't leak. If you want to climb to the top, the best "trail" (such as it is) begins at the shoreline going up at the part of the island closest to Oʻahu, to the right of a bare dirt spot. The second part of the climb is ridiculously steep—scramble to the peak at 206 feet while holding on for dear life. Otherwise, just hang around near the lower levels and pass new laws or whatever it is that new rulers do. Your kingdom may be invaded by kayakers. (But remember, only those who swam here can truly be rulers.)

As a fallback, if your conquest of Chinaman's Hat isn't possible, Goat Island (see page 148) is a worthy candidate for occupation.

NIGHT SHIPWRECK DIVE

Perhaps simple SCUBA dives seem too tame for your adventurous blood. Fair enough. How about diving a shipwreck—at night? It's hard to describe the feeling of discovery that you experience when the top of a ship—even one sunk just for divers—suddenly falls across your flashlight beam cutting through the darkness. There are several wrecks dotting the island (see SCUBA on page 206 for more). The biggest problem you'll have is arranging your dive. Companies usually do these when they have an advance open water class, and you can tag along with them, but you'll need to call them in advance to coordinate. **Ocean Concepts** (677–7975) and **Aaron's Dive Shop** (262–2333) do this dive the most. Aaron's is inclined to dive the Corsair (an airplane), whereas Ocean Concepts in Waiʻanae has their pick of shipwrecks.

The dive lights they use are usually not the best. We prefer bright LED lights. If they won't provide you with a good light, consider splurging and buying one to enhance the experience.

First step to ruling your own island—find one that's uninhabited.

It's hard to beat this romantic table at La Mer.

By their very nature, restaurant reviews are the most subjective part of any guidebook. Nothing strains the credibility of a guidebook more. No matter what we say, if you eat at enough restaurants here, you will eventually have a dining experience directly in conflict with what this book leads you to believe. All it takes is one person to wreck what is usually a good meal. You've probably had an experience where a friend referred you to a restaurant using reverent terms, indicating that you were about to experience dining ecstasy. And, of course, when you go there, the food is awful and the waiter is a jerk. There are many variables involved in getting a good or bad meal. Is the chef new? Was the place sold last month? Was the waitress just released from prison for mauling a customer? We truly hope that our reviews match your experience. If

they don't (or even if they do), please drop us a line. Readers help us *tremendously* to keep tabs on the restaurants, and we read and digest (so to speak) every e-mail.

We often leave out restaurant hours of operation because they change so frequently that the information would be immediately out of date. These decisions are usually made quite capriciously in Hawai'i. If you're going to drive a long way to eat at an establishment, it's best to call first. Restaurants that stand out from the others in some way are highlighted with this ONO symbol.

In some restaurants around the island you'll see guidebook recommendation plaques, guidebook door stickers and signed guidebooks, but you won't see ours. The reason? We *never* tell them when we're there. We review everything on the island *anonymously*. We're more interested in being treated like everyone else than in copping a free meal. How could you trust our opinion if the restaurant *knew* who we were?

By their reviews, many guidebooks lead you to believe that *every* meal you eat in Hawai'i will be a feast, the best food in the free world. Frankly, that's not our style. O'ahu, like anywhere else, has ample opportunity to have lousy food served in a rotten ambiance by uncaring waiters.

There are *tons* of restaurants on O'ahu, and we could only include so many. If you have a favorite you want to recommend, send us an e-mail and we'll check it out. We love finding new places.

For each restaurant, we list the price *per person* you can expect to pay. It ranges from the least expensive entrées to the most expensive, plus a beverage and sometimes an appetizer. You can spend more if you try, but this is a good guideline. *The price excludes alcoholic beverages since this component of a meal can be so variable.* Obviously, everyone's ordering pattern is different, but we thought that it would be easier to compare restaurants using actual prices than if we used symbols like different numbers of dollar signs or drawings of forks or whatever to differentiate prices between restaurants.

When we give **directions** to a restaurant, *mauka side* of highway means "toward the mountain" (or away from the ocean). The shopping centers we mention are on the maps to that area.

Most restaurants don't care how you dress. A few discourage tank tops and bathing suits. Some restaurants have dress codes requiring **resort wear**, meaning covered shoes and collared shirts for men (nice shorts are *usually* OK), dressy sportswear or dresses for women. Only a few require jackets.

It's legal to bring your own alcohol to restaurants in Hawai'i, and many restaurants, especially inexpensive ones, have no objections to letting you B.Y.O.B.

Local food can be difficult to classify. Basically, local food combines Hawaiian, American, Japanese, Chinese, Filipino and several other types and is (not surprisingly) eaten mainly by locals.

Some restaurants have the annoying and presumptuous habit of including the tip on the bill automatically. Be on the alert for it, or you may double-tip. And what if you get horrible service and don't *want* to tip? Then you're left in the awkward position of making them remove it.

Dining at the resorts is expensive, but you probably aren't being gouged as much as you think because their costs are exorbitant. One resort GM we know confided that they had over $7 million in revenue for their food and beverage department one year, but they only made $100,000 in profit. (And this was the first year they had ever made *any* profit on food.)

When we mention **parking**, you should assume it'll cost you money. Free parking is uncommon and is mentioned when it's available.

Many of the restaurants in the Waikiki area make their entrées available to delivery services, such as **Room Service in Paradise** (941–3463). For under $10 (depends on where you're staying), they'll pick up your order and bring it to you, which can be *waaay* convenient.

ISLAND FISH & SEAFOOD

Below are descriptions of various island foods. Not all are Hawaiian, but this might be of assistance if you encounter unfamiliar dishes.

Ahi–Tuna; raw in sashimi or poke, also seared, blackened, baked or grilled; good in fish sandwiches. Try painting ahi steaks with mayonnaise, which *completely* burns off when BBQ'd but seals in the moisture. You end up tasting only the moist ocean steak. Generally most plentiful April through September.

Lobster–Hawaiian spiny lobster is quite good; also called "bugs" by lobster hunters. Maine lobster kept alive on the Big Island are also available.

Mahimahi–Deep ocean fish also known as a dolphinfish; served at lu'au; very common in restaurants. Sometimes tastes fishy (especially if frozen), which can be offset in the preparation.

Marlin–Tasty when smoked, otherwise can be tough; the Pacific Blue Marlin (kajiki) is available almost year round.

Monchong–Excellent-tasting deepwater fish, available year round. Usually served marinated and grilled.

Onaga–Also known as ruby snapper; excellent eating in many preparations.

Ono–Wahoo; *awesome* eating fish and can be prepared many ways; most plentiful May through October. "Ono" is also the Hawaiian word for "delicious."

Opah–Moonfish; excellent eating in many different preparations; generally available April through August.

'Opakapaka–Crimson snapper; great-tasting fish cooked several ways. Common October through February.

'Opihi–Using a specialized knife, these must be pried off rocks at the shoreline, which can be hazardous. Best eaten raw mixed with salt.

Poke–Fresh raw fish or octopus (tako) mixed with seaweed (limu), sesame seed and other seasonings and oil.

Shutome–Swordfish; dense meat that can be cooked several ways. Most plentiful March through July.

Shrimp–Kahuku shrimp or prawns are farm-raised on the North Shore.

Walu–Also goes by other names such as butterfish and escolar. Be careful not to eat more than 6 ounces.

The Hawaiian nickname for this oily fish is maku'u, which means—*ahem*, this is awkward—"uncontrollable bowel discharge." Eat too much, and you may pay more dearly than you intend.

LU'AU FOODS

Chicken lu'au–Chicken cooked in coconut milk and taro leaves.

Haupia–Coconut milk custard. Tasty, but too much will give you the… *ahem*.

Hawaiian sweet potatoes–Purple inside; not as sweet as mainland sweet potatoes but very flavorful.

Kalua pig–Pig cooked in an underground oven called an imu, shredded and mixed with Hawaiian sea salt (outstanding!).

Lomi salmon–Chilled salad consisting of raw, salted salmon, tomatoes and two kinds of onions.

Pipi Kaula–Hawaiian-style beef jerky.

Poi–Steamed taro root pounded into a paste. It's a starch that will take on the taste of other foods mixed with it. Consider dipping your pipi kaula in it. (Now *that* sounds bad if you don't read it right.) Visitors are encouraged to try it at least once so they can bad-mouth it with authority.

OTHER ISLAND FOODS

Apple bananas–A smaller, denser, smoother texture than regular (Williams) bananas and a bit tangy.

Barbecue sticks–Teriyaki-marinated pork, chicken or beef pieces barbecued and served on bamboo sticks.

Bento–Japanese box lunch.

Breadfruit–Melon-sized starchy fruit; served baked, deep fried, steamed or boiled. Definitely an *acquired* taste.

Crackseed–Chinese-style spicy preserved fruits and seeds.

Guava–About the size of an apricot or plum. The inside is full of seeds and tart, so it is rarely eaten raw. Used primarily for juice, jelly or jam.

Hawaiian supersweet corn–The finest corn you ever had, even raw. We'll lie, cheat, steal or maim to get it fresh. Kahuku-grown corn is often available from stands around the North Shore.

Huli huli chicken–Hawaiian BBQ style.

Ka'u oranges–Big Island oranges. Usually, the uglier the orange, the better it tastes.

Kim chee–A Korean relish consisting of pickled cabbage, onions, radishes, garlic and chilies.

Kona coffee–Grown on the Kona coast of the Big Island. Smooth, mild flavor.

Kulolo–Steamed taro pudding. (Tasty.)

Laulau–Pork, beef or fish wrapped in taro and ti leaves, then steamed. (You don't eat the ti leaf wrapping.)

Liliko'i–Passion fruit.

Loco moco–Rice, meat patty, egg and gravy. A hit with cholesterol lovers.

Lychee–A reddish, woody peel that is discarded for the sweet, white fruit inside. Be careful of the pit. Good, small seed (or chicken-tongue) lychees are so good, they should be illegal.

Macadamia nut–A large, round Australian nut grown on the Big Island.

Malasada–Portuguese donut dipped in sugar. Best when served hot.

Manapua–Steamed or baked bun filled with meat.

Mango–Bright orange fruit with yellow pink skin. Distinct, tasty flavor.

Manju–Cookie filled with a sweet center.

Musubi–Cold steamed rice rolled in black seaweed wrappers, sometimes with sliced Spam.

Papaya–Melon-like, pear-shaped fruit with yellow skin; best eaten chilled. Good at breakfast. Don't eat too much or you'll...be sticking close to home.

Plate lunch–An island favorite as an inexpensive, filling lunch. Consists of "two-scoop rice," a scoop of macaroni salad and some type of meat, either beef, chicken or fish. Sometimes called a box lunch. Great for picnics.

Portuguese sausage–Pork sausage, highly seasoned with red pepper. Tastes weird to some people.

Pupu–Appetizer, finger foods or snacks.

Saimin–Noodles cooked in either chicken, pork or fish broth. Word is peculiar to Hawai'i. Local Japanese say the dish comes from China. Local Chinese say it comes from Japan.

Sea salt–Excellent (and strong) salt distilled from seawater.

Shave ice–A block of ice is "shaved" (*never* crushed) into a ball with flavored syrup poured over the top. Best served with ice cream on the bottom. Very delicious.

Taro–Found in everything from enchiladas to breads and rolls to taro chips and fritters. Tends to color foods purple. Has lots of fluoride for your teeth.

WAIKIKI AMERICAN

Included in this category are **Pacific Rim** (sort of a fusion of American and various cuisines from around the Pacific, including Hawaiian and Asian) and **Seafood**. This is because so many restaurants on O'ahu blend these categories together, and it just doesn't make sense to try to separate them.

A special note on breakfasts: Many of the resorts in Waikiki will be happy to hose you with sickeningly overpriced breakfasts—often buffets—with the assumption that you won't want to venture too far first thing in the morning. $20–$30 breakfast buffets of mediocre food, or $10–$15 pancakes are common. Our philosophy is if you're gonna get your pockets picked in the morning, let it at least be at an oceanfront location, where the sounds of the surf might drown out the groans of fellow patrons discovering that the check isn't really a typo after all. We've tried to present you with viable options to the usual hotel fleece job.

The Beach Bar
2365 Kalakaua Ave. • 922–3111

This is the perfect beach bar location. Sure, service is scant and drinks are expensive (good mai tais, though), but the intimacy with the beach is great. Look for the corner table on the left side. Burgers, sandwiches, ribs and shrimp tacos. $18–$25 for lunch and dinner. At the Moana Surfrider next door to the Waikiki Beach Center.

Bogart's Café
3045 Monsarrat Ave. • 739–0999

One of the best cafés on Oahu. Breakfast is their specialty here, and we always get the waffle with Nutella (chocolate hazelnut spread) and strawberries. The omelettes are consistently incredible and expertly packed with gourmet ingredients. Nobody can beat their roasted potatoes. Then there's the coffee and the milkshakes and the smoothies and…well, we're impressed every time we eat here. Lunch is slightly cheaper, but they certainly don't skimp on the quality. (Try the avocado chicken salad.) Only drawbacks are no bathroom, and their music selection can be annoying. $10–$16 for breakfast and lunch. Cash only. They're in a small strip mall on Montsarrat Ave. just north of Leahi St., east of Paki Ave. (see map page 49). You can walk to it from the east side of Waikiki.

Chart House
1765 Ala Moana Blvd. • 941–6660

Dinner is a real treat here. Not part of the national Chart House chain, they have a classic steakhouse style (gas lamps on each table, polite service and high prices) with great seafood and a killer pupu menu. Their prime rib borders on perfection and sells out nightly. Some worthy alternatives are the stuffed ahi or the famous garlic steak. For more intimate seating, try to get one of their booths. A larger pupu menu is served in the lounge for $10–$30. The dinner menu is $30–$75. On the corner of Hobron and Holomoana overlooking the Ala Wai boat harbor.

Cheeseburger in Paradise
2500 Kalakaua Ave. • 923–3731
1945 Kalakaua Ave. • 941–2400
226 Lewers St. • 924–5034

A bamboo-laden restaurant with a south seas/Caribbean atmosphere that started on Maui in 1989 as Cheeseburger in Paradise. (Jimmy Buffett sued them because he has a song by that name. They settled and changed the name of future locations, and Buffett launched his own chain by the same name, but it's unrelated to the Hawai'i locations.) The menu is the same for all three locations. Burgers start at $10 and don't include fries (which are almost $6, but the portions are large enough for two). Lots of burger options plus other sandwich and salad choices. Figure $15–$25 for lunch and dinner. The 1945 Kalakaua location, called **Cheeseburger Waikiki**, at the corner of Ala Moana, has parking. For the Lewers location, called **Cheeseburger Beachwalk**, park at the Embassy Suites Waikiki Beach Walk and have it validated.

Cheesecake Factory
2301 Kalakaua Ave. • 924–5001

A ridiculously easy restaurant to like—if you don't

mind waiting. Their menu is all over the place. You can bring your Thai grandmother here and she'd love it. (We'd crawl over hot coals for the Thai lettuce wraps.) Their Italian is also good; Uncle Vito will love it. (We brought an Italian relative here, and she was impressed with the farfalle.) And the factory burrito grande is huge and *delicioso*. Plus there's seafood, exceptionally good sandwiches, steak and lots of salads. This is a chain restaurant, and we find it amazing that they can serve 1,000 dinners a night in this 14,500-square-foot restaurant and keep up the quality, but they do. Oh, and the cheesecakes... three dozen that'll rock your world. Portions are very generous—consider sharing an appetizer. The atmosphere is noisy. The only hitch is that you won't be the only one trying to eat here. Waits can be unacceptably long; 30–60 minutes is common—sometimes more—and they don't accept reservations. (If you eat between lunch and dinner, you probably won't have to wait.) If you see one of the tall tables in the bar open up, grab it and hand in your beeper. **$13–$25** for lunch and dinner plus a few pricier steaks. In the Royal Hawaiian Shopping Center. You get three hours of parking validation at the Royal Hawaiian.

Chuck's Cellar
150 Kaiulani Ave. • 923-4488

Perfectly named. Located in a dark, thick, jazz-filled cellar, the atmosphere really works. The food is steak and seafood and includes their soup and salad bar, baked potato or rice. We had to pull their ONO for this edition because it feels like they're cutting corners. And when you're in a cellar in Waikiki—even one with a cool atmosphere—you gotta be firing on all cylinders for this price. Chuck's ain't right now. **$30–$50** for dinner. Park at the Ohana East on Kuhio Ave. Don't drive too far in their garage; it dead ends with no place to turn around. Their other location at the Outrigger Waikiki on the Beach called **Chuck's Steak & Seafood** (923-1228) has a *stellar* elevated view overlooking Waikiki to the south and Diamondhead. Typical steakhouse menu with some seafood and lobster. Prices are breathtaking. If money is no object (and you don't want to adopt me), give it a go for the view. **$35–$50** for dinner. Also at the Marriott's Ko Olina Beach Club.

Cream Pot
444 Nui St. • 429-0945

Ya gotta start with the ambiance. It's like being inside a French fairytale cottage house. But it's novel. You'll either love it or hate it. If only there were some soft surfaces to soak up some of the loud ambient noise. Next, no description would be complete without warning you that there's usually a wait. Sometimes really long, or as they'll put it, "Just a few minutes," even when tables are empty. Earlier arrivals may get luckier. Don't hesitate to remind them you exist. We've seen people forgotten and *visually age* in the process. Last comes the food. Not your typical Denny's breakfast. Crêpes, Belgian waffles, hand-rolled omelets, baked eggs, and usually some creative specials. Sweet items abound as do more savory dishes. It's not about heartiness here, it's about quality. The soufflé pancakes are delicious but take approximately *one lifetime* to deliver. The menu is what you get in a French dream from a Japanese chef from Southern California. If you can forgive the thin service and the time it'll take to complete your meal (don't say we didn't warn you), you'll be happy with the results. **$12–$22** for breakfast or brunch. Closed Tuesdays. At Niu and Ala Wai. Open 6:30 a.m.—2:30 p.m. Park in their building, and they'll partially validate.

Duke's Canoe Club
2335 Kalakaua Ave. • 922–2268

As legendary as its namesake here in the islands, Duke's has the sort of dreamy atmosphere that's synonymous with Waikiki, and it's one of our favorite places to eat breakfast. Some of the tables overlook a pool, some overlook the famous surf spot. (Duke Kahanamoku was the sport's first ambassador, the guy who introduced surfing to the American mainland.) Most, however, overlook other tables. Get there close to their 7 a.m. opening time to get a coveted railing table. Koa wood is everywhere, and the ambiance, though a bit loud and crowded, is pleasing. As for the food, it's dependably well prepared. Fresh fish, steak, pizzas, sandwiches and burgers. Many items have an Asian or Pacific twist. You can eat at the restaurant or the Barefoot Bar; each has separate menus. The breakfast buffet with an omelette station, at **$15**, is a no-brainer to recommend—better than Shore Bird. What a great way to start the day! Lunch is either a **$15** (plus beverages) buffet or off the menu for **$12–$18**. Dinner is **$20–$35**. Consider the fish sautéed and herb crusted—excellent! Try the huge hula pie for dessert. Reservations recommended for dinner. In the Outrigger Waikiki on the Beach.

Eggs 'n Things
343 Saratoga Ave. • 923–3447
2464 Kakakaua Ave. • 926–3447

They've been around since 1974, and there's probably been a line outside from day one. Expect a wait. That's because they have a good breakfast selection of pretty tasty and hearty food with huge portions for relatively cheap prices. But what you don't pay with dollars, you often pay with your time. Open 6 a.m.–2 p.m. for breakfast, there's usually no wait the first hour. Inside it's cramped and worn. They're also open for dinner, but their DNA fingerprints are all over it with items like steak and eggs or chicken fried steak. **$10–$15** for breakfast. **$11–$15** for dinner (double if you get dessert, which is made from pancakes.) Their other location is on Kalakaua and Liliuokalani. Same menu, but you're better off getting it to go instead of dealing with the lines.

Giovanni Pastrami
227 Lewers St. • 923–2100

It's kind of a cross between an upscale sports bar and a Roman bathhouse. Italian glass-covered columns line the entry to a central bar surrounded by plasma screens. If you like reuben sandwiches, they make a real juicy one. They really want your $16, because so many items are priced just that—omelettes, salads, sandwiches, pasta, etc. The fancy décor doesn't justify paying the same price for a ham and eggs breakfast as you do the shrimp fettucini. Happy hour is your best bet. You get a free slice of pizza with every drink (3–6 p.m., Mon–Fri). On Lewers Street across from the Waikiki Beach Walk. **$13–$23**.

Happy's Grill at the Hale Koa
2055 Kalia Rd. • 955–0555

Although Hale Koa is a military hotel restricted to active duty and retired military, a little-known loophole in the rules allows *anyone* from the beach to walk onto their property and eat at their restaurant by the pool, the snack bar farther into the resort or at the beach cart (where burgers are under $5). This means the cheap food (with no sales tax) is available to *you*. So if you're irritated at the thought of $20 burgers at other resorts lining Waikiki, head over here and pay around $5. Burgers, hot dogs, chicken sandwiches and similar items at the cheapest prices around. (Their other restaurants are not available to the general public.) Grab a bite, plop yourself onto the beach and pat yourself on the back for your ingenuity. **$4–$9** for lunch and dinner at the pool.

Hau Tree Lanai
2863 Kalakaua Ave. • 921–7066

ⓞⓝⓞ You ain't gonna get out of this cheap, so let's get that out of the way. Their location is next to San Souchi Beach at the extreme southeast end of Waikiki in the New Otani Kaimana Beach Hotel across from Kapiolani Park. This puts them away from the more hectic part of Waikiki with beautiful views of their beach. The lanai is dominated by enormous low-hanging local hau trees which make beachside/railing tables very cool, but tables farther back have more telescopic views of the beach and ocean. This is an old time restaurant, and a lot of people have eaten under these hau trees. Lunch brings the best views. Dinner skies are cut off by the trees but lighting of the trees partially makes up for it.

The food is simply excellent. The level of care that goes into the ingredients is obvious, and the results will not disappoint. Breakfast has several types of benedict, in addition to their egg dishes. At lunch, sandwiches are along the lines of furikake ahi burgers, steak sandwich, grilled portobello mushroom and burgers, as well as a tasty shrimp scampi and those delicious benedicts are also available. Dinner has a revolving fixed menu of around $65 plus the regular menu that stresses fresh fish served a variety of ways, steak and lobster, many with rich, decadent preparations. Breakfast is **$13–$20**, lunch is **$20–$25**, dinner, besides the fixed menu, is **$35–$60** or more with the pricey appetizers.

House Without a Key
2199 Kalia Rd. • 923–2311

A serene, mostly outdoor setting beside Waikiki Beach (which you can't really see from your table—just the ocean). Dinner features well-dressed, well-lit live musicians performing low key Hawaiian music. The menu is small (as is the wine list), and it doesn't really appear to have a theme. A little seafood, a steak, a pasta. The cost is not nearly as high as we'd expect at the über-pricey Halekulani. Portions are small but the quality is excellent. The coconut cake is a great way to top things off. Their signature mai tai is disappointing. **$20–$40** for dinner, lunch is **$15–$25**. Evening attire required, but they won't take reservations.

Hula Dog
2301 Kuhio Ave. • 924–7887

ⓞⓝⓞ Similar to pigs in a blanket, it's an unusual way to deliver polish or veggie dogs. They are inserted in a bread sleeve with their "secret sauce" (though I'm partial to their spicy garlic pepper cheese sauce) with a number of tropical relishes on top. Pretty tasty. To drink, you have lemonade, water or whatever you brought with you. **$7–$11** for lunch and dinner. At the corner of Kuhio and Nahua at the Waikiki Town Center.

Hy's Steak House
2440 Kuhio Ave. • 922–5555

ⓞⓝⓞ A wonderfully elegant steak house that serves the best steak on the island, *bar none*. They clearly use top-notch ingredients, and their preparation skills are superb. The excellent steak selection is augmented by some seafood, including lobster. The staff seems happy and relaxed, not stuffy. (They wear tuxedos, but you'll be fine in collared shirts and long pants.) The glassed-in grill room is a beautiful addition to an upscale yet comfortable atmosphere with music some nights. Overall, though the price is almost as high as Morton's, we don't feel gouged here and look forward to re-reviewing whenever we can justify the price. **$35–**

$60 for dinner. Reservations recommended. Valet parking only. On Kuhio Avenue near Uluniu.

Internat'l Market Place Food Court
2330 Kalakaua Ave. • 971–2080

OK, it's not *really* American, but we couldn't classify it. A huge selection of deep fried stuff from a variety of mostly Asian vendors for cheap cheap. "Healthier" options include burgers, ribs, gyros, pizza, smoothies and more. But if super cheap is your goal, and you've got some wiggle room in your cholesterol level, this is the place for you. Also, bring cash 'cause most of these vendors aren't interested in your plastic. Entrées will run you $6–$10.

Jimmy Buffett's Restaurant & Bar
2300 Kalakaua Ave. • 922–4646

(ONO) Outrageous, over-the-top interior and very cool. The theme is ocean meets volcano meets tiki. They have amazing eye candy. The decor must have cost so much…only Buffet himself could have afforded it. (though some props were not working with no plans to fix them at press time). And the food? It's reasonably good. You won't be offended, but you won't be licking your chops afterward either. Some good items (great, *huge* nachos and tasty ribs) and some disappointments (like the mac nut mahi mahi). Otherwise, it's burgers, pasta, shrimp, steak, fish tacos and other Buffett comfort food. Overall, it's a bit pricey, but you're paying for some of Jimmy's toys, so come on, kick in, you parrotheads. And it's this setting that's memorable enough to garner them an ONO, not the food. (The ONO is for nighttime *only*. Daylight kinda ruins the decor.)

We haven't seen Buffett himself here (but we did run into him once at the Santa Barbara airport, and he has yet to "look us up" like he promised). But the ambiance reeks of the laid-back one. Consider for the novelty. And yes, the margaritas are fairly good. $15–$35 for lunch and dinner. In the Holiday Inn Waikiki Beachcomber.

Kuhio Beach Grill
2552 Kalakaua Ave. • 921–5171

Let's see…pancakes for over $14, omelettes for $18 or a breakfast buffet for $23. Must be right on the beach, right? No! Despite the name, the restaurant is essentially in a hole. You can't see diddly from here except people's legs as they're walking by. You'd be hard pressed to find a worse choice for breakfast in Waikiki given the ridiculous prices. Dinner is steak and seafood for $20–$40. At the Marriott Waikiki Beach Resort.

Lulu's
2586 Kalakaua Ave. • 926–5222

(ONO) Of the three Lulu's in the state, this one is the nicest. The menu is similar at each location, so you can always count on the wings, coconut shrimp, burgers, quesadillas and one of our new favorites, the ahi melt. Unlike the other locations, this one serves breakfast daily and has a refined dinner menu. Also they're the only place in Waikiki with a view of Kapiolani Park, Kapahulu Groin and the beach all in one panoramic corner. We just wish they would serve mints with their garlic fries (man, they're powerful). Beware the lava hot wings (so hot, you'll want a *liquid nitrogen martini* to go with 'em). $10–$18 for lunch and $15–$30 for dinner. On the corner of Kalakaua and Kapahulu Avenues. Park in the zoo parking lot on Kapahulu.

M's Oceanfront Restaurant
2176 Kalakaua Ave. • 971–1766

(ONO) OK…we lied. Forgive us. It's not *really* called M's.

If we called it by its real name—*McDonald's*—you'd never read this review. But these golden arches, on Kalakaua and Liliuokalani Street, are across the street from Kuhio Beach. Grab your McMuffin and coffee and take it to one of the beachside tables. Two people—**$12**—eat on the beach. Yeah, works for us. A similar option at "Royal Burger" (ahem, Burger King) exists at Kalakaua and Ohua Street.

Mai Tai Bar at the Royal Hawaiian
2259 Kalakaua Ave. • 931–8383
A good place for an afternoon cocktail since it's right next to the beach. (Oddly, their mai tais are wildly inconsistent— sometimes way too sweet, sometimes like gasoline.) Nothing's great here. Not the food (overpriced thin pizzas and burgers), not the service and not the drinks. (Overall, we've had bad luck with their tropical drinks here, though out of a sense of duty we'll keep trying.) But what a great location to overpay. At the Royal Hawaiian, Waikiki. **$20** burgers and **$18** salads— that's the pricing scheme here.

Moose McGillycuddy's
310 Lewers St. • 923–0751
A pretty hoppin' place at night with live music and dancing upstairs. The food is ordinary pub food—nothing special. Burgers, sandwiches and lots of pupus (appetizers) at lunch, add some Mexican, chicken and beef at dinner. They have a long happy hour from 4–7 p.m. Go for the music and night life, not for the food. **$10–$17** for breakfast (unless you order their *12-egg* omelette for $19), **$12–$22** for lunch and dinner. On Lewers Street just mauka (toward the mountain) of Kalakaua.

Ocean House
2169 Kalia Rd. • 923–2277
 It's so nice when you have a restaurant with a beach-front location, good food and good service that doesn't *completely* soak you on prices. Don't get us wrong. It's not cheap, but you get your money's worth here. It's mostly seafood with some steak, and the seafood selection is impressive with portions that are more than generous. (Their awesome coconut lobster skewers make a wonderful appetizer for two.) Flavor combinations are well chosen and commensurate with more expensive restaurants. An easy place to recommend. Their early bird prime rib special for $20 is a very good deal. **$15–$20** for breakfast, **$25–$40** for dinner. At the Outrigger Reef on the Beach at Kalia and Beachwalk. Reservations recommended.

Oceanarium
2490 Kalakaua Ave. • 921–6111
 You decide to open a restaurant in ultra-competitive Waikiki. If you don't have a killer beachfront location, how can you stand out? Answer: Build a 3-story, 280,000-gallon saltwater aquarium, stock it with enormous stingrays, reef fish and maybe a shark or two. Each day (at various times) you send in a SCUBA diver to feed the fish. Then spread the tables around this ultimate restaurant eye-candy. The results are impossible to resist. Breakfast buffet for **$20**, the Friday lunch buffet is a good deal for **$18**, it's **$27** for Sat. and **$30** Sun. brunches, which include seafood (which we felt a little guilty ordering since their friends might notice through the glass). Dinner is a nightly prime rib and seafood buffet for **$40**. plus some off the menu. (We got a headache just trying to figure out their schedule. Call to confirm.) Oceanarium is a perfect place for breakfast and lunch, and you can usually get a table without a reservation then (but you might want to make one anyway). Dinner reservations are recommended. In the Pacific Beach Hotel on Kalakaua near

Lili'uokalani. If you have something special (proposing marriage, birthday, etc.), they'll lower a sign about it into the tank if you ask 'em to.

Pineapple Room
1450 Ala Moana Blvd. • 945–6573

(ONO) Local rock star chef Alan Wong opened this place on the third floor of Macy's at Ala Moana Shopping Center. Of all island chefs, we'd be hard pressed to think of one who earns our trust more. Food and service are always superb, and we've never had a negative reader email about his flagship namesake location. The ambiance here is not noteworthy—it's all about the dining. Lunch will bring items like furikake-crusted tombo ahi sandwich, sweet chili-glazed monchong (a local fish), gourmet burgers or kalbi short ribs. Dinner is beef and seafood with Asian and local flavors. Lunch is **$17–$27** for lunch, dinner is **$30–$45**.

Pronto Pickle
2005 Kalia Rd. • 949–4321
Handy location to grab some simple grinds while you're hanging at the Kahanamoku section of Waikiki Beach. Their best offering is the tasty Italian panini. They also have sandwiches, teriyaki chicken and burgers. We can't give an ONO to any place that charges $10 for a hot dog (and still look ourselves in the mirror), but the food is decent, and the location is convenient for a grab and go. Just behind Tropics at the Hilton Hawaiian Village. **$12–$18**.

Ruffage Natural Foods / Ahi Bowl
2443 Kuhio Ave. • 922–2042

(ONO) A long-time natural food store that has a number of very tasty hot items ranging from the gluten-free (very tasty curry chicken) to vegetarian items (good veggie chili dogs or grab their breakfast tofu scrambler) to sandwiches (not all of which are flavorful). Just a few tables overrun with traffic noise—might want to get it to go. On Kuhio Ave. between Uluniu and Liliuokalani.

Rum Fire
2255 Kalakaua Ave. • 922–4422

(ONO) A cool, trendy upscale bar atmosphere (lots of rum, lots of fire) with tons of well-conceived drinks and a killer rum selection (We're *plowing* our way through that list, just so you know—currently liking the *Ron Zacapa* and the *Zaya*.) Also a good beer and wine by-the-glass selection. Oh, yeah, and food. The selection is modest, and there's no real theme. Think of it as high-end bar food with a definite local flair. Portions aren't huge, and the appetizer list is pretty meager. But the food's tasty. **$12–$20** for lunch, up to **$30** for dinner. In the Sheraton Waikiki.

Shore Bird Beach Broiler
2169 Kalia Rd. • 922–2887

(ONO) The sort of place many people are looking for. Excellent location next to a beach without getting hosed on the prices. Railing tables are especially good (since you can almost hang your hand onto the sand), but even tables farther back take good advantage of the view. The breakfast buffet by itself is adequate—nothing more. But the price (under $15) and location makes this an easy ONO. Lunch is a salad bar for $15 or entrées. Dinner is steak and fish served rare...very rare... OK, raw. You cook it yourself on their enormous grill. Salad bar included. If you don't feel like cooking (or want to eat from the railing tables), you can order off the lunch menu at dinner, which is sandwiches, burgers, fish and chips, or fish tacos. **$15** for breakfast,

$13–$18 for lunch, $20–$30 for dinner. At the Outrigger Reef on the Beach at Kalia Road and Beachwalk.

Tiki's
2570 Kalakaua Ave. • 923–8454
Their trademark is the retro-Hawaiian decor—sort of a '50s look. The food's so-so; not great, not bad, but they tend to over-salt things. Huge menu of fresh fish, sandwiches, pasta, fish tacos, short ribs, fish and chips, and burgers at lunch. Add prime rib, steak and shrimp at dinner. Some tables have nice views of the Kapahulu Ponds across the street. Try the coconut butterscotch bread pudding. Decent at lunch, a touch better at dinner. Their best deal is off the lanai menu, which is souped-up bar food. **$10–$20** for lunch, **$10–$35** for dinner. At the corner of Kalakaua and Paoakalani at the Waikiki Beach Hotel.

Wailana Coffee House
1860 Ala Moana Blvd. • 955–1764
A long-time landmark since 1970. Despite the reputation among locals, the food's merely average—nothing more. The breakfast selection is pretty good (the Jamboree is a good deal and includes coffee). Lunch and dinner (served any time) is a large selection of steak, seafood, burgers, soups, local dishes and salads. At Ala Moana and Kalia in north Waikiki. **$7–$12** for breakfast, **$9–$16** for lunch and dinner. Open 24-hours daily.

Wolfgang's Steakhouse
2201 Kalakaua Ave. • 922–3600
First of all, this does not refer to Wolfgang Puck. This guy was the head waiter at a famous New York steakhouse and came out to Hawai'i to open his own. The atmosphere *looks* classy (especially with the huge wine room), but it's loud inside, and the service is not particularly responsive. You'll be paying big bucks (their cheapest steak, NY, is $50), but their menu stresses family-style steak—for 2, 3 or 4—so hopefully everyone likes it cooked the same way. Everything is à la carte and sides are crazy expensive. ($11 for mashed potatos or steamed broccoli or cream of corn?) Overall, it's the kind of experience where you walk out saying, "For that kind of money I expected a lot more." **$70–$90** for dinner. In the Royal Hawaiian Shopping Center.

Yard House
226 Lewers St. • 923–9273
ono A small chain with a powerful trademark. They have 130 beers on tap. (Mainland locations have over *200* on tap, so ignore the sign out front saying they have the largest selection in the world here.) They use some impressive technology and infrastructure to keep the beer cold here. The chain is named after the 3-foot-tall glasses they *used* to offer. (You'll now have to settle for a half-yard of beer.) As for food, they have a huge selection of steak, rib, seafood, burgers, pizza and more, and the quality is pretty good. Expect it *loud* in here. **$12–$35** for lunch and dinner. Easy to spot on Lewers mauka of Kalia Rd.

WAIKIKI CHINESE

China Buffet
1830 Ala Moana Blvd. • 955–8817
Just like the name says. Cheap-tasting food for a cheap price. The breakfast buffet is avoidable, but if you're hankering to get your fill of Chinese and don't want to spend much, you could do worse. Come to think of it, maybe you *can't* do worse. **$8** for breakfast, **$10** for lunch, **$16** for dinner (which includes seafood and a beverage). Next to the Ramada Plaza Waikiki on mauka side of Ala Moana.

Fatty's Chinese Kitchen
2345 Kuhio Ave. • 922–9600
A Chinese take-out (with less than a dozen seats inside) that serves mostly plate lunches (which are cheap, filling and tasty) and fried noodles (which aren't as good). The atmosphere isn't the Ritz, but neither are the prices. Not a bad place to grab a bite on the run. **$6–$11** for lunch and dinner. Cash only. Next to the Miramar at Waikiki near the International Marketplace.

P. F. Chang's
2201 Kalakaua Ave. • 628–6760
(ono) Part of a nationwide chain, but this *super*-prominent location and their two stories of usually-full tables command some attention. The gourmet Chinese food is consistently tasty and the selection more than ample. Chinese food can be hard to order. How many dishes? Portions here are mostly large enough to allow one per person plus a side or appetizer. They have a pricey 4-course option, but it seems like overkill. The best secret here is their happy hour food. Come in before 6, and you can feast on their cheaper lettuce wraps, crispy beans and more and make a meal of it. Too bad their adult beverages are often disappointing. **$20–$30** for dinner. At the Royal Hawaiian Shopping Center. Entrance on Lewers St.

WAIKIKI FRENCH

La Mer
2199 Kalia Rd. • 923–2311
(ono) One of the most expensive meals you'll find in Waikiki. Most appetizers are a wallet-choking $35. But it also has a dreamy, romantic atmosphere, excellent service and well-crafted French food with local ingredients. A great place to propose to that someone special. Reservations recommended and long sleeves or jackets for men. **$50–$140**, they also have a 9-course sampler that takes 3 hours and costs $165 *per person*. In the Halekulani resort.

WAIKIKI ITALIAN

Arancino
255 Beachwalk Ave. • 923–5557
A small Italian café with a half-dozen or so pastas and some 12-inch pizzas with thin crust and more traditional Italian toppings. The prices are reasonable for what you get, and the place is always full by 7 p.m.—often 6 p.m. They're pretty efficient at turning the tables—perhaps too efficient. **$15–$35** for dinner. On Beachwalk, paid parking at the Royal Hawaiian. There is another location at the Marriott Waikiki Beach Resort.

Round Table Pizza & Sports Bar
150 Kaiulani Ave. • 944–1199
1020 Keolu Dr. • 261–4644
(ono) It's part of the Round Table chain, and they have good pizza that's reliable and not horribly overpriced (for a Waikiki hotel restaurant), plus lots of beers. In the Ohana Waikiki East at Kaiulani and Prince Edward. **$10–$17** for lunch and dinner. Delivery in Waikiki. They also have a location in Kailua in the Enchanted Lake Shopping Center.

Taormina
227 Lewers St. • 926–5050
(ono) A vast menu bolstered by a huge wine selection (by the bottle) with lots of great Italian reds. Flavors are bold and memorable and, being Sicilian, lean more toward red sauces. The seafood bruschetta appetizer is amazing and makes me want to come back just for that. Entrées are bursting with flavor here. When the food is this tasty—even when you're not hungry—you know you've

found a home run. Service can be slow and the outside patio table ambiance is not as good as the indoor seats. On Lewers St. makai of Don Ho Lane. Parking at the Embassy Suites and they'll partially validate. **$20–$45** with a couple pricier steaks and some cheaper items at lunch.

WAIKIKI JAPANESE

Benihana of Tokyo
2005 Kalia Rd. • 955–5955
Part of the Benihana chain of teppan-yaki restaurants (where the food is prepared in front of you by a knife-wielding chef). The sushi is not the best, but the cooking show is kind of fun, and the chefs are sometimes pretty engaging. It's expensive, but if you've never done teppanyaki, it's an interesting experience. Overall, the food's not bad, but not remarkable. Steak, lobster, shrimp and vegetables on a sizzling grill. At the Hilton Hawaiian Village. **$12–$25** for lunch, **$22–$80** for dinner. Reservations recommended.

Japengo
2424 Kalakaua Ave. • 923–1234
It's not exactly Japanese. A trendy, upscale, smooth atmosphere with slightly different themes in each room. Some are lounge-like, a sushi bar, banquet tables, moody restaurant, etc. The food is pricey, flavorful and is sampled from Japan, Korea, Vietnam, China and Hawai'i. The menu is not as extensive as the geography sounds, but it's likely you'll find something you like. Dishes will be pretty different than what you're used to and are usually a welcome change. $25 for fried rice will rightly cause you to gasp, but it *is* pretty good. Lots of tempting tropical drinks (consider the super refreshing Kai Breeze). Asian food is not normally associated with good desserts, but their Moloka'i sweet potato cheesecake is a really good way to

end it. We literally agonized over whether to give them an ONO. It's a good experience, but also one you could easily recreate in any reasonably sized city on the mainland. And in the end, it felt too expensive. **$25–$55** plus *super* pricey appetizers. In the Hyatt Regency Waikiki.

Kiwami Ramen
2250 Kalakaua Ave. • 924–6744
ONO Thanks to the reader who tipped us off to this find. It's in the Waikiki Shopping Plaza food court on Royal Hawaiian next to Kalakaua Ave. Forget your perception of Top Ramen (where they deliver the flavor with a bucket of sodium). These bowls of thin noodles in broth are far more authentic Japanese, and their description of how they make the soup stock (which you *might not* want to read) conveys it. Most of their clientele are Asians who appreciate the flavors. Take your time to analyze the different combinations, then take a chance and jump in. We recommend the miso sauce. (They won't let you take it to go because "it won't travel well." Gotta admire the pride.) Prices are cheap for the quality. **$10–$15** for lunch and dinner. (Closed 2:30–5 p.m.) Only beverages are tea, soda and beer in cans or bottles.

Kobe Japanese Steak House
1841 Ala Moana Blvd. • 941–4444
When we contemplated this review, it sounded so close to Benihana's that we decided to focus on their differences. Kobe has been open since 1972, has fewer choices on the menu and valet parking. The building really shows its age compared to Benihana's facilities. They also have annoying photographers who solicit each table before and after your meal. Kobe is behind the Hilton Hawaiian Village on Ala Moana Blvd. Try nearby Benihana first. If you can't get in for some reason, go to Kobe. **$25–$55** for dinner.

Marukame Udon
2310 Kuhio Ave. • 931–6000

ONO This Japanese noodle house draws a steady crowd even when there aren't tour busses lining up out front. You'll immediately see the noodles being made from scratch. Grab a tray and a tempura plate and pick your udon choice—sauce, curry, seasoned beef etc. Choose hot or cold and large or small, and watch 'em prepare your meal. Continue through the cafeteria-style line to begin choosing your tempura and musubi options. Everything tempura is à la carte and cheap. Lines might be long, but they are quick, efficient and clean. The udon noodles are delicious. The broth might be a tad weak if you're raised on packets of ramen noodles. Feel free to add an extra cup of salt if need be. The tempura chicken is borderline addictive. $3.75 to $6.75 covers all udon options. Expect about **$10**, cash only. Don't forget to bus your dishes and feel free to leave yourself a generous tip.

Sansei Seafood & Sushi
2552 Kalakaua Ave. • 931–6286

An impressive sushi-making machine, this local chain is famous for its 50% off early bird special on Sunday and Monday. The doors open at 5:15 p.m., but you'll want to be there an hour early to get in line. They slash their food prices in half until 6 p.m., so grab a to-go menu while you wait and be prepared to order when you sit down. The sushi rolls come out lightning fast. The menu has some inventive rolls and entrées that seem like they're trying a little too hard. But the service is fantastic, and the prices aren't too bad for a resort restaurant. Try the apple tart for dessert. **$14–$35** for dinner, on the 3rd floor of the Marriott Waikiki Beach Resort. They were just shy of an ONO because many of the rolls were too small and a bit under-whelming. Part of the same restaurant,

owner and kitchen is **d. k. Steakhouse** which offers your typical surf and turf options for **$35–$85**.

Todai Sushi & Seafood
1910 Ala Moana Blvd. • 947–1000

ONO Part of an expanding chain of sushi bars, this is an excellent deal for sushi lovers. They have a *huge,* all-you-can-eat lunch buffet for **$16** ($3 more on weekends) and a dinner buffet for **$32**. Kids' prices vary by height (so tell 'em to scrunch down). We're talking 40 kinds of sushi, plus cooked items, including tempura. And they have a great dessert bar. It might not be the best sushi on the planet, but it's good and a great value. At Ala Moana near Ena Road. Pronounced "toe die."

WAIKIKI MEXICAN

La Cucaracha
2446 Koa Ave. • 924–3366

It's a bit gutsy naming a restaurant La Cucaracha (which literally means *the cockroach*), but don't let the name fool you. The atmosphere is bright and festive. Food is pretty authentic with good tamales, an extensive selection of Mexican items such as carnitas, chile rellenos and tortilla soup, and some nice tequilas. Lunch and dinner are **$14–$30**. Pretty good, but not an ONO. On Koa Avenue near Kalakaua and Ulunui Avenue.

Señor Frog's
2201 Kalakaua Ave. • 440–0150

An international chain, we had never been to a Señor Frog's before they opened in Waikiki. We hope their other locations are better than this one. Your waiter's goal is to distract you from the lack of food quality by pouring weak shots down your throat, blaring sirens and making balloon hats. Kids will love it (well, except for the shots). If you have a grade school education and a single tastebud on your tongue, you'll stay away. Later in the evening it takes on a more raucous atmosphere that can be more appealing if you're clubbing. **$12–$35** for lunch or dinner. Upstairs in the Royal Hawaiian Shopping Center on Kalakaua Avenue. Ironically, the one thing we like about Frog's is something the ladies will never get to see. Guys, check out the restroom, and tell her about it.

WAIKIKI THAI

Keo's
2028 Kuhio Ave. • 951–9355
A classic example of a restaurant that built a great reputation back in the day but currently seems to be coasting. You *wanna* like the place, but reality doesn't match the hype. Traditional and non-traditional Thai items. For instance, they make a decent green seafood curry. But their honey-glazed Thai ribs *sound* better than they taste and aren't "falling off the bone" as they claim. The filet of catfish (which is hotter than they say) is a let down, the summer rolls are adequate, and their bartending skills are downright terrible. Service is friendly but not necessarily accomplished. At the corner of Kuhio and Kalakaua. Most items are **$15–$20,** and dinner will probably run you **$5–$10** more when you throw in the rice and/or appetizer.

Keoni by Keo's
2375 Kuhio Ave. • 922–9888
An odd concept: a Thai/American restaurant with two separate kitchens. Their selection is a bit overwhelming, and you can order any of the dinner items at lunch if you wish. The American items include steak, burgers, pasta, chicken and ribs. Full bar. They've picked up the quality, and we've restored their ONO for this edition. Park at the Ohana Waikiki East off Kuhio for parking validation. At Kuhio and Kanekapolei. **$6–$12** for breakfast, (roughly) **$12–$20** for lunch, dinner is **$12–$25**.

Singha Thai
1910 Ala Moana Blvd. • 941–2898
Pretty impressive Thai food in a beautiful if somewhat busy atmosphere. (There's Thai dancing nightly.) The menu is a little different than most Thai restaurants and a bit more limited. They also have a decent number of non-Thai items like steak. Service can be their weak point since the large restaurant capacity—80 indoors and 80 outdoors—can slow things down, and sometimes they completely drop the ball. But the food quality tends to be high, and service disasters are uncommon, if not exactly rare. **$20–$40** for dinner. At the corner of Ena and Ala Moana; parking underneath.

WAIKIKI TREATS

Cold Stone Creamery
2166 Kalakaua Ave. • 923–3866
2570 Kalakaua Ave. • 923–1656
In case you're not familiar with this growing chain, they take whatever ice cream you pick, drop it on a frozen slab and mix any number of a dazzling selection of goodies into it. From boring old sprinkles to Butterfinger candy bars, peanut butter, Heath Bars— whatever works for you. They'll smash 'em up and mix 'em in. The price is uncomfortably high, but you *will* like the results. Lots of locations, including the one on Kalakaua at Paoakalani and on Kalakaua between Lewers and Beachwalk. **$4–$8**.

The Cookie Corner
2570 Kalakaua Ave. • 971–0550
Right next door to Cold Stone Creamery at Waikiki Beach Hotel (which lacks

cookies) is this place, which makes good soft cookies, and the two go well together. Sold by weight ($12 per pound) and average about $1.50 each. **$2–$11**.

Crêpe House
2490 Kalakaua Ave. • 922–2201
Sounds better than it is. Breakfast, lunch and gelato-filled desserts made from huge fresh crêpes. But the ingredients taste cheap. At least it makes for a somewhat unusual breakfast. Shave ice is very avoidable. **$5–$10** for breakfast and lunch. On the corner of Kalakaua and Liliuokalani.

Leonard's
933 Kapahulu Ave. • 737–5591
(ONO) The best place on the island to try malasadas (Portuguese donuts). Fresh, hot and insanely good. Get them filled if you want. (We're predictable and usually get chocolate filling.) Technically, it's just outside Waikiki, but close enough. About a buck each. Outside Waikiki on the Diamond Head side on Kapahulu and Charles. They also have a couple of red and white trucks that wander the island. If you see one, their malasadas are just as good and made fresh on the trucks.

Saint Germain Bakery
2301 Kuhio Ave. • 924–4305
A good place for fresh donuts, éclairs and breakfast pastries. Their specialty desserts in the counter are really good, particularly the chocolate mousse. **$2–$5**. On Kuhio next to the Aqua Waikiki Wave hotel.

Snow Factory
1960 Kapiolani Blvd. • 946–7669
(ONO) This stuff is hard to describe. It's like a cross between shave ice, cotton candy and ice cream with a texture that is really unusual. You'll either love it, or it'll leave you

flat. Can't really say more. They are *just barely outside* Waikiki near the intersection of McCully and Kapiolani behind the Taco Bell. **$5–$8**. Give it a try if you're in an adventurous mood.

Tropical Dreams
334 Seaside Ave. • 922–1214
(ONO) A tiny cubbyhole across from *Ross Dress for Less* that serves the most wickedly delicious ice cream on the island. We've always been a fan of this Big Island-made treat, and we're happy we can get our fix now in Waikiki. **$3–$6**.

Waiola Shave Ice & Bakery
3113 Mokihana St. • 735–8886
(ONO) Also just outside Waikiki, this is the place for shave ice. The fineness of the ice depends on the sharpness of the blade and the pressure, and this place has the finest ice we've ever seen. Frankly, we didn't know you could *make* ice this fine. Add to that the fact that they chill their syrup (keeping it from chunking), and you get an easy-to-recommend shave ice, even if it *is* served without a smile. They also have baked goods. (Check out the delicate almond flakes.) Just mauka of Waikiki. Driving up Kapahulu, when the Safeway store is on your left, Mokihana St. is on your right. **$3–$4**. Cash only.

HONOLULU AMERICAN

Alan Wong's
1857 King St. • 949–2526
(ONO) This is one of those places about which much hype exists. It's one of the *in* places. Sometimes *in* places are good at nothing *but* hype. But not in this case. Simply put, the food's excellent. It's unclassifiable with a Pacific Rim bent. What does that mean? The menu changes often with items such as

ginger-crusted onaga (snapper), steak, an appetizer called da bag (hard to explain but effective), macadamia nut coconut-crusted lamb chops (the *best* lamb we've ever had), and more. Menu changes constantly. The restaurant's small but fairly loud. When you make reservations (which you'll need—they even call you back the day before to confirm), ask for a lanai table, if possible, which has nice views of Manoa Valley in the distance. Alan Wong's is pricey, but the food's top notch. **$30–$60** for dinner. Come out of Waikiki on Kalakaua and turn right on King—it's on your right.

Bubba Gump Shrimp Co.
1450 Ala Moana Blvd. • 949–4867

A chain of theme restaurants based on the 1994 movie, *Forrest Gump.* (Although you wonder if the founders actually saw the movie since few of the shrimp recipes that Bubba rattled off to Forrest are actually on the menu.) Nonetheless, it's a fun theme that works fairly well. Service can be unresponsive until you remember that you're supposed to flip the license plate so it reads "Stop, Forrest, Stop." (If you never saw the movie, this must sound weird.) Anyway, lots of shrimp dishes, steak, burgers, sandwiches and seafood in a campy atmosphere. Food's not great, but not bad. Beverages include lots of smoothies and tropical drinks. **$13–$27** for lunch and dinner. In the Ala Moana Shopping Center.

Dave & Buster's
1030 Auahi St. • 589–2215

ONO A giant, three-story restaurant with the dining room on the bottom floor, a massive game room upstairs and a bar with great views (and pretty generous happy hours) on top. The menu is a good mix of steak, ribs, pasta, fish and chips, burgers, sandwiches, fish, etc. Most items are good,

and portions tend to be ample. Service is friendly but sometimes slow, and waits are common at dinner. (They don't take reservations.) **$12–$28** for lunch and dinner. Lunch specials can bring it down a couple bucks. On Auahi between Kamakee and Ward.

Gordon Biersch
1 Aloha Tower Dr. • 599–4877

ONO A well-run restaurant with a nice menu selection of fish, steak medallions and flat iron frites, pizzas (which make a nice appetizer for two), great burgers, stir fry, salads and sandwiches. Their lobster and shrimp mac and cheese is really likable if you can get past the $20 price. They also brew their own beer here (the Märzen is excellent), but the cocktail selection is bigger. The views overlook busy Honolulu Harbor, but they're occasionally blocked by a large ship if it docks in front. Good desserts. Live entertainment some nights. Not cheap, but you get your money's worth. **$15–$30** for lunch and dinner. A couple miles north of Waikiki at the Aloha Tower Marketplace at Ala Moana and Bishop Street. Make *sure* you have them validate your parking.

Kua 'Aina Sandwich
1200 Ala Moana Blvd. • 591–9133
67-160 Kamehameha • 637–6067

ONO A well-known burger joint that makes great burgers (with 1/3 and 1/2 pound patties), nice thin fries and fairly good sandwiches (which are outshined by the burgers). The fries grow on you as you continue to gobble them up. The place can get pretty crowded. **$8–$14** for lunch and dinner. On the Auahi Street side of Ward Centre near Kamakee Street in Honolulu. Also in Hale'iwa on Kamehameha Highway across from the Hale'iwa Shopping Plaza.

La Mariana Sailing Club
50 Sand Island Access • 848–2800

ono A real find. This is the sort of blast-from-the-past atmosphere where you'd expect to see a young Elvis walking in with a beach babe on his arm. The last vintage tiki restaurant, it's been here over 50 years. The walls are all bamboo and tiki statues, there's an indoor waterfall and huge fish tank, plush booths, Christmas lights, glass globes and puffer fish lamps, all accented by a nightly piano player. The decor definitely works best at night. As for the food, it varies between good and reasonable. A mostly steak and seafood affair with kickin' prime rib and ample mai tais. The atmosphere makes it an easy place to like for those trying to discover the Hawaiian dining experience of yesteryear. Take Ala Moana to Sand Island Access Road and look for a sign on the right. Sometimes skeeters are a problem here. **$9–$16** for lunch, **$13–$30** for dinner. They're part of the nearby boat harbor, and you may find some salty dogs at the bar, which can really add to the experience, depending on which dogs are there.

Morton's Steakhouse
1450 Ala Moana Blvd. • 949–1300

This is a chain that features *insanely* expensive steaks. Here's how it works: You spend $60 for a steak, and you get...a piece of meat. Nothing else. Want veggies? They're $13 extra. Want a potato? It's $11 extra, and they're rather rigid when it comes to toppings. We went with someone who asked for sour cream and chives, and he was told, "We don't offer chives." (Eleven bucks for a potato, and they won't sprinkle some measly chives on it?) Service is friendly and competent, but they seem to go for long stretches where they forget about you. Pardon us, but for this kind of money we'd like a bit more attention and perhaps even a bit of... groveling. (You know, where even if you order peanut butter on your steak, it's an *excellent choice, sir.*) **$50–$75** for dinner. Happy hour in the bar is a much better deal. In the Ala Moana Shopping Center.

Original Pancake House
1221 Kapiolani Blvd. • 596–8213

ono Part of a national chain, this place makes *great* pancakes. They even have some, like the apple pancake and the Dutch Baby, that are *baked* and take 45 minutes. (Call ahead to order.) This place fills up fast, so get there early. They also have omelettes, crêpes, etc. **$6–$11**, open from 6 a.m. to 2 p.m. On Kapiolani between Piikoi and Pensacola. (Their other location is forgettable.)

town
3435 Waialae Ave. • 735–5900

Farro, tatsoi, polenta, mizuna...If these foods sound appetizing, or even familiar, then you might be interested in town. (Yes, you *have* to spell it with a lowercase *t.)* We put it under American cuisine because we don't have a category for *Pretentious Organic.* town prides itself on exclusive use of local and organic ingredients. The menu changes often due to the availability of fresh items, and there are usually just 10 entrées to choose from. Some tasty regular dishes include pan-roasted chicken and gnocchi. The food is actually very good here, well seasoned and healthy, but the experience is slightly out of our comfort zone. For instance, there's no salt and pepper on the table, presumably because you aren't welcome to mess with their concoctions. The artsy atmosphere, plus the pricey menu full of unrecognizable ingredients, is certainly an acquired taste. **$15–$25** for lunch,

$18–$35 for dinner. On the corner of Waialae Ave. and 9th.

Wai'oli Tea Room
2950 Manoa Rd. • 988–5800

ONO Built in 1922, this registered historical landmark was originally a schoolhouse. Today its remarkable setting makes for a great dining experience in Manoa Valley. They serve tea (well, *duh)*, but we found their coffee drinks to be much more appealing (like the caramel latte). It's hard to go wrong on the menu. Everything is fresh and tasty. The turkey on the Eggs Benedict was pulled breast meat, not sliced. (Nice touch.) Too bad breakfast is only served on weekends, lunch daily. The worst mistake you can make here is not to have a reservation. Be sure to ask for an outside table. They also do large parties very well. **$10–$16**. Follow University Ave. until it becomes Oahu Ave. Continue until you reach a stop sign at a 5-way intersection, make the hard left onto Manoa Rd. and find the signs on the right. It's on the grounds of the Salvation Army.

HONOLULU ITALIAN

Assaggio
1450 Ala Moana Blvd. • 942–1935
354 Uluniu St., Kailua • 261–2772

ONO Huge lunch and dinner menus, including lots of seafood, pastas, chicken and sandwiches. The ambiance is restful, if slightly dressy. Items like the fish arrabbiata (which is good) and stuffed baked eggplant (also good) supplement more expected pasta items. Service is adequate, and it's not too horribly priced at lunch. Ask for a table near the fountain. Dinner also works well here. Note that the ONO is only for the Ala Moana and Kailua locations. We haven't been as pleased with the Hawai'i Kai location. At Ala Moana Shopping Center just outside of Waikiki on Ala Moana Boulevard. (Park near Macy's.) **$11–$25** for lunch, **$17–$30** for dinner. Reservations recommended.

Auntie Pasto's
1099 S. Beretania St. • 523–8855

ONO A popular restaurant with both locals and visitors alike. The festive atmosphere is a bit loud. (Tables farthest from the kitchen are the quietest.) The dinner menu has a nice selection of pastas, some calamari, cacciucco (a seafood stew composed of nearly every critter that lives in the ocean—it's pretty good) and eggplant. Try the red pepper calamari appetizer. Desserts are mixed. The tiramisu is real creamy, and the sin pie is as dense and radioactive as plutonium, though somehow somewhat bland...or at least one-dimensional. (Oh, aren't *we* getting pretentious?) Lunch is hot sandwiches and salads. Prices are very reasonable for the quality. They have a late night happy hour with $3 drafts and $5 pizzas. At Pensacola and Beretania in downtown Honolulu. **$8–$12** for lunch, **$10–$20** for dinner.

HONOLULU JAPANESE

Irifune
563 Kapahulu Ave. • 737–1141

ONO As a long-standing restaurant in the Kaimuki area, Irifune is quintessential Hawaiian-Japanese fusion. Since 1974, they've coated their walls with trinkets from the land of the rising sun and pictures of their faithful regulars. You say *garlic ahi,* and most Honolulu residents will think Irifune. Try it on one of their mixed plates with an array of tempura, teriyaki chicken or the garlic crab legs. The service may be slow, but most people come here to gab and commune, so it's expected here. If it's your birthday, be sure to let them know. On

Kapahulu Ave. at Campbell Ave. Lunch is $7–$14 and only served 11:30 a.m.–1:30 p.m. Dinner is $10–$18. Closed Sunday and Monday. BYOB.

HONOLULU LOCAL

I Love Country Café
885 Queen St. • 596–8108

ONO A giant selection of plate lunches, stir fry, burgers, sandwiches, salads, wraps and more. This small O'ahu chain is wildly popular with locals (you may be the only visitor here). Low prices, good food for the money, some relatively healthy recipes for many entrées and big portions. What's not to love? They also have a really good bakery. $7–$11 for breakfast, $6–$13 for lunch and dinner. On Queen Street west of Ward Avenue.

Kaka'ako Kitchen
1200 Ala Moana Blvd. • 596–7488

ONO Very popular with locals. A huge menu of local items, such as Chinese 5-spice shoyu chicken, tempura fish, sandwiches, ahi wraps, salads and a lot more. Reasonable prices for the quality. Order at the counter, and they'll bring it to your table in a take-out container. Their coconut mochi is a wonderful, dense-as-lead dessert, and their pumpkin bread is outrageously pumpkiny. (Is that a word? It ain't in my spell checker. Then again, neither is *Kaka'ako…*) Even if you don't eat your meal here, the desserts (to go) are great. On the Auahi Street side of Ward Centre near Kamakee. $10–$14 for lunch and dinner, a couple bucks cheaper at breakfast.

Nico's on Pier 38
1133 N. Nimitz Hwy • 540–1377

The only way to get fish fresher than Nico's is to catch it yourself. They're located next door to the Honolulu fish auction where all the commercial fishing boats bring their catch to be sold to local markets and wholesalers. Needless to say, *order the fish*. Seating is outside and covered, overlooking the boats that caught your meal. Breakfast ends precisely at 9:30 a.m., if not earlier. Lunch offers seared ahi and local-kine plate lunches. $9–$16 for lunch, closed Sunday. Follow the signs off Nimitz Hwy near Alakawa (see map page 50).

Rainbow Drive-In
3308 Kanaina Ave. • 737–0177

ONO This Oahu icon has been churning out ono grinds at cheap prices for half a century. Plate lunches are the staple here with two scoop rice and macaroni salad. Offerings change daily, but the shoyu chicken and the loco moco are highly revered. At breakfast, try the sweetbread French toast if they haven't run out. $5–$10. Open at 7 a.m. daily. On the corner of Kapahulu and Kanaina.

Willows
901 Hausten St. • 952–9200

ONO Old-time O'ahu visitors may be familiar with Willows. It goes back to 1944, when Waikiki was a sleepy, fairly unknown place that had few dining options. The natural springs on the property were incorporated into a beautiful pool. In the '90s it closed and later reopened under different management. Today its pond and waterfall have been cement-lined, and the menu is all buffet. But if you're looking to slip (just slightly) out of Waikiki and want a fairly good buffet with local-style flavors, such as lau lau, kalua pig, curries and teri chicken, the Willows still works pretty well. The atmosphere is relaxing and peaceful. It's tucked away in a residential neighborhood. From Ala Wai Boulevard take McCully, right on Kapiolani, left on

Hausten. **$20** for the lunch buffet (more on weekends), **$35** for dinner.

HONOLULU MEXICAN

El Burrito
550 Piikoi St. • 596–8225

We like the tamales here, and that's about it. The carnitas is dry chunks of pork, the salsa is cheap, and the beans and rice taste burnt. You can actually hear the microwave being used in the kitchen. Only eight tables inside this hole-in-the-wall, but you're sure to find a seat. Cash only; **$10–$17** for lunch and dinner. On the corner of Piikoi and Kapiolani.

Los Chaparros
2140 S. Beretania St. • 951–6399

Good Mexican food is very elusive on Oʻahu. We like the atmosphere here, but we can't vouch for the entire menu. Some items are excellent. We love the salsa, the enchiladas and the super burrito. (We guessed its weight to be at least 2 pounds.) Their red and spicy green sauces go great with everything, and the fajitas are reasonably good. On the other hand, the pozole is bland, the margaritas are watery, and the tamales are just bizarre. Granted, a good tamale should be moist, but the cornmeal on their tamales has the consistency of cake batter. Stick with our recommendations, and you might enjoy your meal here. On Beretania just past Isenberg. **$10–$20** for lunch and dinner. Closed Monday.

HONOLULU THAI

Payao
500 Ala Moana Blvd. • 521–3511

Disappointing Thai food served by an uncaring staff. Hmm, makes it hard to justify driving to Restaurant Row at Ala Moana and Punchbowl St. It's also uncharac-teristically unkempt for a Thai restaurant. **$10–$15** for lunch.

Phuket Thai
1960 Kapiolani Blvd. • 942–8194

ono Our new favorite Thai near Waikiki. Curries are thick and ultra flavorful, seafood and vegetables always seem fresh, and their tapioca dessert is *mandatory*. Easy to recommend and just barely outside Waikiki in the McCully Shopping Center, Mc-Cully and Kapiolani. **$12–$20** for lunch and dinner.

Siam Garden Café
1130 Nimitz Hwy, A130 • 523–9338

ono Very good Thai food with amazingly flavors. Fantastic green curries, great phad Thai—even if you don't like spicy, the vegetable stir fry bursts with flavor and they have lots of Thai salads. (Only the summer rolls have been disappointing.) If you don't mind the endlessly repetitive Thai videos playing in the background, you'll probably be thrilled with this place (although they do drop the ball *on occasion*). **$10–$18** for lunch and dinner. At Nimitz Center Shopping Center on Nimitz near Alakawa. Open till 11 p.m. most nights.

HONOLULU TREATS

Honolulu Chocolate Company
1200 Ala Moana Blvd. • 591–2997

ono Expensive but well-made chocolates, truffles, pralines and other candy treats. Try a peanut butter praline truffle. **$3–$8**. In Ward Centre at Ala Moana Boulevard and Kamakee. Parking accessed from Auahi St.

CHINATOWN DINING

Chinatown is a cultural and dining destination. Here you will find the most authentic Chinese food on the island, as well as other international flavors. In addition to what we reviewed, there are innumerable opportunities to eat your heart out here. Look at the map on page 115 to orient (if you'll pardon the expression) yourself.

Duc's Bistro
1188 Maunakea St. • 531–6325

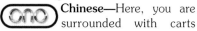 **French/Vietnamese—** This is your best option for fine dining in Chinatown. The menu is a mix of French and Vietnamese cuisine, and they do both genres well. All items are à la carte and sharing is encouraged. Popular dishes include the filet of basa with capers and dill-lemon sauce, lamb tenderloin with tumeric and garlic and the fire-roasted eggplant. There's no written dress code, but the service and atmosphere dictate that you shouldn't come here looking like you just got off the beach. For dessert, if they have it, the chocolate ganache flourless cake is absolutely decadent. **$15–$25** for lunch and dinner. Open for dinner only on Saturdays and Sundays. On Maunakea near Beretania.

Eastern Food Center
118 N. King St. • 536–4121

Chinese—Every street in Chinatown has at least one vender selling roasted meats. They're the ones with chickens, pigs and ducks hanging in the windows. Don't be intimidated by this primitive form of marketing. These meats are usually crispy on the outside and juicy on the inside. Eastern Food is probably the most customer-friendly vender. On King St. between Kekaulike and Maunakea. **$6–$10** (more for the duck).

Golden Palace
111 N. King St. • 521–8268

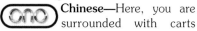 **Chinese—**Here, you are surrounded with carts stocked with dumplings of every kind: steamed, baked, boiled or fried. Don't be afraid to ask questions, though the response might be in broken English. This is an eating adventure, and at the end you will have dined on a range of dishes you can't remember. Take your time, and don't get hung up on a single cart. The dim sum is so cheap **($1.89)** that if you don't like one, leave it alone and order from the next cart. The regular menu's not bad, but the dim sum is what we like. On King Street between Kekaulike and Maunakea Street.

Legend Seafood
100 N. Beretania St. • 532–1868

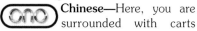 **Chinese—**Absolutely epic Chinese seafood and crisp service. A giant menu of common and uncommon but well-conceived Chinese dishes, including stir fry, prawns in a taro basket appetizer (*highly* recommended), stuffed duck, tofu stuffed with shrimp and ham, braised whole shark's fin soup, etc. The food is fantastic and the ingredients top quality. Lunch is dim sum, which is also good, but if you're looking to treat yourself, go for dinner. **$8–$18** for lunch, **$13–$25** for dinner (more if you push it or order the shark fin soup). At River and Beretania.

Little Village Noodle House
1113 Smith St. • 545–3008

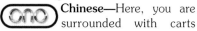 **Chinese—**One of the easiest choices in Chinatown. The food is closer to Chinese-American, but they do it very well. They also have something very rare in Chinatown—*free* parking. The selection is large, each item is described pretty thoroughly on the menu, and the food seems very fresh. Their signature item is the fried rice, and it won't disappoint. **$12–$25**

for lunch and dinner. BYOB. On Smith near Pauahi St.

Mabuhay Café
1049 River St. • 545–1956

ONO Filipino—We're adventurous eaters, and true Filipino food is filled with pretty exotic ingredients. But there are some items on this menu that we couldn't bring ourselves to try. Pork igado is one such dish with numerous organs cooked in vinegar and soy sauce. So why the ONO? Because their pork adobo is so tender and juicy that it truly melts in your mouth. Even the rice that soaks up the adobo's red gravy becomes sumptuous. With smiling servers who may not speak your language, you're in for a treat if you eat here. On River Street near Hotel St. **$9–$15** for lunch and dinner.

Maunakea Marketplace
1120 Maunakea St.
Asian—The vicinity around Kekaulike pedestrian mall is the center of the Chinatown universe. All the best markets are within two blocks of this point. But on the other side of Hotel St., Maunakea Marketplace is the only one with a food court. To get to it, you must run through a gauntlet of veggie, meat and seafood vendors, from the unusual to the downright scary. Look for the fish tanks full of crabs next to the bizarre seafood on ice. The level of exoticness depends on what local fisherman hauled from the deep that morning. Then follow the salty fried smells to the narrow food court with cuisine from all over Asia: Thai, Vietnamese, Korean, Filipino, Chinese, Japanese and some local. Most of the dozen vendors serve 1, 2 or 3 choice plate lunches for **$4–$8**. Cash only. There's seating inside for 80 and 20 more in an outdoor courtyard. Visiting this market is a must-do in Chinatown.

Murphy's Bar & Grill
2 Merchant St. • 531–0422

ONO Irish—This bar has had its liquor license on O'ahu for 150 years, and has been an Irish pub since 1987, annually hosting the St. Patrick's Day block party. If that's not Irish enough for you, may we suggest the corned beef and cabbage? Their Blarney Burger is the best burger on the island. They also have steak, salad, and fish and chips. Lots of stained glass, an ornate wooden bar and real Irish beers on tap make this a popular place to bend an elbow. **$9–$20** for lunch and dinner. On the corner of Merchant and Nuuanu.

O'ahu Market
Corner of N. King St. & Kekaulike St.
Local—An open-air market with the freshest poke (see Island Seafood on page 230) around. The Ishimoto Market counter has different styles, pre-mixed, by the pound. Be sure to ask if it's fresh or frozen. Expect to pay **$9–$12** per pound. You also see pigs being butchered on the street.

Soul de Cuba
1121 Bethel St. • 545–2822
Cuban—This is Hawai'i's home for authentic *Cuban* cuisine. It's casual dining, but the classy atmosphere says otherwise. With all the art and memorabilia on the walls, you feel like you're wrapped up in a Cuban cigar. We can easily recommend drinks and pupus here. Their mojitos will give you goosebumps, and the empanadas are genuine. The sandwiches are a good deal, but the traditional entrées are less than impressive. Most plates include lusciously seasoned meat paired with boring white rice, black beans and overcooked plantains. **$10–$30** for lunch and dinner. On Bethel St. across from the Hawai'i Theater. Gets really loud at peak times.

Tô-Châu
1007 River St. • 533–4549

ⓄⓃⓄ **Vietnamese**—Incredibly popular with locals, they specialize in pho, a noodle dish served in beef broth with vegetables and your choice of meat. There's usually a line out the door the entire time they're open. If you go, you'll find yourself scraping the last drop of soup out of your bowl. Yeah, it's *that* good. **$5–$8** for lunch only. On River St. between Hotel and N. King St.

EAST OF HONOLULU DINING

Once you leave Honolulu and Waikiki behind, heading toward the sunrise, there are quite a few dining choices before you get to Kailua. There are almost as many categories as restaurants in this area, so we mention their category in the description.

Azteca
3617 Waialae Ave. • 735–2492

ⓄⓃⓄ **Mexican**—A local favorite, and for good reason. It's got some of the best Mexican food on O'ahu. The items might be common—tacos, burritos and enchiladas—but they are uncommonly delicious. Try the tamales or the chili rellenos, and top them off with their tasty margaritas. The specialty items seem a bit overpriced for the portions, but they're well-prepared. For dessert, try the flan with a shot of Kahlúa. **$11–$20** for lunch and dinner. On the corner of Waialae and Koko Head Ave.

BluWater Grill
377 Keahole St. • 395–6224

ⓄⓃⓄ **American**—Dote on your spouse or impress your date by making reservations for a table on their deck just before sunset. Then sit back and enjoy the experience. Semi-formal dining with an extensive wine list and great margaritas. Fusion-type entrées make up an extensive menu. Try any of the fresh fish options or the mango guava glazed pork ribs. They have a wealth of drink options (consider the plum-infused li hing margarita). **$23–$35**. In the Hawai'i Kai Shopping Center past Costco over the bridge. Take Hwy 72 to Keahole Street.

Bubbie's Ice Cream
7192 Kalanianaole Hwy • 396–8722
1010 University Ave. • 949–8984

Treats—Locally made ice cream, plus an unusually good selection of ice cream-related items like the wonderful hand-dipped mochis (you gotta get one) and cookie ice cream sandwiches. Flavors like *dark dark chocolate chocolate chip* are delicious, and prices are more reasonable than many gourmet ice cream places. They sell by weight (61¢ per oz.), starting with a "fetal-dip" at 2 ounces, going all the way up to a whole bucket. **$2–$5**. In Koko Marina Center off Hwy 72, Hawai'i Kai. They also have a location closer to Waikiki on University Ave. (Take McCully, right on King; left on University; near Coyne Street.)

Cha Cha Cha Salsaria
377 Keahole St. • 395–7797

ⓄⓃⓄ **Mexican**—Good Mexican food in a small, funky atmosphere. The jerk chicken burrito (don't worry, it tastes better than it sounds) is excellent and has an unexpected hint of cinnamon. Flavors are fantastic, if not exactly authentic. Indoor and outdoor tables next to the water. In the Hawai'i Kai Shopping Center past Costco over the bridge. Take Hwy 72 to Keahole Street. **$8–$16** for lunch and dinner.

Dave's Ice Cream
41-1537 Hwy 72 • 259–0356

Treats—Pretty good locally made ice cream. Love the sweet potato ice cream.

They also have changing local flavors like mango, haupia and lychee. In Waimanalo Town Center on Hwy 72 in Waimanalo. $3–$6. They also have other locations.

Hoku's
5000 Kahala Ave. • 739–8780

ONO **American**—A positively dreamy view of Kahala Beach and the surf rolling in if you're there for an early dinner. This, along with an elegant atmosphere and excellent food, make it a worthy, though pricey, treat if you can foot the bill. Steak and seafood with Asian-inspired flavors. Dinner is $45–$80. Reservations recommended a week *or more* in advance. At the Kahala Resort 15 minutes east of Waikiki on Kahala Avenue. Collared shirts and long pants required.

Kona Brewing Co.
7192 Kalanianaole Hwy • 394–5662

ONO **Italian**—We have a lot of affection for the original Kona Brewpub in Kailua-Kona on the Big Island. While we have to admit this one isn't as good as the Kona location, it's still good enough to merit an ONO, with some caveats. Pizza and beer—that's why you come here. The beer is brewed on the Big Island, and most of it is very good with both permanent and seasonals. The pizza comes with a variety of sauces. We like the cajun for its spiciness (the Pele's Own is a good combination). The Kau Pesto pizza is a nice mix of pesto-based sauce, artichoke hearts, chicken and sun-dried tomatoes, but it doesn't have quite the level of flavor you might expect, and other combinations, like the Greek, are also a bit light on the flavor. Some of the tables have nice views overlooking the waters of Hawai'i Kai. Service has improved. With tasty beer and mostly tasty pizza, it's a likeable experience. In Koko Marina Center, Hawai'i Kai. $13–$30 for lunch and dinner.

Loco Moco Drive Inn
7192 Kalanianaole Hwy • 396–7878

Local—First of all, it's not a drive-in. This place is designed to appeal to locals, and visitors might not find the flavors appealing. Oddly for a local-style restaurant, portions on many items are small. (The teri beef sandwich has so little meat, it could almost be classified as homeopathic.) If you're hungry after snorkeling, consider a plate lunch here—the selection is vast. Otherwise, forget it. In Koko Marina Center. $6–$12.

Olive Tree Café
4614 Kilauea Ave. • 737–0303

ONO **Greek**—Certainly the best Greek food in town but not the easiest to order. Open for dinner only, there's usually a line out the door. Place your order at the counter and wait for your name to be called. Pay for your meal when you pick it up, but only with cash. Follow these instructions to avoid looking like a virgin. Their rigid ways have paid off with consistently good food. We like the fish souvlaki, the dolmas and the lamb shoarma. Service is quick, even if it's busy, and seating is mostly outside. On Kilauea and Pahoa Avenues near the Kahala Mall. $10–$20, BYOB. Easy to like if you can score a table.

Roy's
6600 Kalanianaole Hwy • 396–7697

ONO **American**—Roy's is a hugely successful local chain that got its start at this location. The owner, Roy Yamaguchi, seems to have a knack for combining flavors. It's impossible to classify the menu. They call it Hawaiian fusion cuisine. We're talking dishes like Asian pesto snapper, imu-baked oysters, sashimi, miso-yaki pot roast, mac nut-encrusted mahi mahi, etc. The menu changes *constantly*. Their fish is nearly always great. Ironically, though they're next to Keahole Street, they don't serve Keahole lobster from the Big Island as many other O'ahu restaurants do. The lobster folks on the Big Island told us that, because Roy's is so far from the airport, the beasties would get too "stressed"—and therefore, tough—from the long drive. (Traffic does the same to us.) Portions aren't huge, but the quality of the food is superb. Their chocolate soufflé, which takes 30 minutes to prepare, is deadly—get it with ice cream to actually *counter* the richness. Service is good, though sometimes a bit hurried. (We call it the Roy rush.) If that's the case, simply take control and ask them to slow the pace. They will. The kitchen is exposed, and it can be a bit noisy. Views are of the ocean across the street. In all, Roy's rarely disappoints. At the Hawai'i Kai Towne Center on Hwy 72 and Keahole Street in Hawai'i Kai. They also have a location at the Ko Olina Golf Club (676–7697) and in Waikiki at Beachwalk and Kalia. **$35–$70** for dinner. Reservations recommended.

The Shack
377 Keahole St. • 396–1919
95-221 Kipapa, Mililani • 627–1561
1051 Keolu Dr., Kailua • 261–1191
2255 Kuhio Ave., Waikiki • 921–2255
American—This is a popular local pau hana sports bar with pool tables and games that has a very nice waterfront location in Hawai'i Kai and a tiki theme. (In Hawai'i Kai Shopping Center up Keahole *past* the Hawai'i Kai Towne Center.) Bar food includes lots of burgers (the shack burger is a patty with a hot link on top and tastes *exactly* like it sounds), chicken sandwiches along with the expected appetizers. Food is not bad until they stray from their bar roots, so avoid the ahi wrap and other items you wouldn't find on the mainland. Cheap happy hour and beer. Their Kailua and Mililani locations

are very avoidable. **$10–$15** for lunch and dinner plus a couple pricier items.

Soul Cuisine
3040 Waialae Ave. • 735–7685
ⓞⓝⓞ **Soul**—Totally hidden in a tiny little strip mall on Waialae and St. Louis (you'll probably have to pay to park in the gravel lot across the street), this is the place to get your North Carolina soul food fix. Genuine articles such as jambalaya, gumbo and grits, fried chicken with chili, shrimp and cheesy grits, Carolina pulled pork adobo, and an unusual but effective cole slaw are the kind of items you'll be pickin' from. The menu changes slightly each day. Your surroundings are certainly no-frills and dipped in '70s soul retro and lots of disco music, but it's *the food* you care about. Spicy some of the time, bold flavors all of the time. They call it soul with a twist of aloha, and that sounds about right. The food is real easy to like, and if it resonates with you like it did us, you'll come back at least once for the taste, price (for Hawai'i) and ample portions. Limited service. **$10–$23** for lunch and dinner. Closed Monday. Leaving Waikiki from the southeast, take Kapahulu mauka, right on Waialae, quick left on St. Louis, then curse the minimal parking. BYOB from the 7-Eleven down the street.

South Shore Grill
3114 Monsarrat Ave. • 734–0229
ⓞⓝⓞ **American**—One of the best burgers in town. They top this 7-ouncer (and almost everything else) with their homemade slaw and serve it on ciabatta bread. If that's not good enough, try the East Coast West Coast, a chicken sandwich piled high with pastrami. The plate lunches are great, too, and they bake their own desserts. The bright interior is matched only by the friendly

staff. Prepare to wait in line during peak hours. **$8–$14** for lunch and dinner. From Waikiki, head toward Diamond Head on Kalakaua Ave. Turn onto Monsarrat between the zoo and Kapiolani Park. Look for it on the left just after Kanaina Ave.

3660 on the Rise
3660 Waialae Ave. • 737–1177

ONO **American**—Well known among island residents for their dependably good food. There's no view here, but the service and food make it fairly compelling. Steak and seafood *sound* so ordinary, but the complexity of their recipes and their success at combining flavors usually make for a very good meal. Many dishes have an Asian twist. Impressive but pretty pricey wine list. **$30–$65** for dinner; reservations recommended. Ten minutes east of Waikiki. Take McCully or Kapahulu out of Waikiki, right on Kapiolani, which becomes Waialae. Our only quibble is that the acoustics seem to lend themselves to conversations spilling across the tables more than at most places. Closed Mondays.

12th Avenue Grill
1145 12th Ave. • 732–9469

ONO **American**—This trendy little restaurant has received nothing but praise since it opened. The prices are upscale, but they accurately reflect the flavors and the atmosphere. The entrées seem intricately designed, the martinis are generous, and the desserts will knock you back in your seat. Menu changes seasonally, and you should see what they do with macaroni & cheese. Dinner is **$25–$35**, starting at 5:30 p.m. Closed on Sunday. Located down an alley behind Waialae Ave. From Waikiki, take Kapiolani to Waialae and turn right on 12th just before Koko Head.

Whole Foods Market
4211 Waialae Ave. • 738–0820

American—If you come from a town with a Whole Foods, you already know about the cornucopia of healthy and organic foods they offer. Sandwiches, sushi, BBQ, Asian cuisine, soup and salad bar and a hot bar. Their pizza might have the best crust on the island. The hot bar regularly has spicy Indian dishes right next to turkey with all the fixin's. It's pricier than other supermarket food, but the quality and selection make it worthwhile. **$9–$16** for lunch and dinner. In the Kahala Mall.

KAILUA DINING

Agnes' Portuguese Bake Shop
46 Hoolai St. • 262–5367

ONO **Treats**—A great place for coffee and baked goods in the morning, or to pick up a pie or fresh bread for later. This place is beloved by local windward residents. Especially noteworthy are the coconut macaroons and the apple turnovers, and, although they don't make these here, their chocolate-covered sunflower seeds are painfully addictive. I'm jonesin' for 'em just writing about it. Agnes' has lots of coffees, teas, espressos, etc., as well as Internet access. It's spotless inside, tucked away and hard to find. In Kailua at 46 Hoolai St. at Kihapai Street. Near the intersection of Kailua Road and Oneawa (these are main roads), Hoolai is the side street just mauka of Oneawa. **$3–$5**.

Aloha Salads
600 Kailua Rd. • 262–2016

ONO **American**—A cubbyhole with fantastic salads, subs and wraps with great ingredients for darned reasonable prices. Yeah, that's what we like to hear. Their selection is imaginative, often including various fruits, local vegetables and produce as well as island fish. We've had good luck with their soups of the day, and even kids will love their PB&H sub with bananas. If all this seems too healthy, top it off with the Nutella, strawberry and honey wrap. A easy place to like, unless you want to sit down. (Just a few seats.) **$9–$13**. In Kailua Shopping Center.

Big City Diner
108 Hekili St. • 263–8880

ONO **American**—A small, local chain with a small-town diner feel. The seating is really uncomfortable, especially the vertical booths—pick a chair. The super varied breakfast menu has typical entrées along with items like Mama's breakfast bread pudding (a tasty guilty pleasure), unusually adorned pancakes and kimchee fried rice. Lunch and dinner have just as much variety with lots of salads, sandwiches and burgers, local items and a hodgepodge of assorted selections. With such a broad appeal, there's something for everyone. The food is good and the portions ample. Full bar and some open air seating. **$7–$13** for breakfast, **$11–$23** for lunch and dinner. In the Kailua Foodland Marketplace.

Boots & Kimo's Homestyle Kitchen
151 Hekili St. • 263–7929

ONO **American**—Our endorsement assumes something that probably *won't* happen. It assumes there won't be a ridiculous wait. 'Cause frankly, we don't think *any* breakfast is worth cooling your heels for a hour (or more). This place is popular with locals and visitors. We could almost have classified them as local food. Their specialty is awesome macadamia nut pancakes with a marvelous creamy mac sauce. Definitely try them. Lots of omelettes, so-so hash browns and local dishes in a local sporty environment. Love their strawberry waffles. Breakfast until 2

p.m.; lunch items also served during typical lunch hours. Service can be less than loving. Between Hahani and Hamakua. **$9–$14** for breakfast.

Buzz's Original Steak House
413 Kawailoa Rd. • 261–4661

ONO **American**—Across the street from Kailua Beach Park, its location doesn't take advantage of the potential views. Though it gets fairly crowded and noisy, it has a genuine island atmosphere. Lunch is burgers, fish burgers, chicken sandwich (which needs a bigger portion—we didn't know chickens came that small) and lots of salads. Dinner is steak and seafood. The steak and lobster combo is pretty good, though beef cuts could be a better quality. Love the Cajun-style fish and the Chinese-style fish. *When they have it*, the stuffed ahi is amazing. The artichoke surprise appetizer *can* be awesome, but it's also quite variable. Their "legendary mai tais" are *very* strong—like gasoline. Their BFRD adds pineapple to a taller glass. Same gas mileage, lower octane. Service can be a bit attitudy, and it almost cost 'em their ONO. (Until they bring the check—then they get *soooo* sweet.) **$12–$18** for lunch, **$20–$35** for dinner (more for huge prime rib cuts or lobster). Reservations recommended. Go early or go late. Prime time is pretty hectic. No tank tops allowed after 5 p.m. Buzz's does disappoint on occasion, but overall rates an ONO.

Cinnamon's
315 Uluniu St. • 261–8724

ONO **American**—Open since 1985, you'll want to bring your sweet tooth and your stretchy pants. Open-air seating abounds in the atrium of the Kailua Square on Uluniu. The owner makes all of their cinnamon rolls, biscuits, cornbread and coffee cake in her home. Known locally more for breakfast and brunch, you can definitely expect a crowd. Try the red velvet pancakes or the mac nut cinnamon roll. We also loved the lox benedict, but their corned beef hash can be avoided. The lunch menu consists of salads, soups sandwiches and assorted plates. But it's breakfast that is the star. They will accept your reservation if there are 5 or more in your party. We were told with a wink and a nod that if you made a reservation for 5 and showed up with 4, your reservation would still be honored. Breakfast is **$10–$14**, lunch **$12–$14**

Crêpes No Ka 'Oi
131 Hekili St. • 263–4088

American—Novel food for relatively cheap cheap. So far, so good. All items come on their fresh crêpes with a few breakfast combinations along with their "savory" items, such as the Popeye (lots of spinach, of course), Haole Boy (ham, cheese and pineapple—ironically, on a pizza that's called Hawaiian), and others. Also lots of dessert crêpes, many with the highly addictive (in a good way) Nutella. A huge tea selection. Simple surroundings, ample portions and reasonably quick service. **$8–$10** for breakfast, lunch and dinner unless you snag one of the desserts. Closed Tuesdays. Between Hahani and Hamakua streets.

Island Snow (Kailua)
130 Kailua Rd. • 263–6339

Treats—Good shave ice, though they can be overgenerous with the syrup. Get ice cream on the bottom. This is convenient after a hard day of beachgoing at Kailua or Lanikai Beach. Often served with blank indifference, even if you burst into flames from spontaneous human combustion. At Kailua Beach Center on Kailua Road near Kalaheo; walkable from Kailua Beach Park. **$2–$3**.

K & K BBQ Inn
130 Kailua Rd. • 262–2272

Local—It's a hole in the wall with a disheveled look and the food quality varies considerably, but the selection is huge and they are within walking distance to Kailua Beach Park. Local foods such as chicken katsu, teri steak, sweet and sour spare ribs, saimin and other noodle dishes, plus burgers, fish sandwiches, etc. In short—no great food to be had, but it's convenient for Kailua beachgoers. Nothing more. In Kailua Beach Center on Kailua Road near Kalaheo Road. **$7–$12**.

Lanikai Juice
572 Kailua Rd. • 262–2383

Treats—Expect to wait in line at this locally famous juice bar. Their smoothies are great, and they focus on all-natural ingredients. All orders include your choice of supplement. Try their Mango Mama Mia with bee pollen for strength and endurance, or their strawberry shaka with echinacea for an immune boost. It's hard to go wrong, no matter what you get. **$4–$10** In the Kailua Shopping Center.

Los Garcia's
14 Oneawa St. • 261–0306

Mexican—Huge menu of traditional and non-traditional Mexican items, including fajitas, steak and seafood plus vegetarian items and a full bar. Service is lightning fast. The flavors don't work for us, but they have an unusually loyal customer base who no doubt think we're full of beans. On Oneawa near Kailua Road in Kailua. **$8–$20** for lunch and dinner. Consider parking a block over at the municipal building on Aulike.

Maui Tacos
539 Kailua Rd. • 261–4155

Mexican—This small, local chain is a good place to go

for tacos and burritos. It's not overly expensive (though it ain't exactly cheap), portions are large, and they're totally flexible when concocting items. Don't neglect the sauces to the right of the soda machine to spice things up the way you like them. In Kailua Village Shops at Kailua and Hahani in Kailua. **$7–$10**.

Mexico Lindo
600 Kailua Rd. • 263-0055
Mexican—Good looking—that's the theme. The interior is good looking, the food is good looking, even the menu is good looking. But that's where it ends. It's skin deep. Beyond the looks, everything disappoints. The festive Mexican ambiance gets dampened by the utter loudness inside. The menu is broad and varied, with a fairly good tequila selection, but tastes so bland you may be grateful for that bottle of Tapatío on the table. Service is either with a smile or with a snarl. **$10–$25** for lunch and dinner. In the Kailua Shopping Center.

Moké's Bread & Breakfast
27 Hoolai St. • 261-5565
ONO **Local**—This is a great little offbeat, family-operated restaurant. In- and outdoor seating and a *Mom's cooking* feel. They bake their own bread here and braise their own beef brisket for making reubens and corned beef hash, and it is rockin' delicious. The rest of the usual suspects are loco moco, liliko'i pancakes, waffles and French toast for breakfast as well as pork chops and gravy and a house-cut ribeye with eggs for $11.50. Lunch is sandwiches on their fresh baked bread, soup du jour and fresh green salads. Good service, good ingredients, good folks. Expect a wait, especially on weekends. Breakfast is **$9–$14**, lunch is **$8–$11**. By the way, it's Moké, *not Moke*. In Hawai'i, if you're not from here, and you call someone a moke (espe-

cially if he *is* a moke), bad things will happen to you and your bones. See definition in BASICS.

Pepper's Place
600 Kailua Rd. • 262-3337
ONO **American**—Good sandwiches and cheesesteaks. Try the sausage sandwich—they chop it up and mix cheese, pepper and onions in it. *Excellent!* Hot dogs and baked potatoes also. They are kind of slow, but you can call ahead. **$9–$13**. In Kailua Shopping Center in Kailua on Kailua Road near Hahani Street.

Pinky's Pupu Bar & Grill
970 N. Kalaheo Ave. • 254-6255
American—A vast pupu (appetizer) menu along with lots of sandwiches, some fresh fish, steak, pasta and pizzas. There are winners here—such as the tasty ribs and coconut shrimp along with fairly good burgers—and some losers, such as the edamame or the margaritas. (Decent mai tais, though.) Two people might get the job done with one of their enormous pupu platters and a couple of drinks, most of which come in giant, 18-ounce schooners, so a single mai tai can do a lot of damage. Many of the tables on the left have relaxing views of Kawainui Canal. (Look for ducks.) Right side tables are in a sports bar lounge. Service can be unresponsive, and it's often really loud inside, probably due to the low, hard ceilings. Popular with local residents, Tuesday is kid's night—a great night to avoid if the *endless* sound of twisting balloon animals rubs you the wrong way, as it does me. (That's my hated sound—I'd rather hear a fork scraping on a plate for *hours* or wipers on a dry windshield.) **$9–$20** for lunch (Fri.–Sun. only), **$12–$27** for dinner. Across from the Aikahi Shopping Center where Mokapu Boulevard, Kane'ohe Bay

Drive and N. Kalaheo Ave. converge near the north end of Kailua Beach.

Prima
108 Hekili St. • 888–8933

ono **American**—A wine bar with tapas and brick oven pizzas. Decor is sparse, modern, simple. The tapas are appealing with surprisingly good Brussels sprouts, roasted fingerlings, spicy meatballs and grilled opah. From their genuine Naplese brick oven come pizzas that are thin and flavorful, if a bit salty. The wine selection is not huge (limited space) but seems well-chosen. Lunch is basic sandwiches and the pizzas. Tapas-style share plates from **$4** to **$27**, pasta and pizza **$13–$16** plus any extra toppings you choose. Service is vastly knowledgeable and eager to please. Overall, a really likeable place. Next to Foodland.

Saeng's Thai Cuisine
315 Hahani St. • 263–9727

Thai—If you're in Kailua and looking for excellent Thai food...you're outta luck. The food's not exactly good, the service is not exactly good—the restaurant's not exactly good. Guess that about covers it. But if you're craving Thai in Kailua, it's not exactly bad (and it's better than another Kailua Thai restaurant, **Champa Thai**). Nice vegetarian selection. **$10–$25** for lunch and dinner. On Hahani Street at Kailua Street in Kailua.

Saigon Noodle House
1020 Keolu Dr. • 261–2466

Vietnamese—Large Vietnamese menu that does a pretty good job of explaining your options. All kinds of noodles, rice dishes and Vietnamese sandwiches with everything under **$10**. Service is lightning fast, portions generous and flavors are good. They don't fish from the usual stream of visitors. Nearly all their customers are residents of Enchanted Lakes

subdivision, yet it's only a few minutes from Kailua Beach. We ain't saying it's the best food on the island; we're saying it's a heck of a deal. In Enchanted Lakes Shopping Center.

Sweet Stop
130 Kailua Rd. • 721–5034

ono **Treats**—Tucked away and hard to find in the interior corner of the Kailua Beach Center, this bake shop has incredible cakes, chocolates and truffles made on the spot. They have a great sampler for $10; otherwise, look and read, eat and curse your weakness. It's OK. You're on vacation. **$3–$6**. Closed Sun. and Mon. In the same shopping center is **Bob's Pizzeria** (263–7757). The price of a greasy slice might be startling—$6—but so is the acreage. It's a quarter of a 19-inch pie.

Teddy's Burgers
539 Kailua Rd. • 262–0820
134 Kapahulu Ave. • 926–3444
7192 Kalanianaole Hwy • 394–9100

American—A retro burger joint in the Kailua Village Shops, Kailua. (They also have locations in Waikiki and Hawai'i Kai.) Burgers aren't bad—some of the specialty burgers are pretty creative—and their fries are pretty good, but overall, it's kind of pricey. Nothing to get too excited about. **$7–$12** for lunch and dinner.

KANE'OHE DINING

Boston Style Pizza
46-028 Kawa St. • 235–7756

Italian—An O'ahu chain. Pretty good reputation, but frankly, the pizza is fairly average. Their motto is "size does matter," and you have a choice of a 19-inch pizza...or a slice. Crusts are thin in the middle, thick on the edges. Flavors are simple—gourmet, it's not. Their other locations are in Kaimuki and Hawai'i Kai. This one is off Kamehameha Highway (83) near Windward Mall. Only a few tables at most locations; people usually just take out. **$6–$15**.

Chao Phya Thai
45-480 Kaneohe Bay Dr. • 235-3555

Thai—Sometimes you just want inexpensive Thai food fairly quickly. If that's your goal, you could do worse than Chao Phya. (Now *there's* a tough name to pronounce.) Fairly wide selection, and you get it quick. Portions are good, and the price is right. Avoid the Thai tea—too sweet. **$8–$15** for lunch and dinner. BYOB. In Windward City Shopping Mall, Kamehameha Highway (83) and Kane'ohe Bay Drive, Kane'ohe.

Hale'iwa Joe's at Haiku Gardens
46-336 Haiku Rd. • 247-6671

American—Located in a lush garden setting at Haiku Gardens, it's nice to do a pre-meal stroll in the garden and pond area if you arrive before sunset. In fact, we *strongly* recommend getting there for an early dinner (they open at 5:30 p.m.) since the view of the Ko'olau Mountains is so exquisite in the afternoon. (Plus, the garden setting might bring flying bugs later in the evening.) We like the tables near the railing the best. The food is generally very good. Try the wonderful Thai calamari for an appetizer. Dinner is steak and seafood, plus ribs, pork chops (excellent) and sometimes lobster. The decor includes lots of attractive koa wood. Service can be slow at times, and they don't take reservations. **$20–$40** for dinner. From Hwy 830 (Kamehameha Hwy), turn toward the mountain onto Haiku Road near the Windward Mall. You'll see it on the left a while after Haiku Road crosses Hwy 83.

BETWEEN KANE'OHE & KAHUKU

Once you drive north of Kane'ohe on Hwy 83, your options dwindle until you get to Hale'iwa 40 miles away. Here we've listed the restaurants *in the order that you'll see them*, not in alphabetical order.

Your first opportunity after Kane'ohe is your best bet. **Uncle Bobo's (237-1000)** at 51-480 Kamehameha Hwy is in the tiny town of Ka'a'awa. Uncle Bobo is serious about his BBQ. You can tell because the kitchen is four times the size of the dining room. Luckily he's located just across the street from Swanzy Beach Park with plenty of ocean-view seating. We live for small-town, mom-and-pop diamonds in the rough like this one. The menu isn't big, but it meets all the requirements of a smokehouse. The pork shoulder is an easy favorite, the ribs a close second, and the brisket's not bad either. Get the combo platter and split it with someone hungry. Their homemade sauce is so good, we hope they bottle it someday. **$7–$18** for lunch and early dinner. Closed Monday.

Your next food choice is a disappointment. **Crouching Lion Inn (237-8981)** at 51-666 Kamehameha Hwy is that place that everyone knows you're supposed to stop at. This is considered the place to have lunch on the windward side. Unfortunately, we've noticed a pattern here in Hawai'i. Once large numbers of tour buses start lining up at a restaurant, as they do here, energy seems to go toward processing the numbers—not working toward excellence. So it is in this case. The food's bland, unremarkable and overpriced—period. The view's kind of pretty, overlooking the ocean, if you can ignore the highway traffic and the thick powerlines. Lunch is sandwiches, burgers, seafood, chicken and some veggie items. Dinner is steak and seafood. This place is a well-known institution on O'ahu, and some residents will be shocked at our harsh review. But we suspect it's only those who haven't eaten here in a while. $12–$30 for lunch and dinner. On Hwy 83 in Ka'a'awa on the windward side.

In Hau'ula, there is **Papa Ole's Kitchen (293–2292)** at 54-316 Kamehameha Hwy at the Hau'ula Kai Center. They may have styrofoam plate service, but the grinds are cheap, flavorful, fatty and abundant. It's literally dripping with unhealthinesss. If you get a plate lunch, expect a heaping plate of kalbi ribs or teriyaki chicken, for instance, along with two huge scoops of rice and mac salad. Burgers are priced similar to McDonald's but better. Avoid the fries. $5–$13 for lunch and dinner. Closed Wednesday. It's much better than **Surfin' Tacos (293–4440)**. A roadside stand with surprisingly poor fish tacos, burritos and quesadillas served on tin plates in concrete surroundings by indifferent staff. Wish we could say something nicer, but that 'bout covers it. $10–$15 for lunch and dinner.

Once you get to La'ie, your options expand a bit. There's a large shopping center with a Foodland called the La'ie Village Shopping Center at Anemoke Street (the stoplight) on Hwy 83. Your best bet is **La'ie Chop Suey (293–8022)**. They are fast, efficient, friendly and priced right. An endless, sprawling menu confronts you, but at lunch most opt for either the pre-chosen lunch plate or the dinner plate (available at lunch—spring for that one). We're talking either $6 or $7 for a large portion. If you want to go off the menu, there's almost certainly something for everyone. Not the best food, but it doesn't take much to rise above others in La'ie. Look at the Doctor's Special if you like veggies. Off-the-menu items will cost you $6–$15. Closed Sundays.

Also in that center is a **Subway**, **Pizza Hut**, **L&L Drive-In** (a local drive-in chain

that's not bad), and the **Foodland** has a deli with sandwiches under $7 and hot, whole rotisserie chickens for $8. They also have a bakery with so-so items. Down the highway is also a **McDonald's**.

KAHUKU SHRIMP & MORE

On the side of Hwy 83 in Kahuku, 25 miles north of Kane'ohe. The northern tip of the island has become synonymous with shrimp—shrimp trucks, shrimp shacks and shrimp farming. (Though not all get their shrimp from the nearby farm.)

Giovanni's Aloha Shrimp Truck is the most famous. It may have been an unassuming shrimp truck in the middle of nowhere at one time, but it's become so well-known and heavily visited that long lines and waits can be a real problem. Three shrimp dishes (and a scampi hot dog) comprise the menu with the shrimp scampi being the most popular. They use a delicious (and very garlicky) marinade. Though tasty, many people object to dealing with the shells and the shrimp legs (which you tear off), not to mention burning your fingers in the process. It's $13 and includes rice. The spicy shrimp is so strong it could probably be used to clean the hard water spots off your shower. Definitely avoid the bathrooms ('nuff said about that), and use the wash bin near the tables. This is our second favorite *in Kahuku* (we prefer Romy's), though the service is incredibly indifferent. They also have another location in the Pit in Hale'iwa on Kamehameha. Same menu, same service. Cash only.

This ain't shrimp, but **Uncle Woody's** is a tiny corn stand behind Giovanni's on Burroughs and Kam Hwy Flavors are crazy good. We love the Island Style, but it's the Baja that we dream about. $3. If you've never tried locally-grown Hawaiian Supersweet corn, this place will knock your socks off. An easy ONO. Keep your eyes open for other locations.

While we're here, **Fiji Market (293–7120)** is hard to find behind the gas station at the Kahuku Sugar Mill center. A limited selection of awesome Indian curries for cheap cheap. The chicken, shrimp or lamb curries are flavorful, and the portions generous. Or get a delicious roti wrap to go for a whopping $6. Prices go up to **$13** for lunch and dinner. A no-brainer if you like curries.

The Famous Kahuku Shrimp Truck is junk. Weird-tasting shrimp and squid from a truck that looks almost vandalized, though it's not.

Romy's Kahuku Shrimp Hut (232–2202) is ¾ mile past Kahuku Town (toward Hale'iwa) after you've driven by their competitors. They harvest their shrimp that day, and the freshness shows. Garlic butter (#1) or the sweet and hot (#2) are even harder to peel than Giovanni's, but the eggroll shrimp (#3) eliminates the work. Expect to wait 20–40 minutes unless you call it in. (They take the phone off the hook when it gets busy, though.) You get shrimp and rice for about **$14**. The tables can be windy, so you might want to eat in the car. Cash only. Might want to avoid the fresh sunfish. We've seen 'em dead in the holding tank.

Past Romy's is **Fumi's Kahuku Shrimp**. Similar to Romy's, they raise their own shrimp and cook it fresh or sell it live. Nine different styles (some peeled and fried if you don't want to deal with the shells). **$12**.

BETWEEN KAHUKU & HALE'IWA

You've rounded the top of the island and are on your way to Hale'iwa.

At the Turtle Bay Resort is **Palm Terrace (293–8811)**. They are overpriced and have average food. Breakfast and lunch are a buffet for **$27** or a few à la carte items that will get pretty close. You're a presumed captive audience here at the Turtle Bay Resort, but for lunch and dinner, either hit **Lei Lei's** at the golf course, or head to Hale'iwa, 20 minutes away. You can do better than this place.

Also at the Turtle Bay Resort is **Ola (293–0801)**. This place is so close to an ONO, and yet so far. The setting is one of the best on O'ahu—right on the beach at Turtle Bay. It's so incredible (if you're there for an early dinner to appreciate the scene) and the food so well-conceived that it would be near impossible to not recommend them. Great misoyaki butterfish, fantastic lobster and the best poached salmon we've ever had. But there's a giant gap in the execution. The service reminds us of a beautiful actress who *know's* she's beautiful. There's so little attempt to excel, that we've come to *expect* the should-be-delicious dishes to be served cold, the drinks not to be refilled, the waiter to refuse eye contact, and the phone messages for reservations not to be returned. They have a captive audience at the Turtle Bay, and they know it. And no matter how much of a rock star the chef might be and how great the location, smug or uncaring service will kill the moment every time. **$25–$60** for dinner.

Lei Lei's Bar & Grill (293–2662) is at the golf course at Turtle Bay Resort. Only a few breakfast items (but a tasty croissant sandwich), sandwiches, burgers and salads for lunch, steak, prime rib, seafood and chicken for dinner. In all, it's one of the more reliable eateries in the area. (Certainly better than Palm Terrace.) **$10–$12** for breakfast, **$13–$20** for lunch, **$24–$40** for dinner.

Also at Turtle bay, **Leonardo's** is an Italian place sporting a nice early dinner ambiance with huge windows overlooking the ocean. Food is hit or miss. For instance, they make outstanding raviolis and a good lemon caper pasta, but drop the ball on fresh fish and the chicken Parmesan with gnocchi. Fairly good 12-inch pizzas. Love their dessert shots for around $3, which are delicious but mercifully small. **$20–$32** for dinner.

As you start seeing the North Shore surf sites like Sunset Beach, you'll come to **Ted's Bakery (638–8207)**. They have pies and cakes by the slice. Breakfast is simple and cheap at **$6–$9**. Lunch is great plate lunches, large burgers and shoyu chicken (which always sells out) and good garlic shrimp for **$7–$11**. Grab it and head to nearby Sunset Beach, which is just to the southwest on Hwy 83.

Shark's Cove Grill (638–8300) is super convenient if you're at Shark's Cove or Three Tables (and parking is safer). Burgers, salads, sandwiches or kabobs and pretty good cookies. Overall, it's not bad. (Of course, our judgment has been colored since we usually review this place after we've been diving or snorkeling at these two beaches, and even cat food would taste good after we've come out of the ocean.) **$7–$12**, across from Shark's Cove on Hwy 83 north of Waimea Bay.

HALE'IWA DINING

You'll notice a disproportionate number of ONOs on the North Shore. It's not that we hand them out like candy up here; it's just that the caliber of food and competition seems higher.

Banzai Sushi
66-246 Kamehameha • 637–4404
Japanese—Hale'iwa's only sushi bar and there's a strong North Shore vibe here with surfing movies playing on a projector. They have improved a lot since our last edition. Seating is under a lanai, half western (tables), half Japanese (floor). Some of the combo options are a

pretty good value. And the sushi tastes nice and fresh. **$15–$35** for lunch and dinner. In the North Shore Marketplace on Kamehameha Highway (83).

Breakers Restaurant & Bar
66-250 Kamehameha • 637–9898
ONO **American**—A good menu, good food and a funky Polynesian/surfer atmosphere. An easy place to recommend. Steak, seafood, stir fry, burgers, great fish and chips. Pupus are Asian items like spring rolls and satay, or try the calamari. We've never had a bad meal here. In the North Shore Marketplace on Kamehameha Highway (83). Lunch is **$11–$18**, dinner is **$16–$27** plus pricey appetizers.

Café Hale'iwa
66-460 Kamehameha • 637–5516
ONO **Mexican**—This is a long-time North Shore landmark. The ONO applies to the breakfast, which is a hit with surfers who prefer the "dawn patrol" special (eggs and pancakes for $5.50 before 8 a.m.). The red and green sauces can spice up your morning here. Lunch is not as impressive with simple Mexican items. Service is fast and friendly. **$6–$11** for breakfast, **$8–$14** for lunch. At the mauka end of town near Paalaa Road.

Cholo's Homestyle Mexican
66-250 Kamehameha • 637–3059
ONO **Mexican**—No frills, but flavorful food at reasonable prices. Most entrées have a pretty decent spicy bite to them. Typical Mexican items, plus fish tacos and burritos. Service is sometimes slow, and it's not the tidiest place on O'ahu. Take-out is available. At the North Shore Marketplace on Kamehameha Hwy (83). **$9–$16** for lunch and dinner. (More for fajitas.) They also have a roving food truck.

Hale'iwa Eats Thai
66-079 Kamehameha • 637–4247

Thai—If the line is too long at Opal Thai, this is an acceptable alternative. Their tom ka is creamy and flavorful. The curry is thicker and heartier than you've probably had before and can come with coconut white rice that is very tasty. Prices are very reasonable. We've noticed that if you let your food cool just a tad, the flavors pop more. Near Matsumoto's on the north end of town. **$14–$24** for lunch and dinner.

Hale'iwa Joe's Seafood Grill
66-011 Kamehameha • 637–8005

(ONO) American—A nice menu of fresh fish, ½-pound burgers, coconut shrimp, fish sandwich, a good fish taco, steak and more for lunch plus sushi, ceviche, ribs, etc., for pupus. The sizzling mushrooms are a great appetizer (Ask for some Parmesan on the side.) Dinner is a bit more steak- and seafood-oriented. Consider the covered outdoor tables if it's not too windy. Flies might be a problem, but this is a Hale'iwa-wide problem. This place serves potent mai tais. They would *not* have gotten an ONO if they were in Honolulu because of inattentive service and inconsistent food preparation on occasion, but this about as nice as it gets in Hale'iwa. **$11–$20** for lunch, **$16–$35** for dinner. At the corner of Hale'iwa Road and Kamehameha Hwy (83) across from the harbor.

Jameson's By the Sea
62-540 Kamehameha • 637–6272

American—What do you say about a place that charges $9 for a grilled cheese sandwich or $12 for a cheeseburger at lunch? I guess *overpriced* will cover it. It would be one thing if they used only the best ingredients, but it tastes like frozen fish sandwiches and plain ol' albacore for the tuna melt. They also have $12–$17 salads, $15 summer rolls, etc. OK, enough already—you get the picture. At least the outdoor tables have a fairly pleasing view of Hale'iwa Harbor across the busy street. The indoor tables…don't. On the north side of the Anahulu Stream on Kamehameha Hwy (83) just north of Hale'iwa town. You can do better. **$10–$35** for lunch, **$15–$50** for dinner. Also inside is **Jameson's Fudge Works**. The fudge is the best we've had. Absolutely silky smooth. The only thing gritty is the service. They seem unnecessarily nasty here. They even refuse to take pennies, saying they'll round everything up and refuse your copper. Fudge runs about **$5** for a half-pound, and it's radioactive enough to keep you buzzing all the way back to Waikiki.

Killer Tacos
66-560 Kamehameha • 637–4573

Mexican—It's the place for simple, flavorful Mexican food without high prices. They season things reasonably well here, and you can mix and match to create your own burritos or tacos. In Hale'iwa town on Kamehameha Highway near the traffic circle at Waialua Beach Road. **$4–$8** for lunch and early dinner.

Kono's
66-250 Kamehameha • 637–9211

(ONO) American—Simply a great place for breakfast in Hale-iwa. Their burritos are justifiably famous. Each starts with eggs, cheese and potatoes, then branches off from there. We recommend Wendy's burrito with sautéed onions, peppers and bacon. And always add gravy; you never know when you'll get your next fix. Prices are relatively cheap. They sell their own salt rub, which they are generous with on some of their items, such as the kalua pork. Their baked sandwiches at lunch are *so* hot they need a warning label. Stick with breakfast. **$6–$12** for breakfast and lunch. Cash only. At the North Shore Marketplace on Kamehameha Hwy (83).

Kua 'Aina Sandwich
66-160 Kamehameha • 637–6067

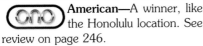 American—A winner, like the Honolulu location. See review on page 246.

Macky's Shrimp Truck
Next to the 7-Eleven on Hale'iwa Rd.

American—We've tried *all* the shrimp trucks on the North Shore, and this one is the hands-down winner. Lemon pepper, butter garlic, original (steamed), coconut shrimp or spicy hot—all plates will run you about **$12** for about 9 shrimp plus 2 scoops of white rice and a small salad. The shrimp are butterflied, delicious and practically fall out of the peel. (Gettin' hungry just writing about it.) Service is friendly and quick, and there is a hand washing station available for when you're finished.

Opal Thai
66-197C Kamehameha • 637–7950

Thai—We loved Opal's food when he operated out of a truck. Now we get to sit down. And if you allow it, a meal at Opal Thai can be the equivalent of being a guest in Opal's home. Opal is the owner. You won't miss him because he'll likely be your host, maître d', server, bus boy and cashier. He'll provide you with a menu, but if you're feeling adventurous, you won't need it. Opal takes time with every table to inquire about his guests' Thai tastes and preferences, then creates a family-style meal based on your responses. The flavor balances, the temperatures and preparation, the presentation—everything here is exceptional. The Tom Yum soup is especially ono. The only detractor to this otherwise outstanding dining experience is that the restaurant is very loud and cramped. With seating for 30–35, expect a wait. Reservations are recommended for peak seating times. BYOB and cash only. **$16–$24** for lunch and dinner. They close between meals.

Pizza Bob's
66-145 Kamehameha • 637–5095

Italian—A somewhat upscale pizza parlor with fairly reasonable prices that also has pastas, burgers, sandwiches, salads and a full bar. Indoor and outdoor tables. They use a five-cheese blend that works pretty well. Consider adding roasted cashews—it creates an interesting flavor. The crust is hard to describe—it…bites easily. (Not very descriptive, but we couldn't think of another way to put it.) Mosquitoes and flies can be a problem, like many places in Hale'iwa. Check the front of the menu for the daily special—it's almost always a good deal. In Hale'iwa Shopping Plaza on Hwy 83 across from Wyland. **$10–$18** for lunch and dinner.

Scoop of Paradise
66-145 Kamehameha • 637–3456

Treats—As the name implies, they have two dozen house-made flavors. It's very creamy, though the tastes are a bit on the subtle side for some flavors. Try the maple walnut. They also sell Bubbie's Ice Cream, which is better. There's much more going on here than just ice cream. There is delicious nostalgia, and the shop has something for kids of all ages from toys to arcade video games. In Hale'iwa Shopping Plaza on Kamehameha Hwy across from Ace Hardware. **$4–$6**.

Shave Ice in Hale'iwa

Treats—There are two good sources of shave ice

in Hale'iwa. **Matsumoto's** is the legendary source with high name recognition (they've been here since 1951), and almost next door to the left is **Aoki's**. *Insanely* long lines are the norm at Matsumoto's, and we've seen times when there was a 45-minute wait there and only a handful of people at Aoki's. Frankly, Aoki's is almost as good (less sweet but slighty courser ice) and, unlike Matsumoto's, they partially chill their syrup (preventing the dreaded ice chunks at the bottom created by room temperature syrups). Both companies are cheap—around **$3** with ice cream on the bottom. So in general, go where the line is shortest. And be careful of bees and wasps who seem to thrive on the dropped shave ice at both locations. In Hale'iwa on Kamehameha Hwy between Hale'iwa Road and the Hale'iwa Shopping Center.

Spaghettini
66-200 Kamehameha • 637–0104
Italian—Lots of spaghettis and pizza by the slice. Though the portions are pretty large for the price, flavors are on the dull side. Not insipid, but you certainly won't be fantasizing about it later that day. They get a lot of spillover from nearby Kua 'Aina Sandwiches (customers who don't want to wait in line at that more popular restaurant). The pizzas are marginally better than the pasta. But hey, you ain't paying much here. **$6–$15** for lunch and (early) dinner. On the Hwy in Hale'iwa.

Waialua Bakery
66-220 Kamehameha • 341–2838
ⓄⓃⓄ Treats—Consummate bakery with authentic surftown style offering fresh baked cookies and pastries as well as bread and buns for your sandwiches. Try their Parmesan garlic bun or the pesto wheat bun for your sandwich, only two of the many delicious

options that are baked fresh daily. Or grab a smoothie or healthy shot of wheat grass, make yourself to home on their patio and people watch. **$3–$6**.

KO OLINA / WAI'ANAE DINING

Your options are pretty limited in Wai'anae because good food's really hard to find. The resort area of Ko Olina has the best food, but it ain't cheap.

JW Marriott Ihilani Resort (679–0079) has some winners. Their **Ushio-Tei** Japanese restaurant is a good dinner place with some non-Japanese dishes. Friday through Monday there's a **$43** buffet. Otherwise, it's **$35–$50**. Resort wear means nice shorts and collared shirt OK. **Azul** is a highbrow Italian and wine bar for **$37–$50**. Some tables have nice views; try to reserve one. Also at the Marriott is the **Naupaka Terrace** for breakfast, lunch and dinner. A pretty good breakfast buffet for **$26**, unremarkable lunch and dinner food. Not bad, not memorable. Their lounge, **Hokule'a**, is a great place to watch the sunset.

The **Aulani, A Disney Resort & Spa (674–6200)** has several choices. The beautiful **Makahiki** has bountiful breakfast (**$27**) and dinner (**$43**) buffets. **'Ama'ama** is their beach-side casual dining restaurant. (No tank tops, no bathing suits.) It's **$35–$60** for dinner. (You know you're paying premium when goat cheese raviolis are **$31**.) **$15–25** for breakfast, **$18–$28** for lunch. They also have a cool lounge called the **'Olelo Room** with pupus and cocktails, where only Hawaiian is spoken. So here's your chance to immerse yourself. (For the record, the ancient Hawaiians never had a word for mojioto—or mai tai for that matter.)

The **Marriott's Ko Olina Beach Club (679–4700)** has **Chuck's Steak & Seafood** (similar to the one reviewed on page 234) for **$30–$45** for dinner.) They also have **Longboards Bar & Grill**. If prices seem high at Longboards; hey, look around. You're open-air right next to lagoon #3 with wicked sunset views. The food is reasonably good, certainly not great. Unimaginative fish, steak, a pasta or two at dinner, sandwiches, wraps and burgers plus salads at lunch. Portions are ample—get an appetizer or an entrée, not both. Drinks are delicious but taste weak. Extensive and selfless research, however, has led us to conclude they aren't as weak as they seem. (That's the Wizard thoroughness peeking through.) The food by itself wouldn't get them an ONO, but this is the sunset view you dreamt of when you imagined Hawai'i. Breakfast is a buffet for $18, lunch is $17–$20. Dinner has the lunch menu plus entrées up to $35 and occasional buffets. Take the road to lagoon #4 and valet park at the Marriott's Ko Olina Beach Club.

Away from the resorts, there's a **Roy's (676–7697)**, similar to the one reviewed on page 254, located at the Ko Olina Golf Club. **Just Tacos (677–7782) is** at Ko Olina Center. The name is strange. They've got a lot more than "just tacos," including queso, ceviche, fried calamari, fajitas, enchiladas, taco salads and steaks. Tacos include The Ultimate Taco (which is actually a burrito) along with the standards of chicken, steak, fish, etc. If you go for the tacos, try the cochinita: shredded pork marinated in citrus juice; not bad. $16–$35 for lunch or dinner. Margarita pitchers looked dangerous at $30–$35. Indoor and outdoor seating with an attractive bar presentation and almost 400 tequila choices. Olé!

Around the corner is **Hawaiian BBQ (680–9888)**. Simple, local-style plate lunches for $8–$12. Nothing to get too excited about, except the price. Nearby **Two Scoops Ice Cream Parlor (489–4350)** serves a relatively unremarkable ice cream. $4–$7.

ISLAND NIGHTLIFE

While it's true that the neighbor islands are a bit lacking in nightlife, no one would ever make that comment about O'ahu. From simple lounges with a single musician playing Hawaiian music on an acoustic guitar to full-blown dinner shows to seedy strip clubs—Waikiki has something for just about everyone.

But people's taste in nightlife varies *tremendously*. This is a section where we feel a little vulnerable, because things change weekly in the world of nightlife. The Friday edition of the *Star-Advertiser* newspaper has an entertainment section (called *TGIF*) that lists what's going on in the coming week. It's *ex-tremely* comprehensive. (It's also online.) Also look for *Midweek* and *Weekly* magazines. Nightlife is one area where the free stuff (seen at news racks everywhere) can come in handy because of the ads. By the way, if you see something playing at the **Hawai'i Theatre** (528–0506) that sounds interesting, jump on it. This has got to be one of the most beautiful theaters you'll see. The restoration is incredible, and it looks like what an upscale theater must have looked like in the 1920s, which is when it was built.

Legendary to Waikiki, **Duke's Canoe Club** at the Outrigger Waikiki on the Beach is always ringing with live music and good drinks. Every Sunday afternoon, master guitarist Henry Kapono plays until sunset, drawing quite a crowd. Also in Waikiki, the **Banyan Court** at the Moana Surfrider has Hawaiian entertainment each night until 9 p.m. Inside the Halekulani is the hidden gem, **Lewer's Lounge**. Nightly jazz piano and top-of-the-line cocktails in a classy lounge make this a favorite place for a relaxing libation. **The Shack** in the Waikiki Trade Center at Kuhio and Seaside has decent food, drink specials and local bands most nights. You can expect to hear Hawaiian, reggae or the occasional rock band.

Chinatown is home to numerous bars that draw people of all types and flavors. Most are found along Nuuanu and Hotel streets. The dueling Irish pubs of **O'Toole's** and **Murphy's** on Nuuanu Street are sharp contrasts. The rowdier O'Toole's boasts live music and a large selection of beers, while Murphy's is a landmark establishment known for their pau hana (after work) and sports bar scene as well as their killer burgers. Also on Nuuanu near Hotel Street is a club with four bars inside, **Indigo**. You can dance, sip martinis, snack on pupus or lounge on comfy furniture in a swanky atmosphere. Hotel Street offers a few more choices from seedy to artsy— something for everyone.

While there's literally no end to the number of bars and lounges in Waikiki, there are also several notable dinner shows and lu'au available.

DINNER SHOWS

You've got a few choices for dinner shows in Waikiki. We were impressed with the caliber of shows overall. Ironically, it's the dinner part of the dinner shows that's usually lacking, so consider eating elsewhere before or after the show.

Creation: A Polynesian Journey (931–4660)

Go for the show, not the dinner. The food is solidly mediocre, and the mai tais are little more than punch. Think of them as homeopathic. Perhaps they simply wave an empty rum bottle over the punchbowl. If you want a cocktail, get one before you come to the show. And while you're at it, eat either before or after (though you won't get as good a table if you don't eat their dinner). The show itself, however, is simply dazzling.

It's high energy, high production value, very professional and ultimately compelling. Don't expect a traditional hula show. This 1-hour show is a pulse-pounding Polynesian spectacular. **$60** for cocktail and show, **$105** for the dinner and show, and a laughable **$155** for the premium dinner and show. At the Sheraton Princess Kaiulani at Kalakaua and Kaiulani.

Magic of Polynesia (971–4321)

We like this show, but not for the reason it's marketed. They tout it as a magic show, but the magic isn't the reason to see it. It's the Polynesian portion— unabashedly Vegasy—which is well done with a high production value. Some of the visuals are stunning. About a third of the show is the actual magic and, though cool, much of it seems to be the same trick several different ways. A curtain goes up and when it comes down, the guy is gone or has switched objects. Impressive the first few times, but it stops surprising you after a while, and big-box magic is a bit less impressive than close-up magic because people inherently distrust props. And there's little personality from the magician—as if he, too, is a prop. But don't let this dissuade you. Overall, the visuals, sound and Polynesian feel make it a fun show, and the magic's interesting, if not overwhelming. It's **$53** for the show alone. They also offer it as a dinner show combo for **$85**, but we recommend eating elsewhere first. At the Holiday Inn Waikiki Beachcomber at 2300 Kalakaua. Reserve in advance.

Society of Seven (922–6408)

Okay, so at press time they had stopped serving dinner at this dinner show. This is a very talented group whose show is mostly imitations of singers past. Although the material feels pretty dated, it's hard not to enjoy the fast-paced, 90-minute show. And although the audience is skewed toward retired people, those of all ages seem to enjoy the performances. **$39** for the cocktail show. At the Outrigger Waikiki on the Beach on Kalakaua.

LU'AU

We've all seen them in movies. People sit at a table with a mai tai in one hand and a plate of kalua pig in the other. There's always a show where a fire knife dancer twirls a torch lit at both ends, and hula dancers bend and sway to the beat of the music. To be honest, that's not too far from the truth. The pig is baked in the ground all day, creating absolutely delicious results. Shows are usually exciting and fast-paced. Although lu'au on the neighbor islands are smaller affairs, on O'ahu you'll be accompanied by 500–1,200 of your closest new friends. To be honest, we've found neighbor island lu'au to be more fun because you're able to wander around more. They feel more like a party than O'ahu lu'au. But two of the lu'au here are pretty good. You'll just feel a bit more processed than on a neighbor island. *Most* include all-you-can-eat food and drinks (including alcohol) for a set fee. If the punch doesn't satisfy you, there's a bar where you can ask them to season it for you or make something more to your liking. Also remember the golden rule at the buffet line—the cheapest stuff comes first, so reserve enough plate real estate for the good stuff at the end.

Different lu'au are held on different nights, and this changes often, so verify the days listed here before making plans.

Polynesian Cultural Center (293–3333)

These guys definitely have the best lu'au show on the island, but their capacity has grown to unbelievable proportions. Their Pacific Theater holds a staggering 2,700 people. And they can feed 1,200 guests at a time. The food has slipped of late, but there's entertainment throughout in a very pretty and relaxing atmosphere. The layout doesn't encourage walking around much, and it's a tad cramped. The dinner show can get pretty cheesy, and their absolute insistence on audience participation can get annoying. Depending on when your table is called, the experience might seem a little rushed, until you realize that you can keep eating and making trips to the buffet even after the show is over.

One thing to remember is that this lu'au is run by the Mormon Church, so don't expect anything in your drinks other than fruit juice. If potent mai tais are your reason for taking in a lu'au, look elsewhere.

After dinner, the evening show called "Ha: Breath of Life" in a dedicated theater is incredible. It has the highest production value of any lu'au show in Hawai'i. The authentic singing and dancing from different countries and in several languages is fantastic, and the performers are crisp and precise. The fire knife dancing is the best you'll see anywhere and is a great way to end the show.

One negative side is that it's a 60- to 90-minute drive back to Waikiki from La'ie on the windward side. Consider taking their bus ride for an extra $22. You should combine this lu'au with a day at the Polynesian Cultural Center (see page 109). Dinner, show and the day at PCC is **$92**, every night except Sunday.

Germaine's Lu'au (949–6626)

Probably the second best lu'au, it's reasonably priced at **$72** (which includes the hour-long bus ride from Waikiki), and they do a very good job. There are around 650 people here, but you can tell that the crew is having fun. The food's pretty good, and three drinks are included. (A tip—if you find the size of the mai tais too small, you can purchase a large glass for $8, and they'll fill *that* each time, instead. Also, you can always ask the bartender to add more seasoning to your mai tai.) The oceanside grounds are pretty, sandy and full of palm trees, and the shoreline has good sunsets most of the year (except the weeks around the summer solstice of June 21 when it sets over land). The interactive show's well done—not too Vegasy—and the audience participation seems to be well received. If the Polynesian Cultural Center's lu'au doesn't sound like it's for you, this is one you should choose. It's about 4 hours at the site and about 2 hours of travel. Located near Ko Olina Resort at the southwest corner of the island.

Waikiki Starlight Lu'au (941–5828)

No amount of potted plants can hide the fact that this lu'au is on top of a *parking garage*. The Hilton Hawaiian Village used to have their lu'au down by the pool, but anyone from the beach could stroll up and watch. Now, six stories up, the ambiance is towers all around and a wall painted like the Ko'olau mountains. Also it's exposed to the wind, so the guests and the food can get cold. Despite the lukewarm entrées, we were impressed by the buffet's best attributes, the non-traditional items: dim sum, sushi rice and paella.

Every guest gets two free drinks, but there's no bar to walk up to. You must order from your server, meaning you can't ask the bartender to spice up your drink (and they need it). If you want a third drink, soft drinks are $5, beers are $9 and mai tais are an outrageous $11. The Polynesian revue is pretty good, but the tables are arranged so that half the seats face away from the stage. We noticed a lot of people squirming in the chairs and uncomfortably twisting their necks to see

the show. The finale is the best part. They have four talented fire knife dancers performing at once. It's impressive, but it doesn't make up for all the shortcomings. $99. Sunday through Thursday.

Royal Hawaiian's 'Aha'Aina (923–7311)

We put this one at the end not because it's the worst, but because it's not your typical lu'au. This is a smaller, more upscale affair. On a grassy lawn right next to Waikiki Beach, about 15 tables (around 200 people) are served gourmet food by attentive staff that conveys *lots* of aloha. The atmosphere is intimate and relaxed. The cultural displays are more authentic, and the food is the best we've seen at any lu'au. (They shy away from that term, instead calling it a "feast" and a "celebration.") Forget kalua pig and dinner rolls; you'll be dining on crab cakes, kona lobster in a curry sauce and osso bucco. The quality is excellent, but they control your portions, not you. Includes two free drinks.

The show focuses on the incredible history of the property, and we found the sound and production as good as the food. But there is a huge catch...The price is an *I-must-have-misheard-you* $169 *per person*. That takes the prize as the most expensive dining event in the state. If money is no object, you'll like the results. Mondays only at press time.

Paradise Cove (842–5911)

Our last choice. It's not that it's terrible. Their location *is* quite pretty, but the food and show are mediocre, and they keep you wandering around the grounds for quite a while before the food and show start. Located near Ko Olina Resort at the southwest corner of the island. $86.

DINNER CRUISES

See OCEAN TOURS on page 205.

(Hotels shown in this color. Condominiums shown in this color.)

Lovin' the lazy life above Waikiki Beach.

Your selection of where to stay is one of the more important decisions you'll make in planning your O'ahu vacation. To some, it's just a place to sleep and rather meaningless. To others, it's the difference between a good vacation and a bad one.

There are four main types of lodging on the island: hotels, condominiums, bed and breakfasts, and single-family homes. Most people will stay in one of the first two types. But B&Bs and single-family homes are often overlooked and can be very good values. If your group or family is large, you should strongly consider renting a house for privacy, roominess and plain ol' value. We don't review individual B&Bs, vacation homes or timeshares, but you can easily find them on the Internet.

The lion's share of visitors stay in Waikiki. There are only a few resorts, condos and hotels scattered outside this area.

Hotels are in green and **condominiums are in blue**. Hotels usually offer more services, but smaller spaces and no kitchens. Condos usually have full kitchens, but you may not get the kind of attention you would from a hotel, like daily maid service. There are exceptions, of course, and we will point them out when they come up. You can find their locations on the various maps.

These are subjective reviews. If we say that rooms are small, we mean that we've been in them, and they feel small or cramped to us. If we say that maintenance is poor, we mean that the paint might be peeling, or the carpets are dingy, or it otherwise felt worn to us.

See all Web reviews at: www.hawaiirevealed.com

SOLID GOLD VALUE The gold bar indicates that the property is exceptionally well priced for what you get.

The gem means that this hotel or condominium offers something *particularly* special, not *necessarily* related to the price.

A REAL GEM

WHERE ARE THE REST?

You'll notice that some of the resorts listed here don't have full reviews. When we review a place to stay, we don't just want to list bare-bones information on them. After all, you can get that kind of info on the Internet. We want to tell you what we *really* think about a place, and that takes space. Also, we wanted to include aerial photos of the resorts. After all, a picture speaks a thousand words (and a thousand words takes too long to read anyway). But in the end we only have so much space we can devote to accommodations.

We had a choice: Give you less info on *all* of them, or do detailed reviews on only a *portion* of them. Neither choice seemed palatable.

So we came up with a *third* way: List minimal info on all (including if they are GEMS or SOLID GOLD VALUES), print detailed reviews on *most,* and post full reviews of all on our website, **www.hawaiirevealed.com**. After all, most people use this section before they come to the islands. And with the Web (which has infinite space), we could do more, like post larger aerial photos of the resorts with specific buildings labeled when appropriate, provide constant updates when necessary and put links to the various rental agents or hotels right in the review, allowing you to go to their sites and get more photos of the rooms. You should remember, however, that resorts post photos to lure you in, and some aren't above posting modified or overly flattering shots when they were new and sparkling. Our aerials don't lie and are designed to give you a feel for their ocean proximity (does oceanfront *really* mean oceanfront?), so you'll know what kind of view to expect from a given location within the resort. Resorts whose review is posted *only* on our website are identified with **WEB REVIEW**

We've reviewed the resorts in Waikiki geographically from left to right (see map on page 49). Please remember that all these reviews are *relative to each other*. This is important. Even staying at a dump right on the ocean is still a *golly gee!* experience. In other words, *Hey, you're on the ocean in Hawai'i!* So if we sound whiny or picky when critiquing a resort, it's only because their next-door neighbor might be such a better experience. It doesn't mean you'll be miserable; it just means that *compared to another resort*, you can do better.

A FEW GROUND RULES

All prices given are RACK rates, meaning *without any discounts*. Tour packages, websites and travel agents can often get better rates. Most resorts offer discounts for stays of a week or more, and some will negotiate price with you. Some won't budge at all on RACK rates, but most told us *no one* pays RACK rates. So always ask, look for discounts or package deals. Prices listed are subject to taxes of around 13.5%.

Unless otherwise noted, all resorts have room safes (for extra—usually $2–$5 per day), air conditioning, empty refrigerators, coin-op laundry facilities, daily maid service, lanais, coffee makers in the rooms, cable TV, self-parking for $5–$35 per day, and local calls from $.75 to $2 a pop. Most resorts have wheelchair-acces-

See all Web reviews at: www.hawaiirevealed.com

sible rooms. A law in Hawai'i has required many resorts to adopt a non-smoking policy, but *some* resorts may allow smoking in your room, on your lanai or on specific floors. If you are bothered by smoking or you can't *live* without it, best check and see if your choice of place to stay will accommodate you. Internet access, if not free, runs around $10–$20 per day. Wi-Fi signal quality in Waikiki varies widely (even at different times of the day or night), so if you need fast, reliable service, opt for a place that offers wired hi-speed Internet. Generally speaking, if a resort is not on the beach, get as high up as possible for the best views and less street noise when staying in Waikiki.

WAIKIKI

Ala Moana Hotel
(800) 367–6025 or (808) 955–4811
410 Atkinson Dr.

1,142 rooms, pool, free free fitness room, steam room, sauna, 3 restaurants, 4 shops, 24-hour business center, 8 conference rooms, valet parking, coffee maker with free coffee daily, free hi-speed Internet access in rooms, Wi-Fi in lobby, lanais on most, day spa. There are two towers—the 13-story Kona and the 36-story Waikiki. The resort rooms were sold off as a condotel, but decor is consistent and on our visit still looking fresh and clean. The room colors and furnishings are relaxing and modern, though not overly Hawaiian in feel, and the flat screen TVs are pretty small. All rooms have microwaves. The property is just outside Waikiki, next door to the Ala

Moana Shopping Center. Business travelers and convention attendees make up much of their customer base. (The convention center is very close by.) Rooms are smaller and less expensive in the Kona Tower and have no lanais, but you can open the sliding door and stand at the railing.

It's a pretty long walk into Waikiki and its beaches and restaurants, but it's also quicker when you're looking to hop on the freeway. In all, you need to decide if the location trade-offs are worth it. Self-parking is $20, valet is $25. Rooms (245–335 sq. ft.) are $269–$349. Jr. suites (700 sq. ft.) are $729, suites (500–2,100 sq. ft.) are $449–$2,499.

Waikiki Marina Hotel
(800) 669–7719 or (808) 942–7722
1700 Ala Moana Blvd.

136 units, pool, spa, tennis court, free continental breakfast, BBQ, free Wi-Fi in lobby, free hi-speed Internet access in rooms, free room safes and free local calls, free polo tickets (in season). This is kind of an odd place. This 40-story building has only 4 rooms per floor, the building is skinny, and rooms are small and weirdly shaped. Not bad, just strange. Most of the rooms have ocean views (some quite expansive), but none have lanais. Kitchenettes in all rooms. The interiors vary widely as each unit is privately owned. Rooms have showers only—no tubs. Parking is $18. Rooms (350 sq. ft.) are $129–$189. A couple of blocks from the beach at the Hilton.

See all Web reviews at: www.hawaiirevealed.com

The Equus
(800) 669–7719 or (808) 949–0061
1696 Ala Moana Blvd.
WEB REVIEW 🏴

Hawai'i Prince Hotel Waikiki
(888) 977–4623 or (808) 956–1111
100 Holomoana St.

521 rooms, pool and spa, hi-speed Internet access and Wi-Fi in rooms, Wi-Fi in lobby, 24-hour business center, day spa, coffee maker with free coffee daily, free 24-hour fitness/hospitality room, free laptop-sized room safes, valet-only laundry, golf course (well…sort of), room service, 3 restaurants, lounge, valet parking, day spa. This resort is set apart from the rest of Waikiki. Located at the extreme edge of Waikiki where the Ala Wai Canal meets the ocean, odds are that whenever you want to wander around Waikiki, you'll either take their free shuttle into the main area, the public bus, or drive and battle for a parking place. Same goes for going to the beach. On the other hand, it's close to the massive Ala Moana Shopping Center—a 10-minute walk away—and there are shopping-starved neighbor island residents who like to stay at the Hawai'i Prince for this very reason.

The resort is composed of twin 33-story towers. All rooms face the ocean and were renovated in 2011 with mixed results—taste aside, they are bright and modern with floor-to-ceiling windows, and a view dominated by the Ala Wai Boat Harbor below you, which is quite picturesque. The buildings are very nicely maintained and appointed and the staff accommodating. Rooms feel smaller than their stated 430 sq. ft., and only 5th floor rooms have lanais. The bathrooms, however, are very spacious with separate showers and tubs (maybe that's where much of the square footage went). They claim to be the only resort in Waikiki with their own golf course. The fine print with that claim is that it's near 'Ewa Beach—20 miles away. (Pretty slick move by their marketing department, though, isn't it?)

Overall, their location is probably a negative. Paying $405 and up per night to stay at a nice resort, then getting on the bus every time you want to go to the beach or eat in Waikiki can be a bit deflating. It's a nice resort, but you're paying beachfront prices…without the beach. Valet parking is $23, self-parking is $17.

Rooms (430 sq. ft.) are $405–$545, suites (839–2,038 sq. ft.) are $620–$2,500.

The Modern Honolulu
(866) 970–4161 or (808) 943–5800
1775 Ala Moana Blvd.
WEB REVIEW 💎

Ilikai Hotel & Suites
(866) 406–2782 or (808) 949–3811
1777 Ala Moana Blvd.
WEB REVIEW

Hawaiian Monarch Hotel
(866) 293–4738 or (808) 945–3444
444 Niu St.
WEB REVIEW

See all Web reviews at: www.hawaiirevealed.com

Aqua Palms Waikiki
(866) 406–2782 or (808) 947–7256
1850 Ala Moana Blvd.

WEB REVIEW

Hilton Hawaiian Village
(800) 445–8667 or (808) 949–4321
2005 Kalia Rd.

3,386 rooms, 6 pools (including a keiki pool), 3 spas, free fitness rooms, free room safes, coffee makers with free coffee daily, about a dozen restaurants, over 90 shops, over 150,000 sq. ft. of meeting space, 24-hour business center, room service, day spa, hi-speed Internet access in rooms, Wi-Fi in some public areas, lanais (on most), children's program, wedding coordinator, wedding chapel, lu'au. Where do we start? We've reviewed every resort in Hawai'i, and this is the biggest kahuna of them all. On a typical day they'll have over 6,000 guests serviced by 1,700 employees, which practically qualifies it as a small town. If you're looking for a pulsating, always-moving resort, this place hums. If you're looking for peace and quiet, you've definitely come to the wrong place. It can get very crowded at the pools, and their multi-level 5,000 sq. ft. Paradise Pool has a 77-foot lava tube slide and a waterfall and is *very* popular. Seven massive towers (the tallest is 38 stories) with the Rainbow Tower being the closest to the water and the Ali'i Tower having the best services. The grounds are strewn with tropical plants, flowing ponds, swimming pools and some exotic birds, including African penguins. (We didn't know they *had* penguins in Africa.)

In some ways they seem to nickel and dime you here. They charge a whopping $16 per day to use the in-room hi-speed Internet access. There's no coin-op laundry (you'll have to valet it), Self-parking is $24 per day and valet is $30. They do give you an option to pay for their Paradise Pass at $20 per day, which gives you free local calls, and other similar discount packages are available.

The Ali'i Tower is the nicest (non-timeshare) tower. It's the best furnished, and there are more personalized services. (Ali'i rooms ending in -05 are particularly nice.) They have their own front desks here and in the Kalia Tower, so you can check in directly and avoid the often busier main lobby.

The Diamond Head Tower is our least favorite, the Lagoon Tower is completely timeshare, and the Grand Waikikian is currently being sold as timeshares. (You can rent a condo there until they are all sold. They're stunning but very pricey). The Tapa Tower rooms are pleasant. All the rooms are clean and contemporary with a Hawaiiana theme and Hilton Serenity Beds. The oceanfront category rooms on the Rainbow Tower—especially those on the Diamond Head side—have smashing views down the beach.

The beach defines the northwestern edge of Waikiki and has the calmest waters. There's a lot to do on the beach and the public lagoon (which is a clean, safer place to frolic). The vendors on the beach rent gear and such for fairly high prices—like $16 for a beach lounge chair and $31 for an umbrella.

They have have a stunning wedding chapel with an on-site wedding coordinator who can help plan events there or on the beach.

See all Web reviews at: www.hawaiirevealed.com

If the prices of the restaurants here scare you off, the Hale Koa's beachside snack bar next door is open to you, but not their other restaurants. The resort is well known for their fireworks every Friday night. They have tons of cultural activities to choose from each day.

Rooms (300–810 sq. ft.) are $199–$469, suites (439–1,826 sq. ft.) are $315–$4,900.

Ramada Plaza Waikiki
(800) 272–6232 or (808) 955–1111
1830 Ala Moana Blvd.
WEB REVIEW

DoubleTree Alana Hotel
(800) 222–8733 or (808) 941–7275
1956 Ala Moana Blvd.
WEB REVIEW

Hale Koa
(800) 367–6027 or (808) 955–0555
2055 Kalia Rd.
WEB REVIEW ▄▄

Ambassador Hotel of Waikiki
(800) 923–2620 or (808) 941–7777
2040 Kuhio Ave.
WEB REVIEW

Maile Sky Court
(866) 406–2782 or (808) 947–2828
2058 Kuhio Ave.

596 rooms, pool, spa, restaurant, pooside lounge, 24-hour business center, hi-speed Internet access in rooms, free Wi-Fi in lobby. Some rooms have kitchenettes; none have lanais. A 44-story tower from 1984 with rooms renovated in 2009. Rooms are very basic but clean. The location is pretty poor—it's only convenient when you want to *leave* Waikiki; otherwise, it's a ways from the beach here—at least a 15-minute walk and a long walk to most restaurants. Business travelers will appreciate that it's reasonably convenient if they need to walk to the convention center. The ocean views aren't worth the upgrade—too distant. Stick with cheaper views. But the highest floors do at least have views that stretch pretty far. Avoid the 26th floor—for some reason they failed to make elevator doors there. (Weird but true.) Their pool is pretty small for a building this size, but they have a nice-sized spa. Some of the rooms are unbelievably tiny, but their 1/1s will sleep up to 6 people. Parking is $18. Rooms (190–215 sq. ft.) are $195–$209, studios with kitchenette (245–296 sq. ft.) are $235–$315, 1/1s with full kitchens (390–575 sq. ft.) are $415.

Waikiki Gateway Hotel
(808) 942–6006 or (808) 955–3741
2070 Kalakaua Ave.
WEB REVIEW

Outrigger Luana Waikiki
(800) 688–7444 or (808) 955–6000
2045 Kalakaua Ave.
WEB REVIEW

The Breakers
(800) 426–0494 or (808) 923–3181
250 Beachwalk
WEB REVIEW

Kai Aloha Hotel
(808) 923–6723
235 Saratoga Rd.

See all Web reviews at: www.hawaiirevealed.com

18 rooms and free local calls, no room safes, free Wi-Fi *possible* from signals nearby and a computer in the office you may use when it is available. A 3-story (no elevator) 1950s building with no non-smoking rooms. This tiny, family-run resort was looking about its age on our recent visit, and without a locking gate to access 1 bedroom units on second floor, you may want to avoid those as there may be some security concerns on this property compared to its neighbors. (First floor 1-bedrooms and third floor studios have a security gate.) The furnishings are old—perhaps the originals in many cases, but with newer slipcovers. You get the feeling it hasn't changed much since it was built—they even have stove-top coffee percolators in rooms. But, hey, you ain't paying for the Halekulani. Parking is $48 for a 3-day pass at Fort DeRussy Park across the street. Studios with kitchenettes and two twin beds (approx. 220 sq. ft.) are $95–$100, 1/1s (approx. 420 sq. ft.) are $105–$160 (depending on the number of people in your party). If you want less street noise, ask for a unit at the back of the building, but trucks delivering to the Trump Towers can be noisy in the mornings. About 2 blocks to the beach. 2-night minimum.

Trump International Hotel & Tower Waikiki Beach Walk
(877) 683–7401 or (808) 683–7777
223 Saratoga Rd.

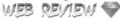

WEB REVIEW ◆

Best Western Plus Coconut Waikiki Hotel
(866) 406–2782 or (808) 923–8828
450 Lewers St.
81 rooms, pool, free Wi-Fi in lobby and rooms, microwave, fridge, coffee makers with free coffee daily, 40-inch HD TVs, free ground-to-order coffee and tea 24/7 in lobby, free room safes, free local calls,

24-hour business center, free fitness room, BBQ. Continental breakfast is free in the lobby at this 10-story building from the 1970s. This is a green resort, but not the way you're thinking. We mean it's bright lime green when you enter the lobby and in the modern decor of the rooms. You'll either find it cool and refreshing, or you'll hate it. You won't get much of a tan by the tiny pool that's shaded most of the time by neighboring buildings, but the patio is large and breezy. The rooms are small, but they made good use of the space. You may notice a large stuffed gorilla dressed in a straw hat sitting quietly in the lobby. We're told he is the third mascot, as the other two have been stolen and have been spotted in the passenger seats of cars roaming around O'ahu. (Perhaps someone uses them to qualify for the carpool lane.) Long walk to the beach. Best views are of the Ala Wai Canal. Valet-only parking is $24. Rooms (250–400 sq. ft.) are $239–$289, suites (650–1,000 sq. ft., but they don't feel it) are $329–$849.

Hokele Suites Waikiki
(800) 367–5004 or (808) 923–8882
412 Lewers St.
WEB REVIEW

See all Web reviews at: www.hawaiirevealed.com

Courtyard by Marriott Waikiki Beach
(877) 995–2638 or (808) 954–4000
400 Royal Hawaiian Ave.
WEB REVIEW

Ohana Waikiki Malia
(800) 462–6262 or (808) 923–7621
2211 Kuhio Ave.
WEB REVIEW

Waikiki Joy Hotel
(877) 997–6667 or (808) 923–2300
320 Lewers St.
WEB REVIEW

The Regency on Beachwalk
(800) 688–7444 or (808) 922–3871
255 Beachwalk
WEB REVIEW

Embassy Suites Waikiki Beach Walk
(800) 362–2779 or (808) 921–2345
WEB REVIEW

Imperial Hawai'i Resort
(800) 347–2582 or (808) 923–1827
205 Lewers St.

270 rooms, pool, sauna, fitness room, conference room, hi-speed Internet access in rooms, restaurant, 4 shops, DVD players (with DVDs for rent in lobby), maid service every 4th and 7th day. There are 26 floors in this 1970s building, and only floors 20 and above give you good views of the ocean. Though this is a timeshare resort, 30% of the rooms are routinely available for rent. 4th- and 5th-floor units have no lanais. The studios have pull-down Murphy beds, making good use of the space. But they don't guarantee the floor or view you'll get when you book—only the type of unit. The rooms themselves are not remarkable and many need updating. Parking is $25 (valet only), and local calls are free. (Sort of—you have to pay $6 per day for "free" calls and room safe.) It's clean and fairly reasonably priced given the location. The beach is only a few minutes walk away. Studios with kitchenette (350 sq. ft.) are $195–$209, 1/1s with kitchenette (450 sq. ft.) are $232–$246, 1/2s with full kitchen (525–575 sq. ft.) are $292–$321, 2/2s with full kitchen (700 sq. ft.) are $337–$351. Discounts are easy to get with studios starting at $108.

Waikiki Parc Hotel
(800) 422–0450 or (808) 921–7272
2233 Helumoa Rd.
WEB REVIEW

Waikiki Shore
(800) 367–5004 or (808) 952–4500
(800) 688–7444 or (808) 923–3111
2161 Kalia Rd.

168 rooms, free hi-speed Internet access, free room safes. A 1960s 15-story skinny building with one end touching Waikiki Beach. Nearly all units face Ft. DeRussy Park, which is good because the back of the building is crammed up against the Outrigger Reef on the Beach. The higher up the better. The first set of numbers is **Castle**; the second set of numbers is for **Outrigger Resorts**, which also manages

See all Web reviews at: www.hawaiirevealed.com

some of the rooms here. This affects things like parking: $18 to self-park through Castle; $30 to valet or $20 to self-park through Outrigger, and their parking is off-property. Outrigger guests also must check in at Regency Beachwalk. All rooms have kitchens or kitchenettes, as well as washer/dryers, and free room safes. Castle rentals have no pool; Outrigger rentals will let you use their frenzied pool next door at the Reef. The condo units themselves are clean, though some could use updating—but they're very bright, reasonably appointed and roomy. Studios (400 sq. ft.) are $205–$320, 1/1s (540–720 sq. ft.) are $285–$431, 2/1s (1,060 sq. ft.) are $415–$525, 2/2s (1,160–1,190 sq. ft.) are $556–$800. The rooms seem pricey to us, and discounts are hard to get because the rates are set by the condo owners themselves. Shop both agents for the best deal.

Outrigger Reef on the Beach
(800) 688–7444 or (808) 923–3111
2169 Kalia Rd.
WEB REVIEW

Halekulani
(800) 367–2343 or (808) 923–2311
2199 Kalia Rd.

453 rooms, pool, free fitness room, free Wi-Fi and hi-speed Internet access in rooms, 24-hour room service, valet parking, 5 shops, 6 conference rooms, 3 restaurants, children's program (seasonal), 42-inch HD TVs, Blu-ray players,

iHomes, free room safes, free local calls, free cribs, 24-hour business center/hospitality suite, day spa, valet-only laundry.

A REAL GEM

Wow, where do we start? This is an awesome and relaxing place. Comprising 5 buildings (the tallest is 17 floors), this is less of a tower resort than most of their neighbors. Services are unmatched here. For instance the check-in: Forget the desk—just have the greeter take you on a tour, then to your room and give you a box of chocolates and an excellent fruit platter. They track your preferences and try to anticipate your future needs. If you order coffee first thing in the morning, next time you stay, they'll already have it covered. This is the way a resort should be run. You want it; you'll get it. Don't like your pillow? They'll get you a different kind. Want to eat at their top-of-the-line fine dining restaurant but left your nice clothes at home? What size do you wear, sir?

Room amenities are high and include deep soaking tubs. The motif is white and pale blue—designed to resemble their name: Halekulani means *house befitting heaven*. Their 2011 renovations will not upset repeat visitors as they are very much in keeping with theme, while giving the rooms a needed lift.

Halekulani's food services are incredible, and everything is created on the premises—pastries, ice creams, breads—you name it, *except* the chocolates. Their spa is so relaxing, you'll think they removed your bones when you weren't looking. It's hard to find much fault here. There is a whole host of attractions around Honolulu, like ʻIolani Palace and the Honolulu Symphony, that you can get into for free because the Halekulani is a sponsor.

See all Web reviews at: www.hawaiirevealed.com

Biggest ding? Their beach occupies the thinnest part of Waikiki—much of it lined by a seawall. (That may change over time if the government steps up a beach replenishment program. The beach facelift of 2012 did *not* benefit the Halekulani.)

You'll be pampered here and may literally weep when you have to leave. The resort exudes a tranquility that's hard to match in Waikiki. Self- or valet-parking is $22. Rooms (519 sq. ft.) are $500–$810, Jr. suites (720 sq. ft.) are $945–$1,030, suites (1,050–1,620 sq. ft.) are $1,240–$3,000. If money is no object, their Royal Suite (4,066 sq. ft.) comes with a personal butler, a baby grand piano, an airport limo ride and breakfast in your room daily for a *mere* $7,000 per night. Their Vera Wang Suite (2,135 sq. ft.) is $5,500–$7,000, and is perfect for a honeymoon, and comes with many amenities. And don't forget the 2,365 sq. ft. Orchid Suite (also $7,000), which is located oceanfront with a private lawn, butler service, bath with steam shower, deep steeping therapy pool and a cold plunge tub, as well as many other amenities. Many packages are available.

Island Colony
(866) 406–2782 or (808) 923–2345
445 Seaside Ave.
WEB REVIEW

Sheraton Waikiki
(866) 500–8313 or (808) 922–4422
2255 Kalakaua Ave.
WEB REVIEW

Holiday Surf
(888) 923–8488 or (808) 923–8488
2303 Ala Wai Blvd.
34 rooms, full kitchens, Wi-Fi in rooms, Internet kiosk in lobby. A 6-story building built in 1963 right across from the Ala Wai Canal and Boulevard (the latter can

be noisy). This is a family-operated condo, and it's pretty no-frills. No room safes, but you can use front desk's. They completed renovations in 2009 and have done some upgrades more recently of new appliances and some furnishings, but it's very basic. The ceilings either have cloud- or ocean-themed murals—good, because you can't see the *actual* ocean from here, which is a pretty long walk. Parking is $15 (cheap). Studios (315 sq. ft.) are $143–$179, 1/1s (350 sq. ft.) are $179–$225. Their online rates usually have good discounts.

'Ilima Hotel
(800) 801–9366 or (808) 923–1877
445 Nohonani St.

98 rooms, pool, free fitness room, sauna, free local calls, 3 conference rooms, free hi-speed in rooms, free Wi-Fi in lobby, 24-hour business center, coffee makers in all and free coffee in 1/1 category and up. A '60s pink building with 17 floors. All rooms have full kitchens,

SOLID GOLD VALUE

See all Web reviews at: www.hawaiirevealed.com

and the layouts are fairly spacious. The decor is pink (*surprise!*) and green, clean but dated. The warm staff and good prices make up for it, though. They even sing Hawaiian songs to the guests in the lobby at 11:30 a.m. every Friday. 1/1s have Jacuzzi tubs. In short, an easy place to get comfortable. Parking is free (that's rare in Waikiki). Studios (530 sq. ft.) are $178–$268, 1/1s (650 sq. ft.) are $230–$280, 2/1s (770 sq. ft.) are $300–$350. 3/2 penthouse with washer/dryer (1,450 sq. ft.) is $560–$600. Lots of discounts available. It's 2½ blocks to the beach.

White Sands Hotel
(866) 406–2782 or (808) 924–7263
431 Nohonani St.
WEB REVIEW

Hawaiian King
(800) 545–1948 or (808) 924–3332
417 Nohonani St.
WEB REVIEW

Aqua Waikiki Pearl
(866) 406–2782 or (808) 922–1616
415 Nahua St.
WEB REVIEW

Ohana Waikiki West
(800) 462–6262 or (808) 922–5022
2330 Kuhio Ave.

659 rooms, pool, restaurant, lanais (most rooms), poolside bar, a conference room, free local and long distance calls to U.S. and Canada, free room safes, free hi-speed Internet access in rooms, free Wi-Fi in lobby and computers for use. An 18-story tower (however, the elevator stops at the 17th floor) from 1973. Rooms could use updating but are well-kept. Views improve with height—but not much. Rooms are clean and simple. Your best view is of the tile mosaic at the nearby Miramar's pool. Tiny showers—good for rinsing your vegetables but not much else. A few rooms have tubs. It's fairly centrally located—three blocks from the beach. Parking is $20. Rooms (264 sq. ft.) are $209, kitchenettes (280 sq. ft.) are $219–$229—worth the upgrade. Kitchenette combos (544 sq. ft.) are $379. These are a standard room and a kitchenette combined via a connecting door. Suites (345–844 sq. ft.) are $249–$489 and aren't worth the money or the walk up from the 17th floor.

Aqua Waikiki Wave
(866) 406–2782 or (808) 922–1262
2299 Kuhio Ave.
WEB REVIEW

Miramar at Waikiki
(800) 367–2303 or (808) 922–2077
2345 Kuhio Ave.
WEB REVIEW

Holiday Inn Waikiki Beachcomber
(888) 465–4329 or (808) 922–4646
2300 Kalakaua Ave.

496 rooms, pool, spa, free room safe, coffee makers with free coffee daily, free Wi-Fi in lobby, free Wi-Fi and hi-speed Internet access in rooms, business center, fitness room, free local calls, 5 shops, restaurant, valet-only parking. A 25-story

See all Web reviews at: www.hawaiirevealed.com

1970 building located in the heart of Waikiki that makes venturing out particularly convenient. The hotel was completely renovated in 2009 with nice results. The rooms are modern and clean; some are small, but most feel larger than the square footage listed. Showers have handheld shower heads and tiny tubs. Their view designations seem pretty fair compared to some of their competitors. 10th floor and above have the best views. You're just a few minutes' walk to the beach. Connecting rooms available. There are several dinner shows here. Valet parking is $30. Overall, if you get a good discount, you'll probably be pretty happy. Next door to the International Marketplace (which is noisy at night) and a block from the beach. Rooms (238–318 sq. ft.) are $329–$399, suites (636–1,500 sq. ft.) are $1,099–$1,500.

Royal Hawaiian (Sheraton)
(866) 500–8313 or (808) 923–7311
2259 Kalakaua Ave.
WEB REVIEW

Outrigger Waikiki on the Beach
(800) 688–7444 or (808) 923–0711
2335 Kalakaua Ave.
WEB REVIEW

Waikiki Sand Villa
(800) 247–1903 or (808) 922–4744
2375 Ala Wai Blvd.
WEB REVIEW

Aqua Aloha Surf Waikiki
(866) 406–2782 or (808) 923–0222
444 Kanekapolei St.
WEB REVIEW

Ohana Waikiki East
(800) 462–6262 or (808) 922–5353
150 Kaiulani Ave.
441 rooms, pool, spa, free fitness room, 3 restaurants, 2 conference rooms, free

room safes, coffee makers with free coffee daily, free hi-speed Internet access in room, free Wi-Fi in lobby and by pool, free local and long distance calls to U.S. and Canada, 24-hour business center, lanais on most. A 19-floor tower built in 1972 that is well-maintained but looking dated. As an Ohana hotel, they cater more to families. Rooms are pretty small and tight. (City-view rooms are a bit bigger and worth the extra $10.) The showers are tiny—drop the soap and you gotta open the door to pick it up. The walls don't block much sound, and if you get a room ending in 00, you may be forced to continuously hear the elevator mechanism. It's two blocks to the nearest beach (Waikiki Beach Center). Connecting rooms available. Parking here wins the *bonehead* award for design. If you keep driving to the top of the garage looking for a space (which is $20), there is *literally* no place to turn around. Rates (which few pay since they have lots of discounts) are $269–$289 (240 sq. ft.), kitchenettes (165 sq, ft.) are $289, suites (375–480 sq. ft.) are $309–$699. Overall, not a bad place if you get a discount, especially since it is smack in the middle of Waikiki.

Hostelling International Waikiki
(808) 926–8313
2417 Prince Edward St.
38 beds, 9 private rooms (includes one family room for up to 4 people), free Wi-Fi, hi-speed Internet available (and computers) for an extra fee, shared kitchen, TV lounge, outdoor garden patio, coin-

See all Web reviews at: www.hawaiirevealed.com

op laundry. Dorms are $25 or $28 (non-members) a night, and private rooms with a bath are $58 or $128 (non-members). Tax included. No phone (other than a pay phone), no a/c (it does get hot—at least they have fans). Parking is $5—first come, first served. Sheets supplied, BYOT (bring your own towels). It's a clean place and well-run. Bring your own padlock for the lockers, which will hold laptops. They loan out beach gear. This is a more laid back hostel than Waikiki Beachside. No smoking, no alcohol allowed, and dorms are not co-ed. 7-day maximum stay. *Not* available to O'ahu residents. A couple of minutes walk to the beach.

Sheraton Princess Kaiulani
(866) 500–8313 or (808) 922–5811
120 Kaiulani Ave.
WEB REVIEW

Moana Surfrider, A Westin Resort
(866) 500–8313 or (808) 922–3111
2365 Kalakaua Ave.
WEB REVIEW

Hyatt Regency Waikiki
(800) 554–9288 or (808) 923–1234
2424 Kalakaua Ave.
WEB REVIEW

Stay Hotel Waikiki
(888) 354–0803 or (808) 923–7829
2424 Koa Ave.
WEB REVIEW

Aqua Bamboo Waikiki
(866) 406–2782 or (808) 922–7777
2425 Kuhio Ave.

92 rooms, pool, spa, sauna, free Wi-Fi in lobby and pool areas, free hi-speed Internet access in rooms, free room safes, coffee makers with free coffee daily, small day spa, 24-hour business center, free local calls, BBQ. A 12-floor 1965 building that's been turned into a boutique hotel. The atmosphere is very tranquil despite being in middle of Waikiki. A nice pool, fresh bamboo, apples at the front desk and Buddhas sprinkled about help add to its appeal, which has sort of a contempory Asian feel. Their saltwater pool is nice with the sound of a waterfall to drown the city noise. Because of the relatively small size, nothing feels too distant. Service is personalized and warm. Some rooms are pretty small but laid out well, so it's less of an issue. (The building gets smaller as it goes up.) The rooms are bright and modern with hints of bamboo sprinkled about. There's a docking station for your iPod, a place to secure your surfboard, and free fresh ground-to-order coffee and tea in the lobby 24 hours a day. Hotel-type rooms have a microwave, fridge and coffee maker—add a burner for the kitchenettes. If you're staying on a lower floor, opt for a room facing the courtyard pool. 2-minute walk to the beach. Self-parking is $20. Overall, we like the place a lot. Rooms (170–215 sq. ft.) are $265, stu-

A REAL GEM

See all Web reviews at: www.hawaiirevealed.com

dios with kitchenettes (214–362 sq. ft.) are $310. Suites (371–1,078 sq. ft.) are $325–$500.

Pacific Monarch
(877) 997–6667 or (808) 923–9805
2427 Kuhio Ave.
WEB REVIEW

Royal Grove Hotel
(808) 923–7691
151 Uluniu Ave.

80 units, pool, 4 restaurants, kitchens, computer in lobby for a fee, older wing has no lanais or a/c. Only 6 stories high at this 1962 bright pink building, and not much seems to have changed since it was built. Maid service is twice weekly for weekly stays or daily for daily stays. Some of the rooms don't have a/c or coffee makers (both equally crucial as far as we're concerned). It's cheap, but it's pretty run down—although they have made some efforts, like new carpets in the hallways and some new furnishings, but don't expect much (like a towel to use at their lackluster pool). We don't see it changing because they are always booked—*go figgah?* On the upside, they do have regular potlucks and a nice staff. The owner plays the 'ukulele with some other locals at the weekly music jams. Parking is $10 at the Waikiki Banyan (a couple of blocks away). Studios are $55–$70 (cheapest rooms are in older building), 1/1s $90–$100. A cou-

ple minutes' walk to the beach. In our opinion, you are better off at the Waikiki Prince Hotel, but they don't have a pool.

Waikiki Prince Hotel
(808) 922–1544
2431 Prince Edward St.
WEB REVIEW

Waikiki Resort Hotel
(800) 367–5116 or (808) 922–4911
130 Liliuokalani Ave.

275 rooms, pool, free room safes, 3 shops, 2 conference rooms, hi-speed Internet access in rooms, 3 restaurants, 24-hour business center, small day spa. A 19-story tower from 1970. Units are fairly roomy compared to their competition with a clean, simple, contemporary decor. There's a lot of aloha with the staff, and they clearly care about your comfort. Connecting rooms are available. Fridays they have local crafters and entertainment. Parking is $20. Plus it's only a couple minutes' walk to Kuhio Beach Park. Rooms (315–348 sq. ft.) are $259–$324, Jr. suites (394 sq. ft.) are $339, suites (696–1,060 sq. ft.) are $414–$794. They have so many specials—including great Internet rates that can knock as much as 35–50% off price depending on the time of year—and few people ever pay the RACK rate listed above if you get one of those discounts, it's a SOLID GOLD VALUE for sure.

Waikiki Beach Tower
(877) 997–6667 or (808) 926–6400
2470 Kalakaua Ave.
WEB REVIEW ♦

See all Web reviews at: www.hawaiirevealed.com

Waikiki Beachside Hotel
(877) 997–6667 or (808) 931–2100
2452 Kalakaua Ave.

70 rooms, free Wi-Fi in lobby, free room safes, 24-hour business center. This 12-story hotel right across the street from Waikiki Beach Center is small by Waikiki standards. The resort has a Euro-Chinese decor and lots of antiques. Fantastic location with some rooms that have killer ocean views, but sadly, the resort was looking run down at press time and badly in need of updating. Valet-only parking is $22. Rooms are small with only double and queen beds available, so they don't allow more than two people per room. Rooms with lanais come at the expense of the interior square footage, so only get a lanai if you really want one. If you want to be able to watch the torchlighting ceremony across the street at the beach from your room, pick a room on floors 3–5 facing the ocean. If you want your view to clear the crown of the large banyan tree across the street, you'll want floors 8 or above. There are two rooms on each floor that have no windows (other than doors with jalousie windows) and no lanai, but you can usually get a good discount on these. No laundry facilities—you'll have to give it to the valet. Bathrooms have showers, but no tubs. Rooms (183–244 sq. ft.) are $165–$335.

Waikiki Circle
(877) 997–6667 or (808) 923–1571
2464 Kalakaua Ave.
WEB REVIEW

Hilton Waikiki Beach
(888) 243–9252 or (808) 922–0811
2500 Kuhio Ave.
WEB REVIEW

Waikiki Banyan
(877) 997–6667 or (808) 922–0555
(888) 565–6411 or (808) 922–0707
201 Ohua Ave.

876 rooms, pool, spa, sauna, hi-speed Internet access in the rooms, Wi-Fi in lobby and coffee shop, rooms safes, basketball and tennis court, putting green, conference room. Two towers (37 & 38 stories tall) from 1979. Parking is $10 per day—a good deal by Waikiki standards. This resort seems geared toward families. They allow up to 5 people per room. There's even a playground next to the pool on the 6th floor, and when kids under 12 arrive, they're given a beach-related grab bag. If you're in Tower 2, be aware that some of your "ocean view" may be dominated by Tower 1, if you have a room directly facing that tower. Aston's rooms (first numbers listed) are being upgraded slowly to a standard look (nothing to *rave* about, but okay), so ask for an upgraded room. There's one thing that got under our skin. They have BBQ grills available, but you'll have to bring quarters, because they're *coin-operated*. Yeah, it's minor, but it's annoying. Check out the snack bar by the pool; it's not the usual fare. They added a $10 "amenity" fee, which pays for Internet in rooms, daily coffee, room safes, DVD rental and some other items.

See all Web reviews at: www.hawaiirevealed.com

The second set of numbers is for another on-site agent—**Koko Resorts**. Their room rates start at less than half the rates of Aston's listed below. The units can be viewed online. Some are good, some fair, but for the money, they are a SOLID GOLD VALUE, and they give $10 off per night for weekly stays. Optional maid service for a fee. No room safes, but there's one in the office. They charge a cleaning fee, but they have free Wi-Fi in rooms and free parking. They also lend beach and sports gear such as bastketballs, surfboards, etc., for free, so you'll have to weigh the options. 3-night minimum.

In general, the resort is not a bad place for families, but child-free travelers might want to look elsewhere. One long block to the beach. 1/1s (535 sq. ft.) are $229–$375.

Pacific Beach Hotel
(800) 367–6060 or (808) 923–4511
2490 Kalakaua Ave.
WEB REVIEW

Marriott Waikiki Beach Resort
(800) 367–5370 or (808) 922–6611
2552 Kalakaua Ave.
WEB REVIEW 💎

Waikiki Sunset
(877) 997–6667 or (808) 922–0511
229 Paoakalani Ave.
WEB REVIEW

Hyatt Place Waikiki Beach
(800) 993–4751 or (808) 922–3861
175 Paoakalani Ave.
WEB REVIEW 🔲

Ewa Hotel Waikiki
(866) 406–2782 or (808) 922–1677
2555 Cartwright Rd.
WEB REVIEW

Waikiki Beachside Hostel
(866) 478–3888 or (808) 923–9566
2556 Lemon Rd.
WEB REVIEW

Queen Kapiolani Hotel
(866) 406–2782 or (808) 922–1941
150 Kapahulu Ave.

310 rooms, pool, restaurant, free Wi-Fi in the lobby and rooms, 24-hour business center, coffee makers with free coffee daily, 42-inch HD TVs, 2 shops, 3 conference rooms, free room safes, lanais on most, day spa. A 19-story building from 1969. This was a grand hotel in its day, but past editions found it *way* past its day. Thankfully new management (Aqua) is bringing back much of its former glory. Rooms and common areas have had many renovations, paint, new carpets, bedding, furnishings, etc., but still keeping with the intended style of the hotel. The restaurant is now open-air on the pool deck, making the entire area feel much more inviting. New staff has brought back the aloha. It was good to see this once-grand lady regain much of her former glory on this visit, including the restoration of many historic paintings dug out of storage. The view from their pool is wonderful, with an expansive vista from Diamond Head to part of Waikiki, and rooms facing the ocean or Diamond Head have awesome views. A short block to the beach. Parking is $15. Rooms (175–355 sq. ft.) are $189–$259, suites (370–615 sq. ft.) are $269–$500. Few pay the RACK rates.

See all Web reviews at: www.hawaiirevealed.com

Hotel Renew
(888) 485–7639 or (808) 687–7700
129 Paoakalani Ave.

WEB REVIEW ◆

Waikiki Grand Hotel
(800) 367–5004 or (808) 923–1814
134 Kapahulu Ave.

180 units, pool, kitchenette, free local calls, free Wi-Fi in rooms, Internet kiosk in lobby, restaurant, lanais and kitchenettes in most. A 10-floor building from 1963. Individually owned units all have different furnishings—some interesting, some quirky island style—but all are clean. Some owners have expanded the interior of the rooms and removed the lanai. The hallways could use a coat of paint. Rooms ending in 00 are inside corner rooms and have a profound lack of privacy. The 10th floor rooms facing the park have an expansive deck outside with lots of lounge chairs and tables. The pool is at the back of the building, but you probably won't use it anyway as the beach is only a minute away. This resort is popular with gay travelers, and there is a gay-friendly bar on the 2nd floor. Parking is $17 and is reserved. Rooms (204–396 sq. ft.) are $165–$325.

Waikiki Beach Hotel
(877) 997–6667 or (808) 922–2511
2570 Kalakaua Ave.
644 rooms, pool, 2 restaurants, 2 conference rooms, free fitness room, free Wi-Fi by pool, hi-speed Internet access in rooms, 24-hour business center. A 25-

story tower with a hot red floral and dark-chocolate bold decor in rooms—sort of a lava color scheme. Breakfast is free with live entertainment—you either eat it at the pool, or you can take it over to the beach across the street in one of their free cooler bags. No coffee makers in rooms for us coffee addicts. Complimentary beach chairs available. Tiny lanais on the Diamond Head side are standing room only. Some connecting rooms available. Overall, the place feels busy and loud most of the time. Parking is valet only for $27. Rooms (288–352 sq. ft.) are $229–$349. Jr. suites (472 sq. ft.) are $329–$379. These prices seem slightly high to us, but few pay the RACK rates.

Park Shore Waikiki
(866) 406–2782 or (808) 923–0411
2586 Kalakaua Ave.
WEB REVIEW

New Otani Kaimana Beach Hotel
(800) 356–8264 or (808) 923–1555
2863 Kalakaua Ave.
125 rooms, 2 restaurants, lounge, conference room, free Wi-Fi and hi-speed

See all Web reviews at: www.hawaiirevealed.com

Internet access in rooms, valet-only parking, fitness room, free rooms safes, free

A REAL GEM

coffee makers with coffee upon request, room service. Two 1964 buildings of 9 and 3 stories (the latter Diamond Head wing has no elevator). Their oceanfront category rooms are extremely intimate with the beach—look straight down onto the sand—and since the tallest room is 9 stories up, you'll never feel completely detached. Room renovations done in 2012 were lovely, clean and modern with bathroom upgrades like hand-held showerheads. It's on lovely Sans Souci Beach. This is the reason for the GEM. Though still expensive, you won't get rooms like that for this kind of price in more centrally located Waikiki resorts. And there's the reason for the lower prices—it's a fairly long walk to the heart of Waikiki, and many will opt to drive and pay to park. But you're also away from the buzz of Waikiki. This is a smaller, quieter resort than others you'll find on the beach. Rooms ending in 17 have wrap-around lanais and grand views of the entire Waikiki coastline. We're told those book out for 4th of July fireworks shows. They have some nice touches like an orchid with your turn-down service, and many of the excellent staff have been around for years. The Diamond Head wing is less desirable (and older room furnishings), but

they have kitchenettes. Their Hau Tree Lanai restaurant is a great (though pricey) place to have your breakfast on the beach. Valet-only parking is $23. Rooms (202–434 sq. ft.) are $180–$440, Diamond Head wing rooms (330–550 sq. ft.) are $220–$380, Jr. suites (395–440 sq. ft.) are $335–$400, suites (420–1,043 sq. ft.) are $530–$1,200. Most rooms are discounted.

Aqua Lotus Honolulu
(866) 406–2782 or (808) 922–1700
2885 Kalakaua Ave.
WEB REVIEW

JUST OUTSIDE OF WAIKIKI

The Kahala Hotel & Resort
(800) 367–2525 or (808) 739–8888
5000 Kahala Ave.

338 rooms, pool and keiki pool, 3 spas, free 24-hour fitness room, 4 restaurants,

A REAL GEM

lounge, valet parking, 3 shops, 8 conference rooms, 24-hour business center, coffee makers with free coffee daily, 24-hour room service, free room safes, valet-only laundry, lanais on half, child care program, Wi-Fi and hi-speed Internet access in rooms, free laptop safes, Wi-Fi in many common areas, 40-inch HD TVs, day spa. A 1964 10-story building plus a low-rise wing. Typically ranked among the world's best hotels—for good reasons. This is probably our favorite O'ahu

See all Web reviews at: www.hawaiirevealed.com

resort. It has all the trappings of a big, fun destination resort without any of the annoyances, like waiting in line or crowds. The Kahala isn't in Waikiki; it's about 15 minutes away on ultra-protected Kahala Beach. The Kahala exudes a relaxed, old world, luxurious feel. There's afternoon tea in the open-air veranda, mature gardens and grounds, and clean, well-tended surroundings.

The resort isn't stodgy, however. For example, no restaurant requires a jacket for men. When you arrive, you're taken directly to your room and asked to please stop by the front desk when it is convenient to give 'em your credit card information. Instead of a pond filled with koi fish, theirs has turtles, manta ray, reef fish and dolphins cruising the waters. (See Dolphin Quest on page 223.) Some of the rooms in the Koko Head Wing are directly over the pond, allowing you to watch these creatures from your lanai. Others, in the low-rise building, are closer to the beach or beachfront. Your preferences are tracked, so your needs might be more easily anticipated. If you order a certain wine at the restaurant, they'll remember the next night and even the next visit. They'll put Christmas trees in your room with special personal decorations at the holidays. If you adored your maid last time, they will make sure you have the same one on your next visit. Many of the staff have been around for years. They have lots of repeat customers, because of the generous (too numerous to list) special touches they provide to each and every guest. The lobby always has some type of free activity going on that guests can watch or join in.

The rooms have the feel of old world Hawai'i meets modern chic in pale shades of yellows, greens and blues. Beds are plush with expensive Frette sheets. Rooms are spacious and nicely appointed. The bathrooms are large with separate deep tubs and showers (except standard rooms), and his-and-hers vanities. Suites are simply two to four different rooms connected. There is a large lanai on every other room (the rest have railings only), so make sure you specify what you want. Many guests open the lanai doors at night and turn on the ceiling fans to enjoy the ocean sounds and breezes.

All the usual beach activities are available at their often bathtub-calm beach, which won't have nearly the level of energy that Waikiki does. Many activities are complimentary, including intro surf or SCUBA lessons. Cabana chairs on the beach are $50 per day.

Their day spa is different from most of the others on the island—10 individual rooms create a luxury and privacy that is hard to find. They have a special menu for dining at the spa. Men can also feel super pampered here and even get their teeth whitened. Couples' rooms are very intimate. The have a wide variety of treatments—some unique to their spa. The fitness center is large and has a personal trainer on staff.

Weddings are popular here, and they have a separate catering department dedicated to them.

Parking is $25 for valet or self, so you may as well let them park it. The views from the two main restaurants are smashing.

Overall, the Kahala conveys a dreamy tropical isolation while being only a short drive to the action of Waikiki. This resort will appeal to everyone, young and old. If this is what you're looking for and you have the budget to afford it, look no further. Rooms (550 sq. ft.) are $425–$1,250, suites (1,100–2,200 sq. ft.) are $1,600–$10,050. They do offer packages that add value, like buffet breakfasts, free nights, etc.

See all Web reviews at: www.hawaiirevealed.com

NORTH SHORE

Turtle Bay Resort
(800) 203–3650 or (808) 293–6000
57-091 Kamehameha Hwy., Kahuku

443 rooms, 2 pools and keiki pool, 2 spas, 4 tennis courts (2 lighted), free 24-hour fitness room, video game room, 2 golf courses, 6 restaurants, lounge, 16 conference rooms, resort-wide Wi-Fi and hi-speed Internet access in rooms, 24-hour business center, valet parking, room service, day spa, 4 shops, horse stables, helipad, wedding coordinators. This 880-acre resort with 5 miles of beaches was built in 1972. On our visit for this edition it was looking the best we've seen it in years. The hotel rooms are nice but not *spectacular*. The place seems to have a very low-key, relaxed vibe overall, and the staff is nice. New owners have slowly but steadily been putting money—over $70 million—into the property. In other circumstances, they might have simply leveled the buildings and rebuilt them. But Hawai'i's current laws would never again let them build so close to the ocean. The result is a roughly polished

A REAL GEM

gem. Out on a point, nearly all its rooms have grand ocean views, though some of the views from rooms in the east and west wings overlook a rather unattractive roof (they are thinking of changing that roof). If you can swing the cost, the 42 oceanfront cottages are as dreamy as any place you'll stay in Hawai'i. They have lots of hammocks by the ocean, deep soaking tubs, separate showers, a mini bar and empty fridge.

The thing that makes Turtle Bay so great is also what hurts it. It's near the northernmost tip of the island—far, far away from Waikiki. Your dining choices are limited to the on-site restaurants, or you'll drive into Hale'iwa 20 minutes (or more with traffic) away. Your nightlife will be almost non-existent unless there is a cool event going on in the Surfer bar. But that's also the charm here. Its beaches (nearby Kuilima Cove and Kawela Bay—a walk but worth it) are wonderful, the grounds are pretty, there are 2 golf courses that are never crowded on weekdays, and the pace is relaxing. This is the only place on O'ahu where you can see sunrise over the water (at least from April to September) and sunset from the same location. Because they're far from Waikiki, they have other activities (for extra) like horseback riding along the shoreline, off-road Segway tours (see ATTRACTIONS) and helicopter flights from their helipad. Their main pool is small for the size of the resort but has a waterslide and small keiki pool.

Their 300 villas (about 22 in the rental pool) were built in 2005 on the footprint of former cottages. They are drop-dead gorgeous and consist of studio to 4-bedroom units with complete designer kitchens, deep soaking tubs, 46-inch HD TVs, Bose stereos, etc. It is obvious they have spared no expense. (And neither will you when you get the bill.) The villas share their own pool and

See all Web reviews at: www.hawaiirevealed.com

have access to exclusive concierge services while still being able to make use of all the resort's main facilities. The catch is that amenities like this don't come cheap, and we felt the cottages were a better deal than the villas.

Their Spa Luana has services for everyone, including keiki. They have a very wide selection of treatments and a private elevator for brides (they do lots of weddings) to get to and from their rooms. Their chapel by the ocean is a small but lovely setting for a wedding and is often used for exercise classes as well. Their fitness center is large and offers personal trainers and classes, such as yoga. They do private dinners in a thatched hale facing the ocean for $555 and up per couple.

There's a *mandatory* $25 a day resort fee that will get you free local calls, Wi-Fi, self-parking, newspaper, laptop room safes, daily coffee, etc. Valet parking is $15. Rates are expensive, but few pay the RACK we list. Rooms (478 sq. ft.) are $450–$495. Cottages (740–850 sq. ft.) are $720. Suites (725–2,200 sq. ft.) are $560–$1,470. Villas (673–2,391 sq. ft.) are $860–$1,670.

KO OLINA

Out near Barbers Point at the southwestern corner of the island is the next up-and-coming resort area.

JW Marriott Ihilani Resort & Spa at Ko Olina
(800) 626–4446 or (808) 679–0079
92-1001 Olani St., Kapolei
387 rooms, 2 pools, 2 spas, 6 lighted tennis courts, 4 restaurants, lounge, 3 shops, 14 conference rooms, valet parking, 24-hour room service, free room safes, hi-speed Internet access in rooms, Wi-Fi in common areas, free fit-

A REAL GEM

ness room, child care program (seasonal), day spa. If you're looking to stay far away from Waikiki and want luxury, this is the place. The rooms are nicely sized and *very* well appointed. The bathrooms have deep soaking tubs, separate showers and two vanities. Bathrooms seem a specialty here as the Ihilani Suite has the one of largest Jacuzzi bathtubs we've ever seen. But it's truly the surroundings that make this property a real winner. The resort oozes a luxurious, tropical feel. The main pool can get crowded, and since they share Ko Olina lagoon with Aulani Disney Resort, that too is now more crowded. Rooms with views overlooking the lagoon (the higher, the better) are utterly fantastic and worth the upgrade if you can swing it. (Ocean view rooms facing north are nice but not nearly as droolable.) Southeast facing rooms have a view of the large Aulani Disney Resort.

Their Ihilani Spa is well-appointed and has a variety of special treatments that will melt your tensions away. If you're hungry during your day at the spa, they'll even provide room service on a patio.

There's a meandering pond with manta rays and sharks cruising around—a nice touch—and a "Reef and Ray Adventure" for kids where they get in the pond and touch the rays.

See all Web reviews at: www.hawaiirevealed.com

Valet or self-parking is $35. Coffee makers upon request, and laundry is valet only. Rooms (515–555 sq. ft.) are $545–$850. Suites (1,069–4,000 sq. ft.) are $950–$7,000. That price feels too high to us. We hope you got a good discount.

Aulani, A Disney Resort & Spa
(800) 626–4446 or (808) 679–0079
92-1185 Aliinui Dr., Kapolei

WEB REVIEW

Beach Villas at Ko Olina
(877) 333–3808 or (808) 225–5590
(888) 410–0410 or (808) 672–2112
92-102 Waialii Pl., Kapolei

WEB REVIEW

WAI'ANAE

Way out in Makaha near the western tip of the island there are several resorts that are rarely spoken of and largely forgotten. Makaha is light years from Waikiki, both in distance and tone. It's not a resort area; it's where many of Waikiki's workers live. You won't have tons of restaurants and activities, but you *will* have world-class sunsets and world-class beaches. See page 103 to see if this area is for you.

Hawaiian Princess
(808) 696–1616
84-1021 Lahilahi St.

120 rooms, pool, spa, tennis court, washer/dryers in the unit, most units have free Wi-Fi, free Wi-Fi in lobby, BBQ. A 16-story tower from 1980. First of all, it's not just a GEM, it's

 A REAL GEM also a SOLID GOLD VALUE. This has the kind of beachfront location that people dream of. It's built right on top of Papaoneone Beach, a very picturesque and surprisingly lightly used half-mile-long beach in Makaha. Views from all of the units are glorious. Some of the rooms here are owner-occupied, some are timeshares, but many are vacation rentals you can find on the Web. The rental agent listed above has units here and is reliable. The 1/1 units aren't spacious, but they're big enough, with the living area adjacent to the lanais. (Some owners have expanded their units by enclosing the lanais.) Corner units are 1/2s and have even better views, if that's possible. The saltwater pool is near the beach but does not have views of it. No room safes, but the property is gated. Though air conditioned, it's done with a heat pump, which doesn't provide the frosty air that a regular a/c does. The units vary a lot depending on the decor of the owner, and some are more updated than others. Parking and local calls are free. 1/1 (535 sq. ft.) are $130–$140. 1/2s (850 sq. ft.) are $160–$175, 2/2s (1,224 sq. ft.) are $200–$225. 4- or 7-night minimum. Longer stays can get discounts.

Makaha Beach Cabanas
(808) 696–1616
84-965 Farrington Hwy
62 rooms, some have hi-speed Internet access, BBQ. These two 9-story towers next door to the Hawaiian Princess aren't as large or well-appointed, but they're a steal, if you

 SOLID GOLD VALUE

See all Web reviews at: www.hawaiirevealed.com

don't mind renting *by the month*. The location is right on Papaoneone Beach, and the sand is straight down below your lanai. Rooms are as varied as their individual owners. Pretty small but pleasant, if their owner has renovated. The bedroom is on the ocean side; living area is away from it. Many units are owner-occupied or timeshare, others are available to rent only from the owners. The phone number above is a good rental agent with some vacation rentals available. No a/c or room safes, and laundry is coin-op. Parking and local calls are free. This property is gated. It ain't the Ritz, but you're living a beachfront dream. 1/1s (456 sq. ft.) are $54–$60 ($1,600–$1,800 per month). Hard to beat that. 30-day minimum.

Makaha Valley Towers
(808) 696–1616
84-740 Kili Dr.
WEB REVIEW

WINDWARD SIDE

Paradise Bay Resort
(800) 735–5071 or (808) 239–1147
47-039 Lihikai Dr., Kane'ohe
37 rooms, pool, spa, no elevators,

lanais on most rooms, conference room, free continental breakfast, free

A REAL GEM

Wi-Fi on lobby lanai and in rooms, free local calls, no room safes (use front desk safety deposit box), maid service is every other day, day spa services upon request. This resort is composed of 10 buildings (two not yet open) of up to 3 floors each built on the slopes of a hill (lots of steps). The area used to be a military barracks during WWII. In the 1940s the first building was built, others followed, and in the 1970s it turned into an inn. This used to be Schrader's Windward Country Inn, but new owners breathed much needed renovations to the common areas and rooms in 2011. The staff is friendly. Some of the rooms have pretty views of the mountains. The units are basic, clean, with nice upgrades in kitchens and baths. The walls at this inn are thin, so expect to hear your neighbor. They offer lots of extra services for their guests, such as free kayaks, paddle boards, boat trips on their pontoon to the sunken island (page 194), and free dinner and mai tais on Wednesdays, free mojitos on Fridays, and they'll even grocery shop for you (for an extra charge). You have to add a 6% "resort fee" onto the room rate that covers Internet, dinner and the other *free* items they offer. The nearest beach is about a 10-minute drive away, but many people take the kayaks out into the bay to snorkel. Free parking and connecting rooms available. Units from studios to 5 bedrooms vary in size from 396–2,400 sq. ft.), though they don't feel overly large. Prices are $145–$750. 2-night minimum. As for the location...this property is definitely the best in the neighborhood.

INDEX

Island Dining Index on page 228, Where to Stay Index on page 272.

Island Dining Index on page 228, Where to Stay Index on page 272.

INDEX

Island Dining Index on page 228, Where to Stay Index on page 272.

Island Dining Index on page 228, Where to Stay Index on page 272.

INDEX

Island Dining Index on page 228, Where to Stay Index on page 272.

INDEX

Island Dining Index on page 228, Where to Stay Index on page 272.

Island Dining Index on page 228, Where to Stay Index on page 272.